TUXEDO JUNCTION

To: David B.T.

From: Claire Nelson

We come as students
We leave as students
and on the way we
learn that we will never
learn all we
need to learn

Xmas 97

TUXEDO JUNCTION

Essays on
American Culture

GERALD EARLY

THE ECCO PRESS

To Florence, my mother

THE ECCO PRESS
100 West Broad Street
Hopewell, NJ 08525
Published simultaneously in Canada by
Penguin Books Canada Ltd., Ontario
Printed in the United States of America

Designed by Richard Oriolo
First paperback printing, 1994

The author acknowledges the editors of the following periodicals in which earlier versions of some of the essays in this book have appeared: *Antæus, The Antioch Review, Callaloo, Cimarron Review, The Forest Park Review, The Hudson Review, The Kenyon Review, Obsidian II,* and *Salmagundi.* Special thanks to Daniel Halpern of *Antæus,* Robert Fogarty of *The Antioch Review,* and George and Phil Wedge of *Cottonwood,* for having been particularly supportive, and to Robert Atwan and Elizabeth Hardwick for selecting "The Passing of Jazz's Old Guard" for inclusion in *The Best American Essays 1986* (Houghton Mifflin). "The Fight: Patterson vs. Liston" by James Baldwin is reprinted by arrangement with The Estate of James Baldwin; it was originally published in *Nugget* magazine.

The author would also like to thank the University of Kansas for providing a two-year minority postdoctoral fellowship that allowed for the completion of several of the essays in this volume, and the Mrs. Giles Whiting Foundation and CCLM-General Electric for awarding writing prizes for several of these works.

Grateful acknowledgment is also made to the following sources for permission to reproduce materials under their control: Don Williams Music Group for lyrics from "1983: A Merman I Should Turn to be" by Jimi Hendrix, copyright © 1968 Bella Godiva Music, Inc., Worldwide Administration Don Williams Music Group, Inc.; Hudson Bay Music, Inc. for lyrics from "Cool Jerk" by Donald Storball, copyright © 1966 by Alley Music Corp. and Trio Music Co., Inc.; Alfred A. Knopf for excerpts from *The Palm at the End of the Mind: Selected Poems and a Play* by Wallace Stevens, edited by Holly Stevens; Newmarket Press for excerpts from *Miss America, 1945: Bess Myerson's Own Story* by Susan Dworkin, copyright © 1987 by Susan Dworkin and Bess Myerson; Random House for excerpts from *The Cat in the Hat* and *The Cat in the Hat Comes Back* by Dr. Seuss, copyright © renewed 1986 by Dr. Seuss; and Unichappell Music, Inc. for lyrics from "Bring It Up" by James Brown, copyright © 1967 by Dynatone Publishing Co., administered by Unichappell Music, Inc. All rights reserved.

Library of Congress Cataloging-in-Publication Data

Early, Gerald Lyn.
Tuxedo Junction : essays on American culture / Gerald Early.
— 1st ed.
p.   cm.
1. Afro-Americans.   2. United States—Race relations.
3. United States—Civilization—1945-   I. Title.
E185.E13   1989   89-31495
305.8'96073—dc20

ISBN 0-88001-232-3
0-88001-233-1 (pbk.)

Publication of this book was made possible in part by a grant from the National Endowment for the Arts.

The text of this book is set in Century Old Style.

Contents

IV

V

Introduction

But then who can ever figure anyone else out?
—Cornell Woolrich, *Night Has a Thousand Eyes*

I. ANTHROPOLOGY

It is a daunting matter for any writer, and especially for those who do not write fiction (because that means they must write something called nonfiction, which means they shall be known by a kind of negative capability), to find himself in the position of having to explain or more precisely justify his work. I am aware that my job here may be more on the order of descriptive rather than analytical, more a simple act of previewing than the more comprehensive one of evaluating, and finally akin to the sort of thing some writers of liner notes for jazz albums do, telling whether a tune is fast or slow, pretty or raucous, all with the aplomb of a salesman selling soft and subtle. I suppose I am attempting to set a mood for the reader, to place or perhaps ease him or her into a state of mind suitable for what comes next. Creating moods is dangerous, for one can hardly tell if, in the end, one has succeeded in creating a hypnotic tamburalike drone or has simply been trying stupidly to attract flies with his tongue. Of course, any description signifies analysis on some even rudimentary level and preview does become evaluation, just as mood-setting is a form of salesmanship: "I feel this way sometimes. Don't you feel that way too?" It is the old snake-oil charm that confidence men and women have used for years to fool people, something called instant and faked intimacy. But I do wish to give my readers pleasure, to make see, to make know, to make understand; not simply to perceive a personality behind the words but a voice resonating both within the words and within themselves as readers. But the pleasure of which I speak is not a desire to be liked as a *personality* or as a *critic,* but to serve my readers as a *writer* by giving them a substantiality that provokes.

Let us begin by assuming that no writer can really explain, justify, or describe a collection of his words simply by offering more of his own words. He can neither plead for his own work nor can he judge it—or at least he cannot plead for it very convincingly or judge it very well. Suffice it to say that this is not the book I really wanted to write. Like most writers, I produced the only book I *could* write when pushed up against the necessity of having to write *something,* and a writer is always pushed up against that necessity for a variety of reasons ranging from raging ambition, to feeding the kids, to a fear that he or she will never write again. I wanted to write another book altogether, not a better one but simply one that would have been, to use Gertrude Stein's phrase, "older and different." I think writers might always be wishing that their present or latest work were older and different. When I was younger and was told, quite to my misfortune, that I could do such a thing, I wanted to write novels. After fifteen years of various efforts at long, short, and medium novels, I discovered that I cannot write novels or even fiction. When one is young, novel-writing is always the dream because all one does is novel-reading and the novel, to the youthful mind, seems a perfect author-centered or author-ized literary work. (As a boy I thought of novels, quite incorrectly, as the only kind of literature, aside from "classics," that people read because of who wrote them rather than for what they say.) It does not matter that I lost time wishing that I could write novels and that I could have written this book when I was younger. In truth, I could not have done so. Like many, I have tried to learn from a kind of negative realization, from understanding what I could not do so that I might better understand what I could do. (As a boy I used to think that if I dropped a quarter on a sidewalk on a very hot summer day it would shrink, raisinlike, into a penny. And now I believe that if thick novels lie fallow they become longish essays.) Writing essays, for me, is not simply a realization of being *unable* to write fiction, it is a clear acknowledgment of being *able* to do something else. Negative capability is essentially an enabling function meant to generate a kind of myth of accomplishment through irony.

I understand this book to be one very long essay made up of essays that are made up of parts that might rightly be called chapters, recitations, or movements—not an anthology, not the best of Gerald Early (a phrase that is meant to be as parodic as it sounds.) Which isn't to say this book is not a fabrication—conventional, certainly, in that it tends, in its parts, to signify a total intelligibility that others might call accessibility or transparency. The book is a fabrication about the mythology of making fabrications.

The essays that make up this volume, pieces written over the last eight years, from 1981 to 1989 (the earliest essay being "Hot Spicks Versus Cool Spades: Three Notes Toward a Cultural Definition of Prizefighting," and the latest, "Jesse Jackson's Black Bottom, or, Crossing the Roads at Tuxedo Junction"), are meant to speak for themselves quite plainly in the expression of their purpose and meaning. And their thematic relatedness, the essence of their fabricating possibilities, lies in the insistent strain of speaking about African-American culture within the wider contexts of both American intellectual/high-brow culture and American popular culture — that should be obvious. (Incidentally, I might add that these essays discuss the reverse proposition: namely, American culture within the wider context of African-American culture.) Little can be said about blacks in this country, their role, their impact, their myth, their drama, without talking at some great length about popular culture, the great basin (or sink, if you will) that exists to commodify and absorb the marginal in American society. (The cultural margins, we Americans have discovered, are fine sources to reinvent and reinvigorate the language; they also provide the necessary background noise for people to buy booze, sex, and a number of other things.) Indeed, it is far from being an overstatement to assert that large components that comprise American popular and youth cultures are to a great extent the inventions of blacks. But there is more to say about the book than merely that.

In illustrating a point, I am reminded of how Frederick Douglass in his second autobiography, 1855's *My Bondage and My Freedom,* described the plantation as "a little nation of its own, having its own language, its own rules, regulations, and customs." In effect, in describing and analyzing where he grew up, the various prison-houses of language and myth — indeed, not a prison-house culture but the prison-house *of* culture — Douglass became something of an anthropologist, the standard field ethnographer (who better for such a job than a *field* hand). Any decent black essayist, and Douglass was often as essayistic as fictional in his autobiography (indeed, I posit that the peculiarly black literary form of the essay grew from Douglass's autobiographies and from black autobiography generally, although it is certainly related to the black sermonic tradition as Martin Luther King's "Letter from a Birmingham Jail" and Baldwin's *The Fire Next Time,* two of the famous black essays of the last thirty years, attest), is not, in effect, literary, or trying to be literary merely, but is trying quite self-consciously to be anthropological. He (or she, as the case may be) cannot help but be anthropological, as there can be no mistaking that for the African-Americans, the place where they live never ceases to be a prison-house of culture (not necessarily a bad prison as prisons go, and sometimes confinement can be strengthening), and in prison one is forced constantly to think about writing as theater. All black essayists, ultimately, with either resolution or resignation, write, as Douglass stated he did, "from sound." It is through sound, uncertain though it may be, that the anthropologist understands his work. The essays in this volume are filled with sound. They talk of little else. They try to replicate nothing so much as the sound of other things, of language bouncing off the prison-house walls. But, for the black essayist, sound must always try to be subversion, the slave's language is always undermining the master's tongue even as it imperfectly replicates it, even as it aspires to be the master's tongue. The perfect image of the black writer is Jim trapped in his prison that is not really a prison in the last chapters of Mark Twain's novel while Huck and Tom cover the walls with language and invent signs for Jim's white captors, all of which has no meaning except that the language and signs refer to novels, romances, literary conventions—that verisimilitude, in this instance and perhaps in all instances, is not a term describing how art is related to life but how life is related to books (and artistic vision), which are, in effect, more real than life. Nothing is more real than our fantasies, Twain's novel tells us. Jim, through his displays of common sense, rebels against being an instrumentality of white consciousness while succumbing to it for lack of anything better to do. I hope this singular dilemma becomes clearer as I go along. But how can one distinguish, in the case of Jim, for instance, subversion from simulation in this vastness of verisimilitude?

Consider how Douglass, in *My Bondage and My Freedom,* appropriates the terms "Nature" and "Nurture" from mid-1850s American pop-scientific, anthropological discourse and uses them to illustrate the slave's humanity, in direct opposition to their contemporary use in the hermeneutical language of the nineteenth-century white intellectual as absences of both a civilizing environment and proper genetic properties (ah, the slave, being property in a world where property was the touchstone of reality, was completely without property, and so was not only completely unreal himself but was forced to see the world as unreality). Douglass achieves this without ever using the words themselves but by appropriating the cultural symbol that compresses and decomposes both terms: mother. Douglass tells two elaborate stories of his mother, who was largely absent from his life: first, how she rescued him from a cruel black "Auntie" and gave him bread, and second, how his literary turn of mind was directly inherited from his maternal (black) side (Douglass always believed his father to be white). So, with Douglass, the absent mother (not "Mammy" or "Auntie," that lover and rearer of white sons and daughters and beloved of them) becomes the presence that repudiates the cultural absences that have been assigned the black. There is a lesson in that bit of fabrication by Douglass (literal fabrication because he could not possibly have remembered the bread incident and how does anyone know, in most instances, which source of genes produced what talents, especially in the case of someone who did not know his father as Douglass did not); a lesson that would stand any black essayist in good stead about playing with language in the prison-house of culture. For Douglass, after all, bread, the staff of life, becomes both nature and nurture and, in effect, Douglass proves the two terms are essentially interchangeable and absolutely meaningless as they both signify "mother," and everyone has one of those, as Douglass demonstrates—you can make of her whatever you wish.

But in the matters of anthropology and language on and reverberating within the prison-house walls no black writer can be more instructive than Zora Neale Hurston, a trained anthropologist/ethnographer in her own right and a novelist of some distinction. In her 1942 autobiography, *Dust Tracks on a Road,* a marvelously and shrewdly fabricated book, she tells of three successive incidents concerning language that occur when she joins a white theater company as a teenager:

> In the first place, I was a Southerner, and had the map of Dixie on my tongue. They [the theater company] were all Northerners except the orchestra leader, who came from Pensacola. It was not that my grammar was bad, it was the idioms. They did not know of the way an average Southern child, white or black, is raised on simile and invective. They know how to call names. It is an every-day affair to hear somebody called a mullet-headed, mule-eared, wall-eyed, hog-nosed, 'gator-faced, shad-mouthed, screw-necked, goat-bellied, puzzle-gutted, camel-backed, butt-sprung, battle-hammed, knocked-kneed, razor-legged, box-ankled, shovel-footed, unmated so-and-so!...Since that stratum of the Southern population is not given to book-reading, they take their comparisons right out of the barnyard and the woods. When they get through with you, you and your whole family look like an acre of totempoles.

As much as the white company liked young Hurston's own colorful language, they enjoyed even more having her saying things which she did not understand:

> Another sly trick they played on my ignorance was that some of the men would call me and with a very serious face send me to some of the girls to ask about the welfare and condition of cherries and spangles. They would give me a tip and tell me to hurry back with the answer. Some of the girls would send back word that the men need not worry their heads at all. They would never know the first thing about the condition of their cherries and spangles. Some of the girls sent answers full of double talk which went over my head.

Finally, this incident with written discourse:

> I got a scrapbook, and everybody gave me a picture to put in it. I pasted each one on a separate page and wrote comments under each picture. This created a great deal of interest, because some of the comments were quite pert. They egged me on to elaborate. Then I got another idea. I would comment on daily doings and post the sheets on the call-board. This took on right away. The results stayed strictly mine less than a week because members of the cast began to call aside and tell me things to put in about others. It got to be so general that everybody was writing it. It was just my handwriting, mostly. Then it got beyond that. Most of the cast ceased to wait for me. They would take a pencil to the board and set down their own item. Answers to the wisecracks would appear promptly and often cause uproarious laughter. They always started off with either "Zora says" or "The observant reporter of the Call-board asserts"—Lord, Zora said more things! I was continually astonished, but always amused.

The passages, taken together, constitute a highly complex rendering of the political realities of blacks and language in the prison-house of culture, explicating and dramatizing all the various issues that a black essayist might think about in relation to what he or she does—for here, to borrow a Roland Barthes phrase, language literally becomes theater. First, there is a political reversal occurring here as Hurston moves from being mascot to becoming something like a scribe to, in fact, something like an anthropologist; moving from being a totem of animal imagery and ritual insult language to serving as a liaison for double entendres about cherries and heads to being a headmistress of a kind of school for scandal or a gossip exchange. Literally, once she controls the call board, the actual script of the lives of the company, she becomes the one who has not only recorded the dialect but actually shaped its creation. That a black should become the central controlling figure for the discourse of whites is, ironically, both a remarkable political feat of assertion-subversion and something genuinely ignominious if we remember Jim as the central and "controlling" figure of the whites at the end of Twain's novel. The method of ritual insulting, which she describes at first as being Southern, she describes later in the book as being particularly female and Negro and refers to it as "specifying." The shift is extremely important because specifying occurs when she is in the all-black southern towns collecting data (folk stories, i.e., oral language) for her books. Among the blacks, she is purely the scientist (the objective subject), evacuating and saving a culture. Among the whites, she is purely the exhibitionist (the subjective object) signifying the tricks and trumps of language. In effect, among the whites, Hurston makes the transition from taboo to totem (which is exactly what Jim does in *Huckleberry Finn*); for Hurston, the writer is the totem who enables the language of others ("the Other") to have meaning. That Hurston should be able to write about this in such a way that she so disguises her seizing the essential instrumentality of an acting company (its language and its script), becoming not simply its conduit for discourse but its source as well while seemingly remaining an instrumentality of the whites themselves (in essence, while still remaining a creation of the white imagination: a folksy innocent) is a masterful stroke of the trickster (although it is the very strength of her trickster dissimulation that is her final undoing—because as the folksy innocent she can do nothing more than either be an exhibitionist or an observer, wavering between the anthropologist as actor to the anthropologist scribe). It is simply the problem of both being there (author) and being here (participant) that black nonfiction writers face as a kind of peculiar hazard of their game. In very stunning ways, the black nonfiction writer as anthropologist exemplifies the point of Clifford Geertz's essay "Being There: Anthropology and the Scene of Writing" better than any academic anthropologist ever could. For Hurston and Douglass—and, by extension, for most black nonfiction writers—"being there" is an ontological conundrum.

The black essayist is caught between acting and writing, between seizing the instrumentality and being trapped by the fact that he is inescapably an instrumentality; as he uses language he becomes both mascot and scribe, an odd, ambivalent coupling of the purloined and the purposeful. Hazrat Inayat Khan, Sufi philosopher and musician, spoke wisely when he said, "The nature of creation is the doubling of one." Perhaps, stated in a different context, it would read, "The predicament of racial politics is the doubling of one." Surely, when Du Bois described in that classic passage from *The Souls of Black Folk* the two-ness of the black, his being torn between his American-ness and his blackness, he did not simply restate a variation of the postmodern divided self. This book aspires to comprehend certain complexities of consciousness that exist among a group of people by considering the very simple idea of "being there" while "being here." I chose the title *Tuxedo Junction* because it is the name of a song by the great black band leader, Erskine Hawkins, recorded July 1939 and a hit with black dancers that became a much bigger hit with whites when Glenn Miller's orchestra "covered" it in 1940. (Tuxedo Junction was the streetcar terminal near a dance hall where the trumpet-playing Hawkins played as a youth.) "Tuxedo Junction" was, to use today's parlance, a crossover hit (although never recognized as such because whites do not "cross over," only blacks do), exemplifying the doubleness of our American culture, the sense of some-thing being there and being here, of being for "them" and for "us" and for all. Those systems of doubleness in our culture are what generates the vital syncretism that makes it function. America's major myth is that of crossing over (ironically signifying both a pure rebirth and a mongrelized syner-gism), from crossing the ocean (the immigrants and the slaves) to crossing the street or crossing the tracks (social and class mobility or going from uptown to downtown) to crossing the Rubicon (irrevocable commitment). But for blacks it has always been the weight of one's previous location bearing down on where you are now, the doubleness best exemplified by the current craze for the self-determining term "African-American" (not the first time blacks have opted for a hyphenated name; in the 1850s the race term shifted from "Anglo-African" to "Afro-American"). Or, as Paule Marshall put it about one of her black characters, crazy Aunt Cuney, in the novel *Praisesong for the Widow,* when Aunt Cuney, as a girl, imagined seeing slaves walking on water back to Africa: "Her body she always usta say might be in Tatem but her mind, her mind was long gone with the Ibos." Alas, the fantasy of the doubleness of being here and being there, of being both an expansive soul while holding earnestly to a specifically located identity, of being pure yet united with an Other. And, paradoxically, Ameri-can blacks have always measured their ideological and biological purity by how much they approached and resembled the idealized, fantasized Other: the African. Crossing over has long been a myth in African-American thought, closely associated with Christian theology, crossing the river Jordan, for instance. Zora Neale Hurston, in her 1939 novel, *Moses, Man of the Mountain,* captures both the racial and the theological aspects of being here and being there, the ontological nature of the black American's consciousness, when she describes Moses's crossing the Red Sea and leaving Egypt in exile:

> Moses had crossed over. He was not in Egypt. He had crossed over and now he was not an Egyptian. He had crossed over. The short sword at his thigh had a jewelled hilt but he had crossed over and so it was no longer the sign of high birth and power. He had crossed over, so he sat down on a rock near the seashore to rest himself. He had crossed over so he was not of the house of Pharaoh. He did not own a palace because he had crossed over. He did not have an Ethiopian Princess for a wife. He had crossed over. He did not have friends to sustain him. He had crossed over. He did not have enemies to strain against his strength and power. He had crossed over. He was subject to no law except the laws of tooth and talon. He had crossed over. The sun who was his friend and ancestor in Egypt was arrogant and bitter in Asia. He had crossed over. He felt as empty as a post for he was none of the things he once had been. He was a man sitting on a rock. He had crossed over.

The myth of fabrication in American culture is crossing over and that is what, in essence, this book is about: the explication of that myth.

II. AUTOBIOGRAPHY

Never to be yourself and yet always — that is the problem.
— Virginia Woolf

It is, perhaps, not so odd that I should write a book of essays and that probably all the books I write shall be books of essays. Although when I was young, in high school and college, I wanted to write novels, doubtless the book that impressed me most during those years was a collection of essays: Amiri Baraka's (LeRoi Jones's) *Home: Social Essays.* Between the ages of eighteen and twenty-two I must have read that book no fewer than eight or nine times. (I cannot recall, either before or since, reading any other book so persistently.) I found the writing to be enormously engaging, both adventuresome and elegant, and I remember after the first reading to have been, to paraphrase Fitzgerald, p-p-paralyzed with enlightenment. No one seemed to say as well or as forcefully the sorts of things that Baraka said in that book (although I don't remember everything he said). I do remember the book stressed the doctrine of cultural nationalism, which enormously appealed to my puritan instincts of renovating the world through a covenant with one's own strength of character and one's sense of election (American millennialism served on the racial half-shell). Muhammad Ali, at this time, was a walking proof of that. Baraka's book was out around the time of Eldridge Cleaver's *Soul on Ice,* and I recall preferring Baraka to Cleaver, a preference that has been subsequently justified, not by the mutability of the political views of either man, but by the fact that overall, regardless of their views, Baraka was the better, and undoubtedly more significant and honest, writer. I am not likely to think so highly of Baraka's book now (and I have not opened it in roughly eight or nine years), but I am sure that this is the work that made me want to write essays.

I mention this, first, because several readers have noted the influence of James Baldwin upon my work, an influence, an impact, if you will, that I would be the last to deny. Indeed, both "Waiting for Miss America" and "*The Color Purple* as Everybody's Protest Art" are self-consciously constructed tributes to Baldwin. But Baldwin did not really inspire me to write essays. I do not recall in high school or college ever imitating Baldwin, although I remember quite well mimicking or outright plagiarizing passages from Baraka. I think partly this particular form of the anxiety of influence occurred because of the times: I came of age in the late 1960s and the early 1970s, when Baraka was in, at least for part of that time, and Baldwin was, more or less, out. I also think that despite my having read *Notes of a Native Son* when I was thirteen, I do not think I appreciated it. I am sure I really did not understand it until I was in my late twenties, or not until I had read a great deal of Henry James and more than a little G. K. Chesterton, the two writers whose styles, I assume, most influenced and inspired Baldwin. (I am certain about James; I am merely guessing about the old Catholic conservative whose views Baldwin would have disliked intensely.) Also, I was not reared in a black charismatic church (I am an Episcopalian and grew up in an all-black Episcopal church), therefore the black sermonic roots of Baldwin's work not only never impressed me; like lost figures in a carpet, they simply never appeared to me. If anything, the appearance of this element in Baldwin's work probably alienated and annoyed me, disturbed and distressed me, and I am sure I gravitated to Baraka because that element was absent. Although I am deeply flattered when critics mention me and Baldwin in the same breath, I have been no more influenced by Baldwin than I have been by George Orwell, Chesterton, Aldous Huxley, Albert Camus (in French and English), Norman Mailer (under whose spell I fell around the time I discovered Baraka; it was fairly short-lived), or Virginia Woolf. If I pay a particular homage to Baldwin it is because his best work made him easily the best American essayist of his time and one ought to place flowers on certain altars. But context is everything: in the late sixties I saw both Baldwin and Baraka on television; I think Baldwin was being interviewed by William F. Buckley and Baraka was featured on a show hosted by David Frost. Baraka struck me far more favorably at the time; he not only seemed more assertive, he seemed a great deal more intellectual. Baraka did not preach; he argued, and quite effectively at that. It was the broad intellectual and literary reaches of Baraka's essays that I wanted, secretly, to match, to attain; I wanted, when I first started writing essays in earnest, to make the language zoom (Baraka's phrase) and to p-p-paralyze my readers with enlightenment, with how much I knew. Of course, actual practice of the art has made me a great deal more humble than I was in my salad days. I might add that I have never forgotten the look of pain and anguish on the face of Baldwin when he was interviewed on television those many years ago and have learned over time to understand that gallant grief, and to hold that picture in my mind may have taught me more about writing essays than anything else—to wish to have such a face as that, a dissipated and despairing face, a gem of a writer's face because it was a face filled with conscience.

The second reason I mention Baraka's collection is that he presented it in his introduction as a kind of intellectual autobiography. I suppose my essays are much the same, unavoidably so, although, despite some autobiographical passages, I am not—nor do I ever imagine myself being—terribly interested in writing autobiography. It is not the primary thrust or purpose of these essays to serve as autobiography. The strictly autobiographical portions are to be approached with caution. This is not to suggest that they are not true, but veracity is hardly the issue or the point. The autobiographical parts often serve the same purpose as notes in a symphony or passage of music: simply to get from one place to another. The personage I am in some of the essays, to borrow Henry Adams's metaphor, is simply a manikin on which I model some suitable clothes for the occasion. Sometimes autobiographical passages are used as authenticating devices, providing me with some authority to say the things I say; at other times, the reader is simply being guided through a particular terrain by these passages; at still other moments, they are meant to serve as a thematic, stylistic, or literary counterpoint to more discursive matters. I am a critic and it is best for the reader never to forget that, even if at times I appear to be playing other roles. All roles are subordinated to the critic; he manipulates all other personages in these pieces to his ends.

But I have spoken of this book as a long essay composed of essays, yet I have not said what I think an essay is. What is it that I write? Before I try to answer, I should say that I learned to write essays, or began the practice of them (my apprenticeship, if you will), by writing for a newspaper, my college newspaper, *The Daily Pennsylvanian*. Starting with personal pieces on the street-gang murder of my cousin in West Philadelphia, I proceeded week by week to crank out a column for more than a year. That what started out with energy and excitement should dull with fatigue and stress goes without saying. But this was very good training indeed (and every good essayist owes more than a little to H. L. Mencken, who has always been one of my heroes; journalism is the essence of the mastering of the art even if it is not the essence of the art itself); first, because I had to write to provoke people to read me in order to continue doing it (I cannot think of a more superfluous writer than someone who is doing op-ed pieces on a college newspaper. I was not simply speaking from rank ignorance, but in almost the basest contempt for knowledge—most students who think they have something to say are too arrogant to be humble). Second, I could write only four to five pages of copy; and third, I had to write even when I did not want to. As Virginia Woolf wrote, "a novel has story, a poem rhyme..." but an essay has nothing but its sheer insistence that the writer knows how to write well enough to make you read something that could attempt to be anything and threatens at any moment to be nothing at all. The essay is, thus, doubly damned; it is a negative function (a nonfiction and a nonpoem but literature of some sort nevertheless) and it is an amorphous beast, serpentine, as Chesterton expressed "elusive, evasive, impressionistic, and shading away from tint to tint." Yet the very best place to learn to write them is at a newspaper, where one learns the three virtues of the essay: to so intensify some aspect of life for someone whose attention is distracted (newspaper readers are always distracted and distractable) as to make that person read with intensified interest; to learn the right number of pages for the subject; and to write persistently. Aldous Huxley spoke of essays being classified in one of three categories: autobiographical; factual, objective/observer; and abstract/philosophical; but after years of thinking and writing essays I find that they are, finally, prose, the common language, stating with clarity and consciousness the startingly human triumph of forthright conviction without story as its aim.

It would be pleasing to know one day that I had written an American Common Reader. This book is certainly meant to be a continuation of that particularly deeply rooted branch of black letters of political engagement, of the Orwellian branch of humanist letters humanely considered, of the Woolfian art of common reading. And that is that.

I

Jesse Jackson's
Black Bottom,
or,
Crossing the Roads
at Tuxedo Junction

I. THE CAT IN THE HAT: A THEORY

Fantastic, isn't it?

—Bugs Bunny at the end of the cartoon "Fresh Hare," when he has been transformed from a prisoner awaiting death into a minstrel

"Greatness" in American politics has always been associated with thin lips.

—Robert Coover, "A Political Fable"

We have with us to-day a representative of Negro enterprise and Negro civilization.

—Georgia governor [Bullock] introducing Booker T. Washington at the Atlanta Cotton States and International Exposition, September 18, 1895

Irving Wallace's 1964 novel, *The Man,* gives us the scenario of a rather intimidated and completely undistinguished black man serving as president pro tem of the Senate who—through a series of fantastic happenstances, namely that the president, the vice-president, and the speaker of the house, all white men good and true, die suddenly and conveniently—becomes president of the United States. That it is not a particularly good novel almost goes without saying, since Wallace is known for writing soap operas, but this book, being the commercially comely blend of speculative fantasy fiction and bad melodrama, has had a fairly long cultural shelf life for the genre. In 1972, during a period when blacks were featured in a fair number of films that collectively have become known as "blaxploitation" movies, *The Man* hit the screen starring James Earl Jones. The film was even worse than the novel and did not succeed at the box office. But one might suppose that the most fundamental reason for continued interest in the book is that it asserts an undeniable and somewhat dismaying truth arising from two views of the same national preoccupation, namely, the capabilities and capacities of the Negro man: first, how it feels to be a black male (gender specificity is important here; women, black or white, in power is a separate consideration) in high places, working in the palace as something more than a cook, cleaner, or clerk; and, second, what our cultural perception of the dark presence in the white tower means.

In truth, Wallace's novel cannot be read without being accompanied by its authenticating text, the book that in fact placed in a vivid historical and personal narrative both the situation (a black man in high government circles) and the characterization of the hero (a black man trying to maintain his dignity through an endless web of contrivances designed to belittle him). To make sure the reader does not doubt the legitimacy of both his scenario and his characterization, Wallace rather clumsily drags in his supporting text in an odd meeting of fact and fiction, source and context. It is in the scene when Douglas Dilman, the hero and first black president, initially meets his white confidential secretary and insists upon leaving his office door open although he knows that his communications with her are privileged and require privacy:

> Dilman hesitated. His eyes were cast downward at his shoes. "Once, President Eisenhower appointed a Negro, E. Frederic Morrow, to his staff in the White House, in an executive capacity. Morrow required a secretary from the White House pool. They were all specially trained white girls. Everyone refused the job. According to Morrow, 'None wants the onus of working for a colored boss.' So Morrow sat alone in his White House office, without a secretary, not knowing what to do. Then, late in the day, a white girl timidly appeared. She was from Massachusetts. She was religious. She knew Morrow was having trouble. She felt that she could not be true to her faith unless she volunteered for the job. When the white girl appeared, Morrow said, 'she kept the door open behind her, as if for protection, and refused to come in and sit down.' " Dilman paused. "I could never forget that. In the Senate I always kept one door open when I had a white secretary or female visitor in. I-I guess I've brought the same feeling with me into the White House. Forgive my sensitivity, Miss Foster. Now, at least, you understand it."

In 1963, less than a year before the publication of *The Man* (which proves, if nothing else, that Wallace is a fast writer; he also had to make adjustments for the death of John F. Kennedy in November 1963, which is referred to in the novel), E. Frederic Morrow's *Black Man in the White House* was published. Morrow had served as administrative officer for special projects in the Eisenhower White House from 1955 to 1961. He was the first black ever to serve on a White House staff. He had originally joined Eisenhower in 1952 as a consultant during the General's first presidential campaign.

In the above-quoted passage, Wallace extrapolates from Morrow's original account to give us an intensified version of the black male's neurosis of inferiority, a neurosis with which Wallace, of course, writing from a liberal perspective, expects us to empathize because this is the era of trying to understand the Negro by placing oneself in his *moral* dilemma (e.g., John Howard Griffin's 1961 *Black Like Me* and Sidney Poitier films). Nowhere in Morrow's book subsequent to this incident does he say that he kept his office door open when his white secretary came in. Indeed, Wallace's scene is a reciprocal reversal in which the white woman's sexual neurosis (fear that a black man might assault her) triggers a corresponding sexual neurosis in the fictional black male (that she might think that he is thinking about her sexually). The open door is the symbol of opportunity and openness in the political discourse of the culture, "The Negro often dreams of things separated from him only by a door, knowing that he is forever cut off from experiencing them." So stated a popular book of the period. Ironically, the door represents exactly that in Wallace's scene: the shuddering repression of both the white woman (displaced in the text from the real-life experience of Morrow; the fictional Miss Foster has no such concern about Dilman) and the black man (displaced in Morrow's text from the fictional experience and account of Dilman, whose little confession implies that he is, after all, merely following a kind of example of behavior, of racial etiquette, which, in fact, does not appear ever to have existed or merited mentioning in the authenticating source). This excessive sexual self-consciousness is almost exclusively the result not purely of racism but of the willingness of people neurotically, even pathologically, to participate in their own oppression. Accepting inhumanity doth make Sambos of us all! In the novel, Dilman's ultimately heroic struggle to overcome his crippling racial consciousness is counterpointed by Sally Watson, a scheming blonde who tries to entrap Dilman sexually (ironically, Dilman's downfall is almost caused by being inadvertently behind a closed door with a white woman) in order to help her boyfriend, Secretary of State Arthur Eaton, ascend to the presidency. She suffers a nervous breakdown, not her first, and must be hospitalized by book's end. There may be at least two possible political interpretations of black man/white woman sexual self-consciousness as exhibited (and that comes closest to the right word as the drama here becomes nothing more than flagrant exhibitionism) in the novel. First, if a liberal such as Sally Watson, who prided in, among her broad-minded accomplishments, having had a Puerto Rican husband and two black lovers, and having served as hostess at several integrated parties, can turn self-servingly in racial solidarity against a black, what hope is there? (And one supposes that Wallace is rather snidely satirizing the complete folly of anyone thinking those liberal credentials mean anything beyond one's fantasizing about sex, but the critique finally seems too clichéd and gender-fixated. Political scheming for women, according to Wallace, becomes another form of hysteria.) We are left, in this instance, to conclude that, in a pinch, whites will pull together to topple a black from any inadvertent rise to power. Second, it is always to the white male's advantage to entangle the black male and the white female in an unholy alliance of sexual self-consciousness and tension; he exploits it, so this novel tells us, to keep himself in power. The latter has the virtue of being correct, to a degree, and sounding particularly contemporary (the evil conspiracy of the patriarchy and all that). The former has the virtue of being a correct assessment of the political reality that blacks have come to know and understand. More about this as we go along.

To speak of one scene of Frederic Morrow's book as being the almost entire thematic unraveling of Wallace's fictional construct is to suggest the considerable influence Morrow exercises over the Wallace text. The very circumstances of Morrow's joining the Eisenhower team must have interested Wallace a great deal:

> Not once during the campaign had I ever talked with anyone about a Washington position with the Administration. I was happy in my job at CBS and confident that it could lead to important advancement. There were personal complications too....
>
> I had many talks with Sherman Adams [governor of New Hampshire and presidential assistant under Eisenhower, who exercised power, especially in his connection to the National Security Council, much as a chief of staff], and he sent me to see several prominent persons to talk about the kind of spot I should occupy in the White House. Finally a letter from Mr. Adams definitely confirmed the fact that I would be notified of this officially.... Mr. Adams advised me to tell CBS that I would be resigning, which I did.
>
> After that I met frequently with Max Rabb [assistant to Adams], and each time there would be a hassle over the salary I could expect in any White House position. I had made it clear that I would not go to Washington for less than $10,000 a year, and I simply could not lower that figure. Max kept trying to induce me to take $1,000 or $1,500 less, and each time I would try to get a firm commitment he would tell me that there were a few more details to be ironed out. By the time the President had moved into the White House my status still had not been established.
>
> The delegation had closed the campaign headquarters at the Commodore, and I began to find it impossible to get in touch with anyone. I phoned the White House dozens of times, only to be told that Mr. Rabb was out or in conference and would call me back. A very distressing period! Several months had passed since I had resigned from CBS, and I was living on savings which were dwindling fast. So was my morale.
>
> Over three months after the Inauguration I finally got through to Bernard Shanley, special counsel to the President, and asked him to please let me know definitely what the score was on my going to Washington. He called me back the next day to tell me that he was very sorry but it had been decided that there was nothing available for me in the White House.
>
> This failure affected me like some kind of complex disease.

Morrow finally is given a position of adviser on business affairs in the Department of Commerce and eventually, through the machinations of Sherman Adams, a position in the White House, which Morrow seemed not to have liked as well. Race, naturally, occupies a good deal of Morrow's attention. It must be remembered that some of the most important milestones in American race relations occurred under Eisenhower: the 1954 Supreme Court decision for school desegregation; the 1955-56 Montgomery bus boycott; the rise of Martin Luther King, Jr., and the Southern Christian Leadership Conference; the intervention of federal troops in Little Rock, Arkansas; passage of the 1957 civil rights bill; the rise of Elijah Muhammad's Nation of Islam; the establishment of the literary careers of Gwendolyn Brooks (Pulitzer Prize winner), Ralph Ellison (National Book Award winner), and James Baldwin (national commentator in white magazines). Despite the fact that most blacks in the 1950s voted Democratic, there were still a fair number of blacks who voted Republican (Eisenhower received 20 percent of the black vote in 1952 and 36 percent in 1956, better numbers than any Republican, with the exception of Richard Nixon—29 percent in 1960, has received since), so Morrow was not ostracized, although there is a great sense of isolation that permeates his book. Morrow is troubled by his inability to please blacks who accuse him of being a mere apologist for an administration that seems anti-civil rights. On the other hand, he is equally troubled by the administration's deaf ear to civil rights concerns. (Eisenhower was not as racist as popular opinion has made him out to be. He once told Morrow the story that shortly after graduating from West Point he was assigned as an instructor to a black National Guard unit in Illinois. As historian Michael S. Mayer recounts, "By his own description a young, spit-and-polish officer, he was dismayed by the poor performance of his black troops. When his rifle team performed pathetically against white outfits in competition, he was 'ashamed and embarrassed.' Eisenhower thought at the time that the men were simply inferior, not improperly trained, and admitted that this association in his early career with black troops affected his thinking on race for years." What is interesting is that by the time Eisenhower told the story to Morrow in 1952, he had become a fairly firm environmentalist, believing education would uplift the Negro. His readjusted focus for black failure was no different from that of most liberals of the time. He certainly may have been in retrospect more liberal in race matters than Adlai Stevenson, his Democratic rival, was. Adam Clayton Powell, Jr., surely thought so, as the Democratic congressman backed Eisenhower in 1956 instead of Stevenson, the break occurring solely on the issue of civil rights. As Powell wrote, "I campaigned for [Eisenhower] from coast to coast. After Eisenhower won, he lived up to each of the pledges [he made in a meeting with Powell] and the nation received its first civil rights law in eighty-two years." Eisenhower must have had a natural inclination to do this since he certainly did not need Powell's support to win.

Morrow, like many blacks of the time, was impressed by Indonesia's

President Sukarno, probably because that country hosted the 1955 Bandung Conference of the colored nations of the world; he was annoyed by the discrimination in Washington that prevented his renting a decent apartment, amused by the whites at parties who mistook him for a servant, truly awed by the presence of Eisenhower. Finally, because Morrow was dark-skinned and from a respectable though not famous background, he was not likely to be either arrogant or burdened by history as was the most famous black politician of the day, Adam Clayton Powell, Jr., the charming and brilliant scoundrel who was too good-looking and too afflicted by the presence of a famous father not to be a tragic nova. Powell was not the kind of black man Wallace could comfortably envision as president; the singularity of his personality alone would overwhelm what was for Wallace the major point of the story: the act of a Negro inadvertently, not through his own will, ascending to power. It was not the story of some particularized black man's rise to power and prominence. Thus, Morrow made an ideal model for Wallace's characterization of a black man in power. (Wallace makes a point of describing Dilman as a very dark black man.) It is hard to imagine Wallace being able successfully to imagine the character of Dilman without having had Morrow.

So the key terms in the above-quoted passage about Morrow's brusque denial of a job are not only his characterization of his cavalier treatment as a "complex disease"—an odd compound, for in his anguished ruminations about his rejection he indeed suffers from a disease that is a complex and a complex that is a disease, a combination of feeling victimized and degraded, inferior and unsure—but also the use of the word "failure," which is not quite an accurate description of what happened to him. But it is to be expected that at times the black bourgeois male would be so traumatized by his mistreatment that he would begin to think of it as failure which, obviously, makes protest against it impossible. All of this is something that only a black man trying to occupy some real "position" in the white world would feel. And it is this sense of complex disease and the attendant feeling of failure that runs rampant in Wallace's novel. His hero, Douglas Dilman, is nearly consumed by this utter uncertainty of position and status despite having become the most powerful politician, albeit by accident, in the land. He does not wish to be the oversensitive Negro, yet he cannot help but feel he is persecuted because of his race. He wishes to be a good president but he cannot help but think his failure is not only looming but fated. It is no accident that the book is called *The Man,* for if the two previous fictive white presidents before Dilman were known simply as The Chief and The Judge, honorifics of white male authority, then the whole business of black manhood is encapsulated in the ironic honorific The Man, used so often by blacks, in fact, when talking about white men in authority and never used by white men in this country when referring to black males who always, even in hoary old age, were boys. Dilman is literally The Man by virtue of being president, and the book becomes nothing more than a not very plausible set of tests by which he can prove he too can be as much a leader of fortitude as the men who preceded him. The articles of impeachment drawn up against Dilman at his trial (he avoids being kicked out of office by one vote) seem in part to read like the standard indictment against the black male in high places: improper advances to a white woman, an immoral relationship with a black woman, irresponsible dismissal of a more capable white man (Secretary of State Eaton), an inability to transcend racial identification, particularly in relation to a fictional African country called Baraza and a militant black group that attracted his son as a fellow traveler. The fact that the impeachment trial and indeed the entire presidency of Dilman refer openly in the text to Andrew Johnson (His Accidency, as sharp-tongued, bewigged, clubfooted Thaddeus Stevens, Johnson's most tenacious enemy, called him, which reminds us of the whole issue of inadvertence) is, presumably, intentional, as the shadow of the Reconstruction seems to shade the entire novel. There is an obvious irony in having the fictional presidency of a displaced, ill-at-ease black man who could not, even if he wanted to, court favor from blacks, recall the presidency of a displaced, ill-at-ease southerner who wanted to even if he finally could not quite court favor from southern planters. But the allusion to the Reconstruction is more important still: it was the first time in America that some blacks found themselves, momentarily and inadvertently, in high places.

James S. Pike's report *The Prostrate State: South Carolina Under Negro Government* (1873) stands in much the same relation to Thomas Dixon's novel *The Clansman* (1905) as Morrow's *Black Man in the White House* stands to Wallace's *The Man.* (D.W. Griffith's 1915 film, *Birth of a Nation,* based on Dixon's *The Clansman* and *The Leopard's Spots,* published in 1903, completes the parallel pattern to Morrow-Wallace film.) Pike is not simply a source but a historical legitimation of Dixon's psychosexual southern interpretation of Reconstruction. Dixon's theme of whites, northern and southern, united in holy war against barbaric, overbearing Negroes who had taken over South Carolina's statehouse after the Civil War, needed the external verification of and symbolic ideological union with the northern newspaperman's account that had such a great impact on the nation. Pike's book is simply a detailed narrative of the South Carolina legislative sessions in the months of February and March 1873, including extensive eyewitness reports and numerous quotations from hearings and official documents. Pike's opening description of the South Carolina Assembly was quoted widely:

> Yesterday, about 4 p.m., the assembled wisdom of the State...issued forth from the State-House. About three-quarters of the crowd belonged to the African race. They were of every hue, from the light octoroon to the deep black. They were such a looking body of men as might pour out a market-house or a court-house at random in any Southern State. Every negro type and physiognomy was here to be seen, from the genteel serving-man to the rough-hewn customer from the rice or cotton field. Their dress was as varied as their

countenances. There was the second-hand black frock-coat of infirm gentility, glossy and threadbare. There was the stove-pipe hat of many ironings and departed styles. There was also to be seen a total disregard of the proprieties of costume in the coarse and dirty garments of the field; the stub-jackets and slouch hats of soiling labor. In some instances, rough woolen comforters embraced the neck and hid the absence of linen. Heavy brogans, and short, torn trousers, it was impossible to hide. The dusky tide flowed into the littered and barren grounds, and, issuing through the coarse wooden fence of the inclosure, melted away into the street beyond. These were the legislators of South Carolina.

What may come as a surprise to the modern reader is that Pike's work is actually a liberal book, a forerunner of the muckraking exposes of Lincoln Steffens, Ida Tarbell, Stephen Crane (*Maggie: A Girl of the Streets*), and Upton Sinclair during the Progressive era. Pike's book was written in the spirit of revealing corrupt, mismanaged government, a reformist book. (Everyone knows, of course, that the Progressive era was a very ambivalent one, its reform efforts motivated by a rock-hard conservatism and tenacious racism as much as a liberal bent for social justice.) Pike believed, as a standard liberal measure, in the education of the Negro: "Education means to educate them out of themselves, to undo the habits and practices and modes of thought and want of thought engendered by centuries of slavery." (Here we have the restated origin of the abolitionist construct of the "maimed black," which was to be restated again as part of intellectual liberal thought by Myrdal and other post–World War II sociologists as well as by 1950s liberal historians of slavery and Reconstruction such as Stampp, whose books were open refutation of the conservative historians Phillips and Dunning, and Elkins, an interpretation of such political magnitude and cultural endurance that blacks, rightly or wrongly but certainly understandably, were to resent it greatly from the 1960s on.) Yet oddly enough, the legislative measure that Pike most strongly condemns that was passed by this Reconstruction government involves black education and the University of South Carolina:

> In execution of the steady purpose of putting blacks on an equality with the whites, a measure was passed at this session to throw open the library [of the University of South Carolina] to the colored students of the Normal School, and to take one of the college buildings for its uses. And in pursuance of the same purpose a majority of the trustees of the college were recently chosen by the same Legislature from the ranks of the blacks. In this case it was color rather than qualification for the post that was sought. This destroys the usefulness of the college so far as the white youth are concerned, as the young aristocratic blood of the State will decline the proposed amalgamation. The movement will eventuate in the substantial destruction of the university, as the black population will afford an inadequate supply of students. It is a damaging blow to the interests of education in the State, and a significant step in the process of Africanization.

How it is against the interest of South Carolina to educate its uneducated slave population, to strengthen its Normal School to do this by providing teachers for the freedmen, to improve the Normal School by giving it access to a better library (or to a library at all, since it is quite possible that a black Normal School had no library to speak of at this time) is quite beyond anyone whose racism has not transcended the boundaries of common sense. In fact, among the most notable achievements of most Reconstruction governments were their policies concerning public education. They provided public schools for both races. Of course, the fear is "Africanization," and it must have done Thomas Dixon's southern heart good to know that a white northern liberal felt about the subject of blacks in high places the same as he himself did. As Eisenhower's sister-in-law wrote to the president during the Little Rock crisis: "We can never upgrade the negro [sic] to our level. Consequently, we must drop to his level." But it is the sentence that follows that reveals the fundamental Freudian preoccupation with Africanization: "And this may be putting it crudely," she continues, "but I hate to think of the many pretty pink-and-white 'Susan' [Susan Eisenhower, the president's granddaughter] type of girls who will fall victim to the passionate instincts and desires of their coal-black classmates!!" No wonder Frederic Morrow spent six years as the spook who sat by the door in a constant state of distress. And in large measure, Eisenhower's sister-in-law's formulations were made possible by the very popular rantings of Thomas Dixon.

Dixon, just as Wallace did with Morrow, extrapolated from his source text, Pike. Dixon discounts the theory of educating blacks as he makes them out to be literally beasts (quite significant in the age of Social Darwinism in which he wrote; in *The Clansman,* he also bestializes the granddaddy white radical, Thaddeus Stevens; for Dixon, liberalism in racial politics is simply the unbearable release of an unreclaimable id: a society without standards or morals which is obviously self-evident if one believes that Negroes have the right and capacity to have power. In some quarters, a milder, more erudite version of this argument has been used to criticize affirmative action and to defend a traditional, Western Civ. liberal arts education à la Allan Bloom and the Grand Traditions). This, at least, took care of the liberal argument that blacks were victimized by environment. They were by nature what they were. Pike does not mention much, if anything, about sex crimes perpetrated by black men against white women. For Dixon, Africanization's lone reality is his own psychosexual fantasy of virginal white girls being raped and of black legislatures passing intermarriage laws. (One naturally would think that most black men had more pressing and immediate problems during the Reconstruction than a concern for the acquisition of white wives and white sex, neither of which, over the years, has been proven to be a substantial improvement over black wives or black sex, although this culture seems bent on using all its advertising and programming muscle to convince us differently.) The transformation is extremely important because in Pike the blacks are seen as hapless tools of ambitious whites. What makes the blacks so monstrous in Dixon is the

muting, though not total absence, of inadvertence. The rape was encouraged by the preachments of social equality by the likes of Thaddeus Stevens,
but the act has its own independent and hideous political force because of its
volitional nature. Rape is an act of making someone submit to you against
his or her own will. In *The Clansman,* the only book of Dixon's that I have
read that I remember very well, because repeated viewings of *Birth of a
Nation* tend to reinforce it, although there are significant and important
differences between book and movie, the climactic sense of the black male's
insane use of political power over the whites during Reconstruction col-
lapses into a generalized, unintentionally feminist scenario of the male's
insane use of power over the female: a violent interracial rape by a black
soldier, Gus, of a fifteen-year-old white virgin, Marion. Indeed, this dis-
places what was supposed to be the central, climaxing scene of the novel,
which was the opening description of Pike's book: the blacks have taken
over the hallowed halls of government. That business becomes secondary
for Dixon. The sexual self-consciousness of the white man's own psychosis
projected outwardly on the black male and the white female is the real
subject here. And we get another reading of how the white man keeps
power, this time through the counterrevolution of the Klan avenging the
illicit meeting of the black male and the white female behind a closed door
(or through a closed door broken open, as in this instance, which is Dixon's
metaphor of the blacks' rise to power).

And so we have come full circle in seeing the white cultural propositions
of the black male in power. The white conservative Dixon points to the
actuality of the Reconstruction (he insisted strenuously on the historical
accuracy of his Reconstruction novels; Pike and other reporters and historians of the period were not simply sources for Dixon, in the end, but
competitors of a sort) as demonstrating that the black in power is simply the
mad Emperor Jones. Inadvertence is neither innocence nor exculpation; the
Negro's inadvertent rise to power is the path to societal degeneration. The
contemporary white liberal, Wallace, relying on the promise of the civil
rights movement and thus giving us speculative fiction with a historical
veneer, views the black male in power as a kind of bourgeois fulfillment of
his manhood (see the characterization of Walter Lee Younger in Lorraine
Hansberry's *A Raisin in the Sun* [1959]—a title that must be a pun of both
bourgeois male ambition and Christian theology—or the characterization of
Joe Starks in Zora Neale Hurston's *Their Eyes Were Watching God* [1937] for
a black woman's critique of the thesis). For Wallace, inadvertence leads to
resolve and the decisive and responsible use of power. After all, Dilman,
after a few initial missteps turns out to be, by white liberal and white
conservative standards, a pretty good president. The black male in power is
the fulfillment of the promise of American democracy which, after all, is
what the civil rights movement as an ideology espoused. Dixon convicts
the Negro under the very same Articles of Impeachment that Wallace uses
to exonerate Dilman—on the basis that the charges are trumped up.

So we are stuck in a kind of nowhere talking about the absolute and utter contradiction that Twain so tellingly phrased in his *Pudd'nhead Wilson* (1894), another novel about blacks inadvertently (but is this so? For Tom, the misplaced black son, it is all inadvertent, but for Roxy, the scheming black mother, it is all planned) being in high places: high-bawn niggers. "Dey ain't another nigger in dis town dat's as high-bawn as you is," Roxy tells her mulatto son who is inadvertently passing for white. And what in the world is the oddity known as a high-bawn nigger, the ultimate oxymoron? Twain's novel, which can be rightly understood only as a satirical gloss on both slavery and the Reconstruction, gives us sexual self-consciousness in its historically correct nineteenth-century American version: between white men and black women; white men because, as Twain shows, their obsessive codes of masculine honor were not simply amusements but the very foundations of the political and economic assumptions that governed their society, and black women because they were both, as the book graphically shows, the mothers and the lovers of white men. What is Tom, the misplaced mulatto: a dastardly white man because of his rearing, a cowardly Negro because of his birth, a white man because he looks as such (when he murders his uncle he wears burnt cork and thus becomes a Negro or at least something black; the episode brings to mind Tom Delamere's murder of his Aunt Polly in Charles Chesnutt's *The Marrow of Tradition,* published in 1901, a book that seems clearly to be the black's response to *Wilson*)? Is he a man or a woman (he dresses as both)? Is he an eastern dandy or a provincial in the dress of Dawson's Landing? Twain so confuses the issue of the liberal's argument about environment and the conservative's of inherent and adhering nature, that the whole epistemology of class, race, gender, the origin of human identity becomes satirized, is, in fact, made absurd with the entrance of the Siamese twins. All power and all human motivation are inadvertence that is both absurd and providential, says Twain. And, of course, all power and all human motivation are intentionality that is both tragic and comic. Ah, you say, what has all of this to do with Jesse Jackson's running for president?

What is the epistemology of the black male's sense of ambition? Suppose, in the end, that a good many cultural propositions in America hinge on precisely how we conceive that and why we conceive it. Jackson gives the best laboratory case since Booker T. Washington of the public enactment of a black male's unabashed quest for power as the bourgeois fulfillment of masculine ambition. For Jackson, inadvertence goes out of the window, as he has had his fill of talking about the black male's ego in relation to his inability to control anything. His compulsion is to have what white men have: complete and relentless control over his own fate and everyone else's. It is a kind of remorseless and single-minded envy that drives him. This is what he preaches to "the locked out": Act, don't react; make deals, not compromises. Jackson is our real-life Cat in the Hat.

In his brilliant short story about presidential politics, "A Political Fable" (1968), Robert Coover tells us that the Cat in the Hat is a trickster. He strolls into the lives of some middle-class white kids, invades a white middle-class home, and wreaks havoc for a time while the parents (Mother's absence is particularly emphasized) are away. Then he magically fixes everything up. The first time was bad enough, with Thing One and Thing Two being set loose from a box and running around the house flying kites, but the second time he leaves a pink cat ring all over the house, and he brings helpers, little cats A through Z, who simply compound the chaos, killing pink snow spots with pop guns, and finally he unleashes something called VOOM! Does all of this sound familiar? Everyone as a child has read this subversive stuff that, in effect, predicts the coming of, to borrow a title from an old Art Ensemble of Chicago album, *A Jackson in Your House*. (Remember Seuss's *Yertle the Turtle* and *The 500 Hundred Hats of Bartholomew Cubbins*? Perfect campaign literature for the bourgeois liberal.) And so like the Cat in the Hat, Jackson brings his chaos and his VOOM! and his pinko cat ring, as well as his aching ambition and his hatred of inadvertence, into our house. He is, as David Walker called himself in his 1828 *Appeal to the Colored Citizens of the World*, "a disturber of the public peace." He is also, unlike his fictional counterpart, quite likely to return more than twice. Of course, we have learned from the famous Warner Brothers trickster, Bugs Bunny, that anything can happen in a cartoon. And we learned in our elementary school civics class that anything can happen in American culture. (Ah, the social uplift of the story of American immigrants and the welling inspiration of Martin Luther King, Jr.'s, Dream: it is all about dreams here and all about wishing on stars so that your wish, too, can come true. Just play the state lottery and it could happen to you.) Or as the Cat says in Coover's story, a direct quotation from *The Cat in the Hat* (1957):

> *"Look at me!*
> *Look at me!*
> *Look at me NOW!*
> *It is fun to have fun*
> *But you have to know how."*

But Jesse Jackson is smarter than Pudd'nhead Wilson. And he is surely smarter than we are who are no smarter than the citizens of Dawson's Landing who do not think you can kill half a dog. Jackson knows it doesn't matter whether you can or cannot as long as you keep telling everyone you just did.

II. THE CAT IN THE HAT COMES BACK: SOME PRACTICES

On their faces they all wear a smirk
'Cause they know I'm the king of the cool jerk.
— The Capitols, "Cool Jerk"

Jesse Jackson is one of the brightest hopes for the future. Jackson, who worked

for Dr. King in Chicago, setting up the successful Operation Breadbasket there, has brains, looks, charisma, and is a gifted orator besides. I see him as the only man on the horizon who can come forward and provide leadership, not only for black America but for blacks and whites together.
—Adam Clayton Powell, Jr., *Adam by Adam*, 1971

I have hopes for Jesse Jackson. I think he offers the most viable leadership for blacks and oppressed minorities in America and also for the salvation of our national decency. I think Jesse's leadership is potentially one of majestic proportions. He is totally dedicated and if we are to arise out of this deepening pit of polarization between us as a people, it will be by supporting the kind of leadership Jesse Jackson offers.
—Jackie Robinson, *I Never Had It Made,* 1972

Within a year of each other, the old dark-skinned, retired fatherless ballplayer turned Republican businessman who was haunted by his repressions and the old light-skinned, aristocratic father-obsessed preacher turned Democratic congressman who was haunted by his excesses both predicted the success of Jesse Jackson, both praised his leadership. To win praise from such widely divergent corners of the black bourgeoisie is quite a feat, which probably only Jackson could pull off. If Malcolm X had lived long enough he probably would have liked him too. Martin Luther King, Jr., lived just long enough and knew Jackson just well enough to be unsure. It is difficult to tell, from the distance where King is now, whether, in looking down on Jackson, he is smiling or smirking.

"Oh-oh!" Sally said.
"Don't you talk to that cat.
That cat is a bad one,
That Cat in the Hat.
He plays lots of bad tricks.
Don't you let him come near.
You know what he did
The last time he was here."
—Dr. Seuss, *The Cat in the Hat Comes Back*

So what does Jesse Jackson want? The question of the age for this past political season and for the season of '84. Surely, he cannot want simply to be famous. He is already that and it would be beneath his ambition to want more of it, simply to want more notice. That is rather like a man wanting more fuel to burn his life up with, a costly way to give off heat and light, if only for a little while. Just ask Muhammad Ali, who enjoyed for a time the kind of fame, the intensity, the shearing whirlwind of adulation and hatred that Jackson now has. The connection with Ali is not accidental metaphor. In the April 5, 1988, *Christian Science Monitor,* columnist Godfrey Sperling, Jr., likened Jackson's stature and reception in the black community to that of

Joe Louis back in the mid to late 1930s through the Second World War.

> He is the blacks' champion. Like Louis, he is standing up to white contenders and besting them. His victories are theirs. It's the way blacks feel when they see outstanding black athletes. It's only a beginning, they know. But it gives them needed assurance that blacks can achieve in a world where whites hold so many of the top power positions.

The assessment is correct but the comparison is not. Jackson, during those heady days of the spring primaries of 1988, was more like Muhammad Ali reborn. Jackson is a champion who not only bests the whites, but brags about it. He is audacious and brash. The very extravagant nature of his manner and presence, the sheer daring quality of his challenge, the Muslim over-tones of his ideology (not only pro-Arab and pro-Palestinian but pro–black entrepreneurial development), his ability to speak cleverly, to rhyme and "to speechify," as the old black folk say, remind one not of the young Ali but of the mature, post-exile Ali. Like Ali, Jackson wants fame, a platform, some enlarged mythical self that becomes interchangeable with the real self. He desires not a public career but an absolutely public life, a public persona that vibrates within the culture like a perpetually struck tuning fork. But he has this now and, unlike Ali, who became simply a gorged parody, a missionary who soon became his own failed, his own unfulfilled mission, Jackson knows that he must not simply and rampantly express ambition (a subversive act for a black man in many spheres of activity in our culture); he must constantly reinvent the stuff that constitutes his craving. He really cannot afford to become so famous that, as Ali ultimately hurt boxing by drawing attention only to himself (while Monzon, Valdes, young Duran, Bob Foster, and others toiled away in the shadows), Jackson deflects notice and oppor-tunity from other capable black politicians on the national scene. Young plants do not grow well in the shade.

So what does Jesse Jackson want? He wants what every social reformer wants: to humanize economics, which is largely considered to be inhuman and something that acts upon passive human beings; he wants to redis-tribute the food supply. As the great black theologian Howard Thurman, whom Jackson greatly admired, wrote: "Indeed, the most fundamental characteristic of life is its search for nourishment." Jackson wants to ensure that everyone has the same opportunity at the trough, that everyone has the same opportunity not simply to eat but also to understand what that unconscious, nay, helpless common vow, "We all have to eat," means for us as a collective reality. None of these desires is new; they are the old trial horses of Christian socialism or democratic socialism. It is, in fact, the very worn nature of these truisms, clothed in a strident moralism, that is greatly appealing to the bourgeois intellectual class because it manages, dismayingly, to stimulate and assuage guilt simultaneously. It is because of this moralism that social reform in this country is the decidedly dreary and deadening business that it is. Jackson stands as probably the only person in the Western world who can mouth these positions with such energy, who has the demagogic potential actually to make a mass movement from positions that intellectuals find to be so purely upstanding as to be constricting. (The have-nots hear Jackson saying only that he wants to take something from the snobbish haves and give it to them; people who have nothing are less interested in having something than in bringing those who have something to the dirty trenches, the infantry of living.) Jackson wants, to borrow Ludwig Lewisohn's list of bourgeois desires, "security, dignity, privacy, liberation from sordid care for the sake of cultural disinterestedness," for those who do not enjoy those things. In short, he wants a kind of massive bourgeoisation of the "locked out" (a curious phrase implying doors; see part one of this essay for more about the image of doors) or those who cannot now enjoy the fruits of the bourgeois life. He frequently calls in his speeches for a Marshall Plan for the poor. Once again, there is nothing new in this, as virtually all social reformers in America have wanted this. They scarcely know how to desire anything else; they can imagine the human race only as a huge, gorgeously pluralistic family with each member contributing gifts that everyone else accepts with great gratitude. ("America is more like a quilt," Jackson said once, "many patches, many pieces, many colors, many sizes, all woven and held together by a common thread.") Jackson's Christianity makes this kind of reform a very safe thing to want because it is absolutely impossible to have it. Which is, at last, precisely the point; desire becomes a politicized but humanized act, economics without inequality because no one will ever be hungry or dirty again. The world will then look very like those postmillennial drawings in the Jehovah's Witnesses' *Watchtower* magazine with nuclear families eating picnics with the bosses on endlessly sunny days while trees groan with vegetation and lions lie down with lambs and play with the kids.

Jackson's blackness makes all the difference in our buying this message as we see, before our eyes, his own personal drama and struggle of bourgeoisation being played out upon the national stage. For the black, the business of his personal bourgeoisation is the business of white acceptance. It is fine if the whites will accept the black as one of their own, even better if he is accepted *because* of his blackness and not *despite* it. This is why Thomas Landess and Richard Quinn, who wrote *Jesse Jackson and the Politics of Race* (1985), and Julius Lester, who wrote a scathing anti-Jackson article a few years back in *Dissent,* are wrong when they accuse Jackson in his presidential tries of simply running for the national leadership of black America. Jackson quite clearly wishes to be the first black leader of white America and wishes to do this by fairly much talking to whites in the same way he talks to blacks and convincing them to let him represent their interests. To spend the time and energy to run for president for anything less would be sheer imbecility. He could already influence the opinions of blacks before he ran for president. He was unable to change their lives (or his own very much, except to acquire fame and money). He decided that the real business of shaking things out in this country is by influencing whites, indeed, actually leading them. Undoubtedly, the general acceptance by whites of his PUSH-Excel educational initiative, which ended so disastrously, gave Jackson a real taste of what being a white leader feels like. Yes, Jackson wants to be the Wizard, as they used to call Booker T. Washington, because he was the last great African-American politician who could really shake things out in the world of white folk. He wants to be Washington and he even believes most of Washington's rhetoric about black businesses, moral decency, hard work, and the like. In the end, however, he must spend a great deal of his time repudiating Washington (whose disciples now are black conservative economists such as Thomas Sowell and Walter E. Williams: segregation does not matter; economics is a force like God that eventually rights all evils through the presence of his only begotten son, the market-place) because he must always sound like a national conscience and he must never lose touch with the bourgeois movement of moral sentiment that validated him, civil rights and the pietistic, fervent denouncement of inequality.

Thus the distinctions between Jackson and Washington become strategi-cally important, differences that can be measured by how both men wished to be seen and accepted publicly, differences that can be measured by their cant words: "accommodation" and "cooperation" for Washington, "access" and "empowerment" for Jackson. Jackson's speech before a joint session of the Alabama legislature in Montgomery on May 24, 1983, seems a real revisionist version of Washington's 1895 Atlanta Cotton Exposition speech, although both speeches, addressing white southerners, have the same theme: finding common ground. Certainly both speeches claim the same national significance as black leaders with southern roots define or redefine the American South. The difference is most clearly presented in the openings: Jackson reminds his audience of how, in this room, 122 years before, Alabama seceded from the Union, about how the white masters divided the nation: "On February 6, 1861, in this very chamber, the Confederacy was formed. Three days later it elected Jefferson Davis its first provisional president. It unified the South, but it divided the *United* States and thrust the nation's regions into war against each other — South versus North, North versus South." Washington says: "Ignorant and inexperienced, it is not strange that in the first years of our new life we [blacks] began at the top instead of at the bottom; that a seat in Congress or the state legislature was more sought than real estate or industrial skill; that the political convention of stump speaking had more attractions than starting a dairy farm or truck garden." Washington joins with his southern audience in denouncing the Reconstruction as an expression of overweening inadvertence (an impossible oxymoron) on the part of degraded people. Jackson wishes to tell the southerner that sectional division is the master's fault, while Washington tells us that racial division is the slave's fault, sort of. But it should be said that Jackson has no more intention of upsetting white southerners with his speech than Washington did. Jackson says at the end: "Today, this is a marvelous place from which to speak. A place where Jefferson Davis stood, where Martin Luther King, Jr., should have stood." But Jackson's act of rhetorical reconciliation is an attempt to appease the southerner by accepting the white hero as long as the black hero is accorded his place as well. The histories—black and white—must merge, which is a direct refutation of Washington's cagey insistence that there can be separation in union: "In all things that are purely social we can be as separate as the fingers, yet one as the hand in all things essential to mutual progress." Which of these is really *e pluribus unum*? Jackson most insistently distinguishes himself from Washington in his use of the rhetorical figure: "We must lift the boats that are stuck on the bottom," a figure he apparently is quite fond of, as it has appeared in a number of his addresses. It is a very pithy revision of Washington's long central metaphor of the distressed ship captain being told to cast down his bucket where he is. For Washington, there are no boats on the bottom, simply poor managers of ships who do not see the riches before their eyes. But Jackson's tangled metaphor is curious. Boats on the bottom are usually wrecked and beyond rescue. They are salvaged but not often renewed or refitted. They may be raised for some hidden treasure but not to be made seaworthy. And the image of treasure hunting suggests a kind of exploitation of the class he is describing, which he vehemently opposes. Yet his metaphor subsumes subtly the very sense of exploitation that Washington's openly asserts. Perhaps Jackson likes the phrase because it suggests submergence, which is an appropriate enough way to think of the underclass in America. Washington is far too much the genial turn-of-the-century optimist to think in those terms. Jackson has a greater sense of tragedy.

> *"Look at me!*
> *Look at me now!" said the cat.*
> *"With a cup and a cake*
> *On the top of my hat!*
> *I can hold up* TWO *books!*
> *I can hold up the fish!*
> *And a little toy ship!*
> *And some milk on a dish!"*
> —Dr. Seuss, *The Cat in the Hat*

But is Jackson really the direct descendant of King? Although he was created by the Southern Christian Leadership Conference, there is a great sense that Jackson wishes to embody the entire spectrum of black politics: separatist, integrationist, legalistic, humanitarian, Pan-Africanist, Muslim, capitalist, socialist, egalitarian, Victorian moralist, anti-establishment outsider, shrewd insider. He is disliked by many because he has managed to negotiate these various roles fairly well over his career. Most black people, whatever their persuasion, will listen to him, an absolutely amazing feat for a man who represents a people among whom the smallest doctrinal differences are often the cause of disputes as frenzied as seventeenth-century churchmen fighting over how many angels can dance on the head of a pin. It must be recognized, first, that King's cant words, "love" and "freedom," were different, like Washington's too, from Jackson's. The change signifies not only a difference in history but a difference in bourgeois perspective, a so-called hard-edged realism that refutes the previous age's mystification and ineptness at implementation. It is this so-called hard-edged realism that makes Jackson popular with blacks today. His speeches are filled with dubious statistics and the jargon of political briefing books. He talks of making deals and sharing power and sitting at the table with the *misuse of meaning.* decision-makers. Yet he cannot abandon his mystical origins completely or else he would lose the very charismatic fetish that makes him a leader with blacks (and whites as well). He must be prophetic in the American vein, *emotive* which is often why the cataloguing in his speeches sounds much like Whitman and the aphorisms sound like bad television jingles. He must be prophetic in the African-American vein, which is why the speeches often sound like sermons and reach a degree of impassioned flight that is rare for American political discourse. As one old black church woman told me many years ago: "I like to see my minister sweat, then I know he is as moved by what he is saying as I am." Or as an old numbers runner I knew used to say: "Prophesying is working, jack." Thus he must constantly exploit the idea that he is the heir of King to authenticate his prophet's voice and prophet's calling. The fact that he is a Baptist minister and that he does not hold a political office makes this implied claim credible and generally acceptable to the public.*

Black political scientist Lucius Barker in his *Our Time Has Come: A Delegate's Diary of Jesse Jackson's 1984 Presidential Campaign* (1988), a book that straddles journalism and scholarship, groupie affection and personal narrative, mentions Jackson as heir to the civil rights mantle and

---

*As this essay is being composed, rumors circulate about the possibility that Jackson may run for mayor of Washington, D.C., replacing a beleaguered and at least partly discredited Marion Barry. Jackson supporters point out that by becoming mayor of Washington, it being a foregone conclusion in all quarters that he would win if he decided to run, Jackson would then acquire the political experience his opponents say he now lacks and thus can be a more creditable and, very possibly, successful presidential candidate in 1992, aside from conferring enormous benefits on Washington through his inspirational leadership. There are a few problems with this scenario: First, by becoming mayor of a virtually all-black town, Jackson would have proved only what most people are convinced of already, that he can get blacks to vote for him. Becoming mayor of a politically diverse place like Chicago or successfully winning a statewide office as governor or senator would be much more impressive to the public and more helpful for Jackson's presidential hopes. Second, no one in American politics has ever ascended straight from the office of mayor to the presidency; it is simply too big a jump, and the electorate is generally not convinced that running a city is anywhere close to being the same thing as running the country. So I think the question of qualifications will still dog Jackson even if he becomes a successful mayor. Last, by becoming mayor of Washington, unless Jackson is the most extraordinary politician in the history of the republic, and certainly some of his followers seem as convinced of that as cult followers are of the messianic powers of their leaders, he is bound to have a record that can be used both *for* and *against* his future office-running efforts even if he is a successful mayor. Frankly, becoming mayor of Washington seems a bit puny and Jim Crowish for Jackson, rather like becoming mayor of Harlem. (Move over, Bill "Bojangles" Robinson!) Jackson is supposed to represent something distinctly radical in American politics. What is so radical about a black politician having a black constituency?

King's throne at least a dozen times: "I too saw the Jackson effort not just as a political campaign but as the most dramatic holistic strategy that could be developed to remind us all of the unfulfilled objectives of Martin Luther King and the civil rights movement and to warn us that the movement's earlier gains were in danger." Another black political scientist, Adolph L. Reed, Jr., in his reasonably argued and generally anti-Jackson book, *The Jesse Jackson Phenomenon* (1986), couches his observation of Jackson as figure from the civil rights/protest wing of black politics, "the protest elite," as a criticism, stating that his campaign was nothing more than the creation of a personality cult: "The initiative's center was the candidate rather than a discrete issue agenda. The Jackson phenomenon thus figures into that context primarily as a cathartic diversion grafted onto regular political processes." Michael Thelwell, the Jamaican activist-writer, in his pro-Jackson essay "God Ain't Finished With Us Yet" reminds the reader too that Jackson and his entire presidential campaign grew out of the civil rights movement. He, like Jackson in his 1984 address to the Democratic National Convention, tells of Fannie Lou Hamer and the 1964 Freedom Democratic Party, the civil rights origin of the National Black Political Self: "In the best possible sense of that term he *was* a *black* candidate, articulating a higher vision of American reality and moral possibility, a vision sorely tested and tempered by the fires of generations of struggle, disappointment, and persistent hope for this nation. His forthright attack on the principles of Reaganism was not a liberal position or a left position—it was fundamentally a black critique" (the emphasis is Thelwell's). All three writers are, in a way, correct in their assessment of Jackson because the real subject of their concern is Jackson's authenticity. Whence his authority to speak on behalf of blacks? Despite Reed's criticism, blacks will never fully accept or completely endow a black leader validated by the electoral process: First, because it is the white folks' way of validating and authenticating their leaders; blacks voted for Jackson not to validate him as a leader but to demonstrate that he could be validated in that way that made many whites fearful. Second, blacks' strong Christian roots make a leader who speaks against the scribes and pharisees, who self-proclaims his authority ("*I* say unto you..." in the King James New Testament; "But *I* tell you the truth" in the New International Version New Testament) quite irresistible and empowered in the only relevant way a leader can be empowered, by God. Because black leaders, since Frederick Douglass, have made their reputations almost exclusively through speeches (Wilson J. Moses's interpretation of Ralph Ellison's *Invisible Man* in his *Black Messiahs and Uncle Toms: Social and Literary Manipulations of a Religious Myth* [1982] is based on this understanding of African-American culture's tempering of its leaders), their authenticity is ultimately *meant* to be both charismatic and messianic. Reed finds all of this to be pre-Modernist and pre-bourgeois with overtones of demagoguery and fascism, all of which is true, although his brother political scientist, Barker, in the final analysis endorses Jackson fairly much on the grounds of his personality. Barker thinks Jackson is a hero, pure and simple, as does Thelwell. And it is sheer enthrallment of that heroism, which for Reed is only the thralldom of those who wish to be captured by a magnetic personality, that excites those intellectuals. Jackson certainly understands the limits of mystification, as do Barker and Thelwell, which is why he has revalidated himself through the electoral process. But he also understands, after all, that blacks are a people in need of national mythology. In a most vital way, Jackson is both neo-King and post-King, and virtually all revisionist contemporary black politics in America owes something to Jackson's synthesis of the black national identity (and black national purpose) of both folk religious tradition and the expression of the American civic self.

> Jesse Jackson, in fact, more than any other politician now on the scene, resembles Reagan in his appeal and in his use of intelligence to expand that appeal. Both men are believers in a cause they embody, so that self-promotion and ideological commitment are fused. Both think, always, of a way to turn each situation, each event, into a vehicle for increasing the acceptance of their message. Both make claims that are one-sided, partial, over-simple, but deeply felt and almost hypnotically convincing to any listeners not actively determined to resist them (and even to some who are resisting). They both need to believe they are selling something far larger than themselves, but that the only way to do that is *through* themselves. They carry the message. Without them, it does not arrive.
>
> —Garry Wills, *Reagan's America*

Had not Ronald Reagan been president both times Jesse Jackson ran for the office, Jackson would not have done nearly as well as he did. Indeed, it is doubtful whether Jackson would have or could have run at all without Reagan. The huge advantage Jackson had was that he was able to run against the Reagan record without running against Reagan himself. Moreover, he was able to do this in a way that Reagan would have done if he had had to run against himself. That is to say, he did not just tell people what they wanted to hear; he transfixed them with the utter seductive power of simply expressing dissatisfaction through an attractive candidate. Since it was impossible for him to win, he convinced people that the mere act of voting for him was not just registering a complaint, it was engaging in the romance of political empowerment. So it is not simply that Reagan's intense conservatism made a more extensive and more disgruntled class of the "locked out" which Jackson so expertly tapped; it was Reagan's method as a politician that opened the door for Jackson, the seemingly "untrained," "natural," committed communicator whose mere presence in the race was the sign and signifier of radical and humane change in American politics that the public was willing to buy. Reagan seemed to transcend politics by simply being himself, and so Jackson thought he would give it a go. Both men gave speeches that were the equivalent of a coach's rallying his players at a pep session: Reagan exhorting to win one for the Gipper, Jackson to win one from the devil, from the forces of darkness. That is why the sports background of both men looms large here. Reagan had been an expert swimmer and a baseball announcer and played athletes (George Gipp and Grover Cleveland Alexander) on the screen. Jackson had been a high school and college football star. Indeed, references to football still pepper Jackson's speeches: "While much progress has been made to eliminate the external barriers denying our right to vote, there are still some barriers remaining. We can't even play the game adequately until our entire team shows up on the field. We have sixteen million black people eligible to register and vote, but only about nine million are in political uniform." Or, "A football team that *runs* all its plays on the ground and never throws a pass can be defensed and stopped. A team that runs the same play all the time doesn't need to huddle. We've got to diversify our game plan." Or, "Wise political parties and politicians exploit (in the best sense) the openings in the other team's offense and defense." Or, "We must run a multiple offense and defense." Or, "To use a football analogy, we are now in the exhibition season looking at various game strategies and assessing the players on the field. During the primaries we will play the regular season, and at the convention we will conduct the Super Bowl. But if you do not think and plan in advance, and then do not play during the regular season, you cannot participate or even get a good seat at the Super Bowl. If blacks focus all of their attention on the Super Bowl, and do little planning and do not play during the regular season [the primaries], blacks will end up basking in someone else's glory or crying in someone else's beer. It is not enough just for our conference [Democrats] to win; our team [blacks and the rejected] must also win. And for our team to win, everyone must help prepare the game plan [party policy] and be in the huddle when the plays [the platform] are called." There is something peculiarly American about this, something that sounds competitive, masculine, tough yet fair. No wonder Jackson became the first politician in recent memory whom so many people referred to by his first name, as we do with some of our celebrities, such as Elizabeth Taylor, Willie Mays, and Ozzie Smith.

He came down with a bump
From up there on the ball.
And Sally and I,
We saw ALL the things fall!
—Dr. Seuss, *The Cat in the Hat*

And Jackson built a coalition as tenuous and unlikely as that which Reagan built. Yet Jackson ultimately is not as strong as Reagan and will have difficulty keeping the pieces together. Jackson's constituency, as he himself described it, is, first, blacks, his strongest and most loyal followers and his weakest in terms of providing him leverage; in 1984, blacks voted for him in strong numbers in the primaries and party caucuses yet left the convention in San Francisco angered by what they felt was Jackson's unfair treatment at the hands of Mondale over the inclusion of the minority planks in the party platform. In a speculative mood while at the convention Lucius Barker wrote:

What might have happened *if* Jackson had not started his campaign so late, or had had more success in uniting black leaders and others for his candidacy, or had developed and instituted more systematic fund-raising activities during the early pre-campaign period? I wondered how different the campaign might have been *if* more time and resources had been put into the development and operation of the campaign organization and the consequent development of a more holistic campaign strategy. I wondered what might have happened *if* it had been possible to devote more time and effort to building the Rainbow Coalition, to push issues and programs that appealed in a real way to all or most of those locked-out groups that Jackson wished to bring into his coalition. I wondered what might have happened *if* there had been a more obvious systematic development of policy papers and more careful planning for concrete alternatives to deal with problems and conditions which Reagan was being criticized for exacerbating (hunger, unemployment, poverty). I wondered what might have happened *if* the Hymie incident had not occurred or *if* Jackson had immediately acknowledged his error in making such remarks. I wondered what might have happened *if* Jackson had had sufficient funds to mount an aggressive media campaign to compete with those mounted by the other candidates. I wondered what might have happened *if* the media had not tabbed Jackson as a black candidate and repeatedly minimized his chances of winning.

All the conditions and events that Barker had hoped for in 1984 actually occurred or were fulfilled in 1988: Jackson united black leadership; he worked with Ann Lewis and Bert Lance and other experienced white political operators to help run his campaign; he drowned the world in position papers that no one read; he broadened his appeal by repackaging his presentation of the issues; he received a great deal more money; he said nothing about Jews; and the press gave him quite laudatory coverage. The result of all this was quite a few more votes but no more tangible accomplishments at the convention in Atlanta. Blacks still left the convention upset and angered. This time because Jackson had not been chosen by Michael Dukakis, the nominee, as his running mate. So in effect, with the best possible scenario imaginable short of Jackson's winning the nomination, blacks still gained nothing from his second run at the presidency.* It may be so, as white Democrats see it, looking back over the last several presidential campaigns, that a Democrat cannot win without the black vote. But it has

---

*Ron Brown became the chairman of the Democratic Party and that was probably largely because of Jackson. The fairly unrealistic response of blacks to Brown's endorsement of democrat Richard Daley, Jr., for mayor of Chicago may indicate that some segments of national black opinion feel that blacks will gain nothing from having one of their own as head of one of the major parties, that strange species known as East Coast Oreos being what they are. And some blacks now believe that Brown may be a chicken who won't be coming home to roost.

also become a fact that he may lose badly with it too. Thus, the politics of ethnicity, on a national scale for blacks, so far at any rate, have not worked. Voting for white presidential candidates has gotten them nothing (so they feel) and voting for black presidential candidates has gotten them little or nothing (which they will not admit).

The next Jackson group is women (presumably white, since he would have black women as part of his black constituency). He failed in his initiative to get the feminists in 1984 although he offered to select a woman running mate and by so doing forced Mondale to select Geraldine Ferraro; although he did better with women in 1988, the National Organization for Women never backed him, and generally only the most liberal-minded working women voted for him. Jackson was, by and large, though not exclusively by any means, a hot number on white college campuses, where young whites have fallen for everything from Dave Brubeck and eating goldfish to civil rights marches, compact discs, and acquiring MBAs. Women are just too wide a constituency to be able to lump together very effectively as an interest group. Moreover, the segment of women Jackson has managed to capture is likely to abandon him if and when an attractive liberal candidate, particularly a woman, comes along. It is a group that is partially committed to him only if there is absolutely no viable white alternative.

Next come minorities, the catchall for all nonwhite Americans who are not black. Jackson has never done particularly well with Asians, who do not wish to be identified with the locked out, which classification socio-economically would not be accurate for them in any case, and Hispanics, while much more supportive, are not a group he is likely to win over entirely, because he is not Catholic nor does he speak Spanish. He can identify with their poverty and their experiences with racism but he cannot identify with them culturally, nor is his position strong in dealing with the intense Hispanic–black tension in such places as Miami. It simply stands to reason that Hispanics will, very soon, begin to develop their own national leaders.

The gays, another group Jackson did well with, especially in 1988, have pockets of strength but they are fairly negligible in national politics now. After all, how many gay people even see themselves as a political entity on the basis of their sexual orientation? Possibly a great number, but I would imagine that gays cross the political spectrum from conservative to liberal to radical. To be gay, it seems to me, does not automatically make one radical, although nowadays it seems to make many self-interested. The presence of AIDS has surely accelerated political organization in gay communities, but that is crisis management as well as, dare I say it, a civil rights issue in this country. And every group that feels itself discriminated against now wants to replicate the civil rights struggle of blacks; there are so many moral crusades being launched today against virtually the entire human species's inclination to dislike anything that it might be recommended that we all become Jainists. Certainly gay political activism will dissipate once a cure is found for AIDS. It is not natural for most human beings to be politically active when there is no crisis or for excessively long periods of time.

> *"So you see!" laughed the Cat,*
> *"Now your snow is all white!*
> *Now your work is all done!*
> *Now your house is all right!...*
> *And so, if you ever*
> *Have spots, now and then,*
> *I will be very happy*
> *To come here again."*
>
> —Dr. Seuss, *The Cat in the Hat Comes Back*

keep using this word w/out any clear explanation as how he defines it)

What Jackson symbolizes is not so much an ideology or a politics but a mood—a bourgeois angst. In the end, you see, he wishes to do exactly the opposite of Reagan. Reagan turned the politics of mainstream consent into the politics of radical dissent, an endorsement of a conservatism that had no program, just an intense itch to be in power and stop whatever programs it did not like. Jackson wants to take the politics of radical dissent and turn it into the politics of mainstream consent. Jackson wants a purer welfare state where, first, everyone benefits according to his need (bourgeois morality) and then everyone benefits according to his merit (bourgeois aesthetics). For Jackson, bourgeois democracy is like a very long line of waiters. Those who wait must be rewarded for waiting their turn although it must be determined if anyone jumps ahead unfairly. And those who cannot wait in line must be fed as well. Reagan wanted a purer marketplace that would benefit those who controlled it because they, in the end, deserved to be rewarded if they controlled the marketplace, a sign of their higher worthiness. It is bad politics and bad moral vision, according to Reagan, to assume that a culture of inequality is wrong, especially when it is precisely what the bourgeoisie crave. Reagan ran the government partly on the notion that smart people do not wait in line. They simply demand service immediately. Reagan succeeded, in part, because it was clear to everyone he wanted the office for a program of change. Jackson has not succeeded, in part, because no one is sure if he wants the office to create change or if simply electing him to the office is the change; even if he does nothing, the culture has experienced something dramatic. Reagan never gave the impression he wanted the office for himself. Jackson, at times, seems unable to convince people that he wants it for anything but a tribute to his amazing feat of winning it.

This is equl —eye not class

> *"But I like to be here.*
> *Oh, I like it a lot!"*
> *Said the Cat in the Hat*
> *To the fish in the pot.*
> *"I will NOT go away.*
> *I do NOT wish to go!"*
>
> —Dr. Seuss, *The Cat in the Hat*

lot of words meaning nothing!

[Jackson embodies the bourgeois angst, the uncertain ego, an ambition that is unsure what its epistemological notions are.] His moral exclamations of indignation coupled with the so-called bargaining sessions of oligarchic concessions are what have endeared him both to white liberals and to blacks. [Ironically, Jackson is the symbol not of action but of the utter bourgeois anguish of the impossibility that action can accomplish anything.] Jackson has not demonstrated that his politics have at all benefited the class he purportedly represents and wishes to help. Indeed, there is no evidence whatsoever that if Jackson did not exist the underclass would be worse off. The sheer irrelevance of his presence in the realm of *materially* affecting the fortunes of our misbegotten sons and daughters, brothers and sisters, is not simply a sign of institutional intransigence, it is a sign of the complete impotence of bourgeois social reform to improve significantly the lives of the poor despite their having such proximity to such enormous amounts of wealth. Jackson thus comes to represent the complete bourgeois political irony—a man who desires to be self-created and to construct an environment sprung whole from the moral consciousness of his desire while being totally dominated by his culture and his culture's view of him. Jackson is a man of many intriguing tensions, stresses, cracks, contradictions. He is probably not a good man, although he is probably not a very bad man either. He is a man who wants to be good. But what is more troubling is that he may be a man who would rather be successful than good, who would rather be heard shouting foolishness than sit quietly in a corner of wisdom.

Jackson still may be a man who can, in fact, accomplish something quite extraordinary in the end. He stands poised on the same edge that Father Divine, the great con man cum social leader or perhaps the great god cum messenger, once uneasily walked, a man consumed by his vision of social reform, emboldened by his considerable accomplishments, and consumed to the point of impotency by his own ego. Between 1932 and 1936—Divine's great Harlem years, after the great triumph over reactionary and racist forces at Sayville who tried to undermine his movement by running him out of town as a public nuisance, only to have the judge who sentenced Divine drop dead suddenly a few days later—Divine was the most significant black leader in America and possibly the most revolutionary force in American politics. He had all the components for social change that Jackson now desires: a racially integrated group of followers who challenged prevailing Jim Crow social customs, a tremendous mass appeal that exceeded that of any left-wing politician of the day, a comprehensive economic program of self-help and cooperation that made it possible for his followers not only to weather but to prosper during the Depression, a political and moral vision for the American poor that included educational programs and reformation of the family structure. What makes Jackson so essential to the hopes of left-wing American reform is that he has Divine's potential to radicalize American politics by radicalizing black Christianity or by making a number of people see black Christianity as radical political force. Jackson can do what no other current politician or reformer can do and what only Father Divine did for a brief time and on a relatively small scale: he can make masses of people contemplate seriously, first, *the possibility of living differently in both a material and moral way* and, second, *the possibility that the country can enact a different mission.* And Jackson's potential is so much greater than that of Divine who, after all, was nothing other than a cagey, if courageous, cult leader shrouded by mystification. Yet at this stage, Jackson's achievements have been so much more modest and he has had so much more with which to work, so many more advantages. Jackson's politics have conclusively shown two things: that black Christianity is the ideological foundation for black nationalism, and that black nationalism, far from being rooted in anything African, is indeed the American reformist impulse, a mixture of conservative ethic and liberal sociology that has always been the root of populist social action. Jackson, like Divine and, of course, King, is showing that black Christianity is one of the greatest forces of populism in the culture. Yet, as with Divine, we are forced to wonder how committed Jackson really is, or is all of this the blandishments of a colossal ego? And as in the case of Divine, do we ask this question only of a public black man? We wish for Jackson to be, to borrow a favorite phrase of Divine's, whose rhetorical excesses Jackson often replicates, "a sample and example" of what?

What makes Jackson so vitally important for our culture is precisely that on a public stage he is trying mightily and sometimes nobly to work out, on moral and psychological levels, what human commitment is and, on political and pragmatic levels, what black male ambition means. It is the struggle of, in the words of Howard Thurman, "a man to yield the nerve center of his consent to a purpose or cause, a movement or an ideal, which may be more important to him than whether he lives or dies." To achieve this surrender may satisfy his sense of Christian commitment, but the cause to which he surrenders must be in the end wholly his and wholly unable to be what it is without him, in order to satisfy his sense of ambition. So the public black man must renounce himself while forever acknowledging only the insuperable power and isolation of his solipsistic wonder. Jackson is showing us on a public stage how to make ourselves sovereign by saying yes everlastingly; a black man is trying to tell us what having a kind of moral energy is. That he may not in the end do much with it is not the point for us. It is a struggle to do anything except waste it; to recognize that life is nothing more than the quest to be committed in some way, shape, or form to more life is the final lesson. We should not expect public men to be saviors, only to be less timid versions of ourselves. They are there to show us everything about bourgeois life that is bad, then to show us everything that is good in it as well, to show us that its goodness and badness are inextricably bound, as ineluctable as our being here on this planet together, as the judgment that ultimately our commitment and our ambition force us to endure from the God who has cursed us with a love everlasting that we are too afraid and weak to face. "ME-YOU, ME-YOU" was the rallying cry of the cat in Coover's story and it is, in effect, Jackson's cry too. What other cry can there be? Who else is there here with us? Despite all his faults, as Stanley Crouch roundly enumerated, it is nice to have Jackson around. Just as Bob Marley told us about reggae, Jackson is "another bag."

I I

1a – Why does he see film as a mediocre art & what is the basis for this disparagement?

1B – He's so keen on being hypercritical doesn't understand that there is some similarity bet Hindu & Christian virtues.

1C The 'oughts' in hist. are precisely what we dwell on to seek to learn avoiding falling into the same pitfalls it is because hist is actions reaction that it lends itself to the cinema epic.

1D In fact the unbelievable nature of this change has nothing to do w/ historical changes but the failure to provide us w/ the interior motivations at work in the character.

1E What horrendous intellectual snobbery. Even if 'non-literary' readers gain some enjoyment from their reading which the intellect can sneer at the pt still remains its obtaining some response in their minds or emotions. Indeed why does he assume there is any 'subversive' focus by Alice Walker to what end. She simply wanted to focus on the horrible brutality some Blk women endure from their men.

2A Irritates me no end by his outré generalisations such as men being favoured by mothers & sisters in Blk families. Perhaps, but how does this lead to their brutalization of Blk women

2C p99 Revolt is by itself an expression of negation against the prevailing e'lte, tonal mores / cult. attitudes.

2D p100 The desire for love is universal – it always involves romance the expression by the races / cult may differ but the aim is the same – a happy union. What is appalling is his v. low opinion of poor Blk men who ~~would have been suitable~~ Prince Charmings. What rot?

3A   Once again pontificating on sthg which he has little knowledge of. No boxer goes into the ring seeing any morality lesson on capitalism. The aggressive nature of this sport lends itself purely well to the psyche of Blk manhood where the sense of inferiority is overcome thru a dominating strength. No way does a Blk boxer reflect white values in taking up the sport. p134 Fails to consider that boxing attracts those w/ mental psychosis who feel a need to physically dominate & inflict pain

4A p226 Once more into the breach of his own fantasy → nothy at all to do w/ Melville's depictions of class as expected by a white Am. apart from his notion of paternalism

4B p227 Ds always mangling terms & mixing their meaning paternalism is meant to be benevolent w/in structure of authority. If it becomes authoritarian it can no longer be paternalistic

4C If this is the case why bother to use lang. –

The Color Purple
as Everybody's Protest Art

I. REFLECTIONS IN THE DARKNESS
OF THE THEATER

But on the other hand, if you can believe I am in Africa, and I am, you can believe anything.
—from one of Nettie's letters in Alice Walker, *The Color Purple*

The Color Purple, by black feminist writer Alice Walker, is not a good novel. Therefore, one had every right to expect that it would make an excellent Hollywood film since Hollywood has never been able to make great films from great books. And because the film has been recognized rather lavishly with awards and nominations for awards, not to mention a very strong box office as well, it is safe to assert that the novel has indeed been transformed into an excellent Hollywood film. A book like *The Color Purple* lends itself to the glossy and excessively sentimental treatment that Hollywood is so capable of providing for its "serious subjects" or those endearing pop-culture literary attempts at some sort of social protest. *The Color Purple* offers Hollywood, rather like a traditional trifle on a wedding gown, a bit of something old and a bit of something new. The old stuff is race, which, in this post-Dr. King age of a perfectly integrated society, when indeed a Negro can marry his boss's daughter, is not only unworthy of any trenchant discussion but scarcely worthy of notice. Blacks have long ceased to be exotic or exciting or even interesting, largely because it has been determined by an act of cultural fiat that, except as nostalgic objects of some ahistorical past, they no longer exist. Dr. Kelly Miller predicted back in 1925 in the New York *Amsterdam News* that the Negro race would die out, and I guess in the 1980s we can hear, to use an old black folk phrase, "the death bell toning." So, it is a perfect age to make a movie about a race when one is no longer confronted with the question, Which side are you on? and racism is something that occurred long ago and far away. Feminism, though, is something quite lively and intriguing for Hollywood and it has been pursued by the filmmakers out there with all the naive gracelessness and enervating bathos that will eventually make it not an object of real thought but rather a shrewd diversion from thought itself. Feminism becomes for us through our films not even something remotely identifiable with a "social problem" but the mere cause for shocks and quakes to the nervous system, something to keep us from being bored, which will become part of a collected fund of contemporary boredom. I sometimes think the sole purpose of the film *The Color Purple* is simply to stave off boredom with, ironically but not unexpectedly, all the elements of boredom.

There has been in recent weeks a good deal of teeth-gnashing and hand-wrenching in some quarters of the black community over the film, Hollywood's latest treatment, among other things, of Afro-American life. One might almost be happy that this decidedly inept film had been made if the ensuing debate in the black community about the meaning of the depiction of black men and black women in American popular culture would produce anything like critical clarity. It will not. So black folk will simply experience another round of frenzied name-calling and posturing, the sort of emotionalism that passes for constructive argument in the black community, a place where many people still innocently think that mere outrage over insults means something in this world.

The Color Purple is one of such a long line of inept Hollywood films about black life—a cultural enterprise that started with King Vidor's *Hallelujah* in 1929—that this sort of thing has become a cherished tradition. *The Color Purple* is a very bad film, so undeniably bad that one wonders how Steven Spielberg—its director—ever acquired any sort of reputation as a competent artist. (I suppose it is, finally, its utter mediocrity that makes *The Color Purple* such an outstanding Hollywood film in much the same way that *Lilies of the Field* was. In Hollywood films about black folk, the powers that be usually hit what they aim for.) Spielberg is well considered because, in part, his films make enormous amounts of money, which means that they cease to be films at all and become entrepreneurial events. This ability to make money has always been consistently mistaken by Americans for talent or genius, depending upon how much money is made. Also, Spielberg is loved by American audiences because he makes very expensive B movies, which means that he combines hokum and splendor, that indeed he cares very much about richly etching the details of hokum, corn, and trash. As a result, he has bestowed an enormous significance on a mediocre art. His [handwritten: 1A] purpose is not to make the B movie any less mediocre but to make it a more grandiose spectacle. He does not remind me so much of David Lean or Cecil B. DeMille, who also loved the epic, the grand spectacle; Spielberg brings to mind the late jazz orchestra leader Stan Kenton: Give me a cast of thousands and I will give you not order but the degenerative excesses of order. This art of the maximum, which is supposed to heighten one's sensations by playing so blatantly upon the emotions, becomes in the end merely prosaic. Spielberg's films essentially have the same moral and artistic visions as a professional wrestling match: the experience of an exaggerated morality in an excessive spectacle that is, I think, not an experience of art, but an experience of the negation of art. [handwritten: 1B claptrap]

In *The Color Purple* clichés fall upon one another, trip over one another really, in such a tumble that one is forced to think that Spielberg was really directing a parody or a comedy and was not succeeding. There is no need to waste the artistic significance and power of such excess by taking it seriously; but apparently he does, just as Stan Kenton did in jazz orchestration. Sunrises and sunsets abound; children are seen running through grassy meadows of flowers that exist nowhere in the South of the black farm worker; Africa is the land of wild animals and huts. We even have a brief "coon" episode of singing in a church, a barroom brawl, and a happy ending, this last being the only aspect of the novel that Spielberg used unaltered. And, of course, in Spielberg, as in the novels of Henry James, everyone has enough to eat and money is, at best, only a moral abstraction. The whole did not resemble a movie so much as an interminably long television program, which I think for Spielberg was perfectly the point of all those clichés. They may not have succeeded as comedy but they did succeed in intoxicating the audience with the comfort of things familiar. In the end, the film is like a very expensive, very large greeting card; and a card, after all, has no meaning except in the experience of receiving it. *The Color Purple* has meaning only in the experience of having *watched* it. The audience emerges from the theater in much the same frame of mind in which fans emerge from a wrestling match, saying collectively, "*I* cried," "*I* laughed," "*I* was angry." It is not the experience of catharsis but rather something more akin to the experience of receiving therapy or counseling (the white 1980s version of mojo hands, voodoo, and St. John the Conqueror root: psychoanalysis and self-help for the masses). The film does not purge one's emotions or free one's secret self; in short, it does not produce the true power of dream. It simply, in the absolute darkness of the theater, allows one to evoke endlessly a series of absolutely trite responses to a series of emotional, manipulative, trite situations; for the film does indeed trivialize its themes by condemning the modes of irony, ambiguity, and, ultimately, realism; so instead of being searing, it is merely heartwarming. And a chronically insecure American audience is reassured about its bourgeois pretensions and moral integrity of the society itself. *The Color Purple* does not broaden one's ability to respond but reduces it, and the audience finds this both charming and soothing. The characters on the screen have meaning only insofar as they provide this insular, protective, and narcotic experience for the audience. They mean nothing otherwise.

But the fact that *The Color Purple* might be dismissed as bad art, as kitsch, is, on one level, the least significant aspect of this quite important film. For what this film brings to mind more significantly is Richard Attenborough's tribute-epic about a large portion of the nonwhites of the world: *Gandhi,* a tableau that actually has less to do with the life of Gandhi than with the West's romantic love of Indians. Gandhi sits in this film as a sort of centerpiece on an elaborately decorated table, resembling for the most part nothing so much as the late-nineteenth-century representations of Uncle Tom, the white West's other famous gentle dark man. And probably for the Western mind, Gandhi does indeed become the dramatic, ahistorical, fictional Uncle Tom of the stage plays: his Hinduism washed clean by its similarity to Christian beatitude and humility, his virtue being that he has endured nobly (like Faulkner's Negroes) and thus can be petted perpetually by condescending whites. This supposedly historical film seems constantly on the verge of not only eschewing history but denying it. Years are denoted on the screen, but little can be made of the significance or lineage of the conflicts that are dramatized; they possess no resonating depths. So history itself becomes worse than confused; it is utterly senseless. What is the meaning of the British raj? What is the meaning of the war between Hindu and Moslem? What does it mean to be Hindu, other than, as the film simplistically and tautologically points out, that one is obviously not a Moslem? And what does it mean to be Moslem? This is not a question of whether history *ought* to mean something—a philosophical and theological concern that this film and most other commercial art do not remotely approach—but rather, whether it *can* mean something intelligible in this framework. Human beings, apparently saddled with both the responsibility and the need, must by virtue of their humanity make history bear intelligible meaning; otherwise why bother talking about history at all? So concerned is Attenborough with giving us the sweep and splendor of history that its meaning becomes not only displaced but irrelevant. History is simply a grand parade of picturesque, loosely connected events that fail to mean anything aside from being grand and having "changed the world" in some unfathomable way, largely because, one supposes, it was grand enough to do so. Attenborough's film, like most of its type, gives us history as panorama. That is to say, history as an unintelligible spectacle of the making of history.

The Color Purple is not a historical film in the same sense as *Gandhi,* but it seems, by necessity of the setting of the subject matter, as preoccupied with history as any "period epic." *The Color Purple* gives us a fictive historical sense by, like *Gandhi,* denoting years on the screen, arbitrary years to all appearances, to indicate the passage of time. But here the alienation from history and from lineage seems even more compelling and distressful than in *Gandhi*. The years roll by in *The Color Purple* and they signify nothing for either the audience or the characters on the screen. One can overlook such anachronistic details as Shug Avery playing a blues record in 1916, when blues did not become a recorded art until 1920, or Celie drinking champagne on a Jim Crow car in the 1930s. But what cannot be over-looked are those dumb dates themselves. Time, to paraphrase Rodgers and Hart, might just as well have stood still. The characters are totally untouched by history itself and so is the audience, much to its relief. The changes that occurred in America from the turn of the century through the 1930s (particularly changes in the American South) have no effect upon the characters. The financial fortune of Mr. Albert as a black southern farmer is not affected by politics; it is not even affected by the weather. The charac-ters remain immaculate, severed from their parents, as is true of characters in nearly all American films, and signifying a purity, an innocence that white Americans wish to maintain in their view of history, of blacks, and of themselves as a people. There is more than a bit of truth in the bitter assessment of this film by one black nationalist who said, in effect, that whites have been unable to portray honestly their own history in American films, so why expect them to handle anyone else's any differently?

But there is more at stake here than merely *that*. History has become for the white American that which occurs away from home and mother. And all changes that are wrought upon people are individualistic, internal, and inner-directed, never generated by the outward events in a society. Thus, this "liberal" film winds up purporting a very conservative ethic: We must all pull ourselves up by our own emotional bootstraps. The victim, in essence, cures herself. Even if it is argued that the brutal treatment of women by men is such a "universal" and ageless concern that it transcends history, we are then left, by such grandiose admission of true futility, with the utter impossi-bility of either understanding or changing such treatment. It would seem as much a mysterious given in the world as air, water, and light. It would be, in short, unintelligible. This view once again endorses another conservative ethic: The way things are is the *nature* of the way things are. This is a huge conundrum for both the film and the novel because neither makes an attempt to explain the nature of the problem or evil against which they are supposedly protesting. So the ending, which gives us the transformation of Mr. Albert, is not simply far-fetched, which would have been acceptable, but utterly impossible since nothing in his society as we are given to understand it would generate or support such a change. The question is not only why would he change, considering the social conditions under which he lives, but how could he change if his moral sense is so utterly and inexplicably debased? This is why, incidentally, considering the novel alone, a character like Joe Starks in Zora Neale Hurston's *Their Eyes Were Watching God* is an infinitely superior depiction of a brutal, repressive, wife-beating black man.

Starks is a deeply complex man whose bourgeois aspirations we find, in spite of ourselves, to be attractive. And it is that essential attractiveness that ultimately makes the reader realize the horror of Starks's misogyny. Starks wants what every man in bourgeois culture desires: control, ownership, position. And the male reader slowly but surely grows to know that Starks is really himself. There is a great deal at stake in the war between the black sexes involving the man's sense of values and his ego and his refusal to lose face before other men; so much is at stake that the reader discovers in the end that men like Starks, and that is most of us, would rather die than change. Starks does not give us much hope but he is not unintelligible.

But much as white Americans may find the great ahistorical sense of the film comforting, black Americans, I think, a significant number of whom liked the film, find it comforting as well. Blacks have shown just how much they have come to resemble other Americans in their alienation from their own history. Nothing indicates this as clearly as Black History Month, when history becomes a series of dates and faces, notable persons who have achieved something noble or useful, and who are remembered in a vacuum seal of pious duty that simply announces itself as a sanctimonious unease with the past. What else has the celebration of Black History Month become but an empty spectacle? What else but a kind of secret loathing could characterize a people's labored and self-consciously defensive response to its past?

I think one reason many blacks enjoyed this movie is that it allowed them a certain luxury they had never truly experienced before: to see their past not simply as a story of noble (and local) uplift but as a kind of metaphysical triumph over history itself. *The Color Purple* has all the historical sense of "Cinderella," not quite a folktale because there are no real folk in it, but a superbly realized feminist cartoon about a woman, victimized by cruel relatives, who is transformed into a princess. It is the triumph of the race without precisely being about race, so it has all the overtones of being "universal." And one has become "universal" in America when one's history is something one lives *through* but not in.

The absence of real folk only intensified the enjoyment for those blacks who liked the film because they were not reminded of their greasy, soiled, and messy past. This production goes out of its way to eliminate any trace of folk reality from black southern life. Consider the film score by Quincy Jones, one of the film's producers and a former jazz trumpeter and arranger who has gone on, in recent years, to fame and fortune arranging tunes for such rock and pop stars as Michael Jackson and Frank Sinatra, and issuing his own albums of bland, finger-snapping dance music. The music in this film is as bland, uninteresting, and offensive as anything to be found in any of Jones's albums. The horror of this is not that the score is anachronistic but that it absolutely *refuses* to be, in any way, authentic period music. Shug Avery, one of the film's principal characters, is supposed to be a blues singer during the early decades of this century, cut from the same mold as, say, Ida Cox, Victoria Spivey, Bessie Smith, or Ma Rainey. In those days, as the autobiographies and biographies of such early-twentieth-century black artists as Louis Armstrong, Bessie Smith, Ma Rainey, Willie "the Lion" Smith, Scott Joplin, and Sidney Bechet will attest, in black juke joints the songs were very slow (to give the prostitutes a chance to slow-drag their clients into arousal) and quite dirty—for example, this famous 1930s blues song performed by Lucille Bogan (Bessie Jackson) called "Shave 'Em Dry," which, as one commentator pointed out, seems to out-Sade Sade:

> *Now your nuts hang down like a damn bell-clapper,*
> *And your dick stands up like a steeple,*
> *Your goddam ass-hole stands open like a church door,*
> *And the crabs walks in like people.*

The rough audience at juke joints, consisting of prostitutes, pimps, gamblers, hustlers, and black men and women who had spent the previous week doing back-breaking work in turpentine factories, railroad yards, farms, and white people's homes, would certainly not be interested in the sort of mild fare that Jones presented in the film. Regardless of Jones's temperamental inclinations or artistic taste, he knows enough about Afro-American music to know that songs at least as outspoken as Ma Rainey's "Black Bottom," "Nobody in Town Can Bake a Sweet Jelly Roll Like Mine," "Hear Me Talkin' to Ya," and "Hard-Driving Papa" are true representations of black women's blues of the period. He also knew or at least sensed that a soundtrack of authentic black period music would have alarmed and offended the black audience he hoped the film would attract. Louis Farrakhan, Jesse Jackson, and Benjamin Hooks, to name a few of our nation's "black leaders" and keepers of the black bourgeois flame of achievement and respectability, would have been united in their joint denouncement of a score by a black man for a film directed by a white man that displayed such crude, vulgar, and "filthy" music. The silly music for *The Color Purple* simply underscores the discomfort with and the distance from their folk past that black people are unwilling to admit. And to deny that past, as this film does, is simply to say that blacks have no spiritual or historical genealogy. But what is truly crude and distasteful is not the authentic *vulgar* black music of the past but the insipid soundtrack of the film, which reflects an even more insipid and dispirited contemporary *popular* music that basically indicates that E. Franklin Frazier was right: the black bourgeoisie is nothing more than a class of philistines. Jacques Barzun explains the difference between the vulgar and the popular in European art, which I think is quite lucid and applicable to Afro-American art as well: "What had been rough became falsely polished, pretentious, apish, and cheap. The common people of former ages had made folk songs and folk tales and had sung them themselves; the new plebs had cheap songs and cheap tales made for them by hacks in imitation of the high-class product."

So the film has become for black people what it has become for everyone else: the ideal American protest art, freeing Americans from any criticism of their social or political order by denying that the film presents a problem open to any implication of a social or political solution. It is protest art that moves an audience without disturbing it, the most dangerous kind of narcotic art in many instances. And it selects as its villain the black male, the convenient and mutable antihero of the white American psyche for the past 150 years. There is nothing wrong with the black male's being a villain in a film about a psychotic wife-beater, but it is too facile to be truly credible in a moral way. He is too easy a mark as the villain; and his villainy will, of course, disturb no one because the black male in America has simply come to symbolize all that is degenerate and pathological in the male himself. But those black men who have complained about the film are wrong: it is not an insult to black men. It is, indeed, a perverse tribute to them, for it is their thundering demonness, their smoldering sexuality, and the still pressing need on the part of whites to mask this in buffoonery that is on everyone's mind. Toni Morrison was quite right in something she expressed in *Sula*: the black male will never suffer psychological neglect from white men, white women, black women, or himself. He is always, in some way or other, the essence of the everything that is on every American's mind.

II. AND REFLECTIONS IN THE LIGHT

O Mary, don't you weep
And tell Martha not to moan.
—Black gospel queen Inez Andrews, "O Mary, Don't You Weep"

A good friend and colleague, Elizabeth Schultz, pointed out in passing not very long ago that Alice Walker's *The Color Purple* has a certain similarity to Harriet Beecher Stowe's *Uncle Tom's Cabin*—something to the effect that both novels have suffered from the popularity they have had to endure. I think she meant that both novels have been burdened by their pop-culture status and, as a result, both mass audiences and the critical elite have tended to misinterpret these works. The misinterpretations have arisen partly because these have been extremely popular works of social protest, indictments about the ways we live, written by women who, many believe, cannot really write, and so they have been subject to the most intense and awkward forms of admiration and suspicion. The popularity of the works has tended to blunt and distort the response of some critics by antagonizing their snobbish sensibilities, convinced as they are that these works could be popular only by pandering to certain mass expectations. For these reasons, among others, I suppose it is not surprising that my colleague should begin to think of these novels along the same lines. It may be the judgment of literary and cultural history that these books will be condemned to be yoked together and exist in that limbo of literary reputation between hack work and greatness.

I have said that *The Color Purple* is not a good novel, but it does articulate one useful observation that I can dispense with quickly. The book utterly condemns the black male's glorification of his pimp mentality, and for this we should be thankful. For an insufferably long time, the black American male has been convinced, both by himself and by white males, that he is the monstrous stud on our cultural block. It is one of the few contemptible misrepresentations dreamed up by the white male that the black male has taken to heart, has clutched feverishly. Perhaps he has taken an unseemly pride in this perversion because it has titillated some white women (which in turn has titillated him) or because it has endowed him with the power of the slave master and permitted him to turn his community into a kind of brothel filled with "bitches" and "'ho'es." Whatever the case, Walker was quite right in linking that attempt to the oppressive attitude of the slave master, to the attitude of a rapist. It is appropriate that the lazy Mr. Albert should run something akin to a plantation with a big house as he remained a pimp in his soul.

Despite this, *The Color Purple* remains an inferior novel not because it seems so self-consciously a "woman's novel" and not because it may be playing down to its mass audience, guilty of being nothing more than a blatant "feel good" novel (just the sort of book that is promoted among the nonliterary) *The Color Purple* is a poor novel because it ultimately fails the ideology that it purports to serve. It fails to be subversive enough in substance; it only *appears* to be subversive. Indeed, far from being a radically feminist novel, it is not even, in the end, as good a bourgeois feminist novel as *Uncle Tom's Cabin,* written 130 years earlier. Its largest failure lies in the novel's inability to use (ironically, subversively, or even interestingly) the elements that constitute it. Take, for instance, these various Victorianisms that abound in the work: the ultimate aim of the restoration of a gynocentric, not patriarchal, family; the reunion of lost sisters; the reunion of mother and children; the glorification of cottage industry in the establishment of the pants business; bequests of money and land to the heroine at novel's end; Celie's discovery that her father/rapist is really a cruel stepfather; the change of heart or moral conversion of Mr. Albert, who becomes a feminized man by the end; the friendship between Shug Avery and Celie, which, despite its overlay of lesbianism (a tribute to James Baldwin's untenable thesis that nonstandard sex is the indication of a free, holy, thoroughly unsquare heterosexual heart), is nothing more than the typical relationship between a shy ugly duckling and her more aggressive, beautiful counterpart, a relationship not unlike that between Topsy and Little Eva. Shug convinces Celie that she is not black and ugly, that somebody loves her, which is precisely what Eva does for Topsy. For Walker, these clichés are those not simply of the Victorian novel but of the *woman's* Victorian novel. This indicates recognizing and paying homage to a tradition; but the use of these clichés in *The Color Purple* is a great deal more sterile and undemanding than their use in, say, *Uncle Tom's Cabin.* Together, for Walker, these clichés take on a greater attractiveness and power than for the female Victorian, since they are meant to represent a series of values that free the individual from the power of the environment, the whim of the state, and the orthodoxy of the institution. The individual still has the power to change, and that power supersedes all others, means more than any other. Human virtue is a reality that is not only distinct from all collective arrangements except family; in the end, it can be understood only as being opposed to all collective arrangements. But all of this is only the bourgeois fascination with individualism and with the ambiguity of Western family life, in which bliss is togetherness while having a room of one's own.

The heart of *The Color Purple* is this rhetoric of virtue from which its theological propositions spring. The novel is not representing Celie as a powerless victim simply to establish a critique of Calvinist or conservative Christianity, but to create an outright revolt against such inhuman orthodoxy. For Walker, conservative theology endorses weakness, is enthralled by it because the existence of a superior power demands a corresponding submission; an elect is nothing more than a collective power, an unnatural sovereignty symbolized first and finally by the Calvinist male God. Two separate concepts become fused at some point in this book: the subversion of Calvinist Christianity by its replacement, which is something like liberal religion, and the absolute elimination of evil. Thus the resulting necessities of two conversions in the book: Celie's transformation to self-assertion and human dignity denies a Calvinist world, and Mr. Albert's feminization transforms the power of evil. Walker insists on a theology without victims: this must, to be sure, be a theology in which victims can never be possible, dependent on a world where all are equally strong and where all are equally humbled. This is finally expressed in the novel through a fairly dim-witted pantheistic acknowledgment of the wonders of human potential that begins to sound quite suspiciously like a cross between the New Age movement and Dale Carnegie. Nothing symbolizes the overthrow of this male-centered Calvinism more than Celie's refusal, about two-thirds of the way through the book, to write letters to God anymore. She writes to her sister instead. These quotations from various characters toward the end of the novel signify the coming of the winds of theological change:

> I think it pisses God off if you walk by the color purple in a field somewhere and don't notice it. (Shug)

> God is different to us now, after all these years in Africa. More spirit than ever before, and more internal. Most people think he has to look like something or someone—a roofleaf or Christ—but we don't. And not being tied to what God looks like frees us. (Nettie)

> But if God love me, Celie, I don't have to do all that. Unless I want to. There's a lot of other things I can do that I speck God likes.
> Like what? I ast.
> Oh, she say. I can lay back and just admire stuff. Be happy. Have a good time.

> I think us here to wonder, myself. To wonder. To ast. And that in wondering

bout the big things and asting bout the big things, you learn about the little ones, almost by accident. But you never know nothing more about the big things than you start with. The more I wonder…the more I love. (Mr. Albert)

As we can see, the transformation of values among the book's characters has been completed by the end. God has been reduced, though made invisible and nonhuman in a way, and thoroughly accountable to creation. And everyone has, through conversion, been able to become his or her own minister, a community without leaders, all equally endowed with the light: from an oppressive ghetto of political and social unequals to a black Little Gidding. (The sheer vacuity of the theology of the novel undermines what for many critics was one of its unquestioned virtues: Walker's use of dialect. When characters talk about God and faith, the vernacular becomes a kind of gibberish, a baby talk, an insipid mumbo jumbo that ultimately displays the utter blankness of the book's supposed radical politics. Inasmuch as the book preaches social progress, the language, which is supposed to symbol-ize the growth and expansion of human consciousness, is nothing more than an indicator of a giddy regression to the idealized emotional purity—but what is in truth the confounding morass—of childhood. Characters do not grow up in *The Color Purple,* they simply, in the grand tradition of American self-actualization, become transcendental, which means that their motives have become transparent and their desires sincere and uncomplicated. In this instance, alas, as it has always been, transcendentalism is an excuse for Americans to try to sound philosophical while sprouting sophomoric bromides.)

What Walker does in her novel is allow its social protest to become the foundation for its utopia. Not surprisingly, the book lacks any real intellec-tual or theological rigor or coherence, and the fusing of social protest and utopia is really nothing more than confounding and blundering, each seem-ing to subvert the reader's attention from the other. One is left thinking that Walker wishes to thwart her own ideological ends or that she simply does not know how to write novels. In essence, the book attempts to be revisionist salvation history and fails because of its inability to use or really understand history.

There is certainly no lack of history associated with the novel: its title and elliptically rendered episodes hearken back to Jean Toomer's *Cane* (and Faulkner's *As I Lay Dying*); its speech patterns and love of anthropological folklore bring to mind Zora Neale Hurston (its specific imagery of swollen male bellies is a direct reference to *Their Eyes Were Watching God*); and the epistolary style, which may have emanated from the feminists' realization, as Barbara Christian points out, that "letters were the dominant mode of expression allowed women in the West," is more likely the result of the influence of Samuel Richardson's novels of innocent women in distress. And there is also a great deal of history within the novel itself, references to Harlem, Bessie Smith, African emigration, J. A. Rodgers, and European imperialism. The problem with the novel's historicity is that it seems false and unconvincing, a kind of obvious scaffolding. The bits of history seem undigested and set in the text like lumps. Like the film, Walker's novel, despite its historical references, really wishes to deny history by refusing to show what change and passage of time mean in a society. This is why the social-protest aspects of the novel, some nicely worked-up bits of grim naturalism, are inchoate and why the utopian ending must exist. Walker decided that her heroine has no real way to work out her problems within the context of history. And salvation history becomes the utter supersession of oppression history through the assertion of an unoppressed self. The problem this presents for the reader is that Celie does not find a convincing way to reclaim her humanity and to reassemble the values of her world.

It is equally difficult for Stowe to find a convincing way for Tom to reclaim his humanity and reassemble the values of his world. The difference between the two novels is that Stowe does not believe in the necessity of a world without evil in order for Tom to be a hero or in order for his virtue to mean something. Nor does she believe that salvation history is the supersession of the history of the world as we know it or the history of oppression; rather, she believes that we live now in salvation history. On the surface, one might say that the difference is that Tom (like Eva and St. Clair) is sacrificed for the *atonement* of the sin of slavery while Celie is allowed to survive and triumph (and so are the other major characters of the book) for the *supersession* of a male-dominated, oppressive world. Tom dies without changing the worst evil with which he is confronted: Simon Legree. In fact, because he dies resisting Legree's will, he is really protesting against that evil. Celie lives as the victor, ultimately being the source of change for the evil Mr. Albert. Stowe knows from her experience with the abolitionist movement in Ohio and from suffering the death of one of her children that to rid this world of evil will not be simply the act of the good asserting itself, of saying that evil is impossible, but the act of the shedding of the blood of virtue. Walker is unwilling to accept anything less than the conversion of evil and this is because certain pointed theological questions never occur to Walker that are extremely important to Stowe: Is this world worth saving? Should it be saved if the price must be so high? Stowe does not question the nature of the price, as a good Calvinist-tinged Christian would not. A refusal to grant the price its proper respect born of its necessity and its nature would be simply Manichaeanism. Walker refuses to see the necessity of the price itself and certainly does not appreciate its nature as any sort of heroism. Thus she will not have her characters pay it. It seems to me that no matter how much as modern readers we prefer this revised rhetoric of virtue, the Calvinist imagination has a greater grasp of the political and social cost of virtue, a greater sense of the drama of the existence of virtue in a fallen world. Stowe pleads just as strenuously and far more effectively for the humanity and protection of women and children and for the assertion of the values of the home against the values of the marketplace that have dehumanized and debased all human relationships. But her sense of history is greater, knowing that the Revolution of 1848, the abolitionist movement, the Fugitive Slave Act, and African emigration are the result of large social and political trends that affect *all* citizens. Small but significant changes, such as the freeing of all of his father's slaves by Shelby's son, come hard; utopias do not come at all. Stowe knows that conversions like the one experienced by St. Clair are rare; most people who participate in a comfortable social order will not change until they are forced to. *The Color Purple,* book and movie, has become everybody's protest art: an indication of our need to have a bloodless eschatology where there are no devils in the end, no evil that cannot be repented, and, indeed, no final rendering up of things because there will be no sin, only all of us simply going, quietly and softly, into that good light.

Waiting for
Miss America

I. STAND UP AND CHEER

I'm as good as any woman in your town.
—Bessie Smith, "Young Woman's Blues"

I remember well sitting in a barbershop in the not so once-upon-a-time-long-ago past right after the yearly telecast of the Miss America contest. Most of the patrons, who were black and male, decided that they would not let so insignificant a matter as not having watched the program prevent them from discussing it endlessly. In fact, not having seen the show or having any real idea of what the Miss America contest was about seemed to have fueled their imaginations and loosened their tongues in such a way that, in retrospect, any knowledge of the true proceedings of beauty contests may have been found inhibitive. Most of the men spoke of "white bitches parading their asses across the stage" with much the same expression of mixed desire, wonder, and rage that often characterized the way I heard a good many black men talk about white women in my childhood. As the talk eventually died down, one of the patrons, a black man with a derby and a gold tooth and who looked for all the world like a cross between Lester Young and Stymie from the Our Gang comedies, said with a great deal of finality: "You know, there are three things in life you can bet your house on: death, taxes, and that Miss America will always be white." Now that we have a Miss America who is black or who, at least, can pass for a fairly pronounced quadroon, I suppose that the chiliastic inevitability of taxes and death might be called into question. *False combination chiliasm denotes a new age of frightens*

I use the word "quadroon" because it seems so accurate in a quaint sort of way. When I finally became aware of the fact that our new Miss America is black (something that I was not aware of instantly, even though I watched the pageant on television), I immediately thought of the character Eliza from Harriet Beecher Stowe's famed 1852 novel, *Uncle Tom's Cabin.* Our new Miss America has elevated the image of the tragic mulatto woman from the status of quaint romantic figure in some of America's most aesthetically marginal literature to that of a national icon. I thought of Eliza not only because she was very light but also because she was the essence of cultured black womanhood. Her hands, according to the witnesses in the novel, never betrayed her as a slave because she never, unlike, say, Uncle Tom's dark-skinned wife, Aunt Chloe, performed any hard work. She was shaped in the image of her mistress, Mrs. Shelby, and, like her mistress, possessed little that would have enabled her to escape pious mediocrity. She had simply a desperate love for her son and her husband and a desperate wish to be good despite the odds against it. And I suppose if there has been anything that has characterized the light-skinned black woman as cultured mulatto, it has been that air of desperation that has made her seem so helpless and so determined in the same instant. She showed such incredible strength bottled in a welter of outmoded morality. This desperation is quite important; any black woman who would want to become Miss America or, for that matter, the first black woman to do just about anything in our country (where such "firsts" *signify* so much while they *mean* so little) has to be a bit desperate; and in this culture desperation and ambition have become indistinguishable. Any act of that magnitude is always reminiscent of Eliza, feet bloodied and hair flying, clutching her son tightly as she jumps from floe to floe across the icy Ohio River. When this desperation has combined with bitterness, it has produced the true tragic genius of the mulatto personality (the term "mulatto" having come to indicate a psychological mode rather than a racial mixture) exemplified by such women as Dorothy Dandridge, Billie Holiday, and Josephine Baker.

But our new Miss America is as sweet as any of her sisters before her, so she will not, in the end, bring to mind those great images of the mulatto personality like Holiday, Baker, and Dandridge. Her reign will help us forget them; for while our culture can tolerate desperate black women who want success and love, it cannot tolerate bitter black women who have been denied success and love. Our current Miss America will always bring to mind Eliza and she will clutch her crown and roses in much the same way that Stowe's character clutched her son. She will personify the strength, courage, and culture of black, middle-class womanhood, and all of its philistine mediocrity as well. *What is this judgement based on? No evidence of the connection bet Williams & Horche lacerates.*

Far from being the far-reaching, revolutionary breakthrough in race relations (a new chink made in the armor of the annealed idea of white superiority) that such black leaders as Benjamin Hooks and Shirley Chisholm seemed to have thought, I believe it to have been a quaint joke in much the same way that the flights of the first black and woman astronauts were. Surely, no one really believes that the choice of a black Miss America is comparable to Jackie Robinson breaking into pro ball. Or perhaps it is. Professional athletics have always been, in some sense, the male equivalent of beauty contests; because they are a male province, they always have been considered to possess deeper cultural significance. But, leaving simplistic feminist thinking aside, I believe our new Miss America is a bit too ambiguous a symbol to be as powerful a jolt to our racial consciousness as the emergence of the professional black ballplayer.

Suffice it to say that a black girl as Miss America is a joke but not an insult. In the first place, it is difficult to be insulted by an act that is so self-consciously well-intentioned. Vanessa Williams, the young student who won the contest, is such a radiantly beautiful woman that only black nationalist types would find her to be absolutely bereft of any redeeming qualities. Our black nationalists, who constitute a more important segment of black public opinion than many white people realize, have already proffered their opinion that the selection of a black woman as Miss America is a completely negative, conspiratorial attempt on the part of white America further to degrade black people. One might almost wish this were true. What makes race relations in America such a strange and dangerous affair is that white America—at least, the white power elite—never acts in concert about anything. It would be nearly reassuring to be black if only one could always suspect whites collectively of acting from the most malicious, wicked designs.

I heard several black men on a local black radio call-in program complain rather vociferously the Monday following the Miss America pageant. One caller, who writes for the local black newspaper, thought Ms. Williams to be "politically unaware" because she refused to be a spokesperson for her race, and he considered her "a liability to the black community." Another caller voiced the opinion that the selection of Williams as Miss America was further proof that white America wished to denigrate black men by promoting black women. It is with a great degree of dire anticipation that I await the response from these quarters once it becomes generally known that Ms. Williams has a white boyfriend. She will no longer be simply "politically unaware" or "an insulting hindrance to the ascendancy of black men"; she will be a traitor, "sleeping with the white boy just like the slave women used to do on the plantation." One might almost think Michelle Wallace's contention in her sloppy little book, *Black Macho and the Myth of the Superwoman,* to be essentially correct: the final racial confrontation will be between not blacks and whites but between black men and black women. One hopes that the neurotic concern over miscegenation that seems to bedevil blacks as well as whites will not ultimately display itself in a game of murderous recriminations.

Most black women I know were overjoyed about a black woman becoming Miss America; it was, to their way of thinking, long overdue recognition of the beauty and the femininity of black women. "It might show black men that we're as good as white women," one black woman told me, and, despite the humor that surrounded the statement, it seemed to be, underneath, a deeply distressing appeal. Perhaps—and if this is true, then racial psychopathology is more heartbreaking than anyone remotely believed possible—black women needed some giant manufactured event of American popular culture to make them feel assured that they were and are, indeed, as good as white women. Winning the Miss America contest has become, for at least some black women, American popular culture's fade-out kiss of benevolence.

At a time when the very purpose and motivation of the Miss America contest is being called into question, and rightly so, by feminists of every stripe, and the entire cultural sub-genre called the beauty contest is being seen as, at best, irrelevant to modern women and, at worst, an insult to them, one might find the Miss America title to be a very dubious or ambiguous honor. Furthermore, Vanessa Williams was chosen largely because her good looks are quite similar to those of any white contestant. It will take no imaginative leap on the part of most whites to find her to be a beautiful girl. She does not look like the little black girl of the inner-city projects who reeks of cheap perfume and cigarette smoke and who sports a greasy, homemade curly perm and who has a baby at the age of fifteen for lack of anything better to do. (Whose little girl is she? one wonders.) Vanessa Williams will not even in a distant way remind anyone of *that* hard reality and, in truth, she is not supposed to. Her beauty, if anything, is a much more intense escapism than that of her white counterpart. In effect, her selection becomes a kind of tribute to the ethnocentric "universality" of the white beauty standards of the contest; in short, her looks allow her to "pass" aesthetically. It is an oddly bestowed kiss that white popular culture has planted on black women; it is just the sort of kiss that makes the benevolence of white folk seem so hugely menacing. As a friend of mine said, "When white folk get in trouble with their symbols, they throw 'em on black folk to redeem." To be sure, it is for such reasons that the selection of a black woman as Miss America is much more ambiguous and less effective as a symbol of American racial fusion than the breaking of the color barrier in professional sports. So, with angry black nationalists on the one side, with uneasy white and black feminists on the other, with many adoring young black women asking, "How do you do your hair?" and with many adoring older black women saying, "Child, you sing just like so-and-so at my church. Lord, you got a voice," Vanessa Williams is not expected to have an easy time of it.

I would like to think it was an act of God that I should choose to watch (for the first time) the Miss America pageant the very year that a black woman won the crown. I had never watched the pageant before, partly, I suppose, because as a male I have never found beauty contests to be interesting and partly because as a black I have always thought them to be chilling in an alienating sort of way (I have always found very beautiful white women to be oddly frightening, as if within their beauty resonated an achingly inhuman purity; they have always been in my imagination, to borrow from Toni Morrison's *Tar Baby,* the snow queens of this life) and partly because, in the instance of the Miss America pageant, the contest took place in Atlantic City and as a native of Philadelphia I have always found this shabby playground of the Eastern Seaboard to detract from whatever glamour the contest might have possessed. I remember as a kid buying boxes of St. James's saltwater taffy, the only souvenir that one could ever really *want* from this resort, and wondering if Atlantic City had ever been the happy place that was pictured on the cover of the boxes. I certainly cannot recall its being so when I was a child, particularly since one had to ride through wretched Camden, New Jersey, to get there and then walk through the endless blocks of despair that made up the black neighborhood in this little town in order to get to "chickenbone" beach—where all the black folk were to be found. I doubt if the casinos have, in any wise, improved the place. I understand that the Miss America contest was instituted in 1921 as an attempt by local businessmen to extend the resort season beyond the Labor Day holiday. It was certainly sleazy enough in those early years; no pretense was made that it was anything more than a flesh show: no talent show, no scholarships to the winner and runners-up. It was simply a parade of white "goddesses" who were being exploited in the worst sort of way, a "clean" peep show that was dedicated to making money, endorsing white supremacy, and denigrating women in one fell cultural swoop. It is no wonder, considering what the contest stood for, that women's clubs were, in part, instrumental in shutting Miss America down from 1928 through 1932. It is also no wonder, considering what the contest stood for, that it was recommenced for good in 1935.

I watched the Miss America pageant this year largely because the subject of beauty contests was on the mind of everyone who lives in St. Louis. The city fathers (and its few mothers, too) decided that St. Louis should play host to the 1983 Miss Universe pageant in an effort to improve the image of St. Louis and to promote tourism. How much playing host for that beauty contest helped this city remains to be seen. The immediate returns show that St. Louis, a city that can ill afford such losses, will have to have a tremendous boost in tourism next summer to recoup its expenses. What I find most striking is the lack of imagination, the sheer lack of inventiveness on the part of local politicians: to think that a beauty contest, itself a confession of a dreadful social tactlessness, would resuscitate a city where poverty and crime are the unredemptive admissions of failures so vast that instead of being frightened *of* the poor, one is frightened *for* them. I have read in the papers that our fair city may next bid for the Miss USA contest which, for the last few years, has been held in Biloxi, Mississippi. If the Biloxi Chamber of Commerce is to be believed, this contest has increased tourism so much that literally countless thousands of Americans now include Biloxi in their summer vacation plans. I have no idea what staging the Miss

Universe pageant has done for this city's image, but I believe the gang rape of a teenage girl in broad daylight before a score of witnesses in one of our public parks made a deeper impression on the national mind than the wire-service photo of smiling women in hair curlers visiting the Arch (St. Louis's version of a national treasure) a week before they were to be judged in the pageant.

I had no idea while I watched the telecast that our new Miss America, then Miss New York, was black. I was watching the show on a snowy black-and-white television and the girls seemed to be either olive or alabaster. I had, rather uncharitably, assumed all the contestants were white. Actually, I was more curious about the fate of Miss Missouri who was, like Miss New York, one of the finalists. She was a blond girl with a somewhat longish chin named Barbara Webster.

It was a very long program, but surprisingly, not a boring one. I can say this quite seriously even after having watched the talent portion of the program and after having discovered that those young women had precious little of *that*. They made up in earnestness what they lacked in natural gifts, and since they are supposed to symbolize the girl next door or the boss's daughter (the girl every man wants to marry but no one is supposed—pardon the vulgarity, but it is really quite appropriate here—to screw), it is all right if they seem, well, amateurish, like products of a finishing school. The girls fairly dripped sincerity. As a consequence, one cheered them all and felt embarrassed by their shortcomings; they all seemed to be somebody's kid sister or somebody's older sister doing a parody of an audition. Miss Ohio did a song-and-dance number that was as devoid of skill as, say, a first-grader's attempt to write a novel; she tried to do some Fred Astaire sorts of things with her hat, but simply gave the overwhelming impression that she would have been less confounded had she simply left it on her head. I think it was Miss Alabama who played a Gershwin medley on the piano. It is very difficult to convince anyone that you are a serious musician when you have to grin all the time (consider Louis Armstrong, one of the greatest musicians America has ever produced) and your smiles are not in response to the pleasure you derive from your playing but from an unwritten rule that any contestant in the Miss America pageant must never appear serious for fear that someone might interpret pensiveness as a sullen demeanor. Miss Alabama, we learned, had something like fifteen years of piano lessons and played Gershwin very much like someone who had had fifteen years of piano lessons and never learned to play the instrument. Miss Missouri wound up looking even more ridiculous than Miss Alabama: she played a hoedown number on the violin; she played well, but a toothy grin and a tasseled jumpsuit made her appearance seem so incongruous with the music she was playing that it bordered on being avant-garde. She needed only the Art Ensemble of Chicago playing behind her with tribal face paint and laboratory robes to complete the lunacy of it all. Another young woman, I don't remember which state she represented, did a dance number to the theme song from *Flashdance* that very closely resembled a routine in an aerobics class. This exercise, which is the most apt word for the performance, did not end so much as it petered out. And, of course, there were singers. In fact, most of the talent consisted of singing that sounded very much like bad versions of Barbra Streisand: no subtlety, no artful working of the lyrics or melody, just belting out from the gut with arms flung wide and face contorted with melodramatic emotion. The two numbers I remember most clearly are the medley of "Dixie" and "The Battle Hymn of the Republic" sung by a young woman who represented one of the southern states, and "Happy Days Are Here Again" sung by Miss New York. The medley seemed to me to be as silly as someone singing a combined version of "The Star-Spangled Banner" and "Amazing Grace"; someone might as well do such a medley in a future Miss America contest and neatly tie together all the ideological aspects of being American. To be American has come to mean, in popular culture, not so much being alienated from our history, but insisting that our history is contained in a series of high-sounding slogans and mawkish songs—indeed, that our history resembles nothing so much as the message and the jingle of a television commercial. I suppose that Miss New York was the best singer; surely she was the most professionally fervent. The song she chose was interesting; it reminded me of the little shows put on by the children who were featured on the Our Gang/Little Rascals comedy shorts. The song reminded me of those Our Gang segments not only because both are products of the Depression and because they are homely and mediocre, but also because they were both designed to make people forget a harder reality, a more painful reality. The Miss America contest has given us a long line of charming Shirley Temples for a number of years, and now that a black woman has been selected we might assume that she, too, can be Shirley Temple. (Now black women too can be sweet and cloying, dancing and singing automatons like Temple, the most beloved of children in her films, and who, always in search of parents, would teasingly ask, "Whose little girl am I?" and would always find an eager audience ready to answer, "Ours!") Or, perhaps, we might assume that it is getting a bit more difficult for the Miss America contest to protect us from our own reality.

II. BABY, TAKE A BOW

Rich relations give crusts of bread and such.
—Billie Holiday, "God Bless the Child"

For the benefit of those who never knew
I'm a Miss America! How do you do!
I won a prize in '44 and of course all this is through with;
And I have a great big silver loving cup that I don't know what to do with.

I'm Miss America...so what?
They had me posing like I wouldn't
And they photographed me where they shouldn't,
But it's nice to be Miss America, it makes life so très gai,
Now if I could only find a way to eat three times a day.

—sung by Miss Venus Ramey, Miss America of 1944,
    in her nightclub act after her inauspicious reign

Dolgin's is the sort of store that reveals just what retailing will be like everywhere in America's future, a future that will show that expansion is reduction, after all; Dolgin's shelves tell the story of the slouch toward a cunning yet bland anonymity that has made the old style of crass salesmanship through the frenzied pitch outmoded. It is stores like Dolgin's that Sears wants to imitate, creating an ambience like an American consumer's fantasyland where customers buy items about which they know very little because through some sort of subliminal hearsay they were informed that the product was good or needed. American retailing nowadays does not seem condensed so much as it seems compressed; every huge retailing outlet must sell everything from blank tape cassettes to baby food, and the workers are no longer interested in selling anything; they merely "ring you out." One is left almost eerily to the mercies of one's own impulses. It was pleasant to think that at one time a store such as Dolgin's thought the customer needed the services of an informed, trained salesperson; but customers no longer have needs that must be accommodated, simply urges that must be appeased. Shopping, to a large extent, is a tawdry sort of therapy; one can push a cart up and down the aisles of any store now, not just supermarkets, and commune with the self while half believing that America is still a land of plenty. This mass shopping habit, so similar to the vision of retailing in Edward Bellamy's 1888 futuristic novel *Looking Backward,* is simply the intensified loneliness of the herd instinct of popular culture; the alienation we experience these days is not from the strange but from the familiar.

It was at Dolgin's that our new Miss America made her first—and probably only—appearance in St. Louis, giving away autographed snapshots of herself with anyone who cared to be in a picture with her. In fact, the event was advertised as "Have your photograph taken with Miss America." I suppose it was fitting that she should be appearing at Dolgin's; she was, in some sense, another product that everyone should certainly be familiar with. There were no introductions made when she appeared before huge crowds waiting to see her and she said little or nothing to the people who came, one by one, to have their picture taken with her. Words were superfluous for someone who seemed to be more of an emanation from the Godhead than a human being. She smiled beautifully and constantly in a way that was completely expressionless. Her smile was not devoid of meaning; it resonated a rather genteel mocking quality that heightened its bored detachment. I especially liked how she stood on the ambiguous edge of being a tragic mulatto and a conjure woman, on the edge of absolute love and absolute power; for, at that moment, sitting in that store, she was the most loved and most suspect woman in America. She was loved as all Miss Americas are loved; she was, after all, no different from her predecessors: a sweet girl with ambition and a more than ardent belief that anyone in America can make it by working hard enough. She was the most suspect woman in America because she is black and, as such, is as inscrutable a symbol of American womanhood as one could hope to find. In other words, some blacks don't trust her motives and some whites don't trust her abilities. Yet she became, for those people in Dolgin's, America's version of a princess without a realm or, to put it more precisely, with a limitless realm since it was the entire fantasy of American popular culture. Doubtless, Dolgin's never had so many black folk pass through its portals or, at least, so many black folk pass through who had absolutely no intention of buying anything. There were young black men with fancy cameras, young black women with little sons and daughters dressed in their Sunday best, older black women who giggled with excitement every time they saw Miss America smile. It was as if they had all come to pay homage to some great person instead of merely having a picture taken with a young woman of twenty who had done nothing more notable than win a contest, which, I suppose, was more an act of chance than anything else. Yet these black people, who had come out in frightful rush-hour traffic in a tremendous autumnal rainstorm, must have felt that it was an act of destiny that this girl was crowned Miss America.

"This is history, man," said one young black man to another. "I would've come through a hurricane to meet *this* Miss America. They sure ain't gonna pick another black woman to be Miss America no time soon."

"That ain't no lie," replied the other. "White folks might be sorry they picked this one before the year is over."

"She sure is pretty," said a grandmotherly-looking black woman. "I never thought they'd pick a black girl to be Miss America during my lifetime."

"Hey, white folks gonna think we taking over," said another young black man. "First, we get a black mayor in Chicago, then we get the Martin Luther King holiday, and now we got Miss America. The man who run Dolgin's figure the only time he see this many niggers in his store is if he was giving away watermelons or Cadillacs."

People standing nearby laughed at the last remark.

"That's just it," said a young black woman. "They're not use to *black* people coming out to see Miss America."

And indeed that young woman spoke truer than she knew. In the past, I would imagine that the few black people who bothered to see Miss America when she made a public appearance were motivated only by the most disinterested sort of curiosity, a curiosity approaching the immaculate objectivity of the scientist: for, of course, a white woman as Miss America was merely an object for conversation, not veneration. For the first time, black people can now be motivated to see Miss America for the same reason that whites would crowd stores like Dolgin's to see her in the past: out of admiration, that sort of public love that, in the instance of black Americans, is so dammed up because they have so few public figures they can love so unconditionally and totally because nothing more is expected of them than that they look beautiful and act in some remotely "cultured," polished way. To be sure, a good many black people will seek excuses to hate our new Miss America, but a much greater number will love her obsessively.

There were many white folk standing and waiting as well, and while some probably came out of curiosity, most seemed to esteem truly and deeply our new Miss America. One blond woman, looking as though she had just escaped a dull office and a duller job, was positively flushed with the electricity of the moment. A mother had her son rehearse these lines to say to Miss America when he would finally meet her: "I think you're very beautiful and I'm glad you're Miss America." Another woman had her young daughter, perhaps ten or twelve, wearing a blue dress, patent leather pumps, stockings, a tiara, and a banner draped across the shoulder that proclaimed "Miniature Miss." This youngster, possibly a future Miss America, certainly a future contestant in somebody's beauty contest, was the only person to curtsy before Miss America as if she were meeting the Queen of England. I heard a thirtyish white man speaking to a young black fellow: "I just had to come and get a picture of Miss America. I think this is wonderful. My wife won't believe that I saw Miss America unless I get a picture. I think this is wonderful. I can't believe it." I think that Miss America must have been gratified and grateful that so many whites were there, not so much because she sought their approval but because she sought their acceptance. Their presence might assure that her reign would not be a separate but equal one. The importance of this cannot be overstated, for she has probably unconsciously conceived her symbolic stature as a force to fuse, if only momentarily, our divided culture. Since her black skin, by virtue of the historic burden it carries, brings the element of "social relevance" to the dazzling idiocy of beauty contests, our new Miss America must be aware that she can do more with the title than any white woman ever could, that she can greatly enhance the symbolic yet antique meaning of young womanhood in this culture simply because she is black. She has effectively done two things: she has encouraged blacks to participate in this fairly sterile cultural rite of passage; she has revitalized white interest in the contest by forcing them to see the title in a new and probably more deeply appreciative light. For whites who relish the idea of a black woman as Miss America, she simply serves the artless assumption that America is truly a land without racism, a land of equal opportunity at last. After all, so goes the reasoning from these quarters, twenty-five years ago, if Dolgin's existed in St. Louis, blacks probably could not shop there; they certainly could not work there. Now a young black woman as Miss America is signing autographs in such a store. Racial progress moves apace. Whites who detest the fact that a black woman is Miss America will simply campaign all the harder to make sure that such a lapse does not occur again. For more whites than one might care to imagine, the Miss America crown and the heavyweight title in prizefighting are the flimsy supports for the idea of racial superiority along sexual lines.

The last time a woman who was chosen Miss America was even slightly enmeshed in a similar welter of social and cultural complexities was in 1945, when Bess Myerson, another Miss New York, became the first Jew to win the pageant. Admittedly, only *Life* magazine (of all the publications that ran stories on Myerson during her reign) briefly mentioned her religion; it was never an issue of public discussion because it was never an object of publicity. Yet with the ending of the Second World War—a war fought, in large part, against the absolute nihilism of pathological racism—and with the holocaust and the subject of war trials still fresh on everyone's mind, the selection of a Jew by the Miss America judges strikes one as being, at least, self-consciously but subtly profound or momentous; it was a contrived but important effort to legitimize the contest. Since the 1945 contest was the first in which scholarships were given away, it was essential that the winner also have some real talent. Myerson had already received her B.A. degree in music from Hunter College when she entered the pageant, and during the talent segment she played Gershwin on the flute and Grieg on the piano. There was little doubt that she was not only the most skilled contestant for *that* year, but probably the most gifted entrant in the entire history of the pageant. As *The New York Times* stated in an article printed the day after she won: "The only reason she entered the contest in the first place was... the lure of a $5,000 scholarship that would enable her to continue for another four years her twelve-year study of music." Myerson was not simply another pretty face; she changed the entire nature of the contest from being a gross flesh show to being, of all things, a scholarship competition. Vanessa Williams is seen by the people who run the Miss America contest as another possible legitimizing force. The selection of Myerson did not change the fundamental spirit or intention of the contest; nor did her winning enhance the general caliber of the average contestant who came after her. Myerson simply eased the way for the contest to return to its fantasy, pop-culture preoccupations and continue to select gentile mediocrities. Williams will most likely serve the same ends; the judges can, with a cleaner con-science, return to selecting white women almost exclusively. None of this is exactly sinister; it is, in fact, the bald, guileless stupidity and pointlessness of it all that galls one more than anything.

I stood in line for nearly an hour, along with my wife and two small daughters, waiting to be photographed with Miss America. I might not have gone through all of this had my children been boys, but I knew I simply had to have my daughters in a photograph with the first black Miss America. They would, at least, find it amusing to see the picture when they were older and they might even think it "significant." The photograph turned out to be less than I hoped for. My four-year-old, who would have infinitely preferred having her photograph taken with Michael Jackson, was a bit confused by it all. My two-year-old was completely terrified of the crowd; she never even faced the camera when the picture was taken. So the picture shows a smiling, demure, quite lovely Miss America with a blue and black suit, light brown hair, and green eyes as bright and brilliant as slightly moistened, clear glass beads; a young father smiling slightly with his two children on his knees—one faintly nonplussed and greatly surprised, the other faintly annoyed and greatly distressed. I suppose I am the most humorous figure in the photograph, looking like nothing so much as a candidate for Father of the Year. Miss America probably felt a bit of sympathy for the valiant young father and his uncooperative children—but not half as much as I felt for her, traveling to all the stores like Dolgin's all over the country, signing autographs by the hundreds of thousands, surrounded by more guards than the president, seeing the worst of America as a grotesque phantasmagoria of shopping malls, hotels, and airports. As she sat there in Dolgin's, smiling benignly as each person stepped forward to have his or her picture taken, I could not help but think of her as a courtesan receiving her clients with graceful indifference. All of this was surely immaculate enough; no one was allowed to touch her. But that seems only to have intensified the perversity of the service she was providing; for to maintain the purity of her presence, the public was, in some way, being reminded that it could only defile her, if it had its druthers. And perhaps we would have, since nothing brings out American bloodthirstiness more boldly than the victimization of the innocent.

We are secretly driven slightly mad by the fact that Miss America is sweet and wholesome because it reveals our tremendous preoccupation with our own vehemently stated innocence. Miss America is sweet and wholesome because she symbolizes our deep neurotic obsession with chastity (which is really the only quality that makes a young girl truly sweet and wholesome and *desirable* in our culture). Watching our new Miss America with her beautiful, overly made-up face and perfectly manicured hands, I thought of the direct counterpart to the question that was posed to James Baldwin, as he relates in his description of his conversion experience in *The Fire Next Time*: Whose little girl are you? And because Vanessa Williams's eyes answered dutifully to each person who came forward and silently posed the question: "Why, yours of course," it occurred to me that the ease with which the answer was given belied the sincerity of the response entirely. The Miss America role is tough work; one must have the beauty and charm of a princess, the elegant fortitude of a courtesan, and the cheap hustle of a tease. She is not America's dream girl, she is America's sick fantasy of girlhood and innocence.

As we were leaving the store with our photographs and our two rather relieved children, my wife turned to me and said, "Wouldn't it be something if one of our girls became Miss America twenty years from now? This photograph would be sought by all the papers: 'New Miss America photographed as child with first black Miss America.'"

"Yes," I said, "that would be something."

Although in one very obvious way it is very wonderful now that black mothers can tell their young daughters, "Yes, my darling, you too can become Miss America," one wonders what might be the larger psychic costs demanded by this bit of acculturation. Despite the fact that I do not wish my daughters to grow up desiring to be Miss America, I take a strange pleasure in knowing that that contest can no longer terrorize them; and this pleasure is worth the psychic costs and dislocations, whatever they might be. After all, black folk knew for a long time before Henry James discovered the fact that it is a complex fate to be an American.

Postscript: In July 1984, shortly before this essay was published, Vanessa Williams became the first Miss America to be stripped of her crown, when *Penthouse* magazine published sexually provocative photos of Williams taken a few years before she became Miss America. Her replacement, Suzette Charles, Miss New Jersey, became the second black woman to become Miss America, which means that blacks are, on the whole, doing better than Jews in this business, as Bess Myerson remains the only Jew to have won the contest. Or perhaps blacks are doing worse, as some have perversely joked that it takes two light-skinned black women to equal the reign of one white woman.

The Return
of Miss America

I. MIS-UTTERANCE

The Americans refuse everything explicit and always put up a sort of double meaning.

—D. H. Lawrence, *Studies in American Literature*

The whole Pageant was set up to convince us that we had to behave like ladies. It was like a coming-out party, a debutante ball, with a sorority installation at the end. Then when you had finally become one of the debutantes, what did they want? They wanted you to smile and wink and pull your skirt higher and sell hair tonic for them.

—Bess Myerson, Miss America of 1945

He stood there before us, the assembled multitude of waiters, looking very much as one might expect some middle-management person in the retailing business to look, earnestly dedicated to the company, in this case a St. Louis department store called Famous-Barr. (And perhaps it is his look that makes loyalty so unesteemed in our time: it seems such a denial of breeding, taste, and, finally, personality. It is too egoless a passion in the age of ego.) One might imagine even that he was rather pleased he was no longer merely a head of a department such as boys' clothing or electronics but that he was fired with the same desire as when he told the underlings and the part-timers in his department that they must always be busy; must always stuff racks that were already overflowing with cheap merchandise; must always ask the customer who pays with cash, "Wouldn't you like to open a line of credit with us?"; must never ask a customer, "May I help you?" but rather say, "This is a very nice item that we just got in today." Or perhaps this Mr. Wilkerson was never a department head, perhaps he started as a buyer in toys or junior-miss wear, this executive who stood before us. Or perhaps he never started as any of these, although everyone knows in the retailing business two fairly sure facts: that men are the top managers although women make up the large number of clerks (I once met a woman who had been a buyer for more than twenty years without having been even mentioned for a promotion to executive management; I thought it a long time, those twenty years, to stand on her feet for twelve hours a day every day during the five-to-six-week Christmas shopping season and eight hours a day for the rest of the year) and that even if one comes in with an MBA one must get experience working as a buyer or a department head or even a clerk for a time.

It was a partly cloudy but warm day, a Sunday in November as I recall, and I stood with a fairly good-sized crowd waiting for Miss America 1988 to appear as part of a fashion show sponsored by the "Crafted with Pride in the USA" council, a clothes consortium that is one of the principal backers of the Miss America contest, such a principal backer that Miss America 1988 was to tour the entire year—this being the mere beginning, as she had just been crowned in September—in a wardrobe bearing this label. Miss America, clearly, was not there to model clothes, nor even to provide running commentary about the clothes while they were being modeled; she was, with her two male bodyguards and her chaperone, meant only to introduce herself, give a short preface to the afternoon's proceedings, and then spend the rest of the day being a presence. The show, Mr. Wilkerson told us, was to commemorate the remodeling of three Famous-Barr stores including the one we were in, located in West County, a largely white, middle-class area of St. Louis County. It was reassuring to know that at least for now the department store as a marketing concept was far from dead. Some of the sweetest times I had as a child with my mother were spent strolling in a large department store in Philadelphia called Strawbridge & Clothier, a place that opened up before my child's eyes, my child's mind, reeling with possibilities, giddy with vision, like the grandest bazaar in the world. It was the only place where my mother had a credit card, probably the only place that was assured enough, classy enough—and it was a classy store—to give one to a widowed black woman who earned the salary of a school crossing guard, and when she used that delightful "open sesame," I sensed that I could have throttled the entire fullness of the store, as if chastising my own genie. Ah, for shopping to ever mean *that* again!

There were, in a crowd of 200 or more people waiting, exactly eight blacks, four of whom happened to be me and my family; two others worked for Famous-Barr and were monitoring the show, and the other two were models in the show. It was just something I noticed in passing while standing there because, of course, when you are just standing there waiting without much to do except consider the other people who happen to be standing there waiting with you, you wonder if they are waiting for the same reason you are waiting. And the department store, from my childhood, had always been a white world. I remember those old white women clerks (when being a retail clerk was a career for some women) at Lit Brothers, Gimbels, Strawbridge & Clothier, and Wanamaker's who waited on my mother in those days back in the fifties and how some were kind, some coolly efficient, and some flatly rude. But how they acted was scarcely the point; one simply felt quite alien standing in front of them with purchases. It is a curious fact of our cultural history that the civil rights movement was largely an attempt to win for blacks the right to be mass consumers. In the fifties, when the right was far from gained, I felt quite strongly the sense that some people thought it quite presumptuous of my mother to shop in a downtown department store. And it was always a cause for celebration if one saw a black working as a clerk in those days. Sometimes, if my mother saw one, she would buy something from that department, if it were possible, just to be waited on by someone black.

Some black shoppers walked by as I stood waiting, read the sign that announced Miss America's appearance, and looked at me and my wife and children in a decidedly odd way, as if wondering what kind of fools we were for standing there. "Humph," said one black woman quite loudly who was quite close to me, "you wouldn't catch me waiting for any Miss America." But I, alas, had been caught in an act in which one could not be, after all, in the least bit uncatchable although that would have been preferable. I suppose we stood out and were easily noticeable to passersby who cared to note who was waiting. (Most, of course, both black and white, were indifferent.) A certain self-consciousness is inevitable because you are aware that it means something to nearly everyone that blacks are waiting to see a white celebrity who, in all honesty, is a celebrity for whites as, in effect, all famous white people are. (Someone said to me shortly after Vanessa Williams became Miss America, "Well, you guys finally got a Miss America." I looked at him, rather puzzled. "Don't you have one, too?" I asked.) It does not wash wholly to say that you are here because this is the first time in four years, since Vanessa Williams, the ill-fated Miss New York, Miss America of 1984, that a Miss America has visited St. Louis. Neither Sharlene Wells, Miss Utah, Miss America of 1985, nor Susan Akin, Miss Mississippi, Miss America of 1986, nor Kellye Cash, Miss Tennessee, Miss America of 1987, came here. So it was no common event, a visit by Miss America, and Miss Michigan, Miss America of 1988, may be the last Miss America in St. Louis for the next several years. That does not wash wholly because everyone wonders why any of that should matter to me as a black. Yet it matters a great deal because she is my Miss America too and the Miss America of my wife and children. Or perhaps our standing here, waiting, will make her so. Perchance it was a new civil rights gesture, this wait-in for a white celebrity. A small white girl, perhaps six or seven years old, standing in front of us, kept looking back at us as if she too could not comprehend why we were waiting with everyone else. But as the moment neared for Miss America's appearance she lost interest and never looked at us again, or perhaps she simply resigned herself: After all, why shouldn't they be interested too? The family next to us was videotaping the entire event (the postmodernist replacement of the diary, through which events are not remembered and shaped but captured and preserved: the bourgeois narrativity of history ends and we are left with the bourgeois technology of the camera endlessly photographing); they thought it the most natural thing in the world for us to be there. "Isn't it exciting!" the woman said to us before anything had happened. "Wasn't it wonderful!" she said to us after something had happened.

And something did happen. Mr. Wilkerson finally introduced Miss America in a way that seemed utterly confounding: he mispronounced her name. He called her Kate or Kathy. In fact, he changed her entire name to something else, and although when she appeared some in the crowd were a bit nonplussed, knowing that the retail executive misspoke her name, she seemed unruffled. It was a strange moment of dislocation, a gross miscue thrown into this ritual of conventions. As soon as she stepped up to the microphone, this quite striking, nay, beautiful blond woman, wearing a very handsomely tailored suit, gently and smoothly corrected Mr. Wilkerson by repeating her name: Kaye Lani Rai Rafko, the mere act of which brought to mind the Miss America pageant she had won two months earlier, for it was there, along with fifty other girls, that she introduced herself by stating first her name and then her title and finally the city where her state pageant was held. So we all know, by common consent, that the women of the Miss America pageant hold a double meaning, a double identity as both themselves and as symbols of the womanhood of their states, thus endowing two not abstract but meaningless categories: womanhood and a geographical location that supposedly engendered or spawned both it (this species of womanhood) and them (as distinct persons). By winning the contest Miss Rafko did not cease to be herself exactly; the contest insisted on identifying the contestants by their names and not just by their titles. Moreover, everyone remembered that she was the finalist who did the Hawaiian dance number, an undeniable proof that these contestants are not as much talented as they are conditioned and practiced, that they are not inspired as much as they are aimed and directed—all the qualities of the doggedly persistent middle-class professional. She was also winner of the swimsuit competition, and aside from her ardent and undoubtedly sincere desire to be a first-rate nurse with her own hospice, she seemed a quite undistinguished contestant. Yet it was the sheer fixity and humility of her professional drive to be an accomplished nurse, the fact that she was clearly less talented as a performer than her sisters who seemed to have spent their lives taking music and dance lessons—woe be unto any young woman whose talent is not a performing art—that won the contest for her. Like the previous three white winners, she was an insistent, implied criticism of Vanessa Williams, the failed Miss America. Miss Rafko was not likely to tend to hubristic excesses and, like the other three, she did not aspire to be a performer or entertainer. (Indeed, Miss America of 1985, a Mormon, aspired to be only a housewife.) We all knew that much about Miss Rafko, knew she was those aspects of ourselves.

But she became, inevitably, a great deal more than herself, an embodied conceit of the sublime. She would have been, in another age, the figure, the muse, whom all the nation's poets, for one year, would use as the subject and creative force for their poetry. In still another time, she may have been the personification of the Lorelei. Now, for us, she symbolizes the commercialization of both bourgeois adoration and, even more important, bourgeois ambition. She is adored because she is successful, which is the end, the final stop on the huge organ of America's ideal of ambition. For Americans ache for success not simply in the quest of some paltry fame but in truth for some sense of personal empowerment. In this regard Miss Rafko or any Miss America becomes a reduced Lorelei, not a seductress exactly but an embossed carnal imprint of bourgeois yearning fulfilled not through notable achievement—which is ultimately how we have debased the idea of ambition as the longing for recognition, not significant accomplishment—but simply through, paradoxically, acts of both chance and the will. Miss America becomes such an irresistible emblem for us as Americans because it is such a perfect meshing of an individual ego's search for personal validation with a corporate will for mythic and mystical signification. To borrow Anita Loos's brilliant phrase from her novel about the great American Lorelei, *Gentlemen Prefer Blondes* (1925), for Miss America both the person and the mythic, institutional entity, success is simply "a fate that keeps on happening." The chosen woman herself, supposedly, has doors of opportunity opened for her, a real future, so to speak, while Miss America as a personification of young bourgeois womanhood everlasting becomes, well, everlasting and, more important, indispensable to the public and its vision of the culture. Thus, Miss America, in her beauty, is meant not to inspire but to reassure. For the commercialization of ambition is simply the worship of the selling of the act of selling as a value from which all other American values spring. The self is nothing more than the series of renderings it can evoke of anything. The world becomes for the self, as Hemingway wrote, merely a good place to buy in. And so Miss America is meant to remind us of that, and the dual identity (and we are reminded also that Loos's American Lorelei had two names as well, one bestowed upon her by a judge just as beauty contest winners get their title names) symbolizes "the exchange of values," to borrow from Hemingway again, that is the essence of the commercialization of human experience that is bourgeois culture: to render and to sell the components of seduction, which is finally all the articulation that bourgeois culture has left. And all the articulation it needs since we, the public, wish to be guaranteed every year that the world remains one of buyers and sellers, of buying and selling, of Yankee barters, swindles, trades, and getting one's money's worth. It seemed fitting that I should see this fourth in a series of white Miss Americas who were meant to redeem the contest that is "the largest single source of scholarships for women in the world" from the sullied reign of the first of its two black winners—we tend to forget that Vanessa Williams's replacement in 1984 was Suzette Charles, also black. Alas, poor Vanessa Williams was fired because she did not know how to make a hard bargain. Perhaps black folk need to learn about being mass consumers, so perhaps do some young women. It was in such a place, a retail establishment, that I saw Vanessa Williams four years earlier, and somehow this closure seemed proper: Miss Rafko, unlike Miss Williams, who did not speak when she appeared and whose silence spoke volumes about blacks and articulation as empowerment, telling us of irrevocable bargains in the house of irrevocable bargains, herself symbolizing a bargain of sorts, all on a Sunday afternoon. Our Puritan forefathers and foremothers must be turning in their graves at such a flagrant violation of the Sabbath in so many ways. It is not our play on the Sabbath that they would find as distressing as that we desperately work it so. How far we have come and how far must we go! And so in re-uttering her name, Miss America simply renders herself as she has been rendering herself as a public act, a stylization of American ambition and the professional art of selling, since she entered her first local beauty contest.

II. THE MISS BLACK AMERICA CONTEST

I felt a need for someone to want the black baby to live—just to counteract the universal love of white baby dolls.

—Toni Morrison, *The Bluest Eye*

I got a sweet little black angel and I love the way she spreads her wings.

—Blues singer Robert Nighthawk

He wants to buy her. He's offering to trade six of his women for Ann.

—Discussion between male leaders of an island tribe and white filmmaker Carl Denham, concerning a proposed trade for Fay Wray's Ann Driscoll character in a scene from *King Kong*, Adolf Hitler's favorite movie

It is the most mysterious aspect of that collection of the cultural postures which we might designate the grand American Vanity that so much blatantly commercial and degrading idiocy is found so seductive as to be longingly imitated with the sincerest affection by people who should know better. The Miss Black America contest (or perhaps the black Miss America contest is a more apt name) is just a fawning imitation that exhibits the most deeply felt sincerity, which is undoubtedly also the most deeply felt jealousy, while, of course, it fancies itself making a social protest, a politically inspired gesture. This pageant exists in part as a protest against the glorification of white feminine beauty in the Miss America contest. (There were no black contestants in the most recent—1989—Miss America competition, but a year earlier two blacks—Miss Mississippi and Miss Colorado—were awarded fourth and third runner-up scholarships, respectively, a sign that, among the Miss America officials, there are no hard feelings about the Vanessa Williams scandal and a sign not to be taken lightly, as black folk are well aware that the race burden falls equally on the righteous and the unrighteous when some prominent black screws up.) What the designers of the Miss Black America contest naively fail to note is that the Miss America contest is not simply a cultural act that glorifies white femininity. It is a cultural act that *reinvents* the mythology of white femininity every year for the quite crass purpose of selling things, virtually anything. The economy of our culture is based ideologically on several maxims, one of the major ones being: Whiteness sells anything that, no matter how absurdly, adheres to it. Not only have whites managed to convince themselves of that; they have managed to convince the entire world of something that borders on being a self-evident truth. The quixotic idea of a Miss Black America contest is doomed to failure because, based as it is upon the white model, it will ultimately, in its search for sponsorship, discover that blackness cannot sell anything: it can hardly sell the reality of itself; it certainly cannot sell a fantasy. There is, to be sure, a complex grid of mythologies that surrounds the black American's blackness but there is absolutely no mythology of his or her physical beauty. In the practical sphere, Miss Black America's only real hope is to have the backing of Johnson Publications (publishers of *Ebony* and *Jet*) and its cosmetic wing, Johnson Products, which it does not have and is not likely to get, possibly because the powers at Johnson think the Miss Black America pageant to be a silly idea, probably because it wants no real competition for its own big black woman's event, the annual Ebony Fashion Fair, or what is even more likely, because the Johnson people would prefer a black winner of the Miss America contest (they have been Vanessa Williams's biggest boosters both during and after her reign) to a black winner of a self-segregated contest. A black winner of the Miss America contest has, in the eyes of Johnson, proven something in the mainstream culture where, as far as they are concerned, all reality that is worth thinking about is located; a black winner of the Miss Black America contest, in this culture, has simply proven that a black can win a black contest which, in the end, is a perfectly ridiculous proposition to set out to validate, a neurotic tautology that tantalizes many blacks in their search for self-respect; for that is the only reason *that* version of the contest exists: so that a black can be proclaimed the winner. It is like cheating at cards and letting everyone know you are cheating for worthless stakes; white folk have been cheating at cards for years, and while they have not convinced everyone of square dealing, they've fooled enough; besides, as the saying goes, they are playing with real money, or at least everybody's willing to believe they are. One of the sponsors for the telecast of the Miss Black America 1987 contest was a quarterly publication called *Black America Magazine,* which strenuously (and with maddening frequency) promoted itself as the alternative to *Ebony* and *Essence* (not a Johnson publication but not a critic of Johnson either) that unlike those black staples had the "guts" to examine the important issues facing the black community. That sort of criticism, which has been leveled so shrilly and so often at Johnson Publications that it has become virtually a reflex thought-cliché among black intellectuals and has tended to blind some people to the obviously comforting virtues of Johnson's philistinism — they are all magazines for the masses, let us recall — well, that sort of criticism is not likely to endear the Miss Black America pageant to Johnson in any case.

From the opening scenes at its 1987 venue, West Palm Beach, Florida (unlike Miss America, which is always held in Atlantic City, the Miss Black America pageant seems to move from place to place; in fact, one of the commercials for the program was a plea for someone to sponsor it anywhere in 1988), to its announcement of a winner, the Miss Black America contest mimicked the white beauty contest in many of its most vile features. Indeed, one might say the difference between this contest and the Miss America pageant is about $5 million, a good sound system, and several weeks of rehearsals. And undoubtedly that difference is everything, the difference between black and white in America, one might say, or the difference between playing for worthless stakes and what passes for real money. The Miss America contest has all the studied and tasteless professionalism of a Las Vegas revue while Miss Black America has the all quaint disheveledness of a competition being held in the basement of an urban black church. If Miss Black America fades from the cultural scene, it will be in part because a large number of blacks, both lower and middle class, are actually ashamed of its amateurish quality. "It seems just like something niggers would do," is precisely what many blacks among themselves, secretly, chafing from the blinders of their oppression and degradation, are likely to say. "Why can't we put on something the way white folks do?" Why can't we indeed.

The 1987 show opened with a big production number involving all the contestants just as the Miss America show opens, and each contestant was introduced, although because there is no network of state pageants that feeds contestants to a national competition as with Miss America, many of these young women were from the same locations and none, to my knowledge, held any other titles. So despite the fact their cities were announced, the girls really represented no other entities but themselves. Indeed, many, probably most, I would venture, had never been in a beauty contest before. Their general lack of poise made such an observation apparent. The opening number buoyantly announced the theme of the contest: "Reflect Positivity in My Mind." The word "positive" has become the most brutal cant word in black American discourse, signifying that large segments of the black American's cultural ideology are nothing more than reworked pep talks of Norman Vincent Peale and Dale Carnegie. It is this craven, unimaginative, bourgeois Christian nonsense that often makes attending a black-sponsored public event such a horrendous experience: it is the uncompromised fear that one is going to get preached at, attacked with a bunch of meaningless bromides that are uttered not just with sincerity but with a dismaying tenderness. Thus every black public event becomes a high school commencement where some young girl sings "Climb Ev'ry Mountain" and everyone is moved to weep. Blacks love to wallow in the sentimentality of their myth of endurance. The Miss Black America contest of 1987 had all the earmarks of bourgeois Christian sloganizing. The lyrics to the opening number included this inane redundancy: "The positive look in my eye will always indicate the self-confidence and positive spirit inside me." Positive within and without; one can scarcely tell if it is the glowing mantra of Kundalini Yoga or the slogan for Amway. "I can perform any task," the song continues, "I can sell any product. I can succeed in any job." Even a downtrodden people can stand only so much of that trite, insubstantial optimism. But it may very well be that blacks, postmillennial as they seem to have become, are more American than any other people here. A people tortured and ridiculed for their imperfections must, even more than any other Americans, believe in their perfectibility.

The contest offered the usual "peepshow" swimsuit and execrable talent competitions as well as something called a projection competition. Its counterpart in the Miss America contest is the interview that the contestant is put through during the week preceding the actual televised event. This is coupled with the woman's answer to one or two questions during the televised portion of the contest. I am unsure if the Miss Black America contest conducts lengthy interviews with the contestants during the week but the women are certainly put on the spot with several questions for the television cameras. The questions, which are meant to demonstrate the contestant's ability to think on her feet but really thwart the ability to think at all, are to be answered in thirty seconds, and some of the women stumbled badly here. The scores are computed by an accounting firm, the judges are pillars of the community, sometimes even famous. And as in Miss America, this scrupulous engineering is to free the viewer from any sense of the beauty contest as a genre being a sleazy fraud or a breeding show for women like contests we hold for dogs and horses. In the case of Miss Black America, all this seems a bit too much for prize money that amounts to two scholarships, together worth $2,500, to Roosevelt University in Chicago. At least the Miss America corporation gives away enough scholarship money to some of its contestants so that it might be said that enduring the competition itself is at least somewhat profitable. Besides, for a time, at any rate, a woman can actually be famous as Miss America. But what does this poor imitation of the Miss America contest really mean? And why, finally, does it exist?

It is, of course, an uplift project, which means that for some considerable number of blacks it is something in the realm of realpolitik, that the rectification of the race—and something like the Miss Black America contest helps to rectify and edify the race—is something that will affect materially the larger culture itself. Jesse Jackson's presidential campaign is somewhat similar in its intention and its ideological sources, although its impact has been markedly different, in large measure because it has been quite a great deal more successful as a popular cultural gesture on the part of a black than the Miss Black America contest.

The idea of the national black beauty contest that would celebrate some representative racial standard and would also be some bourgeois vision of realpolitik, that is to say, an amalgam of both acculturation and black nationalism that would alter the black's status as American, is not new at all. Blacks apparently have been tormented by the Miss America contest since its inception in 1921 and have been convinced for nearly that length of time that a black version of that distinctly commercial enterprise would be a positive social and psychological good. On October 9, 1925, in, appropriately enough, Atlantic City, the winner of the first Miss Golden Brown National Beauty Contest was announced. A Miss Josephine Leggett of Louisiana, "scintillating star of the race stage," we are told, became the first Miss Golden Brown of America (and to my knowledge may very well have been the last). The contest was sponsored by Madame Mamie Hightower (a competitor of the famous Madame C. J. Walker) and her Golden Brown Beauty Preparations and Chemical Company, located in Memphis. The nearly full-page ad that announced the winner of the contest appeared in an October 1925 number of the New York *Amsterdam News,* an African-American newspaper, and read in part:

> The first annual national Golden Brown Beauty contest has concluded. The curtain falls. The lights are dimmed. The audience sits enthralled. For among the hundreds of hundreds [*sic*] of beautiful girls entered by our group in every nook and cranny of the nation, one, by her fascination, by her beauty, by her charm, has earned the coveted title and queenly crown. . . .
>
> At the Golden Brown Ball, given in Walzdream Ball Room, Atlantic City, October 9th, four other girls, nationally popular, also received the acclaim of the assembled multitude. And Miss Texas, (Mrs. Lula E. Booth); Miss Ohio, (Miss Mabel Peoples); Miss Columbia, (Miss Gladys Randolph); Miss Wisconsin (Miss Linda Gray), returned to their homes conscious of having played stellar parts in one of the most stirring spectacles in the history of our race.

The fact that there were 39 other state winners who were contestants in this competition (which means a total of at least 44 state winners out of a possible 49: 48 states and the District of Columbia; there were, for instance, only 40 contestants in the 1945 Miss America contest that Bess Myerson won) indicates that the Golden Brown beauty contest was quite well organized, possibly better organized than the current Miss Black America contest. It is unlikely, if the contest closely followed other white beauty contests of the day, that there was either a talent competition (Miss America did not add talent until 1938) or any interest in college women or awarding scholarships (Miss Golden Brown awarded the winner a "wonderful, luxurious Hudson Super-Six Coach Automobile" and the Miss America contest did not award scholarships until 1945). It is likely that the winner of Miss Golden Brown went on a tour promoting Golden Brown beauty products and perhaps even played black theaters just as her white counterpart went on a vaudeville tour. That the beauty standards for blacks of the day were a "light, bright complexion that is the heritage of our race" and "soft, wavy hair that can be dressed in any style," as the Golden Brown ad reminds us, should not strike anyone with some awareness of black American cultural history as unusual. Moreover, it is actually irrelevant what the standards were since that contest, like its current counterpart, Miss Black America, is meant to make blacks, particularly black women, feel good about themselves by asserting two distinct and important realizations: first, that the Miss America contest is a race or ethnic contest that does not celebrate female beauty universally but merely white beauty; second, that understanding and shaping one's own ethnicity to one's own political and social needs is everything in this country. It is good to know that dark-skinned women are not discriminated against in these contests anymore, although black Americans still clearly value light skin and soft, wavy hair.

One is sure that the Miss Golden Brown contest was an uplift project of tremendously philistine, smug, and prescriptive proportions. One supposes, at last, that the Miss Black America contest is meant to be particularly a bourgeois uplift project for black women as well, saying something to the effect that we are proud of our women too. This might not be a bad idea if the contest truly honored the achievements of black women instead of simply degrading the contestants in something that is a cross between a local community center's amateur night and some prudish sorority's version of a poorly rehearsed burlesque skit. Alas, the Miss Black America contest would be no more acceptable, no more tolerable, if it were an exact glossy imitation of the Miss America big show, for the expropriation of the beauty contest is not an act of empowerment for the black women as a cultural image; it is an act of belittlement. But there is at least small comfort in the fact that for the foreseeable future it is impossible for Miss Black America ever to menace us by approaching that mad magnitude. To be sure, black women as both sexual and rational beings have been denigrated to a heartbreaking degree in this culture, but how can replicating a contest that degrades white women help black women at all? As tempting as it may be, if only to shout back in some kind of defiant anguish, to have black women considered as sexy as the latest white, blond nymph from Hollywood, it will not answer to have black women become commodities in that way, even if it were possible, which it clearly is not at the moment. When Bess Myerson, during her campaign to become Miss America of 1945, met Jews who told her how intensely proud they were of her and how fervently they wanted her to win, we are aware that ethnicity and self-respect, ethnicity and mythic self-image, ethnicity and marginality are not simply archaeologies of the culture, so to speak, but honest-to-God trench-warfare politics. Jazz singer Leon Thomas was smarter than he knew when he once sang, "It's my life I'm fighting for..." But we must ask ourselves the essential question of what womanhood, a womanhood of blackness, an African-American womanhood, really is (a question that must be seen as a freedom, a liberation, simply to ask it and perhaps a disengagement from sheer reactive bourgeois ethnicity which has never signified freedom but rather carnal and inexorable entrapment), and to think that a beauty contest can simply ask the question, let alone resolve it, that a beauty contest can help black women realize their womanhood and express it, to think that having women perform a few tawdry exploits in the manner of a poorly conceived test would give blacks some politically or culturally useful image of womanhood indicates how frightened many of us, both men and women, must be of a true womanhood coming into being. And so we have come to acknowledge what we have always known: that it is the peculiar dilemma of the oppressed to be seduced by the very rituals and concepts that dehumanize them and, in this instance, what beauty contests represent, in truth, beyond female degradation or racial mythmaking is this bourgeois deception upon which the foundations of bourgeois culture have been built: that human worth must be *proven,* a bit of brutishness that the bourgeoisie insistently deny by pointing to their historical documentation, which signifies a free humanity. But the most self-reflexive and self-fulfilling problematizing trademark for all bourgeois culture is precisely that: the irreconcilability between consciousness and condition. To deny the fundamental moral primacy that bourgeois culture grants to its own expediently produced (for the ruling classes) tragedy is for blacks and all thinking people to deny, among other things, the beauty contest, which denial gives us this affirmation, this to assert: that all human worth must be *assumed* and *defended.* Humanity must be free in condition as well as in consciousness. For blacks to ignore beauty contests instead of replicating them would be a first step toward true cultural hegemony. It is time to start playing for real stakes and not for funny money.

III. WEIGHT WATCHING:
A COURSE IN WOMEN'S STUDIES

Moreover, when we fast, be not, as the hypocrites, of a sad countenance: for they disfigure their faces, that they may appear unto men to fast. Verily I say unto you, they have their reward. But thou, when thou fastest, anoint thine

head, and wash thy face. That thou appear not unto men to fast...
—Matthew 6:16-18

I know exactly how she feels; I see her strained face and hear her say that she is not hungry, that she does not need to eat. I know what she is undergoing.
—Cured anorexia nervosa patient speaking about another suffering from the disease, quoted in Hilde Bruch, *The Golden Cage*

During the starvation I put myself on a regimen that I felt was very unpleasant, but I endured it because I had imposed it upon myself.
—Anorexia nervosa patient, quoted in Hilde Bruch, *The Golden Cage*

My wife, who has been a sometimes ardent, sometimes unfaithful member of Weight Watchers for the past several years, asked me just recently whether I would attend an open meeting, designed not only to entice new members but to allow "significant others" or "partners," as the terms go in these pansexual days, to understand the experience and struggle of losing weight. I looked up briefly from a book I was reading and replied, "Sure," not really thinking at the time that I would go. That is to say, it was a sort of put-off answer to a question that one does not take seriously.

Surprisingly, when the Saturday morning of the open meeting came around, I went quite willingly, docilely in fact. I was curious to know what people talked about at this sort of meeting. Several years ago my mother married a man who had been an alcoholic for a number of years. Those familiar with the drinker drinking can imagine how painful some of those years must have been. She has attended many of the meetings of an Alcoholics Anonymous affiliate, Al-Anon, designed for people who are related to alcoholics. As I considered Weight Watchers to be, and surely its founders must admit this, nothing more than a kind of parodic imitation of Alcoholics Anonymous—the encounter-group way to end self-destructive habits through rehabilitative discourse, the psychotherapeutic séance of shedding light into the dark night of the dark soul—I thought it might be, actually, quite important to go. I thought that in some mild way I might understand my mother's relationship with my stepfather if it were, in some harmless and amusing way, a cognate of some aspect of my relationship with my wife.

It is of course a peculiarly American optimism that evil is nothing more than a series of bad habits that can, through an exercise of self-control, be broken or at least made less compulsively excessive. I wanted to go because I had no understanding of people's bad habits and hence no patience with them. Ironically, it was because the emotional stakes were not nearly as large as they were with my mother and her life with an inveterate and awfully conspicuous consumer that I wanted to take my wife's concern about losing weight seriously.

No one would think my wife is fat or overweight from simply looking at her. One might think her to be bordering on having a weight problem but not having arrived. Since the birth of our first child over nine years ago she has been struggling with her weight, up and down, but mostly a steady creep up until she was nearly forty pounds heavier than when we married. At one time I supervised a diet for her, during which interval she lost about twenty pounds or so in about six weeks. She missed her period for one month as a result of the strenuous nature of the diet. The fact that strenuous dieting causes amenorrhea or what amounts to a kind of fictive pregnancy has been noted by physicians and scholars who have studied anorexia nervosa: a striking irony how denial can signify a sort of fulfillment. My wife soon missed her periods for the next nine months; it was discovered that she was, indeed, pregnant again. She also lost the urge to diet because she was pregnant. As a result of having a legitimate excuse to be freed from deprivation, she ate voraciously. She gained more weight than she should have. The delivery did not produce much weight loss, which is what she was hoping.

Since that time, seven years ago, my wife has been trying to lose, quite unsuccessfully, the weight she gained during that pregnancy. She owns many clothes that she cannot get herself into, she thinks she looks bad, she feels fat and ugly. She loves to read the comic strip *Cathy* whenever it deals with dieting. This is a typical kind of self-absorption that overweight people suffer from. Turns of self-pity and self-denouncement. It is not unlike a religious preoccupation with sin, with grace, with sanctification.

"How do you stay so thin?" she asks me, "What's your secret? You seem to eat anything you want."

Of course, I don't eat anything I want, exactly. In fact, there are many times, especially during stressful periods, when I eat nothing at all for an entire day. We are both on a diet together now; she feels the only way she can stay on it is if I go on it as well. We eat all of our meals together. Because of that, I have eaten more food in recent weeks than I normally do; as a result the diet is helping her to lose weight while I gain it. The fact that I may gain a little weight makes her feel good, as if she is not, finally, some freak of nature.

When she saw magazine pictures of Walter Hudson, believed to be the world's heaviest person with a weight of over 1,000 pounds, she was quite happy to know that she was not, at least, pathologically overweight. But this sort of thing seemed a long way 'round the mountain to achieve a bit of self-esteem. Her passion for eating would never make her a deranged glutton any more so than her passion for dieting would make her anorexic. But esteem comes a bit easier when she can compare herself with the overweight women who work around her. The problem here is that there are simply not enough of them.

She laughs at ads for weight-reducing products like Dream-Away, a pill that one can take before retiring and that will "melt off pounds the easy way." She knows the proper way to diet is by eating less and exercising more. Yet she dreams, as all compulsive eaters do, that something like

Dream-Away really does work. The business of selling diets in this country has always been the business of selling illusions (everyone knows that, even the dieters themselves, but of course everyone's theme song in this country is "When I Grow Too Old to Dream"), reality being something that Americans generally have a hard time living with; but the business of selling to women, more so than to any of the rest of us, is the surrealism of posing desire as the Platonic perfection of yourself with a price tag. The real question for a woman as intelligent as my wife is not how to lose weight sanely but why eat foolishly in the first place. It is an especially intriguing one for one such as me who is not tempted by food and cannot understand people who are.

The meeting was just what I expected but was nonetheless startling, which means of course that it was everything I hadn't really thought about wrapped in the rhetoric of everything I knew. It was quite crowded, close to 100 people in a fair-size room in a bank building. There were only three other men present, the rest were women, which one expects because weight loss is an obsession with women in this culture, and the weight-loss industry — from pills to diet foods and drinks to exercise programs and health spas, from bottles of mineral water to self-motivation tapes — is all really directed to women, to make women feel insecure about their looks, their health, indeed, about the very phenomenon of being a woman, and thus, predictably, insecure about their sexuality, about their ability to capture men. Walking into a health-food store or a diet salon and seeing row upon row of magical bottles containing elixirs of all sorts for dieting and health (for women are in a perpetual need of losing weight and taking vitamin supplements), as if being a woman, in the end, is a condition of which one must be cured, convinces one that bourgeois woman's culture truly is a culture of bottles.

Lois Banner, in her study *American Beauty* (which should have been called *White American Beauty* since she does not, by her own admission, deal with blacks — who, after all, are American — but let's not quibble over such trivialities), talks about the nineteenth- and early-twentieth-century standards of feminine beauty: the thin, pale steel-engraving girl; the voluptuous chorus-line dancer and actress; the Gibson girl; the flapper; each the dialectical supersession of the other. I suppose today we are caught between the athletic, fresh-looking Gibson girl (Heather Locklear and other Hollywood actresses who play romantic leads; Cher, for instance, who does ads for Vic Tanny and whose body makeover was the subject of articles in women's magazines) and the superthin steel-engraving type (virtually any model). But generally the desirable look is thin, hence the interest in dieting, since most women cannot achieve the thinness of our feminine cultural icons without real persistence and effort. Of course no one cares if they do achieve thinness, only that they want to.

Certainly, few women want to look like the famous woman bodybuilder Bev Francis, the "star" of the documentary *Pumping Iron II: The Women,* who has the physique of a man, because I think it frightens women in some way to think that they can, indeed, be as strong and muscular as a well-built man. For the average woman, where would the epistemology of womanhood be located if women could *look* like men. So, the current craze among women with working out is not really intended to assault, or even call into question, standard sexual roles. Florence Griffith-Joyner has proven that one can be a sexy athlete even in as sweaty a sport as sprinting.

As I walked in and saw the women, two popular-culture remembrances sprang to mind: an old science fiction film called *The Attack of the 50-Foot Woman* and an episode of the old television series *Thriller* called "A Wig for Miss Devore." The first is about how the mad, hysterical woman becomes a kind of outsized monstrosity—a deceptively remarkable look at the pathological narcissism that men believe is the root of woman's vanity. The second had a theme familiar in the 1950s and 1960s: an old woman finds a way of remaining young by wearing a magical wig; of course, she must kill her male suitors as part of this ritual, which includes, incidentally, taking off the wig and revealing herself as a horrible hag. ("Devore" must be a play on the word "devour.") That whole business is what some commentators have aptly called the woman as menopause monster, the woman willing to kill for her insane vanity and her sexuality. And it is, alas, their sexuality, their ability to approximate the look of whores—think of such currently popular women as Dolly Parton, Tammy Bakker, and Tina Turner, who look like better and paradoxically more lurid versions of the average streetwalker— that make women interesting in this male-dominated society. And if they are not whores, they are nothing more than crows on a clothesline.

It is a major mystery to most men what makes women interesting to each other. Perhaps it is not a mystery, though. Perhaps what makes most women interesting to each other is exactly what makes them interesting to men. I have often been told that women wear makeup for other women and not for the benefit of men. (I have been told that women dress for other women as well.) This, I am sure, is true in the sense that men cannot and do not appreciate the aesthetics or artistry of feminine making-up, if one can assume that this totally contrived commercial invention by cosmetics companies is indeed an art. (When one sees the exquisitely made-up young women salesclerks at cosmetics counters in department stores dressed in white lab jackets as they commonly are these days, one is not sure if it is an art or a science, a craft or a technology.) Yet I remember watching a documentary about pornographic films where a former actress in this genre said that makeup made every woman sexy and appealing. To be sure, in the scene where the actress was wearing makeup while filming, she did look a great deal more appealing, more beautiful in the way we have become accustomed to thinking women, particularly white women, in this instance, beautiful in this culture. Obviously, men respond to makeup, or one might say this make-believe, as well. For men, it seems so much more alluring to "screw," so to speak, a made-up woman, which is why so many men want their wives or girlfriends to wear makeup to bed. In this regard, I find it striking how heavily made-up the contestants for the Miss America contest are, where the most prized value of the competing women is supposed to be their innocence. The made-up contestants look older than they really are (Miss America contestants are generally quite young; few are older than twenty-two or twenty-three, many as young as eighteen or nineteen); without makeup many would probably look no older than adolescents, so the makeup may serve a dual purpose: to give the women the "professional" look of the model and actress so that they will photograph better and to give them a mature veneer so that their youth will not make us uncomfortable. Makeup may not quite mean making oneself a tart, as it did in the middle of the nineteenth century, but it has become a sign for a certain type of sexual suggestiveness, a deeply troubling woman's minstrel face or stage mask for the sexual come-on. But this is nothing new; too many feminists have said as much. Let's go on.

Most of the women at the Weight Watchers meeting were older, probably from their mid-thirties on. There were many who were in their fifties. There were a few young girls there under the age of twenty-five or twenty. To be a man in such surroundings is a quite extraordinary experience. I cannot recall, offhand, being anywhere in recent years where I was outnumbered by so many women. And they were, by and large, a very ordinary-looking group of women, middle class and lower middle class, mostly white, who were probably either housewives, receptionists, secretaries, schoolteachers, or low-level administrative bureaucrats of some sort. The sort of group in whom one expects to find, and usually does, an intense degree of mediocrity and philistinism, which makes being middle class the very dull and exasperating experience of unfulfillment that it is for most of us. But it was just this tempered boredom, this cloud of anesthetized frustration, that made being there of great interest for me, made me see the women as being deeply human—touching, wise, and foolish—and not simply as lust fixations or, even worse, nothing at all.

The meeting itself, which took a while to start because all the members had to pay their dues and be weighed in, had all the combined characteristics of an encounter-group session, a Dale Carnegie self-improvement class, a confirmation lesson complete with catechism, a high school varsity team meeting, and a religious service, a combination of elements that is, must be uniquely American because only Americans can bring that much righteous and earnest determination to a project of such small virtue. The teacher, a woman, opens the class by asking how the weight loss went for members that week. People raise their hands and various responses are given: two pounds, three, four and a half, to which she gives appropriate words of encouragement like a proud parent working with a child on her mathematics. One man, the only one present who I think was really a member, responded that he lost ten pounds, and that produced a hum and buzz of comments. The woman next to my wife and me said disdainfully, "Men always lose weight like that."

That seemed to be the consensus in the room: that the ease with which men lose weight or appear to lose it made them aliens in this enterprise. It was the *struggle* of losing weight that was the real subject of concern here, and it was something, this struggle with an unwilling body, that was peculiarly and exclusively female: the struggle of having periods, about which my wife complains bitterly ("You're so lucky to be a man and not have to go through this every month," she says to me); the struggle of giving birth and giving your body over to a child; of being addicted to sweet food and fashion-model clothing; of having your body mutilated through breast-cancer surgery or hysterectomies; of having to go through menopause. The life of a woman is her rite of passages with a very demonstrative body that, possessed by its biological imperatives and locked in the childish imaginations of men, seems to exist both beyond her will and to spite it, as a commandment and a punishment. One thinks of the edict of nuns: a life against nature; and the dieting practice of a young woman suffering from anorexia nervosa: "It's like forcing yourself to do something that doesn't come naturally." It is, perhaps, how women understand not only their will, but will itself, as one's inner force against nature. And so in some sense women have defined the act of becoming themselves in many instances as being something that makes them cease being women at all or at least cease being themselves. They enact quests to become invisible. But it is the great American heroine, Scarlett O'Hara, of Margaret Mitchell's *Gone With the Wind,* who gives polemical challenge to this when she says early on in that novel: "I'm tired of everlastingly being unnatural and never doing anything I want to do." "Why is it a girl has to be so silly to catch a husband?" Scarlett asks. Why is it, in so many respects, that a woman has to be silly so that we might know her to be a woman?

The teacher or leader, who was by turns a coach, a minister, an orchestrator, and a judge, built this week's lesson around jargon: she wrote words on the board such as "garmites," "telepression," and "retinus pigmentoastus," and had people try to guess their meaning. The fact that Weight Watchers would have its own discourse is not unusual and is indeed undoubtedly helpful to the women, as it permits them to think of their experience as being special enough, and of their attempts at reforming their self-nurturing habits as being as profoundly critical enough, to merit a language. There was talk of "red-light foods" and "red-light moments"—taboo foods and taboo periods of temptation in one's social activities—that made one think of the term "red light" in connection with prostitution and as a kind of stark symbol of taboo and woman in our culture. But naturally Weight Watchers does not believe in taboo foods: a member can eat anything; there is only the taboo moment of wanting the food that is so alluringly placed before you, like a seduction that holds unbearable consequences and unutterable gratification. How much fun is there for any of us in this culture when we are clothed unless we are eating?

And obviously the real subject at these meetings is the meaning and ritual of woman's self-nurturing, for the new religion being offered here is not simply a new obsession with the body and the self but an attempt by these women to talk their way through being able not to eat in order to compensate for a starvation of another sort. For the eating does make up for other things, is a kind of make-believe in which the woman can escape other make-believes of a more sinister and demanding sort. To be fat affords one the pleasure of not having to worry about being thin but only if one can live in peace with one's fatness. It is impossible for most women in America to be able to do that, tormented as they are by the illusion of beauty in the mass marketplace and by the guilt of the sin of gluttony. The women are here every week to have the sin of gluttony made a venial offense, to take comfort in knowing that, after all, one can be cured, which, in this secular age, is the equivalent of being forgiven. Counselors now confer grace instead of priests. Ah, so perhaps coming to this Weight Watchers meeting is as close as I will ever get to witnessing the *culpa* of the convent when the nuns gather to proclaim each other's sins before the Mother Superior, the Living Rule. But more about nuns momentarily.

There is the usual self-reliance discourse here involving words such as "momentum" and "motivation" borrowed from the male worlds of business and sports, but there is also the emphasis that eating within bounds, eating only your fair share, which is I think a particular moral preoccupation with women, is a way of life.

"There is no end," the teacher reminds them. "It isn't over when you have reached your ideal weight."

Indeed, for many of the members, the real struggle would have only begun at that point. After the conversion, one must fight the temptation of backsliding. And there is an interesting emphasis on assertion. Many of the women, during the course of testifying at the meeting, spoke of how food is pressed upon them, how people around them expect them to eat, how their families push cake on them, how friends at parties insist on their eating. To say no to this is a very important step in the lives of these overeating women; for the denial of self-nurturing gone neurotic is the first step for them to realize the bounds and limits of woman's nurturing ability in society itself.

Incentives for these women come from many sources but most particularly from the examples of famous, admired women: fat actresses and singers such as Dolly Parton, Oprah Winfrey, Elizabeth Taylor lose weight and it becomes a celebrated event in American popular culture. But this brings to mind something else. Two of the most popular novels for women readers by women writers in twentieth-century America, both of which were made into highly acclaimed Hollywood films, are Margaret Mitchell's *Gone With the Wind* (1936) and Kathryn Hulme's *The Nun's Story* (1956). It is quite enlightening to think how much the plots and themes of these two novels, which center largely on women characters, involve food and its consumption. We learn, for instance, in *Gone With the Wind* that the women eat tremendous amounts of food before dinner parties, a custom apparently, so that at the parties they eat very little and appear more delicate. As Scarlett's personal slave, Mammy, says: "Ah has tole you an' tole you dat you kin allus tell a lady by dat she eat lak a bird." Presumably Mammy's fat body and mammoth breasts are a sure indication that she is no lady. But of course the ladyhood business, in relation to food, is just a deception. It isn't that women do not eat; it is simply that they do not wish to be seen eating by men. But connections between women and eating abound in this novel: Mammy's concern for Scarlett's mother, Ellen, the good Catholic, because she does not eat enough; Scarlett's dreams of food during the difficult days of Reconstruction and her famous vow that she "will never be hungry again"; Melanie Wilkes, Scarlett's moral counterpoint, who is "too thin" and "too white" and who gives up her food but continues to overwork, exhibiting all the symptoms of someone suffering anorexia nervosa, her small breasts and boyish figure slowly etherealized; Scarlett's days with Rhett Butler when she begins to eat huge meals with all the table manners of a child; and of course there is Scarlett's constant preoccupation with her eighteen-inch waistline.

Hulme's *The Nun Story* is a thinly fictionalized biography of her friend, Marie Louise Habets, a Belgian nurse and a nun who asked to be released from her vows to join the Resistance underground during World War II. Here too food is everywhere. When Gabrielle, who will become Sister Luke, first enters the convent, the thoughts of the outside world that seduce her most are not about sex but about food; her last meal with her father, who opposes her entering the convent, is his attempt to call "for all the temptings of life to speak to her where he had failed"; she grows particularly to dislike eating her meals on the hard wooden benches at the convent; one of her acts of penance required by her superior is that she take a beggar's bowl and go from nun to nun during mealtime and beg a spoonful of soup from each; when her father visits her he invariably tells her how thin she is getting (indeed, the novel seems to be one long journey into thinness for Sister Luke); in fact, it is food that finally forces Sister Luke from the convent, when, during the Belgian occupation, when everyone thought of food because there was so little of it, the convent-hospital where she is serving takes in the mistress of a German officer (who turns out to be a British spy) and in exchange for this the convent is sent a great deal of food. The mistress, a spoiled and irritating French collaborator, angers Sister Luke so that one day, during a phone conversation with the woman's lover, she responds to the woman's complaints about anal suppositories by saying customized ones are not manufactured in Belgium. The woman's lover is so amused by this that he sends a side of beef to the convent with Sister Luke's name on it. It is then that she makes her final request of the priest to be released of her vows, opening her last confession with him by saying, "I'm a food stamp, Father." I mention these books in passing only to show how much food is on the minds of women in this culture. So it is not surprising that ordinary women think of famous women by thinking about the ways these women handle food; food has become the essence of the struggle for selfhood for many of America's mythic and fictive women. In *The Nun's Story* and *Gone With the Wind,* food is connected with the epistemology of religious devotion, with the carnal world, with capitalistic enterprise, with the sanctity of private property. In short, food is the quiddity of woman's ambition in Western bourgeois culture.

"Liz Taylor really looks good since she lost all that weight," my wife said to me about a year ago. "I think I might buy her book." She also told me she might buy her perfume, Elizabeth Taylor's Passion, which is apparently one of a line of toilet items. But when I was last standing and gazing at a department store beauty counter, I was so overwhelmed by the numberless rows of bottles of colognes, perfumes, talcs, nail polishes, lipsticks, eye shadows, mascaras, rouges, liquid soaps, makeup removers, astringents that I felt myself lost in a wonderland of bottles. I did not think it possible to find Elizabeth Taylor's Passion in a bottle, but I never asked for it.

But why should she care about Liz Taylor at all, and most strangely why should she care about something as absolutely trivial as Liz Taylor's weight? Yet Liz Taylor's weight struggle, inextricably bound up with her love life, seems to speak deeply to many women. Her struggle is their struggle, with food and with men. Her latest book, *Elizabeth Takes Off* (Taylor has written two other books and one hopes the world is found sufficiently unworthy so as not to merit a fourth), is, in some ways, the most perfectly wrought woman's autobiography imaginable. It is about food and dieting from beginning to end. As Richard Watson points out in his delightful *The Philosopher's Diet,* "The diet industry [philosophical analysis reveals] is part of the entertainment business. It belongs to the specialized branch that manufactures unnecessary things to do." So when the acting career goes fizz, why not write a dieter's autobiography? Simply shift from one form of entertainment to another, a relatively easy move for Taylor, who, bless her heart, has never been under the conceited impression that she is an *artist.* Pictures of Taylor, both from stages in her career and from stages in her consumption of food, are side by side with recipes and exercise tips. Her book offers what will undoubtedly become an increasingly popular genre with women: the autobiography and the advice column, the how-to book and the confession. It resembles nothing so much as some older boxing autobiographies such as Jack Dempsey's first, Jack Johnson's, and Archie Moore's first, with their dieting and training tips, male athletes being the most conspicuous members of the male population who have been traditionally as interested in diet as women. (Incidentally, it must be remembered that the weight and dieting habits of some famous men have had a bigger impact in this culture than those of women: during his heyday Muhammad Ali's weight was the subject of almost daily conversation, and everyone knows that singer Mario Lanza dropped dead because of too many crash diets, just as everyone knows about the weight problems of Elvis Presley, the constant fasting of the once overweight Dick Gregory, who has now gone into the diet business with a

clinic and a special line of diet drinks, the ups and downs in weight of singer
Luther Vandross, that Orson Welles's death was caused by overeating, that
Marlon Brando's weight has prevented him from acting in recent years
but that Raymond Burr's has not. Reports of a Brando resurgence have then
connected to rumors of his dieting.) Even more closely Taylor's mixture of
forms resembles certain juvenile (didactic) biographies. Perhaps what we
have with Taylor, in our subjective age, is the stridently anti-intellectual rein-
vention of Parson Weems. The symmetry and descriptive exactitude of the
subtitle, *On Weight Gain, Weight Loss, Self-Image, and Self-Esteem,* isolates
the proper subject of the book, the twin modes of the womanly self and the
twin obsessions of consumption: eating and its renunciation. Although Taylor
can frankly admit about her acting that she has "no techniques" and that she
never took lessons, a confession that applies to her ability as a writer as well as
to her expertise on the subject of weight loss and the psychological well-
being of women, it is the sheer nonprofessionalism, antiprofessionalism of
Taylor's work that makes it endearing and appealing, its authority, as in
fundamentalist faith, emerging from the heart (so Taylor's dieting is tied to
her story of her marriages) and from experience (and dieting is tied to her
career and her celebrity status). That unaffected naturalism seems both
sincere and authentic, inspiring and practical problem-solving. A few passages from the book may explain its popularity:

> Weight loss can provide an immediate boost to our self-esteem. And every
> woman knows it takes less effort to diet when she is happy.
>
> In my late forties, weight gain became a primary factor in my feelings of
> self-worth. And when I finally had the courage to do something about those
> added pounds, I was forced to acknowledge that loss of pride played a large role
> in the reasons I put on weight in the first place.
>
> One of the reasons I decided to write this book was that I was so disturbed by
> the hundreds of articles saying that my weight gain—and by implication other
> women's—was the result of outside forces I couldn't control. This simply isn't
> true. . . . During the time I took off all those pounds I learned a lot about self-
> image and self-respect—most of all that I was in control.
>
> You and only you can take charge of your self-image and weight loss.
>
> None of us really changes to please anyone except ourselves.
>
> Even as a child, I insisted on determining my own fate.
>
> I'm convinced the inner strength that rescued me from my destructive slide
> many years later was forged during those early studio years when I determined
> always to maintain control over my personal life regardless of studio demons.

The passages indicate that the book is really about what is the only subject
of interest to women in American popular discourse, personal empowerment.
High self-esteem signifies empowerment, and dieting becomes the path to
that holistic, unburdened selfhood. One of the most important passages in
the book is Taylor's discussion of her conversion to Judaism in 1959. "It

had absolutely nothing to do with my past marriage to Mike [Todd] or my upcoming marriage to Eddie Fisher, both of whom were Jewish. It was something *I* had wanted to do for a very long time" (emphasis mine). The idea of freely converting as an act of self-expression (most people assumed she converted to please her Jewish husbands) becomes of a piece with the will to diet and the ability to form one's own image. In essence, Taylor's book tells us that dieting is the womanly restatement of Arminianism in post-industrial Western society. And since Arminianism has swept most of the Christian world, why shouldn't its promise that the kingdom of empowerment is within you sweep the bourgeois secular world as well? I understand why my wife wishes to read Taylor's book. Black women, in particular, are suckers for tales with that moral.

But black women, burdened with the historical image of being the major feminine nurturers in our culture, have other models and sources in addition to the ones white women have: the regular feature in *Ebony* on some man or woman (mostly women) who has lost an incredible amount of weight; Aretha Franklin's constant, publicized battles with her weight; features such as the one in *Essence,* a black women's fashion magazine, on Angela Davis's health routine; the images of the very slim figures of Whitney Houston and Anita Baker. But there is a greater ambivalence among black women about weight loss and exercise; several prominent black women such as Gladys Knight, Patti LaBelle, Janet Jackson, Kim Fields, Toni Morrison, and Jackee Harry are by no means thin. (There are black women athletes such as skater Debi Thomas, tennis player Zina Garrison, and track stars Jackie Joyner-Kersee and Florence Griffith-Joyner who surely possess goddess-like figures, but they are rarely, if ever, advertised as such. Probably Griffith-Joyner has received more attention in this way than any other black woman athlete, but her beauty has not been unquestioned. During the 1988 Summer Olympic Games, where both Griffith-Joyner and Joyner-Kersee won gold medals, Brazilian Joaquin Cruz was quoted as saying, "Florence looks like a man, and Jackie looks like a gorilla." White male sports writers responded indignantly, if somewhat patronizingly and with certain sexist assumptions. But the question is, Why was this obscure Brazilian quoted in American newspapers to begin with?) Moreover, one rarely sees black women jogging or doing aerobics while one watches through the window of some exercise spa. (I remember a few years back, when Tina Turner's legs were being lionized, as it were, that she remarked that she never exercised or worked out.) I suppose if the weight-loss battle is, in part, tied to the business of sex and men, then the attitude of black women may have something to do with the common expression among black men that they "want a woman with a little meat on her bones." Blues singer Mississippi John Hurt once sang, "Woman, get your big leg offa mine," which may summarize a great deal. But as James Weldon Johnson pointed out many years ago, a point that still has a great deal of force, hardly anyone in this culture, black or white, has ever thought that black women were or could be beautiful. It has been said by scholars that one of the things that blacks taught whites about living during the days of slavery was how to slow down. When I see many of the white women running, jogging, and race-walking in my neighborhood, looking distraught and impatient, I think that there might be a kind of beauty of motion that they could learn from their black sisters yet.

So I wonder what my wife thinks of this: There was a white woman at the meeting who I suppose was in her fifties and who had lost a considerable amount of weight. In fact, she was quite thin, nearly anorexic. Her hair was dyed black, her face was heavily made-up, and she wore a sleeveless, low-cut leotard with leather pants (she had also some sort of fur, possibly mink, jacket) on a day when it must have been little more than ten or fifteen degrees outside. She was clearly one of those women who was trying to dredge up her lost youth. She wore the type of clothing she did because she was quite vain about her weight loss and her current figure. Looking at that woman made me think, oddly enough, of the first babysitter my daughters had when we came to St. Louis, a quite overweight black woman who took care of children in the basement of her home. She was also a hairdresser on the side but, having few customers, would spend most of her time doing her own hair, which, apparently, never ceased to fascinate her. She had a hot comb in her hair every day. Indeed, aside from food, hair seemed her most consuming passion. Her own daughter suffered from a disease that prevented hair growth, which was a cause of great anguish for the mother. Many medications were tried with the daughter, and whenever some small hair growth resulted, it was the cause of great celebration and a doing up of the daughter's hair in grand style. Perhaps the pencil-thin white woman and the heavy black woman were more alike and more in need of sharing their differences than anyone could imagine. I stood before *those* expressions of womanhood struck dumb with a kind of wonder, but my wife intensely disliked both women.

My wife told me that Weight Watchers encourages members who have reached their goal weight to continue to come to meetings by making them life members and absolving them of having to pay dues. They are meant to serve as models for the other women who are struggling to reach the end. "It can be done, and here are some who have done it." One has to find one's models where one can, I thought. But there are still some lessons that are too hard to be learned well that way. Or, to put it another way, when one considers what black women and white women can teach each other, when one considers the significance of these ordinary women sharing experiences in this way, the choice for women between eating and not eating is more fraught with a kind of feminist philosophy than many of us ever dreamed it was. Near the end of the meeting, when the teacher had whipped up more than a bit of enthusiasm and had her students shouting out what they needed to do to get through the next week of dieting, the resolve and strengthening that was required to resist the temptation of food; well, I must admit that that bit of womanly determination to be better women gave me a thrill.

Her Picture
in the Papers:
Remembering Some
Black Women

To my mother and sisters

She wants her mind to be like that. Solid, contained, and black as a sheet of darkened ice.
—Jean Toomer, *Cane*

I. "THE WORLD IS BLOOD-HOT AND PERSONAL..."

It was with the greatest reluctance, a reluctance bordering on real discomfort, that I attended a showing of *The Color Purple*. I have always felt somewhat justified in having this kind of bracing and protective cowardice whenever I decide to see or not to see a film with, to use the quaint 1930s phrase, an "all-Negro cast." This is, after all, the sort of film that is obviously aimed at a black audience, aimed that way not because producers could not hope to find enough whites who are willing to see a large number of blacks in Technicolor, but because it was and still is thought that blacks might find it refreshing or merely curious to see themselves doing something meaningful on the screen, or at least what the operators of mass culture think is meaningful; and this prospect can be, frankly, terrifying. My justification for my fear stems from the real possibility of being insulted by one of these artistic events; and commercial films with black actors performing major and demanding, one might even hope exciting, roles are so rare that they do constitute something epochal for the culture itself, since it means that we are thinking seriously or trying to think seriously about something that might be important. Indeed, it is the fact that such films are so rare that makes them so problematic and so much the essence of insult. That burden of serious and earnest statement is the flip side of the coin of comic sentiment which has always typed the black actor, nay, the black person, as an image of American popular culture.

The Color Purple, directed by Hollywood wunderkind Steven Spielberg, is not only a poor film; it is not even interesting. It seems small and mundane like a television production. Possibly the only creative phenomenon that could have given it any lasting value would have been a woman director, especially a black woman director—Maya Angelou comes to mind right away as a possibility. But one can never be sure about predicting births and deaths in art. What place will *The Color Purple* occupy in the black American artistic legacy of commercial film? Will it ultimately come to be seen as having lesser significance than such works of black directors as Emmet J. Scott's answer to *The Birth of a Nation,* the 1918, NAACP-financed *The Birth of a Race;* Oscar Micheaux's various films; Melvin Van Peeble's *The Story of a Three-Day Pass, Watermelon Man,* and *Sweet Sweetback's Baadassss Song;* Bill Gunn's *Ganja and Hess;* Gordon Parks's *The Learning Tree, Shaft, Shaft's Big Score,* and *Leadbelly;* Michael Schulz's *Carwash* and *Krush Groove;* Sidney Poitier's *Buck and the Preacher, A Warm December,* and the Uptown Saturday Night series; Spike Lee's *She's Gotta Have It,* among others? Will *The Color Purple* be considered more significant than other white-directed black films such as *Stormy Weather, Carmen Jones, Porgy and Bess,* and nearly all other major and minor Hollywood vehicles of that sort, from King Vidor to Sidney Poitier, from Stepin Fetchit to the black exploitation era of the 1960s and the early 1970s, from Joe Louis in *The Spirit of Youth* in the 1930s to Muhammad Ali in *The Greatest* in the 1970s, because it has a black literary source? (And one wonders where the adapted works of black writer Willard Motley—*Knock on Any Door* and *Let No Man Write My Epitaph*—will wind up.) How will *The Color Purple* stack up against such serious white-directed dramas and fantasies as *Nothing But a Man, A Soldier's Story, Black Orpheus, The Brother from Another Planet, A Raisin in the Sun,* or *The Great White Hope* (the latter two adapted from successful plays, one by a black woman and the other by a white man)? The fact that *The Color Purple* is based on a novel by a black woman writer may not, in the end, be all that important. Kristin Hunter's *The Landlord* was the first novel by a black woman to be made into a commercial Hollywood film, but, because of the dismal quality of the conversion, I think it has become more a cause of embarrassment for Ms. Hunter than any reason for celebration. The film was made in 1969 and has largely and rightly been forgotten. All of these questions bring to mind one very critical point, a sort of epistemological inquiry: What is a black film? However that question is answered (and probably Professor Thomas Cripps in his *Black Film as Genre* answered it best), it is certain that if the definition is that a black film must be an artistic enterprise passing through black hands only from script to screen, then there have been virtually no black films ever made in America. That may be a consummation devoutly to be wished by some black folk, but I suppose we, both black and white, must face the reality of a mixed, mongrelized heritage at last.

The Color Purple continues to be, if Darryl Pinckney's review of Ishmael Reed's latest novel, *Reckless Eyeballing,* in a recent issue of *The New York Review of Books* is any indication, the center of a very bitter though bloodless dispute in the black community. The issue is quite a bit larger than feminism, either black or white, or the artistic merits of Alice Walker's work or the film that bears her title. All manner of artistic and political flotsam and jetsam swim in the waters of the black community—from Prince's songs and movies to the videos of such black artists as Jeffrey Osborne and Cameo (a few too many white women for some black women's taste), from the novels of Gayle Jones (over which I heard Professor Richard Barksdale struggle in a lecture, after which he was promptly eaten alive by the white feminists in the audience) to the overabundance of black women in ratio to black men, from black-against-black violence (which is often manifested in horrible crimes committed by black men against black women and black children) to what is perceived by many as a conspiracy against the presence of the black male in America (it is a statistical fact that a black male between the ages of twenty and forty is six times more likely to be murdered or imprisoned than a white male in the same age group; it is also a fact that a black male in America is more likely to make less money, have worse health, and die younger). All of this is taking place among a group of people whose differences of opinion involve nothing less than the highest emotional stakes, an utter necessity born of the fact that blacks are probably the only folk in this country who know precisely that what it *means* to be an American is exactly what it *costs*. Black people live in a very personal and precariously structured world, a world of uneasy marginality, easily threatened by any bump or wave on the graph of white American popular culture, as if every moment, every event were the brink of the *fatal instant.* There is a question for the black American more horrible than, Must I be what the white American says I am? It is, Must I be what the white American has made me?

Let us consider for a moment Spike Lee's low-budget hit, *She's Gotta Have It,* which must for now, whether intended or not, bear the burden and the instructive duty of being construed as a reply of sorts to *The Color Purple* (a less ambiguous reply, to be sure, than the recent film remake of Richard Wright's 1940 novel, *Native Son*). Lee's film seems to offer some ingenuity in its handling of the social implications of the problem of black sex. Yet, although it is a superior film to *The Color Purple,* its politics are in fact a good deal less daring.

One of the reasons for Lee's artistic triumph—that is, for his succeeding in making a film about black life that did not divide the black community — is that he did not try to say too much or be too grand (there are indeed hidden virtues in the constraints of a meager budget). Aside from the obvious appeal of seeing black men and black women making love on the screen, what must have struck black audiences was the film's sheer and clean simplicity. There was a certain sense of relief in knowing that Spike Lee was not, after all, trying to make a feminist or even an overtly political film at all but rather a work that was making fun of the male ego. The distinction is important as it will help us understand that Lee's film is in the conservative Hollywood comic tradition of ridiculing the excesses of the male ego, a tradition so safe that Clint Eastwood, one of the leading actors and box-office attractions in the macho idiom of the American tough guy, can make a parodic version of his Dirty Harry thrillers, *The Gauntlet,* and return in later films to a nonparodic portrayal of a similar character without risking any loss of audience.

She's Gotta Have It, a rather spirited sex satire about a young black woman named Nola Darling and her three lovers, is actually based upon a doggedly asserted sexist assumption that most blacks, male and female, viewing the film would recognize instantly: black women have no sexual alternatives to black men. Homosexuality is only for the small daring fringe (being dismissed by most black women as being too unconventional or "freaky"), and white lovers, in this age when black women no longer possess a sullen provocativeness because they are no longer sexual contraband, are virtually a social impossibility. White men, by and large, have nothing to say to black women these days. Having no leverage in the battle of the sexes, the black woman, according to this black male fancy and undeniable sociological truth, is in an utterly powerless position. For Nora Darling, like most black women, white lovers are never remotely considered and homosexuality, in scenes that announce a kind of astringent prudery or sexual conservatism on the part of Nola that black women for the last few decades have generally been accused of, is completely rejected. Lee is not interested in attacking or criticizing the injustice of the implications of the assumption; thus, Nola Darling never becomes a figure of feminist uplift as Celie does in *The Color Purple.* She never transcends or revolts against her position as a black woman in modern bourgeois society and never seems to want to. Lee's film never aspires toward feminist implications because it never criticizes or attacks the adversative nature of sex relationships which, of course, is the major preoccupation of feminist thought. The film works on the idea of simple reversal: a woman is shown to be obsessed with sex in much the same way that a man might be. There are two reasons in the end that this reversal never truly disturbs the audience. First, it is only another example of a woman entering a man's world or assuming a man's sensibilities about something. Historically, this has never been as disconcerting a proposition as the idea of a man entering a woman's world, which is the ending that *The Color Purple* both designs and demands for its revised project of female uplift (much more clearly in the novel than the film). Second, like Celie, Nola Darling is better than any of the men who want her. She is honest and not possessive. She is, blandly speaking, a nicer person. This moral superiority is comforting to both male and female viewers as it makes a woman sympathetic in about the only way we can bear and certainly the only way we can admire.

Lee's film, in short, is about a group of bourgeois characters who are trying in a more or less entertaining series of comic encounters to come to grips not entirely with sex but with the moral implications of their own black middle-class existences. The Thanksgiving dinner scene where Nola invites all three of her lovers to share her table is vitally important in this regard: Is it possible, the scene is asking, to group together the discrete element of black male middle-class existence into one consolidated bourgeois sensibility? Is this the new black family plot? Both Lee's film and *The Color Purple,* each with their lengthy and important family dinner scenes, may be offering something like a new black family plot. Consider that both films give us, finally, the interesting irenic solution to the black sex contest: the idea of accepting woman as the analogy of polarity. In *The Color Purple* she symbolizes a better version of humanity and in *She's Gotta Have It* she is a better, a more self-assured version of sexuality. In either case, whether old-fashioned moralist or modernist aesthetician, she is a kind of ideal bourgeois conception, the romance of the humane alternative to competition, production, and technology (the male world). That has been the solution that the bourgeois Western mind, both male and female, both black and white, has been tending toward since at least the nineteenth century. And there is something expressly reactionary about it all, as if the only way victims can be understood is that somehow they must be better than those by whom they are victimized.

I attended a showing of *She's Gotta Have It* one Sunday afternoon at an art-house theater that normally attracts very few black patrons. Upon entering, my wife and I discovered that the place was filled with no one but blacks of every class, age, and description. We saw the film with an older, respectable black couple from our church, a physician and his wife. As we left the theater the physician's wife expressed her confusion and dislike for the film: the blunt sexuality was appalling, the comic silliness of the plot seemed disturbing. My wife, on the other hand, loved the film, its images of black lovemaking, and wants, even now, to see it again. The two women are about thirty years apart in age, and their being members of different generations undoubtedly accounts for the difference in perception.

When I first read *The Color Purple* I thought it seemed, oddly enough, to point to Fanny Hurst's famous 1933 novel, *Imitation of Life.* I felt it almost perverse to consider these two books as part of the same sensibility. They would seem to bear so little in common on the surface. So I was quite surprised when I read *The Color Purple* a second time and still thought about *Imitation of Life* and the poor ugly black woman, Delilah, whose cooking and demeanor become both the substance and the icon upon which Bea

Pullman, determined, ambitious, Calvinist-inspired white woman, makes her money. It is distinctly disquieting, painful to read at convenient intervals that Delilah is "black, gargantuan, a tent," that she wore a cape that gave her "the appearance of a slightly asthmatic rubber tent." There are no ugly white women in the novel. How preposterous this all seems, this incredibly black-skinned woman having a white child. It seemed more a wish than anything else. Perhaps for Hurst that was precisely what it was supposed to be: the wish that black women harbor in their hearts—to bear white children, to have the whiteness that is buried in their souls, that is yearned for in their hearts emerge in the form of white-skinned youngsters, reformed sexuality, reformed femininity. (The sexual nightmare of the black male is precisely that: that black women really want to sleep with white men, bear their children as they did on the plantation. The sexual politics of the oppressed depends upon a charged sense of inferiority.) Except, of course, for Hurst this whiteness is a crime, a manifestation of the unconscious desire to be white and beautiful and female instead of the black woman accepting her place "in her great fluted white cap, and her great fluted white smile on each box[.] Delilah, who, though actually in no more than her late thirties, looked mammy to the world"; the place that through the magic of automation and business can produce in capitalistic mass precision a "corps of ample, immaculate Negro women graduating into the Pullmans of various large cities." Smiling Pullman women to match the smiling Pullman porters. And they might in their deaths, these armies of mammies, begin "suddenly to pour hot broad kisses against the bare ankles" of their white mistresses.

Imitation of Life seems to be nothing more than an elaboration of the subtext of *Uncle Tom's Cabin.* To be sure, Delilah's literary ancestors are the Shelbys' cook and Tom's wife, Aunt Chloe, and St. Clair's cook, Dinah: two big ugly black women who know they are in fact lesser beings than their mistresses. It is Chloe who says to Mrs. Shelby: "Now, Missis, do jist look at dem beautiful white hands o' yourn, with long fingers, and all a-sparkling with rings, like my white lilies when de dew's on 'em; and look at my great stumpin hands. Now, don't ye think dat de Lord must have meant *me* to make de pie-crust, and you to stay in the parlor?" The scene that most graphically details the position of white mistress over black woman is that in which St. Clair's exacting northern cousin, Ophelia, tries to reorder Dinah's kitchen "to a systematic pattern," obsessed with the fact that the women servants under Marie St. Clair seemed "indolent and childish, unsystematic and improvident." Ophelia's act seems to be one of cultural imperialism and psychological oppression and although a modern black reader may see the scene in this way, it is not a certainty that Mrs. Stowe intended it so. It is during this same scene that the reader is informed that Mrs. Shelby, the same woman of the soft white hands, was able to bring her kitchen, and her black female help, "into harmonious and systematic order," that she was, indeed, an ideal housekeeper. The white woman's function is not to get into the kitchen to work with black women but merely to supervise them at their labor. Gillian Brown discusses this scene in an academic article on *Uncle Tom's Cabin* that appeared a few seasons back in *American Quarterly* ("Getting in the Kitchen with Dinah: Domestic Politics in *Uncle Tom's Cabin*") that makes me think that she has never read *Imitation of Life;* otherwise she might have tempered her analysis a bit. She says, for instance, that "what makes *Uncle Tom's Cabin* a particularly striking domestic novel is that Stowe seeks to reform American society not by employing domestic values but by reforming them." This statement seems frankly untenable. If it weren't, Brown might have accounted for the fact that Eliza, the runaway mulatto, has hands that are as soft as those of Mrs. Bird, one of her white bene-factors, who happens not to be living in the corrupted world of the slave economy. As the other Dinah, the Birds' free servant, observes when Eliza arrives, "Never done much hard work, guess, by the looks of her hands." And the reader can suppose only that she has never done any hard work because she is almost white and the hard kitchen work is for the "stumpin hands" of Dinah and Chloe. I think that Mrs. Stowe's is not quite a supreme vision of black and white sisterhood together in the march toward the matriarchal utopia, as some white feminist critics have claimed. It is difficult to tell precisely what Mrs. Stowe's feelings are about all of this but perhaps Cassie, the privileged octoroon working the fields on Legree's plantation, means something by way of balance. But she does not have to be there and *that* makes all the difference. Alas, poor Topsy, benighted, abused black woman-hood made whole and Christian by the spinster New England white woman. Are black women, in this racist, feminist dream, what benevolent white women have made them?

The Color Purple is not supposed to recall *Imitation of Life*. It is supposed to bring to mind those nineteenth-century black feminist works by maids-in-bondage, Harriet Wilson's *Our Nig* and Harriet Jacobs's *Incidents in the Life of a Slave Girl*. The reemergence of its suppressed, atomized black family brings to mind another nineteenth-century black work that centered on the Victorian holy of holies, family life as humanized economics: Frank Webb's 1850s novel, *The Garies and Their Friends*. But I think Walker's novel suggests *Imitation of Life* because in some way I imagine Celie's story to be the revisionist autobiography of the Delilahs and Chloes in American litera-ture, which is why she, too, like them, becomes successful in a cottage business, so to speak. They were cooks; Celie is a seamstress. But Celie runs her own business and is hired out not simply to provide the labor and substance for a white (male or female) manager:

> I sit in the dining room making pants after pants. I got pants now in every color and size under the sun. Since us started making pants down home, I ain't been able to stop. I change the cloth, I change the print, I change the waist, I change the pocket, I change the hem, I change the fullness of the leg.

Celie works with the compassion, compulsion, and autonomy of an artist.

What was seen as disorder in Dinah's nineteenth-century kitchen or the mere crude material for white inspiration for a capitalistic venture in rationalism (compared to Robinson Crusoe and Friday and those homely modes of production) in Delilah's twentieth-century kitchen is for Celie the richness and diversity of a self-sufficient expressive life. Thus, the black-skinned woman no longer has to see herself in relation to white men or women as Delilah saw herself: "a washin'-machine and a ironin'-board…to save [them] ever havin' to shuffle a bone again." And her relationship with the older, more experienced black woman, Shug Avery, is a reformation of the emotionally crazed, pathologically servile relationship that exists between the white mistress and her black hired or purchased women. Celie, as the revised Chloe, Delilah, and Dinah, has brought the lowly, ugly, black-skinned woman to a holistic self-awareness. In short, Celie is the revised black-skinned woman of American popular culture.

"I never did set very well with women," Billie Holiday writes in her 1956 autobiography, *Lady Sings the Blues,* in what amounts to a very revealing half-statement, as women never set too well with Holiday either. In the book, coauthored by William Dufty, the husband of her manager, Maely Dufty, Holiday employs a stream of invectives to describe women: *bitch, broad, lezzie, dame, dyke,* and *chick,* accompanied by some very unflattering adjectives: *fat, lazy, dogass, greasy,* and *freakish.* Some of this language, particularly the terms for women, was part of the underground in which she moved, the world of the whorehouse, where she first heard jazz, and that was, as she put it, "about the only place where black and white folks could meet in any natural way"; the world of the nightclub, where Holiday earned her living as an adult and created her art; the world of lower-class blacks among whom she grew up; the world of the masculine hip, which is largely what most significant segments of the jazz world are, all worlds in which women are particularly devalued and in which women participate in their devaluation by using such language in reference to themselves. Holiday was well known for her, to borrow Zora Neale Hurston's word, "specifying" ability, that is, the ability to curse someone out with rapier adroitness, a skill she particularly honed on women.

But Billie Holiday was also incarcerated several times, first when she was placed in a Catholic institution as a ten-year-old girl when her mother's boarder tried to rape her. Subsequently, Holiday was arrested for prostitution and, several times, for possession of narcotics. All of these arrests resulted in stays of varying lengths in reformatories, drug rehab centers, and prison. In every instance, she was, naturally, confined within an all-woman environment: women inmates, women guards, women supervisors, even, on two occasions, a woman judge, "a tough hard-faced old dame with hair bobbed almost like a man's," who was lenient the first time and very harsh the second. (She is the only judge who is described at length in the book.) I would think that the source of much of Holiday's attitude toward women and the language that symbolizes it was formed and forged among these various collections of wayward women or the instances of a woman possessing state-recognized authority, indeed, who was the state, a judge in juvenile court. She had, in some sense, to come to realize that waywardness among women was something of a crime against the state. Or that illness in women (female trouble, one might say)—and for Holiday, deviance, at times, seems to be described as a disease—was something of a crime against authority and the state. After all, her plea for drug addicts in the book is a cry for understanding an illness or disease, the liberal's cry. Thus, in one respect, the way she describes women takes on the quality of speaking about something disfigured, something that is ill or damaged in some way. Perhaps she wrote more tellingly than she knew when she said of one of her drug trials: "It was called 'The United States of America versus Billie Holiday.' And that's just the way it felt," as if to be a sick woman and to have that sickness recognized by society as such was to be engaged by the state in war, in adversative contest.

Billie Holiday was also Catholic, having been given the name St. Theresa when incarcerated as a girl and having noted on more than one occasion the intensity of her mother's piety. This too, I am sure, played a role in her attitude about women and sin. The way she describes women often makes them seem as if they are *unnatural* (her particular fascination with lesbianism in the autobiography underscores this point, as she insists that she herself was not a lesbian, probably an arguable assertion in some quarters, while pointing up how she attracts lesbians as a star woman singer and how much she was exposed to them in the various institutions where she stayed); dirty and despicable, women are like the deformed sinner.

Of course, she had bad experiences with women from childhood. Her cousin Ida, with whom she lived when her mother went north from Baltimore, the city where Holiday was born, to work as a maid, beat her constantly "not with a spank on the ass, but with her fists or a whip" for the doings of Cousin Ida's son, Henry. The worst offense was wetting the bed, which Henry did regularly but for which Billie, who slept with him, was blamed. The entire scenario of the mother whipping the girl for the sins of the boy with whom she is forced to sleep is so fraught with psychosexual implications that one might think it was entirely imagined by Holiday. Certainly, having been reared in an atmosphere where boys are privileged and protected and girls must bear and indulge the boys' weaknesses, a quite common occurrence in the households of the lower class (where male prerogative is especially entrenched because the underclass male is so unmanned in the larger masculine world) and the middle class as well, would explain Holiday's attitude later when she was often accused of being victimized by her first husband, Jimmy Munroe, and led by him into drug addiction:

My marriage was coming apart. And it was during this time that I got hooked. But one had nothing to do with the other, really, and Jimmy was no more the cause of my doing what I did than my mother was. That goes for any man I ever knew. I was as strong, if not stronger, than any of them. And when it's that way, you can't blame anybody but yourself.

Here is the defiant cry of self-reliant womanhood ("I did not become a drug addict because my heart was broken or because I felt it would help me keep my husband," she is in effect saying) that is as much a part of the Billie Holiday myth as the whimper of the torching jazz singer who cowrote or became closely associated with such songs as "Don't Explain," "Good Morning, Heartache," and "My Man," the last line of whose book is in fact a lyric from the last-mentioned song: "Tired? You bet. But all that I'll soon forget with my man." (On the flip side are the songs she cowrote or was closely associated with that had elements of social or personal protest, such as "God Bless the Child" and "Strange Fruit.") It is one of the arresting and complex paradoxes of this book that Holiday can appear both weak and strong, defiant and maudlin, tough and sentimental almost simultaneously. And she is almost always likely to be weak, sentimental, and maudlin in relation to a man, despite her talk about being stronger than any man she knew, which is, too, fundamentally a correct self-assessment. First, she learned from a young age that men really are weak (bad bladders) and spoiled (by their mothers) and so must be pampered and excused. Second, it must be remembered that as art-jazz singer in her later days, as a big-band "canary" in her youth, she was, when not incarcerated, surrounded by "cats" (cats and canaries, the predatory world of sexual conquest in microcosm), enveloped in a world of men, something about which she must have had mixed feelings. For although she greatly admired the male musicians with whom she worked, both black and white, she realized the precariousness of being a woman in this business and even understood a certain kind of negative solidarity that did exist among women in the business. (For example, she told Helen Forrest, when both were denied an opportunity to perform with the Artie Shaw band at a New England boys' school, "You're so fine and grand. You may be white, but you're no better than me. They won't have either of us here because we're both women.") And she admits that solidarity should exist (as when she helps Sarah Vaughan: "It's the easiest thing in the world to say, 'Every broad for herself.' Saying it and acting that way is one thing that's kept some of us behind the eight ball where we've been living for a hundred years"). Despite this, there was little chance of any real camaraderie among the women singers in this business, as Holiday herself disliked most of them, black and white, even those who worshipped her, and she had more than a slight cult following during her career. It was apparently not jealousy or insecurity that generated Holiday's attitude. She was, at times, simply regal, with the aloofness of a potentate and the glamour and allure of a big-time Hollywood actress even if, to borrow Martin Williams's phrase, she never had an act. She was, far and away, the grandest female gesture and most hypnotic actress of the century.

What most easily explains the paradox in Holiday's autobiography is her own persistent belief in ladyhood. This attitude might be expected from someone who, as an adolescent, scrubbed the steps of white homes or turned tricks to make a living, caught between being an underpaid performer of degraded housework and a disrespected sex object. Holiday is proud of herself when she earns the nickname Lady at the nightclub where she works as a teenager, when she refuses to take the customers' tips from the table in the way that was demanded of her. Saxophonist Lester Young makes it official by giving her the nickname Lady Day. Her mother is given the name Duchess. As she writes earlier, when her mother comes back to retrieve her from Cousin Ida's: "When my mother came back to Baltimore one day she had nine hundred dollars she had saved. She bought a real fancy house on Pennsylvania Avenue in north Baltimore. We were going to live like ladies and everything was going to be fine." Holiday is also proud of being able to return to Baltimore and show up a girl she grew up with named Evelyn:

> I drove up in my white Cadillac in front of the house where Evelyn used to live. I parked it where the junk wagon used to sit. This saintly bitch who was going to be a big dancer was still living there. She had six kids and none of them by the same father and she was still funky and greasy. The kids lined up in the street and I bought them ice cream and gave them fifty cents apiece. They thought it was a big deal and I was a big star.

So what partly motivates Holiday (and to become a successful performing artist is an exercise in motivation and ambition of gigantic proportion, it is to aspire for weighty achievement in a treacherous realm) is the inferiority complex of the lower-class black woman who has been told she is nothing by both the white women for whom she works and the light-skinned black women with whom she is forced to live. She realizes that her labor as both maid and housekeeper, as a whore, her comparatively dark skin in fact, makes their ladyhood possible because it is defined by not being what she is.

On the other hand, Holiday reveals through her constant references to slavery that she must have known that the whole ladyhood business was nothing more than a fiction, just as through this same imagery she clearly knows that being a working black jazz musician is being nothing more than being a slave to white nightclub owners, record companies, booking agents and the like. The story of her great-grandmother's being a slave and a mistress for her master is repeated several times in the book: "Mr. Charles Fagan, the handsome Irish plantation owner, had his white wife and children in the big house. And he had my great-grandmother out in back. She had sixteen children by him, and all of them were dead by then except Grandpop." She writes later that "the white women didn't have as much to do with [the making of the world of slavery] as the men. But they only had to look out their windows to see what was going on. There was damn little 'segregation' on the plantations in the daytime, even less at night." In truth, there were no ladies on the plantation, just mutually exclusive social tiers of women who exist as indulgences and economic helpmeets for the planter who becomes simply a Cousin Henry writ large, surrounded either by women who see and are powerless to say or by women who are in fact powerless even to acknowledge the act of seeing, for whom being blind is an act of volition of the most extraordinary magnitude. Moreover, this is the same great-grandmother who dies with her arm tightly wrapped around young Holiday's neck as an image that slavery and the past cannot be forgotten, that it in fact has a stranglehold on the present that can be broken only with the force it takes to break the grandmother's arm.

But if being a black jazz musician is like being a slave, Holiday does not advocate a revolt; she in fact admires the power of some of the men who control the technology that makes her art possible and feels that a kind of collaboration is best. In describing an aspect of her experience as an actress while making the film *New Orleans,* she makes an apt analogy to her act as a jazz recording star:

> I got along fine with the cameramen. I dug from the beginning these were the most important cats around. They're like the boys in the control room when you're making records. You can turn in the best performance in the world, but if those cats in the control room aren't with you when they turn those little knobs or twist those little dials, you might just as well have stayed in bed, Jack.

On the one hand, this statement is nothing more than an essential acknowledgment that art is a collaborative enterprise; on the other hand, it does ironically recognize the relative powerlessness of the artist in relation to the creation, form, and structure, indeed, to the sheer intentionality of his or her art. It is the same recognition of the powerless artist that is repeated throughout the book: the film editing that reduces her part in the film which she cannot protest; the inability to collect royalties for her recordings; the humiliating nature of road life for a black musician; the helplessness of the artist when faced with unscrupulous managers, demanding or unappreciative fans, and greedy nightclub owners.

Finally, Holiday described the passage from uptown to downtown when she became a success with "Strange Fruit" at Café Society around 1939:

> I found out the main difference between uptown and downtown was people are more for real up there. They got to be, I guess. Uptown a whore was a whore; a pimp was a pimp; a thief was a thief; a faggot was a faggot; a dike was a dike; a mother-hugger was a mother-hugger.
>
> Downtown it was different—more complicated. A whore was sometimes a socialite; a pimp could be a man about town; a thief could be an executive; a faggot could be a playboy; a dike might be called a deb; a mother-hugger was somebody who wasn't adjusted and had problems.
>
> I always had trouble keeping this double talk straight. And sometimes when I messed up, the fur and feathers would fly so you'd think nobody around there ever called a spade a spade before.

The last sentence ends with a pun, obviously enough, as one can rest assured that the whites downtown had called enough spades by their unrightful names and surely a spade herself ought to be accorded the same privilege in speaking about white folk. But as Holiday should have known, it is a signal impossibility to keep "double talk straight"; the singular power of language is that it can be the manifestation (even the manifesto) of dishonesty while in fact also being the root of it as well. And all of this talk in the end is about class and class interest. Uptown, Holiday's invectives are the proper descriptive terms for social dregs; downtown, there is an unbreachable disjuncture between the language of social degradation and the economic station of bourgeois respectability. Mastering languages may be a sign and symbol of social mobility but languages themselves are not mobile, entrapped by the political and social powers they serve and signify. Holiday's book, the very richness of its vernacular, is ultimately the sign of its undoing as a political work not simply because of her attitude toward women but more because she, in her obsession with honesty, a point she makes more than once in the book, rehearses invective as the language of stigma. But she is, by far, the most stigmatized person in her narrative, so her language becomes only a kind of cul-de-sac from which she cannot liberate herself except through the arty and witty poetry of her jazz songs. It is one of the most profound statements ever made by an American, living in a culture where languages whirl by demons, to speak of the struggle of trying to keep it all straight.

I grew up in a family of black women. My father died before I was a year old and my mother never remarried until I was twenty-six. So I was surrounded in my mother's house by her indomitable presence and the lesser but nonetheless strong presences of my two older sisters. In my extended family, my many aunts were always more dominating and domineering than my few uncles; my maternal grandmother was and is a more fearful and powerful being than my grandfather. She could outtalk him, outcurse him, and outfight him. Yet she is no stereotypical matriarch. She is not religious and was not particularly loving with her children. I remember her in my youth sitting on plastic-covered sofas eating huge dishes of ice cream and watching her latest, newest color television or reading the *National Enquirer.*
It was impossible not to be shaped and stamped by the characters of these quite extraordinary women and it was also impossible not to be thoroughly distressed and vexed by what I thought, at one point in my life, the overbearing authority of a bunch of loudmouthed, frustrated females. Several years ago, when my great-aunt Virginia died, well in her seventies, I remember how sorry my mother felt, the deep arcs of sorrow that were etched by the memory of the two women's having lived together for several years when my mother was just a young widow with three children and no high school diploma. The sorrow was all the more aching, I think, because my mother knew that my great-aunt Virginia was a selfish and foolish old woman who constantly petted and supported a ne'er-do-well, no-account son at the expense of her other children. Alas, that is the story with all black sons, as

2A.

Lorraine Hansberry's *A Raisin in the Sun* shows so convincingly, we are all petted and supported by the women in our families. That is why we are so capable of mistreating and brutalizing women. We secretly suspect that they may always show themselves to be our superiors; for black women do not say simply "We endure" but, more pointedly, "We endure our men." But it was my great-aunt Virginia who opened her door to my mother and her brood when my mother had no place to go and it was she who told my mother never to remarry while her children were young: "You got girl children and you know how these stepfathers is. They ain't about being nothing but dogs. Promise me you won't marry." And my mother kept her word.

My grandmother loved the blues and, I am told, used to play them loudly on her phonograph so that the whole neighborhood could hear, back during the days of the Depression when she was the only one on the block who had such a wondrous device. And her favorites were Bessie Smith and Memphis Minnie. She doesn't listen to the old music from the old country anymore, good old Alabama girl that she was. She spends her days watching hours of game shows and soap operas.

My mother loves gospel music and on Sundays used to be able to listen to it by the hour on the radio. Her favorites might have been the Caravans. I know she has always worshipped Mahalia Jackson and Aretha Franklin.

First my younger aunts, then my sisters started to listen to rock and roll. And it was always the girl singers who were the favorites: the Shirelles, the Jaynettes, Ruby and the Romantics, LaVern Baker. Different generations do have different perceptions. How my grandmother loved the first film version of *Imitation of Life* and Lena Horne in *Stormy Weather* and how my mother would always weep when Mahalia Jackson sang at the end of the second screen version of *Imitation of Life* and when Dorothy Dandridge's character died at the end of *Carmen Jones*. But *The Color Purple* is the film that speaks for and to my sisters and their generation, for it is not about the black woman's triumph as comedy or death but as satire and the death weapon that will allow a whole life.

What follows—the stories of the Shirelles, the Caravans with Inez Andrews, and Memphis Minnie—is what some different generations of black women have taught me; is about the black woman's struggle to create her own metaphor of herself—the saying one thing and meaning another—within the confines of American popular culture. And the stakes are exorbitant, for as Norman O. Brown writes, "Meaning is new, or not at all; a new creation, or not at all; poetry, or not at all." This is the stuff I learned while traveling the mansions of my mother's house.

II. "WHAT ELSE IS THERE TO SAY
BUT EVERYTHING?"

But most radio stations, they won't let ya sing th' real songs.
—Woody Guthrie, *Bound For Glory*

Life is water that is being drawn off.
—Jean Toomer, *Cane*

THE SHIRELLES

One of the girls used to say that all the time. "They should give us the key to the city." I said, "I'd rather have the keys to a car."
—Shirley Alston

I remember those old Scepter 45s that my sisters used to buy when we were kids. They are part of the same set of memories that have frozen forever the image of Chubby Checker riding around our neighborhood in South Philadelphia in a bright, new yellow Cadillac, flushed with the success of having pulled off a quite common theft in pop music: stealing, note for note, vocal inflection for vocal inflection, a song by Hank Ballard called "The Twist," a theft that was symbiotically useful for both men; the words of a Hank Ballard song that my mother liked so well, "Annie had a baby/Can't work no more"; Jesse Belvin's high pompadour of processed hair as he sang so sweetly and richly the ballad "I Do Believe the Masquerade Is Over"; and all those dedications such as James and Bobby Purify's "I'm Your Puppet," going out for Jimmy who wants to make up with Lil' Sister; Gene Chandler's "Duke of Earl" for all the guys down at Earl's barbershop; Lee Dorsey's "Working in a Coal Mine" for the sanitation crew on Twenty-first and Tioga; Billy Stewart's "I Do Love You" for all the fine mamas at Pearl's beauty shop going to the fish fry tonight; Aretha Franklin's "Respect" for Lulu and the crowd heading for the cabaret; Mary Wells's "You Lost the Sweetest Boy" for Dottie, Ruth, and Sheila, who want a kiss from your local DJ; and Wilson Pickett's "I'm Gonna Wait 'Til the Midnight Hour" for the Anthill Mob.

It was the wild and woolly days of black American popular dance music, when poor black kids in the neighborhood did not desire to be athletes; everyone wanted to be a lead singer in some group like the Cadillacs, Earl Lewis and the Channels, the Diamonds, the Impressions, the Flamingoes, the Drifters, or the Jive Five. And everyone who could carry a tune was singing on the street. As Ben E. King, former lead singer with the Drifters and a successful single act in the sixties—"I (Who Have Nothing)," "Stand by Me," "Spanish Harlem"—recalled about those days:

Remember, it started as a *neighborhood* thing. And your buddies, the guys who sang with you, they were your *heart.* You could get so in tune it seemed you all had but one heart between you. Those street years were the best of my life.

And I suppose those girls singing secular songs in church basements and on schoolyard steps and in tenement halls felt the same closeness, the same friendship, dreamed the same dream of success and fortune as the boys dipping and do-wopping did. Shirley Alston remembers: "We were like a street-corner group, only being girls, we weren't allowed on the corner, so we'd go down to the basement of Beverly's house." It is a fine reassurance about the ultimate quality of being alive that even the essentially vile and ugly profile of street-corner life with its superficial bonding and cutthroat betrayals can produce its own romance of sentiment.

Here we go again ZA [margin note]

I do not remember the names of any artists who recorded for Scepter, a small label, except two: Dionne Warwick and the Shirelles. My sisters liked those old Warwick sides such as "Walk On By," "Make It Easy on Yourself," "You'll Never Get to Heaven (If You Break My Heart)" "Don't Make Me Over," and "Anybody Who Had a Heart," but they loved the Shirelles. These were the records they would dance to together, holding hands, showing each other certain steps, laughing as only young girls can, endlessly and easily talking about the cute boys they had met. I always remember myself outside their room, listening, rather angry at the camaraderie, jealous really, and chafing a bit at simply being "the kid brother." It was not my room, alas, and it was not my music. The sound of the Shirelles was the music of the young girls of our culture, the music of the summertime of girlhood, contrived tunes about an unreal innocence that actually touched a very real and vital innocence: "Dedicated to the One I Love," "Will You Love Me Tomorrow?," "I Met Him on a Sunday," and "Soldier Boy"; the titles nearly tell the whole story; what the songs say completes the tale. "Tonight's the Night" and "What a Sweet Thing That Was" are tritely rehearsed adventures in youthful sexual anxiety and the quest for the ideal (and idealized) boy: "You say you gonna kiss me/Tonight's the night" or "You said hello and loneliness said goodbye then." These tunes became the prototype for later songs by black girl groups or groups fronted by a black female voice such as the Chiffons' "He's So Fine" ("If I were a queen/And he asked me to leave my throne") and the Ad Libs' "The Boy from New York City" ("He's the most/From coast to coast").

Content such as this makes this music, in some sense, truly an art form of despair, as I have always considered black popular dance music to be. I realize that such an idea runs contrary to the dominant belief that rock and roll or rhythm and blues is largely an existential art form of the underground which features frank sensuality and the hipster's orgasm of the moment. Before this music was completely coopted by the bourgeois world and transformed into a well-greased engine of money-making kitsch, when it was largely the expression of poor black folk (and poor white folk) in revolt, one could almost be enthralled by this powerful and crude art that made the bourgeois and the upper-class elite think its makers and fans were *totally* vulgar and at least *half* mad. Rock and roll is, of course, the black music of the city, of urbanity's and anonymity's battle with the ego, of the urban age and the urban rootless traveler. It is, as well, the music of resentment, occurring as it does after the explosion of the atomic bomb and that event's confession of the failure of rationalism and positivism and of a world that could never hope to make sense; what was left for blacks (and for the whites who rebelled and finally exploited the sources of this music) but a stance of resentment and a longing for the primitive romance of adolescence (singing on the corner)? And what has the generalized popularity of rock and roll meant but the possibility for all Americans, black and white, nowadays to have the most extended adolescence of any people in the history of the world? Inasmuch as this interpretation of rock and roll as the music of the existential is true when it is more cognizant of its sources in gospel and blues music, it still remains not an art form of revolt but an immature expression of negation caught largely between the strophe of escapism and the antistrophe of a juvenile realism that evokes only parents, sex, dance, and the lone institution of school; this is appealing not simply because it is descriptive of the world of the teenager and possesses at best an inchoate political criticism but because escapism and juvenile realism of some sort are the twin towers of the bourgeois American imagination.

But the music of the Shirelles alludes to an even greater complexity inasmuch as this type of R & B has always approached in sentiment and in lyrics the American popular song of Broadway and Hollywood. S. I. Hayakawa, in his famous essay "Popular Songs vs. the Facts of Life," explains quite well the popular song's tendency toward "wishful thinking, dreamy and ineffectual nostalgia, unrealistic fantasy, self-pity, and sentimental clichés masquerading as emotion." It is at least in part a music of neurosis, an art form of a bourgeois sensibility that is unable to reconcile its idealizations about love with its desire for down-and-dirty sexual expression.

The double tension is in the music of the Shirelles. First, it is a black music conceived and written by whites. This is certainly not new in the history of American music, nor is it necessarily bad or undesirable. From its very beginning in slave songs, black American music has had its white publicists, in effect, its white collaborators, from critics and writers of all sorts (collectors to historians) to nightclub owners and record-company executives. In the specific artistic instance of the black jazz musician, both singer and instrumentalist, the white popular song has been almost the exclusive element of the repertoire. But for the black jazz musician there is a greater sense of artistic control, that he or she is using these songs in the way he or she wills to achieve a different, even alien art that defies or rebels against the sources and implications of the original. In rock and roll, there was and sometimes is the latent element of a real minstrelsy, of mimicry, as if everyone were blacker than he or she truly ought to be, as if its naturalness and authentic ethnicity were being determined by people who have decided this is not a natural or authentic expression for themselves, as if the very vision and nature of the performance were being controlled by alien hands. The second tension is that, as stated earlier, the music of the Shirelles is an art form for the underground overladen with the ethos of the bourgeois, popular song. It is a sex song trying not to be a sex song. Or a song about bourgeois romantic love that is always on the edge of denouncing itself. If we can accept Herbert Gans's thesis that the poor are not merely receptive, uncritical dolts whose lives are simply the swing of the birch from bread to circus, then we can see this latter tension as the cause for much anxiety in the lives of the poor black girls who listened to this music and for whom it was primarily, although by no means exclusively, intended, accepting some elements, rejecting others, and feeling, with keen awareness, that the sentiments of this music were dishonest.

On one level, to hear Shirley Alston's lead voice again, sometimes unable to negotiate certain phrases well, sounding as flat and as innocently incompetent as any young girl's voice, is almost a moving experience not in spite of the huge faults of this music, its vacuity and its danger, but because of them. One wishes to be seduced by this music, to be seduced by what it can evoke; for its evocations are not those of either love or sex but of the utter impossibility of true sex or true love; so impossible is it that one is temporarily relieved by the blatant fantasies celebrated in this music. Thus, it is not nostalgia that frames and echoes this earliest and quite successful girl group that spawned the few other black ones like the Supremes, the Marvelettes, and Martha and the Vandellas and the few white ones like the Shangri-Las, the Ronettes, and the Angels.

It is a very simple shimmering joy and aching sadness that surrounds and emanates from the voices of these black girls who really could not sing: they sang to the hearts of every young black girl of a generation ago, telling them that they too could wish and hope for a black Prince Charming even if everyone, the girls singing and the girls being sung to, knew that there was no Prince Charming. Every black girl, for a moment while the song played on the radio or on the little tinny hi-fi, could have access to what most white girls could think about: the dream of the white world of romantic love. But being aware of how untrue the songs were (an advantage the poor black girls had over the middle-class white ones) made the final knowledge of fraud on the part of the artist and the listener not a source of disillusionment but rather a source of anxiety which in the end was a kind of impressive strength; for both the listener and the artist, poor black girls all, the songs were an unconscious protest not against a world that refused to allow the possibility of the song's realization but against a world that made the songs possible to begin with.

The girls, my sisters and all the others, knew that their hopes were to be dashed in a dreary round of dish washing, television watching, baby making, and bar hopping; for the idea of a Prince Charming was not a homage to men (who these girls knew from early and intimate experience were shabby enough) but rather to the imaginative power of girlhood, to its insistent quest for a moral vision and a moral world. It was small hope, the often futile wish, that one might meet a man who would simply respect one's existence. So these songs, finally, for the many black girls who listened to them, were not escapes from reality but pleas for a less bloodthirsty one. The lies of the art, once placed in the mouths of the black girl singers, became a protest against a world where such lies were necessary for a comfort that denied belief.

What happened to the Shirelles? They faded from the scene when the Supremes, a much more talented act, made it big in 1964, although they continued to cut records throughout the sixties with indifferent success. Girl acts were never very popular on the R & B circuit anyway. "It's a man's world," as soul singer James Brown once sang. Or perhaps it is just another story of theft, betrayal, and misplaced ambition:

"They supposedly had a trust fund set up for us," Shirley Alston said of her managers, "but when we got to be twenty-one, there was no money for us. We never saw it like they said we would. They should have invested the money for us properly. Being the top female group in the country, we should have made a lot of money, and we didn't....We were young; it was a whole new thing—the glitter of show business." Perhaps those girls who sang behind Shirley Alston suffered the same fate as Martha Reeves's Vandellas. As Martha remembers those days of riding in the back of the Motown bus and those girls banished to the hearth:

> When people say, "Where are the Vandellas?" I say *men* broke up my group. Sure. Men. I get one cute and all properly trimmed, you know, the modeling school and etiquette and all. And some men come along and say, "Wow, that's a hot number." And before I know it, she's gone.
> I've loved each one. And I'm godmommy to their babies.

INEZ ANDREWS AND THE CARAVANS

We did a couple of programs with the Caravans and I remember [Inez Andrews] singing lead—she had an amazing voice. She was about six feet tall, very thin, and I remember her standing on stage at the Apollo Theatre leaning on the Hammond organ—she was eight and a half months pregnant—singing "Oh Mary, Don't You Weep," and I cried. I could not believe this woman.
—Madeleine Bell of the Alex Bradford Singers

We have a lot of rock-and-roll singers out in the audience. They come purposely to see what they can learn—or what they can steal....Rock-and-roll singers steal even worse than the gospel singers. Because we had something to steal from the very beginning, while they had nothing.
—Inez Andrews

There was a woman DJ in Philadelphia named Louise Williams, also known as the Gospel Queen, who played gospel records every Sunday morning on the local soul station WDAS. Her theme, I remember quite clearly, was the Staple Singers' "It Takes More Than a Hammer and Nails (to Make a House a Home)." For all I know, she may still be playing gospel on a Sunday morning, although the glory days of that music are gone forever. The passion and the polish and panache those great male groups had—the Dixie Hummingbirds, the Highway QCs, the Five Blind Boys of Alabama, the Soul Stirrers, the Mighty Clouds of Joy, and the Pilgrim Travelers—are not to be found in today's performers such as Al Green, Andrae Crouch, and Leon Patillo (although they are likable enough).

When I was growing up all the great black male evangelists such as Daddy Grace and Bishop Johnson would preach for hours on the radio, contests of endurance for preacher and congregation. And those divine male gospel groups could be found performing at such places as the Met at Broad and Poplar streets: heads greased back, sweat pouring like running water from their foreheads and necks, suits of bright red or virgin white or shining silver, prancing before the spiritually and sexually aroused women in the front rows much like thoroughbred horses on parade, screaming into a microphone like the great blues shouters they truly were:

I'm gonna steal away, steal away to Jesus, hmmmmmm.
Yes, sir, right now, I'm gonna fall down on my knees, hmmmmmm,
And I'm gonna steal away, steal away to Jesus.
'Cause I know he calls me by the thunder, oh yes, he does.
And I hear the trumpets sound within-a my soul.

The greatest of all the female gospel groups was the Caravans. It was organized in 1952 as a background chorus but within the next few years could boast such singers as Bessie Griffin, Dorothy Norwood, and Imogene Greene. By the mid-fifties the Caravans featured three of the greatest women gospel singers in history: Shirley Caesar, Albertina Walker, and Inez Andrews. It is hard to imagine that three magnificent women, each of whose presence is dominating and overwhelming—the petite, nervous, gliding Caesar; the heavyset, still, nunlike Walker; and the tall, haughty, and graceful Andrews—could ever have subdued their egos enough to have worked together for as long as they did. They each possessed a voice that hardly needed a microphone; voices that were and are so booming that they can scarcely be contained in a large hall. And they could each preach a sermon, as all black gospel singers are required at some point in their performance to do for their audiences; in fact, they could preach better than most men who made their living at that trade. I think, in this regard, Caesar might have slightly exceeded her former companions. Her record "Go Take a Bath" is one of the most powerful and effective sermons I have ever heard. Unlike the men, the women would always come on the stage wearing choir robes, muting their sexuality by hiding their bodies under what were little better than old-fashioned habits. This did not prevent them from positively electrifying their audiences by belting out such tunes as "Lord, Don't Leave Us Now," "Running for Jesus," "What Will Tomorrow Bring?," "Comfort Me," and "It Must Not Suffer Loss," this last being for me the Caravans' most stunning song in addition to containing their most cryptic line, "Jesus being the *unnatural* god just kept on coming." With young James Cleveland's arrangements, the group's music was among the finest on the black gospel circuit.

Of the three women, I have always enjoyed the contralto of Inez Andrews, the high priestess, the best of all (even better than Clara Ward, although the latter could outhustle anybody, eventually winding up in Las Vegas as a parody, jumping around on the stage with such a manufactured fervor as to be virtually a comedy act. Besides, what self-respecting black gospel act would play Vegas? Would Mahalia Jackson have played before those philistines and unrepentant sinners? Would the Caravans, for mere pieces of silver?). Andrews seemed perfect for the role of Margaret in James Baldwin's *The Amen Corner,* which means that she has always struck me as a very sensual woman. I think she is a better writer of songs than either Caesar or Walker; her songs always possessed a layered density. After she left the Caravans, she formed her own group in 1961 called Inez Andrews and the Andrewettes. One of their most popular songs, "Look Up and Live," was always played when someone died and the bereaved needed strength to carry on. It was, for instance, played quite a bit on soul stations the weekend following the death of Martin Luther King, Jr., when every black person I knew or met seemed slightly crazy with grief: "Lord, if this be your will, I just want to look up and live."

Andrews's greatest song is "Oh Mary, Don't You Weep," about Mary and Martha asking Jesus to raise Lazarus from the dead. The song has achieved a certain mythical status because Aretha Franklin once recorded it; the recording simultaneously knocks one down and takes one's breath away, a chant not of saints but of the insane and unstoppable Holy Ghost itself. It was very fitting that Franklin sang this song on the album that celebrated her brief return to recording gospel music, a very emotional and stomping tribute from one ungodly good woman gospel singer to another.

I do not keep up with gospel music much these days, so I do not know what Andrews is up to now. If she is still physically well, there is little doubt that she is still singing; her audience may have grown a bit old (the youngsters don't like the old-time, "heavy-handed" style of delivery of the progenitors of this music) but it is loyal and loving, as loyal and loving as it has remained for Willie Mae Ford, Dorothy Love, and some of the other old-timers in the professions.

To hear those old records with the piano and organ playing together, as they always do in a black church, and to listen to the Caravans, is to be reminded of being poor and surrounded by women. Of course, if one is reared in poverty, it will always be in a house of women who, no matter how much they have sinned on Saturday night, will blast gospel music and go to church on Sunday. I was always amazed as a boy at the number of women who attended those gospel shows at the Met on Sunday afternoons and evenings, kicking and screaming and fainting. It is, in fact, a strange psychological or psychosexual truth that in those orgiastic moments of faith witnessing in the black church, it is almost always women who lose control of themselves and often pass out. These same women who, during the week, work cleaning the floors in an office or in some white person's house or caring for some white children or cooking at some cheap restaurant or washing clothes at a hospital laundry. Then would come Saturday afternoons at the beauty shops and Saturday nights at the bars with the men to whom they have to awaken, chastened and bitter, on a Sunday. I suppose I stopped listening to gospel music because it was and is truly the art form of poor black women, no matter who sings it, a music that allowed them to bear their lives for another week, which meant it was a music of the grotesque, a music celebrating a hard, harsh religion whose truth they would never deny although they have never experienced it; a hard, harsh religion that offered release from men, from jobs, from life itself, in a sort of primal scream of alienated wonder, for when is one most obsessed by the need to confess one's loneliness by shouting for God? So, in our society, by going to church, black women come, at last, to language and to its sexual power. They have moved from the enforced silence of the Babel outside to the restoration of the Pentecost. "Speaking with tongues," writes Norman O. Brown, "is fiery speech, speech as a sexual act, a firebird or phoenix."

To hear the Caravans is to hear at least thirty women singing, to experience something quite and deeply surreal. To hear these women singing is not to hear Christianity but rather the absolute inaccessibility of any of its tenets since these voices seem to deny forever the idea of virgin births and sons of God and repressed Jewish prophets spreading the word through jeremiads. If black women's R&B is the music of irretrievability, then black women's gospel is the music of improbability made palpable, made utterable. So there is, finally, no apocalypse in these voices, these singing women, only that which will rescue us from the apocalypse, from the tyranny of minds imprisoned in millennialistic belief. And this will rescue Christianity from its sources of oppression and return us to the utter and complete pagan wonder of totally knowing a sensuous world.

Or as Inez Andrews herself simply put it, "If you've never had an urge to read the Bible, maybe a song will inspire you to. Everybody don't go to church and some people don't want to be saved. But when trouble comes, they want to have something they can reach out to. And most times, if it's not the Bible, it's a song."

MEMPHIS MINNIE

And music, warily, like the golden rose
That sometimes after sunset warms the west,
Will warm that room, persuasively suffuse
That room and me, rejuvenate a past.

—Gwendolyn Brooks, "Piano After War"

It is difficult nowadays to find old records by Memphis Minnie, although she recorded quite frequently during her heyday in the 1930s and 1940s. She died after a stroke, in a nursing home in Memphis on August 6, 1973. There are two pictures of her in Paul Oliver's *The Story of the Blues*. One is a popular publicity still probably taken in the late 1930s, showing a strikingly handsome woman, gold teeth gleaming, with polished nails and strong hands, a guitar across her knee. The other was taken a few years before her death; she sits, confined to a wheelchair, an old woman whose face has seen a great deal of illness. I suppose she is about to burst into tears as well, for she was, in her prime, one of the greatest artists who ever lived in America. In her old age, her mean dotage, her final sickness, she looked like every black person's southern grandmother who had spent too many years doing backbreaking work in some white woman's kitchen or on some black man's farm. In her old age, she was every black person's tragic past. Maybe that is why young black folk do not listen to the blues anymore; that, too, is a memory of a tragic past of segregation, cotton picking, urban and rural shacks. Blues music had something to do with those sociological phenomena, mostly to describe them in certain lyrics. But it is not really a music of sociology. And what influences a blues composer are other blues songs and not only the sorrows of his or her personal life. It is good for everyone to understand that small fact, that the blues is a tradition as well as an exercise in biography, advice, and gossip.

I wish to remember Memphis Minnie's strong hands; they were not an accident. She was considered the greatest blues guitarist of her era and once easily beat that towering giant of blues guitar, Big Bill Broonzy, in a guitar-cutting contest that was judged by blues greats Tampa Red, Sleepy John Estes, and Richard Jones, who wrote the famous blues "Trouble in Mind."

No one is really sure how old she was when she died. Her date of birth varies depending upon one's sources, from as early as 1896 to as late as 1904. Perhaps she lied as she grew older. Perhaps she did not know when she was born. Her birthplace was Algiers, Louisiana, her name Minnie Douglas, and she started "rambling," to use her term, taken from the autobiographical blues "Nothing in Rambling," when she was quite young:

I's born in Louisiana
I raised in Algiers
And everywhere I been
The peoples all say

[Refrain]
Ain't nothing in rambling
Either running around
Well I believe I'll marry a good man
Oh—Lord, and settle down

I first left home
Stopped in Tennessee

The peoples all begging
Come and stay with me

[Refrain]

I walked through the alley
With my hand in my coat
The police start to shoot me
Thought it was something I stole

[Refrain]

The peoples on the highway
Is walking and crying
Some is starving
Some is dying

[Refrain]

You may go to Hollywood
And try to get on the screen
But I'm gonna stay right here
And eat these old charity beans

[Refrain]

This is an unusual blues, a man's blues really. Women almost never wrote "wandering" blues, largely because it was supposed, with a great deal of truth, that women did not (because of more stable employment) or could not (because of children) get wanderlust the way men did. Minnie Douglas traveled, hoboed really, a great deal during her teenage and young-adult years and loved to write such blues. Obviously, from the tale of the lyrics, she wanted to be a performer almost from the start, and her first traveling adventures were unsuccessful in establishing her in that line. It is a song of disillusionment, of poverty, and with the constant repetition of the word "peoples," a song of crowds, of mass reality and a mass sharing of reality, of a lack of individual privacy. It is not a surprise in considering this song that such male commentators on the blues as Paul Oliver, Bruce Cook, and Samuel Charters always refer to Memphis Minnie's singing as "as strong as any man's" or to her demeanor as "as tough as any man's" or her playing as "the equal to any man's." Both in the realm of an instrumentalist and in the subject matter of some of her blues, she was not afraid to walk on a man's turf; in large measure, inasmuch as blues music is an autobiographical music, she had lived, to some degree, a man's life.

Actually, Memphis Minnie's first move was to Walls, Mississippi, at the age of seven, where her father bought her a banjo. By the time she was eleven, she was playing professionally with small jug bands, and by the time she was sixteen she was a tough, street-wise girl, playing on the corners of Memphis and known as "Kid Douglas," a man's moniker. She traveled for several years with Ringling Brothers Circus (Langston Hughes's novel *Not Without Laughter* contains a good account of what blues performers did in circuses) and eventually returned to Memphis to marry her first husband, Casey Bill Weldon, famous for such blues as "Lady Doctor Blues" and "Hitch Me to Your Buggy and Drive Me Like a Mule" and from whom she learned more technique for the guitar (Weldon was an excellent bottleneck guitarist). By 1929, the year she was discovered by Columbia Records talent scouts, she had a second husband, named Joe McCoy, and was singing on the streets of Memphis again as Kid Douglas and sometimes as Kid McCoy. She singlehandedly reintroduced country blues after the death of the classic blues of the twenties, a genre dominated by black women's jazz-vaudevillian styles: Mamie and Bessie Smith, Ida Cox, Ma Rainey. She was to be the pioneering force in blues music, which had become overwhelmingly male again and probably overwhelmingly archaic in light of Basie, Goodman, Billie Holiday, Coleman Hawkins, Ellington, and the era of swing. She was eventually to establish herself in Chicago and to marry twice more. She was also destined to be a major musical act for two decades.

Her biggest hit was a bawdy tune called "Bumble Bee." It was quite common for both blues men and blues women to sing very dirty or suggestive songs, although women became more noted for this, perhaps because it was especially titillating to hear women sing so blatantly about sex. Their audiences loved these tunes but sometimes the performer—Bessie Smith, for instance—did not. Others, like Lucille Bogan (also known as Bessie Jackson; she possessed a sensual face and a mouth full of bad teeth), seemed positively to thrive on singing about sex organs, bull-dykes, and hot action between the sheets (for example, "My pussy's so good it'll make a dead man come") and generally all sorts of pornographic songs that seem quite close to the black street poetry genre of the toast. "Bumble Bee" is not my favorite song by Memphis Minnie in this vein. It was not really her material and her unease with that fact shows in her unsure singing. "Me and My Chauffeur," which plays upon the common blues pun of the male lover as a "driver" (the "soul drivers" of slavery also come to mind, black men who practiced a kind of crude, brutal authority on the plantation), is a much better offering, more sly and more telling, with her own lyrics:

Won't you be my chauffeur
Won't you be my chauffeur
I want someone to drive me
I want someone to drive me downtown
Baby drives so easy, I can't turn him down

But I don't want him
But I don't want him
To be riding these girls
To be riding these girls around
You know I'm gonna steal me a pistol
Shoot my chauffeur down

Well I must buy him
Well I must buy him

A brand new V-8
A brand new V-8 Ford
And he won't need passengers
I will be his load

Going to let my chauffeur
Going to let my chauffeur
Drive me around the
Drive me around the world
Then he can be my little boy
Yes, and I'll be his girl.

Where is the evidence for this?

This song is a good illustration of why the blues is such a compelling, complex art form despite the apparent narrow range of its subject matter (although it is a much wider music than rock and roll). As Paul Oliver has pointed out, "Whole areas of experience and perception do not appear in blues songs; there are only the slightest passing references to children; family life is represented more by its disintegration than by its preservation; appreciation of scenic beauty seldom extends beyond the cliché...; national events and success are seldom recorded; political comment is to be found in a handful of blues, Jim Crow and poll taxes hardly at all." Yet Memphis Minnie's song is quite a compression of images about class, money, and the politics of sex. What is implied in the relationship between a chauffeur and his employer is that he works, in fact exists for her pleasure. It seems, indeed, to be a reversal of the relationship between the whore and her procurer, and such a reversal was quite important and appealing to the women who listened to this song, who often found themselves in subordinate positions to their men. (It is interesting to note how much this plays on the poor men's fantasy of being taken care of by rich women. It was, for instance, Bigger Thomas's dream in Richard Wright's *Native Son* that his job as chauffeur for the Daltons would lead to such a relationship with their daughter.) In this song, because the woman hires the man, she is in control of the relationship, and her purchase of a car for him reinforces the idea that the relationship is based on a financial transaction. If the song were only a reversal of the sexual power roles, then it would be neither comic nor poignant, which it happens to be. She is jealous of him and doesn't want him to ride other girls around; so, as is not the case in an employer-employee relationship or that between a whore and a pimp, he is not replaceable or at least not replaceable without a great deal of emotional trauma and dislocation. He does not possess equality with all other men; he has something unique to offer. The humanizing equality occurs at the end when she becomes a girl and he becomes a boy. They are not equal to others of their sex, which would mean they would essentially have no identity except that of a collective, corporate one, but they are equal to each other as persons of different sexes; hence a fused, powerful symbiotic identity is formed. This song, like so many other blues, is protest against the collective, mass self. Given the nature of the origin of the blues, this emphasis is not surprising, since this art form was invented by a people who were victimized and debased by a corporate identity. The song is a fine example of how good blues musicians used their usual topic of love and sex not only to criticize the way things are but to offer scenarios of how things can be made better.

One of the best blues essays ever written was Langston Hughes's column on a New Year's Eve Memphis Minnie performance at the 230 Club in Chicago. The piece appeared in *The Chicago Defender* on January 9, 1943. She has, by this time, abandoned acoustic guitar blues for driving, urban electric blues, and the music, as Hughes described it, is "so hard and so loud, amplified...by General Electric on top of the icebox, that sometimes the voice, the words, and the melody get lost under the sheer noise, leaving only the rhythm to come through clear." There are other changes as well. In Giles Oakley's study of blues music, *The Devil's Music,* is a picture of a very young, quite sexy Memphis Minnie: a shapely leg thrust beyond the folds of a slit gown, a girlish, "come hither" smile. This photo was probably taken around 1930 and used in black newspapers to advertise her club dates. Hughes describes her in this way in 1943: "She is a slender, light-brown woman who looks like an old-maid school teacher with a sly sense of humor. She wears glasses that fail to hide her bright bird-like eyes. She dresses neatly and sits straight in her chair perched on top of her refrigerator where the beer is kept."

Even the spirit of the music itself has changed. It is the black music of the war and as such it is, for Hughes, a music of deeper resentment, more mature resentment than the blues and jazz that preceded it:

> It was last year, 1941, that the war broke out, wasn't it? Before that there wasn't no defense work much. And the President hadn't told the factory bosses that they had to hire colored. Before that it was W.P.A. and the Relief. It was 1939 and 1935 and 1932 and 1928 and years you don't remember when your clothes got shabby and the insurance relapsed [*sic*]. Now, it's 1942—and different. Folks have jobs. Money's circulating again. Relatives are in the army with big insurance if they die. Memphis Minnie at year's end picks up those nuances and tunes them into the strings of her guitar.

But unlike rock and roll, the urban blues, finally, is not simply a music of resentment but rather a music of remembrance:

> Then, through the smoke and racket of the noisy Chicago bar float Louisiana bayous, muddy old swamps, Mississippi dust and sun, cotton fields, lonesome roads, train whistles in the night, mosquitoes at dawn, and the Rural Free Delivery that never brings the right letter. All these things cry through the strings on Memphis Minnie's electric guitar.

Few black writers have understood as well as Langston Hughes that the power of blues is that it can be a music of remembrance without being a music of the romance of remembrance, a music of the sentiment of remembrance. The narrowness of the range of the blues, it seems to me, has made this possible and given the music its great strength because it has eliminated the very subjects—children, happy families, landscapes in sun-light and moonlight—about which one could tend to wax sentimental. Blues is not a music of regret, a Wordsworthian quest for lost innocence. And what is sentimentality but an excessively structured sense of regret, a homesickness? One can remember truly only as through a glass darkly; the adverse is the real.

Hence, whenever I hear Billie Holiday's girlish 1930s songs, songs so differently rendered from the dark sorrow songs she sang in the fifties, I think of saxist Lester Young and young Malcolm X, old Detroit Red the hustler, putting too much steaming conk on the processed hair and hurrying to douse the burning mess in a toilet bowl. There is a mocking quality in young Holiday's girlish tones, mocking the vanity of men. And whenever I hear Memphis Minnie's tough-voiced blues, I think of singer, dancer, trum-peter Valaida Snow, who, during her heyday in the thirties, according to pianist Earl Hines, "had a Mercedes and a chauffeur...used to dress luxuri-ously and look very, very glamorous"; she was the only black American woman imprisoned and, as jazz historian Frank Driggs notes, eventually broken in body and spirit in one of Hitler's Danish concentration camps during 1941 and 1942. She was freed from the camp weighing under seventy pounds but immediately went back to rebuilding her career. The two women do not sound alike at all; Snow sounds so sweet and campy and much the sage con artist as Fats Waller, singing the better pop tunes of the day such as "I Wish I Were Twins," "Until the Real Thing Comes Along," and "Mean to Me." Yet it seems that the women share a great deal: both were born around the same time (Snow in 1905), in the South (Snow was born in Tennessee and spent part of her childhood in Florida); both were musically influenced by one or both parents (both of Snow's parents were in show business); and both wanted to enter show business at a young age. Snow, too, ran away from home at a young age, married at the age of fourteen (the first of several mar-riages), and reached the big time in Chicago at the Grand Terrace. But what is even more important than some biographical similarities are their inde-pendence, their drive, their mastery of their art, and their ultimate sense of tragedy (Snow, too, died in obscurity and of a stroke, on May 30, 1956).

There are two brief recitations I would like to make in closing. First, I would like to quote the lyrics of Memphis Minnie's most striking and enduring blues, a deeply autobiographical song that tells a black woman's story or some black women's story or a lot of black women's stories. And it is a story about which one needn't say anything except that it is about the achieve-ment of the black woman's *being:* not to accept the morality that condemns her. Then *I* would like to tell a very short story. Here is the song, "In My Girlish Days":

Lay down at night, trying to play my hand
Through the window, out stepped a man
I didn't know no better, oh boy, in my girlish days

My mama cried, papa did too
My daughter, look, what a shame on you,
I didn't know no better in my girlish days

I flagged a train, didn't have a dime,
Tryin' to run away from that home of mine,
I didn't know no better, oh boy, in my girlish days.

I hit the highway, caught me a truck,
1917, when the world was tough,
I didn't know no better, oh boy, in my girlish days.

Now, the other short story. While on a two-year postdoctoral fellowship at the University of Kansas in Lawrence, I was made the guest editor of a literary journal there for the issue that is to celebrate Kansas's 125th year of statehood. Because of Kansas statehood's historical connection with the matter of slavery, the issue was devoted to black writers of the Midwest. It was a nice appointment of a sort, nice in the way that being allowed to head any kind of enterprise is. I suppose I was offered this in part because I am black (always an ambiguous honor at best), in part because I am a writer (the only secular profession that justifies poverty as nobility of the spirit), and finally because the English department needed to give me something to do short of teaching classes (which, after all, makes winning a postdoc a fairly useless experience) but adding to "the intellectual life of the university." Something like that.

I decided early on that an issue on blacks in the Midwest must have something about jazz, especially since Kansas itself is so rich in the tradition with the likes of Scott Joplin, Bennie Moten and his Blue Devils, Mary Lou Williams, Count Basie, Jimmy Rushing, and Charlie Parker either having been born in these parts or having passed through, making some very important music on the way to New York. In casting about for something a bit more than the usual and predictable piece about the history of jazz in Kansas City, I stumbled upon the existence in Lawrence of Audrey Jones, an eighty-year-old black woman who was born in Kansas City, Kansas, and who used to dance and sing on stage back in her youth with Stewart's Darktown Strutters and the Jazz Babies. She currently goes around to nursing homes playing the piano and singing blues and gospel for the patients. She can also play guitar, drums, a bit of trombone, all by ear, she told me when we spoke.

I thought an interview with Ms. Jones might make an interesting piece, so I called her. She was rather surprised and perhaps a bit disbelieving ("Why do you want to talk to me?") but she relented ("I like you. You sound nice. You got a nice voice"). And once I arrived at her small, disarrayed home (she was in the process of moving) that must have been filled with all kinds of bric-a-brac and objects of memory, she discovered that she did indeed have something to say after all and proceeded to say it for the next ninety minutes at a pretty vigorous pace, punctuating her story of working with Stepin

Fetchit and having run away from home at the age of fifteen in order to go on stage, with bits of songs, accompanying herself on the guitar.

She was pretty honest about "running off with young men" and "drinking plenty of whiskey," which I assumed continued after the show-biz phase of her life ended, which it did after a few years. She worked for a while in a steel mill in Chicago and finally resettled in Kansas, this time in Lawrence, and became a cook for a fraternity house, a job she had for over twenty years. We sat on two kitchen chairs with nothing between us except a tape recorder running. I think she was quite pleased that I was black. I believe she thought from the phone conversation that I was white. It was probably nice for her to know that a black person, particularly a black man, thought her memories had value. And being black, I thought it was less of a robbery. After all, I wasn't one of those white guys collecting stuff for a quaint or scholarly publication. At least I comforted myself by thinking I wasn't.

At the end of the interview she showed me a copy of a story that had been written about her a few years before entitled "Meet a Neighbor," which probably appeared in some neighborhood publication. She was quite proud of it.

"I will call you in a few weeks. I think I want to have a photographer take your picture," I told her.

"You really gonna take my picture for this?" she asked, smiling, not believing that she could possibly be *that* interesting.

"Yes," I said, "I think that would be nice. Add a nice touch."

"You really gonna take my picture?" she asked again. "They ain't take my picture when they write this about me," she said, pointing to the piece in my hand.

"Yes, I know," I said, "but I think I would like to have your picture."

As I walked down her pathway, I could hear her dog barking. The moon was out. It was a clear warm night. We thanked each other. She seemed very happy, maybe as happy as she has ever been in the last several years. I suppose it was because, after a long struggle, she was going to get her picture in the papers at last.

III

Hot Spicks Versus Cool Spades:
Three Notes Toward
a Cultural Definition of
Prizefighting

One must have a mind of winter
To regard...

And have been cold a long time
To behold...

—Wallace Stevens, "The Snow Man"

NOTE 1

As we enter the eighties and as the sport of boxing spotlights the lighter weight divisions* where the Latin fighters tend to congregate, a new variation on the old theme of race begins to emerge. The most important, that is, the most symbolic, battles will no longer be, as in the old days of Jack Johnson, Joe Louis, and Ray Robinson, white versus black, nor, as in the sixties and seventies with Muhammad Ali, Joe Frazier, and Ken Norton, black versus black, but rather black versus Latin. No fight could more appropriately have opened the era of the eighties in boxing than the first Sugar Ray Leonard versus Roberto Duran bout for something called the World Boxing Council's welterweight championship.

No title fight of the seventies, with the exception of the Ali-Frazier

---

*Professional boxing currently has twelve weight divisions: Flyweights (not over 112 pounds), Bantamweights (not over 118 pounds), Junior Featherweights (not over 122 pounds), Featherweights (not over 126 pounds), Junior Lightweights (not over 130 pounds), Lightweights (not over 135 pounds), Junior Welterweights (not over 140 pounds), Welterweights (not over 147 pounds), Junior Middleweights (not over 154 pounds), Middleweights (not over 160 pounds), Light Heavyweights (not over 175 pounds), Heavyweights (over 175 pounds). There are currently twenty-three champions, two for every division except the middleweights, where Marvin Hagler holds the undisputed title. Every other division has a World Boxing Council and a World Boxing Association champion, much to the chagrin of old-timers and boxing purists who think that this proliferation of champions

clashes and, possibly the Ali-Foreman tilt, received so much publicity as this one, or reached out so far beyond the confines of the sport's enthusiasts to excite the general public. Yet no fight of this caliber in recent memory was more disappointing. To put it bluntly, it was a failure—perhaps, a poignant signal of what our slouch to the end of the century will be. The fight was surely exciting; despite complaints from some quarters about Duran's mauling and wrestling tactics, hundreds of punches were thrown by each fighter and most of them landed. The fight was performed (the most apt verb that comes to mind) at a brisk pace, and any true boxing aficionado, any dedicated devotee of what was called in 1824 "the sweet science of bruising," found more than enough in the bout to keep his interest and even to elicit his admiration.

But the fight was a failure to the general public, and even the cultural instincts, the cultural radar, if you will, of the boxing aficionado sensed it to be a failure, because it was not conclusive. The fight had excitement but no drama, tension but no true engagement; it ultimately gave the viewer the incredibly weird sense of experiencing a kind of rhythmless syncopation. At the end of fifteen rounds, the question of who was the best—the only relevant question in boxing and, indeed, in all sports—remained largely unanswered. Leonard and Duran seemed as if they had fought the entire fight underwater; once it was over, once they emerged from the deep, there was a lingering sense that they had never touched one another, a feeling that the fight just witnessed had never even taken place. The fight was so close that it became nearly a kind of pointless derring-do on the part of the fighters. To the public mind and to our cultural selves, it was important, to be sure, that one man come forth clearly as the best. Duran was chosen the winner almost as an afterthought.

Some said that this fight would be, metaphorically, the matador and the bull—in other words, the classy boxer against the slugger; old-timers talked about its similarity to the Jake LaMotta–Ray Robinson battles; others reminisced about Carmen Basilio and Ray Robinson or Sandy Sadler and Willie Pep; those of more recent memory said the fight was a scaled-down version of Ali versus Frazier. All of these fights were big affairs, and all of them, except Ali-Frazier, were fights between men of different races. Even the Ali-Frazier fight had a deep and bitter intraracial contrast which I will discuss shortly. So in truth the Duran-Leonard fight was, quite properly,

---

has diluted the significance of holding a title, but much to the joy of promoters and television networks who can create twice as many championship fights. The junior weight divisions are less prestigious than their full-weight counterparts. The rules are the same for all the divisions, although the scoring of a professional bout may differ slightly in different states. Title bouts are often fifteen rounds, non-title "elimination" bouts between two top contenders are twelve rounds, and other non-title fights are ten rounds. A round is three minutes in length and fighters are given one-minute rests between rounds. Generally, a fighter trains six weeks in preparation for a fight, but in some unimportant non-title fights they may train for as few as three weeks, whereas for very important title fights they may train for nine weeks. Gloves weigh either eight ounces or six ounces.

placed in this tradition. The fight was the mythical confrontation that was to apotheosize one particular minority as the underground male image of the American collective psyche. The fight was the super-cool nigger versus the hot-blooded greaseball. Here was the monumental encounter between the hot and the cool, between the classical order of technique and the romantic impulse of improvisation; the inner-city warriors at each other for ownership of the night (one as Clark Kent in a Brooks Brothers suit, the other as Chanticleer in a sombrero).

There was Duran, whose style, like that of a jazz musician, relies so much upon the inspiration of the moment that when he is uninterested in a fight he is worse than mediocre; and there was Leonard, so completely absorbed with the intricacies of his talents that with Joycean dispassion he seemed to watch the beautiful nuances his left jab made as it traveled its trajectory through the air. George Benton, once a world-class fighter, and now the trainer of such fighters as the up-and-coming featherweight Rocky Lockridge, also seemed to be just such a combatant, enamored of the artistry of his style. One imagines that Leonard could overwhelm his opponents while not even realizing that they actually existed. Furthermore, Duran represented the old, perhaps dying order of champions, the young kid who learned his art on the street and went straight into the pro ranks at the age of sixteen. Leonard was the product of AAU meets and the extensive amateur programs in this country that threatened to make the old street-corner art of fighting obsolete (just as the old after-hours jam sessions among jazz musicians are a thing of the past; now young musicians learn jazz in the practice rooms of Juilliard).

The question arises why the first Leonard-Duran fight was the symbolic racial showdown of the black and the Latin or, to put it in the vernacular of the average white, between the nigger and the spick, as opposed to the fight between Wilfred Benitez, a Puerto Rican, and Leonard, in which Leonard won the title by a knockout in the fifteenth round. Benitez, who became junior welterweight champ at the age of seventeen by beating Antonio Cervantes and who became welterweight champ before he was twenty-one by beating Carlos Palomino, certainly had credentials that were as impressive as Duran's. Furthermore, while the bookmakers made Benitez an underdog in his fight with Leonard, it must be remembered that Duran was also an underdog. The answer to our question is that Benitez is black. Moreover, he anglicized his first name from Wilfredo to Wilfred, an act for which most New York Latins, among whom Benitez was once considered a young, reckless god, will not forgive him. More important, Benitez does not fight in what we have come to think of as the Latin-macho style of, say, a Duran, or a Pipino Cuevas; Benitez is a slick, polished boxer, a counterpuncher who slips his opponents' blows very well. In short, there seemed to be no real racial contrast between Benitez and Leonard for the press to exploit and the public mind to latch on.

And racial contrast is what the male politics of boxing is all about, and it has a long history. Jack Johnson, the first black heavyweight champion, avoided fighting such talented blacks as Sam Langford, Joe Jeanette, and Sam McVey during his championship reign because the ticket-buying public—that is, at that time, the white public—was interested only in seeing him fight a "white hope." Even with Joe Louis, certainly the most beloved of all black boxing champions during the 1930s and 1940s, his most important and most publicized fights were those against Max Schmeling, "Two-Ton" Tony Galento, Billy Conn, and the final bout of his career with Rocky Marciano, all of whom were white. Granted that Louis's fights with black fighters such as Ezzard Charles and Jersey Joe Walcott were certainly major contests, one has only to check the various record books and boxing annuals to discover that only Louis's matches with whites get the pictures. Ray Robinson, the great black welterweight and middleweight champion, also had his most important fights against white opponents: Jake LaMotta, Gene Fullmer, Paul Pender, Bobo Olsen, Carmen Basilio, and for the light heavyweight title, Joey Maxim.

The Patterson-Liston bout changed the racial emphasis and then the most publicized title bouts became intraracial instead of interracial. Most of Ali's important fights, unlike Louis's or Robinson's, were against blacks (e.g., Liston, Frazier, Norton, Foreman, and Spinks). This, of course, was because there were very few white fighters left in the game. Just as the Patterson-Liston bout became in the public mind—and, now, "public" means black and white collectively—a fight between a "punk" and a "bad nigger," the first Ali-Liston match became the "crazy nigger" versus the "bad nigger," and the first Ali-Frazier fight, an encounter so fraught with political overtones that many blacks cried in the streets the day after Ali lost, became the "politically hip" black versus the "homeboy." Ali never really needed to fight white men to create racial contrast for a bout since, with the help of the media, he was able to make over his principal opponents into whites by virtue of their politics or lack of politics; nearly every Ali opponent became a representative of the white establishment. Indeed, by the time of the Foreman fight, Ali had become a sort of Calvinist redeemer of the race and Foreman the pork-eating king of the unelect. (We must except Leon Spinks from this process. Spinks's ghetto image made Ali seem the bourgeois, overfed, conservative black. Remember, Ali never bragged, never acted the street-corner clown role, before the first Spinks fight. For the second fight, Ali became the old, wily pro, the "old head," and Spinks was the green amateur, the "young boy." The bout became a classic street-corner lesson in humility for Spinks. Never try to beat an old head at anything, whether it is doing the dozens or doing the dukes.)

Remembering Ali's title fights against white opponents is almost a test to discover how much trivia the mind is unable to discard. During his first championship reign there were George Chuvalo, Henry Cooper, Brian London, and Karl Mildenberger (four forgettable and largely forgotten fights in chronological order, from March through September of 1966); and during his second reign there were Chuck Wepner, Joe Bugner, Jean-Pierre Coopman, Richard Dunn, and Alfredo Evangelista. Between the two reigns there were Bugner, Rudi Lubbers, Jerry Quarry, Jurgen Blin, and Chuvalo. These fights were uninteresting not only because Ali usually did not fight at his best against these opponents, but because they were so suffocatingly passionless.

Black fighters captured Ali's easily distracted attention not only because they were better than the corps of white fighters he faced, but quite simply because they were black and were rivals for the attention of white America. And after all, Ali, since winning the gold medal at the 1960 Olympics, wanted the attention of white America, not even its adoration, though to a large degree he got that as well; but its attention was what he and, perhaps secretly in their hearts, most blacks craved. He wanted to make himself so important that whites could not ignore him, to bring the black psyche out from the underground and onto the stage, the very proscenium, of white consciousness. And he felt that he could do this better than other blacks. Ironically, Ali, while playing the role of the militant Muslim, denigrated his black opponents in ways that one would have expected only from a racist white, or a black ill at ease with his collective identity. He called them "stupid," and "ugly," he said that they "couldn't talk" and that they should not be allowed to "represent the race." In short, Ali's black opponents became symbolically that marauding mass of lower-class tricksters and berserkers who made whites flee the cities in fear, and Ali, a roguish combination of Reverend Ike and Ellison's Rinehart, a sort of jive-time, jive-assed shaman, was the middle-class, brown-skinned black who kept them at bay. If on the part of these opponents there was jealousy and envy against Ali, the "crab in the basket" mentality of the poor, then on the part of Ali there was honest abhorrence of blacks who traditionally made things "hard for the race." In some ways, Ali was as much of a striver as a hard-working, light-skinned hero from a Charles Chessnut or Jessie Fauset novel.

Since the retirement of Ali no other black fighter has been able to make an effective contrast between himself and another black fighter. If two black fighters are in the ring, the white public generally ignores it, and the black public, while on a local level supporting such endeavors of black club fighters and novices, tends to feel a bit uneasy when the fight is for higher stakes, obviously thinking that "two brothers shouldn't be beating each other up for entertainment." In effect, the Leonard-Benitez fight was two black men slugging it out. In truth, racial contrast eases the painful realization that boxing is a sort of vicious exploitation of simply being male; racial contrast gives boxing matches symbolism, a tawdry, cheap, sensational significance that the sportswriter may understate but never leaves unsaid. So with an insufficient white presence in boxing, and lack of general public interest in most black-versus-black fights, the only racial contrast that can be manipulated is black versus Latin. But the Latin must be of a certain sort.

Enter Roberto Duran, the man who, despite or perhaps because of his Indian heritage, looks both so classically and so uniquely Latin, the man with the relentless and uncompromising style—with fifty-five knockouts in seventy fights—who was champion of the lightweights for five and a half years and who exterminated the division's opposition with a degree of fury and disdain that endeared him to the television networks when they decided to recognize the existence of boxing below the heavyweight division. (We will not speak here about the level of Duran's competition while he was champion. Nor will we comment on the distinct possibility that Duran's considerable talents may be vastly overrated. Suffice it to say that it is doubtful that such mediocre fighters as Lou Bizarro, Vilomar Fernandez, and Edwin Viruet would have lasted until the thirteenth, fourteenth, or fifteenth rounds if they had been against such lightweight greats as Benny Leonard, Henry Armstrong, Joe Brown, Carlos Ortiz, Joe Gans, or Ike Williams.) Here was the true Latin fighter, or at least what an uninformed American public thought was a true Latin fighter, since we know nothing about Hispanic culture and Hispanic civilization; but we do know the word "macho," a cliché that describes nothing but signifies everything. Duran is the true Latin, macho almost to the point of irritation, the man who said to Howard Cosell that he would make Leonard "fight like a man." Here was the racial contrast that made the almost unendurable publicity for the first fight possible. Duran became the prototypical Latin fighter, many people forgetting, first, the fact that not all Latins are aggressive punchers, and that the fighters who gave Duran the hardest times in the ring—the Viruet brothers, Saoul Mamby, Zeferino Gonzalez, and Vilomar Fernandez—were all Latins who understood that discretion is the better part of the manly art of self-defense, and chose to box with Duran rather than slug it out; and second, the fact that Duran, over the years, has learned to become a better than passable boxer and actually beat Jimmy Heair in a lackluster bout by outjabbing him.

Very little more needs to be said about either Duran or Leonard; they became the blond and the brunette of the romance of American sports. Duran, we know, was the little tough guy from Panama who knocked out horses as a teenager, quit school at the age of thirteen after having reached the third grade, won the lightweight title in 1972 from Ken Buchanan on a low blow, then refused to honor the return-bout clause of the contract; the man sportswriter Dick Young called "the Animal" (a term he would never dream of using to describe a black fighter) and promoter Don King called "the Little Killer." Duran's bully-boy insouciance brings to mind both the late Bruce Lee and jazz trumpeter Miles Davis, both of whom were also little tough guys, who, at the height of their fame, swaggered and swashbuckled in front of their audiences as if they were preening themselves for some secret fertility rite.

Leonard is the young man who has brought, as Howard Cosell tells us, "class" to boxing. He is articulate and handsome, smiles a lot, never discusses politics, and, aside from having one illegitimate child who was later legitimized through marriage, has very little of the taint of ghetto upon him. He gives talks about good sportsmanship to elementary school kiddies and signs autographs for Jewish ladies vacationing in the Catskills. But in truth Leonard wants so desperately to become a personality, recognizable in the same way that white movie stars and entertainers are, that he seems to be holding himself aloft for the highest bidder. Leonard, in short, wants to end up like such white ex-jocks as Bruce Jenner or Joe Namath. What we are witnessing is not the rise and fall of Sugar Ray Leonard but the selling of "Sugar." Leonard is such a shrewd young man that we can get no real sense of the army of people behind him; he seems to be the only *auteur* of this scenario. He wants to be liked, so he makes himself *likable* in about the only way a black person can in this society, by being inoffensive. (Ali, of course, was terribly offensive to this *Herrenvolk* democracy's taste and values, and he paid a dear price for that.) Leonard is not interested in airing his excesses or becoming, to use the 1920s phrase, "a race man"; he is not mythopoeic material. He is bland and cute, and gives the overwhelming impression of being harmless; his coolness is without subtlety, his manner as polished and chilled as a depthless lake in winter. Unlike other fighters, and most especially unlike Duran, Leonard anesthetizes the general public to the corruption and horrors of boxing because he does not look as if he came from a ghetto and gives the impression that boxing is not the only thing he can do. His presence, unlike, say, that of Leon Spinks, is not a *j'accuse* to the sport of boxing and to the society that supports it.

As a cultural event, as an event that produces a pattern of symbols and meanings, professional boxing, like most sports, is a social ritual, a drama in the most Aristotelian sense that elicits the feelings of pity and fear most vividly. Ideally, deep inside we should fear the winner and pity the loser, and somehow if the match fails to produce these "cleansing" emotions, then it has failed to complete us. By "completion" I mean what Clifford Geertz once said, that the involvement in our cultural forms and rituals gives us definition, finishes an "incomplete or unfinished animal." And in sports, particularly boxing, the ritual is very much like the Christian Communion: we partake of the body and soul of the athlete, the last and exquisite god, vulnerable. We have become so accustomed to racial contrast in boxing matches that they have become nearly meaningless, just so much shoddy and cheerless brutality, without it. The masks of racial identification that our fighters wear are similar to the masks worn by the actor in ancient Greece; they are not masks that hide, not psychological masks, but rather masks that reveal all, masks of the primitive which are, as it were, giant, lurid images of the ego beneath. Probably boxing comes closest, of all sports, to producing the primitive responses of pity and fear because the sport *is* so primitive — so naked, if you will. It is appropriate that boxing should now be the possession of the cool medium of television (boxers, like other athletes, have become "TV heroes"), where the drama has been modernized to adopt a tone of muted stridency.

So in our cultural hearts racial contrast and what is concomitant with it, racial identification, are important for the completion of ourselves. The cultural weight of the first Duran-Leonard fight is that it reinforced the emotional perception, if not the intellectual idea, that men are different physically and psychologically because they belong to different races. Despite the mass of scientific evidence to the contrary, we still secretly wish to believe that the mask we wear, namely our skin color and our racial background, like the ancient Greek mask, makes us what we are. Duran becomes the stereotypical fiery, macho Latin and Leonard becomes the stereotypical cool, slick boxing black.

Racial contrast awakens the still uglier need of racial identification, some-thing that the ludicrous boxing film *Rocky* exploited in such an obvious, almost embarrassing way. Even today in boxing a cry can be heard that goes back as far as 1910: the cry for a "Great White Hope" who, supposedly, will save boxing for its white fans. As an example of how racial contrast brings about racial identification, consider Gerry Cooney, a promising young Irish heavyweight. Cooney has suddenly been propelled to the position of number-one contender in the official rankings of the World Boxing Council and the World Boxing Association, largely on the basis of beating a very inept white fighter named Dino Dennis. Now according to CBS Sports broadcaster Dick Stockton, the public is "demanding" that Cooney fight for the title (or, since nearly every division has two titleholders, it is more accurate to say "fight for *a* title")—a demand based on his very impressive win over once highly re-garded Philadelphia heavyweight Jimmy Young. However, before Young lost to Cooney he was defeated by a young black fighter named Michael Dokes and beaten twice by a black Puerto Rican, Osvaldo Ocasio. The public did not "demand" that either of these fighters should immediately fight for the title. Nor did anyone think that the significance of Cooney's victory was more than slightly diluted by the fact that Young had not won an important fight since his loss to Ken Norton a few years ago. Apparently the catharsis of pity and fear produced by boxing is effected more profoundly when the viewer is of the same race as one, and only one, of the boxers.

World champions from the British Isles such as middleweight Alan Minter and lightweight Jim Watt disguise this urge of racial identification under the cloak of nationalism. Those of us with only a passing acquaintance with the history of Britain are well aware that the British nation is, in truth, the British race and that the British wish to stay as alabaster white as the heroine of an Ann Radcliffe or Jane Austen novel. Besides, when black British junior middleweight champion Maurice Hope has fought over the past few years, no band of brass-playing beefeaters file in the ring before the fight to play national airs and the British fight fans at ringside do not sing "God Save the Queen" with tears in their eyes—which is what actually happened before Minter's most recent defense against Marvin Hagler and Watt's most recent defense against Sean O'Grady of Oklahoma. (Some old-timers might mention Sugar Ray Robinson's black British nemesis, Randy Turpin, as an example that the English love of boxing transcends race. However, Turpin's ghastly suicide several years after his boxing career ended indicates that the love affair between him and his countrymen was short. Turpin died in dire poverty, so his death did not result, certainly, from a surfeit of public esteem.)

And now we must await the article in some leading sports publication such as *Inside Sports* or *Sports Illustrated* or perhaps in *Esquire* or *The Ring* that will ask the asinine question: Are black fighters better than Latin fighters? The article will then offer as possible evidence for an affirmative answer the recent successes blacks have had with Hispanic adversaries: Hilmer Kenty's knockout win over Ernesto España for the lightweight title; Aaron Pryor's knockout win over Antonio Cervantes for the junior welterweight title; Tommy Hearns's devastation of Pipino Cuevas for the WBA's version of the welterweight title; Marvin Johnson's victory over Victor Galindez for the light-heavyweight title;* Jessie Burnet's victory over Galindez to become the number-one contender for the newly created cruiserweight crown;[†] Leo Randolph's upset over Ricardo Cardona for the junior-featherweight title.[‡] But this current trend means nothing. American fighters are coming out of amateur programs better trained than many Latin fighters who fight out of foreign countries. As many of the South American countries improve their amateur athletics, their fighters will generally gain parity with black U.S. fighters. Furthermore, such brilliant Latin fighters as Roberto Duran, Wilfredo Gomez, Alexis Arguello, Wilfred Benitez, and Salvador Sanchez have had a great success against black fighters in the past and probably will continue to be successful in the future. Finally, outside of Muhammad Ali, the two most eminent fighters of the decade 1970–1980 were Duran and now retired middleweight champion Carlos Monzon. No black fighter, aside from Ali, dominated his division the way these two Latin fighters did, and neither man had, through the decade of the seventies, ever lost a title fight. Let us hope that such an article dies before it is written, since the current *slight* superiority of black fighters has absolutely nothing to do with race and we need no sportswriter to make implications to the contrary in a national publication.

NOTE 2

I remember very well that I could not sleep the night that Benny Kid Paret was knocked into a coma by Emile Griffith in a welterweight championship bout in March of 1962. I had watched that fight on television, and when Paret was carried from the ring, unconscious, and, for all intents and purposes, lifeless, I felt myself quivering on the inside. That night I prayed

---

*Marvin Johnson subsequently lost the title to Eddie Gregory, who is now known as Eddie Mustafa Muhammad.

[†]This division, not officially recognized by all the boxing powers that be, is to accommodate fighters between 175 and 200 pounds. Heavyweights would then be fighters over 200 pounds.

[‡]Leo Randolph subsequently lost the title to Sergio Palma of Argentina.

to God to save Paret's life. Indeed, I remember being on my knees and praying very hard, having learned in church that God answers those who truly believe. I thought I truly believed but Benny Kid Paret died anyway. I learned something not only about the inscrutable whimsicality of God but also about the precariousness of the life of a fighter. It was then that I felt professional prizefighting should be banned, not because it was brutal (a kid who grew up in my neighborhood could not be that morbidly thin-skinned and survive), and not even because it was absurd (whether life itself is absurd is debatable but certainly all sports are), but because it was so uncaring. Boxing as an official bureaucracy hates boxers. Some boxing bureaucrats somewhere allowed a woefully out-of-condition middleweight named Willie Classen to fight and die in the ring, allowed a flashy Philadelphian named Gypsy Joe Harris to fight although he was legally blind in one eye; these same officials and bureaucrats now tolerate a parade of bums and stiffs who, fighting under various aliases, endanger their health and degrade the sport by being allowed to fight opponents who are infinitely superior to them. In the past year, seven fighters have died as a result of beatings that they sustained in the ring, the latest being a young Welsh bantamweight named Johnny Owen, who was knocked out by champion Lupe Pintor in the twelfth round of their fight. Owen never regained consciousness and died in a Los Angeles hospital a few weeks later.

So far, the average death rate has been one fighter every two months. And yet nothing has been done to safeguard the fighters; various state boxing commissions have not coordinated their records to prevent, say, a fighter who was knocked out forty days before in Maryland from fighting in Pennsylvania or Nevada; if a ringside doctor is present at a fight, it is almost always a general practitioner, possibly an internist, doctors who are expert at examining cuts, but almost never a neurologist, a doctor who would recognize the signs of incipient brain damage; nothing has been done to change the rules of professional boxing, either reducing the number of rounds or changing the style of the gloves or introducing a standing eight count in professional fights; the only things the WBC and the WBA are concerned about is squabbling over who is the true champion of a division or compiling a ranking system often with the money of promoters and television networks in mind; so, suddenly, a very uncreditable bum becomes a contending fighter—this, of course, means that many a fighter's record is more fiction than fact.

These are the old complaints. Indeed, every few years some hard-boiled, reform-minded sports reporter like the one portrayed by Humphrey Bogart in the 1950s cinéma vérité classic *The Harder They Fall* recites this list as a kind of litany to stir the soul of the great mass of the unconcerned. The fact that these complaints are not new should tend to bother us rather than bore us. After all, these cries of reform reveal that the only major innovations that have taken place in the last 120 years of professional fighting have been placing gloves on the fighter's fists and reducing championship fights from interminable lengths to twenty rounds and, finally, to fifteen. But it should be obvious to all that professional prizefighting cannot be reformed, not with so many bogus and even criminal entities, outlaws to their very bootstraps, struggling for corporate hegemony while the boxers are seen as so much meat hanging on hooks (the most moving scene in the film *Rocky* is of Sylvester Stallone punching a carcass in a slaughterhouse. Heavy-handed but still striking symbolism). The solution for this sport is quite simple: professional fighting must go the way of cockfighting and dogfighting and be banished from our realm. Then, the amateur program, which is more sanely supervised, can be offered in colleges, and poor boys from our mean streets can be given an education and the possibility of actually qualifying for work from which they may get a pension in their old age. We have seen how, as a cultural phenomenon, boxing brings out deplorable urges to see ourselves racially, and we have only to walk into any local gym, get to know any two-bit fighter, to learn that as a nonsymbolic part of our social system fighting is an ugly sport. The one word that comes to mind more than any other watching the fighters work in the gym is "proletariat." These men are honestly, and in a most ghastly way, *toiling,* and what is more striking is how much more grotesque this work is than, say, *the* nightmare of an assembly line. And "proletariat" is such an appropriate word for fighters whom we also call stiffs and bums, words that grew out of the working-class vocabulary—a stiff being someone who is managing to survive in the working world, a bum being a stiff who has temporarily been cast out of the working world and hence is just "bumming around."

As an ardent, I might say passionate, lover of professional boxing, a follower of my boxing heroes since I was a young boy, and as one who appreciates the working-class folklore that surrounds boxing, I find it particularly difficult to call for boxing's demise. I remember listening with intense fascination while patrons in the local barbershop spoke of the exploits of Sonny Liston; I can recall the agonizing disappointment when my uncle failed to take me to see the Joey Giardello–Dick Tiger middleweight championship bout; there comes to mind the anguish when I read that the once magnificent heavyweight Cleveland "Big Cat" Williams, who was nearly shot to death a few years before, was going to fight Muhammad Ali for the title, a hopeless mismatch, and I can remember aggrieved amazement when I heard that the promising young lightweight Tyrone Everett had been shot to death by his girlfriend. Perhaps in the end, only a true lover of the sport can understand why proles deserve a better fate.

NOTE 3

Eugene "Cyclone" Hart was once a prospect for the middleweight title. He had a left hook that was the best that the division had seen since the days of

Ray Robinson; he would whip it around his whole body, producing a crushing blow. Unfortunately, Hart was not a good defensive fighter and tended to get discouraged and disoriented if his left hook failed to produce results within the first few rounds. He had recently lost a fight by knockout to Vito Antuofermo, who was to become, briefly, the undisputed middleweight champ, when I met him in circumstances that were probably not very flattering to Hart. He had been arrested for disorderly conduct and, at that particular time, I was working with the Release on Own Recognizance Program (ROR), which was funded by the Law Enforcement Assistance Agency. My job was to interview prisoners before their arraignments to discover if they were eligible for release on their own recognizance—or as they called it, free bail. I cannot speak about other projects that LEAA gives money to but I certainly can say that my job was a monumental waste of my time and the taxpayers' money. But that topic of discussion must wait for another time. Of course, once I discovered that Cyclone Hart was "in the tank," I made sure to finagle his paperwork so I could interview him. Quite naturally, once I got him to my desk I promptly forgot his bail interview—he did not need one anyway, since he had never been arrested before and the charge was so minor that "free bail" was a foregone conclusion—and we sat and talked boxing.

"Are you still going to fight?" I asked. "Lots of people say you're washed up."

"Well, I'm still gonna try," he said. I remember how hard and strong his body was. He had the hips of a dancer, the shoulders of a halfback. "I think I can still make it. I got a few good fights in me and I might still get a title shot. That's what I'm hangin' around for: a title shot."

"I thought you were going to knock Antuofermo out of the box early," I said.

"Yeah, so did I, but he's a pretty tough cat."

We talked for a while about some other of the local fighters: Jerome Artis, Bad Bad Bennie Briscoe, Sammy Goss. When he rose to return to his cell he said:

"Yeah, I'm still hangin' in. I mean, what else can I do? My luck might change."

I had expected him to make a sort of sign with his fists when he said that, but he merely held his hands relaxed at his sides. His lack of gesture was as surprising to me as walking down a flight of stairs and anticipating a final step when none is there. Cyclone Hart was a washed-up fighter at the age of twenty-seven.

"I still might get a title shot," he said as a policeman led him away.

"Yes," I called after him, from my desk, "that's nice work if you can get it."

POSTSCRIPT: LEONARD-DURAN II

The hardest thing to teach a young boy bent upon becoming a professional prizefighter, according to any cigar-chomping, gibbous old fight trainer, is to get up and continue fighting after being knocked down and hurt. In most cases, a fighter is knocked down by a punch he did not see, and it is only human nature to want to avoid the unknown and not to wish to continue. It takes hours and hours of the most severe sort of training to make a fighter overcome that natural instinct. Robert Jarrett, a black man who is neither a cigar-chomper nor gibbous, explained this to me one winter afternoon. He is a former professional prizefighter who now trains black youngsters in the Richard Allen projects in Philadelphia in the "sweet science." "Once a kid learns this," he pontificated, "he becomes a man." I did not disagree. But when I see a decked fighter get up and continue to fight, or, in most instances, continue to get beaten to a pulp, I know it is not "heart" or courage that makes him stand up, but a sort of Skinnerian conditioning that has effectively dulled his brain so that he has no real idea when he is hurt or how badly.

Professional boxing, in recent months, has come to resemble professional wrestling in the absurd perversity of its demeanor—lacking, however, wrestling's vulgar hilarity. Wrestling, like Roller Derby, realizes its own sense of burlesque and continually teases and insults its lower-class audience with a sort of mock drama as if it were masterminded by some Grub Street exile; boxing has now mistaken its hysteria for the most profound theater. It has, in a word, become not just a joke spoken in poor taste, but a joke gone in the teeth.

The abrupt ending of the Duran-Leonard rematch, with Duran, for whatever reason, walking away from Leonard in the eighth round, was a pathetic ending to a rivalry that had so engaged the imagination and symbolism of our culture. Perhaps Duran walked away because he was "taking a dive," although one would be hard-put to imagine what corporate interest could induce him to embarrass himself so in front of his family, friends, fans, and countrymen, or what corporate interest would want him to; or perhaps he walked away because he experienced an epiphany that revealed at once and at last to his eyes the absurdity of his profession; or perhaps, and this is more likely, he felt very sick: the once poor, lean street urchin, who when he first began as a professional was easily able to make the 135-pound limit for lightweights, may have, in acquiring fame and riches, eaten his way not only out of the lightweights but perhaps out of the welterweights as well. Crash dieting and the use of diuretics are poor methods of training. Alas, this is what happens to those who live life in the fast lane. At any rate, this poetic battle, which was to pit the war machine's frenzy against the body electric's gallantry, became just another tainted, bizarre contest. This fight that was to justify the existence of boxing wound up justifying its swift execution.

This bout kept the spirit of several other recent championship fights: Muhammad Ali's painful return, in which, donning another disguise of Melville's Confidence Man, he paid the price of passing blood for a week in exchange for $10 million and the opportunity to show the world what early male menopause is like. After acting and Third World diplomacy failed, only boxing remained for this most self-conscious man to engage his puerile exhibitionism. More recently, there was the fight for the junior welterweight championship of the world between Aaron Pryor, the black champion, and Gaetan Hart, the white Canadian challenger. Not only did this fight exploit, as usual, racial contrast and racial identification, but the network that televised the fight reminded the viewers at every opportunity that Hart had seriously injured one fighter in the ring and killed another. Implied in this grotesque reporting, and in the whole raison d'être for Hart, an extremely mediocre fighter to be fighting for the championship, was the obscene question: Would Pryor be Hart's next victim? Hart had eighteen losses on his record; normally no fighter with such a propensity for losing would have been even remotely considered for a championship fight, and the two men he severely battered in the ring were even more inept as fighters than he was and probably should not have been allowed to fight. Pryor knocked out Hart in the sixth round of a mismatch.

In early November I went to an elementary school gymnasium in Ithaca to watch a local amateur fight card. The first bout of the evening was between two ten-year-old kids, one black, the other white, representing two different boxing clubs. The white youngster was game and tried very hard but the black boy had real talent, the look and hunger of a possible future professional prizefighter, and he thoroughly thrashed his opponent and easily won the fight. As I watched the black boy being congratulated by his friends and as my eyes circled the gym and viewed Ithaca's lower class out in mass to support its relatives and friends I asked myself, Why? Why does this youngster want to be a fighter? Why would his family be proud if he became one? His chances of having a career like Ali, Duran, or Leonard—boxing's representative men of the moment—are so remote that no bookie would give any sort of betting line on the possibility. And the cost of this misplaced ambition is so much deeper and heavier than if a middle-class kid who plays tennis, another "solitary ego" sport, wished to become John McEnroe.

Tennis is a bourgeois respected recreation, second only to jogging; no stigma is attached to its pursuit by the white middle and upper classes, and failure to succeed as a tennis professional does not affect the middle-class youngster's mobility or the possibility that he can cultivate other humane or profitable interests. In other words, a tennis career and, say, an MBA degree are not incompatible. They are phenomena of the same world and they represent the same bourgeois values.

Boxing is part of another culture, available to a boy who cannot be a singer, a preacher, or a thief (which are really the only other job-training programs

readily available to the lower class). His success is measured by his movement up the fight card until, finally, he becomes the featured attraction, the
main event, and the high rollers of the upper class, caught between ennui
and debauchery, come to watch him fight and to bet on the outcome. For
the poor, any ambition is ultimately to make money, to change their lives,
to make them better. But, as James Brown sang in the mid-sixties, "Money
won't change you." A poor person with money is simply, to the eyes of the
middle classes, the beast displaced, the tolerated savage, the simpleton with
poor taste. And the poor boy himself discovers that the rage that he nurtured
to become champion, the rage that pushed him from his birth, the rage
against that stultifying bourgeois monolith which has made his life miserable,
either still gnaws at him like a burning ulcer or has left him completely
burned out by the absence of desire. Thus he finds himself naked and
vulnerable, in a nest of vipers. And further, he discovers that it was the rage,
and the rage alone, that not only kept him alive but made him human.
Money won't change you, indeed. But as James Brown sang in the same
song, "Time will take you out."

As I watched the youngster in the ring I thought for a moment about
Benny Briscoe, the Philadelphia middleweight, now an aging thirty-eight,
who had several times fought for the title and each time come up empty.
Losses to Carlos Monzon and Roderigo Valdes for the title and losses to such
up-and-coming middleweights as Marvin Hagler (now the champion of that
division) and Vito Antuofermo climaxed a career of frustration and bitterness.
Bennie will never be champion and, although he continues to fight, he must
hold down another job in order to live.

On any given weekday, in any gym in America, there are ten-year-old
boys banging away at heavy bags and sweating in desperation as they
pursue that Belle Dame sans Merci—a professional boxing title.

On any given weekday, Bennie Briscoe hauls trash in the ghetto of North
Philadelphia. The long journey from the gym to the professional prize ring
ended as it began: on the streets. As the corner boys say, Briscoe still
"lives on the block."

"I Only Like It Better When Pain Comes": More Notes Toward a Cultural Definition of Prizefighting

*To all the black boys of Philadelphia
who are the small princes of our wounded order*

I. THE EXILES

On a summer day many years ago Jeff Chandler beat my cousin Gino Fernandez in a fight on the grounds of the Nebinger schoolyard. I think both Jeff and Gino were nine or ten, which means that I was about fourteen or fifteen. I doubt if now it is remotely possible to recall the reason for the fight. I lived in South Philadelphia and my cousin, who lived in West Philadelphia, would from time to time come to visit me and spend a few days. I remember well how we enjoyed each other as boys, finding much to do with our days together. This was to change as Gino grew older; toward the end of his life I rarely saw him and when I did we had little enough to say. In recent years, I have come to feel quite bad about this estrangement even though it was not my fault that it occurred. On this particular day of the fight, I suppose that my cousin's being from West Philadelphia and therefore a stranger in the neighborhood may have had something to do with the antagonism between the boys. Jeff probably instigated the fight because he was always,

---

The title comes from an article that appeared in the March 1983 issue of *The Ring* entitled "1982: The Year of the Notables and Quotables" (pp. 18–29). The full quotation of Frank "the Animal" Fletcher is on page 22 and it reads as follows: "I hate to say it, but it's true that I only like it better when pain comes."

as I remember him, a very tough small boy who took a great deal of pride in his ability to fight.

The battle was not a very long one. It started out evenly enough, but the crowd of boys who nearly smothered the combatants was quite partisan in favor of Jeff, giving him the sort of "home-court advantage" that revealed to me instantly that my cousin was doomed. Gino did, though, fight quite well for several minutes. Suddenly, Jeff hit him with an uppercut to the solar plexus so perfectly executed that any prizefighter would have been proud to have thrown it; its technique was not simply flawless, but rich in artistic refulgence. My cousin crumpled to the ground in agony. He was crying, a sure sign of capitulation. Jeff walked away, surrounded by his cloud of admiring and cheering witnesses. He felt no sympathy for the loser and, in truth, it was proper that he did not. After all, each boy knew the risks of the encounter before it began, and to commit oneself to any action is to commit oneself to the etiquette of promptly paying certain immediate psychic costs for failure. So, after a minute or two of taunts and jeers directed at me about my "punk cousin," I was left alone to tend to Gino, who was now sobbing heavily, deeply ashamed. I picked him up, extricated a balled-up, snotty handkerchief from my pocket, and wiped his face. We walked together almost in the pose of big brother and little brother: I held my arm around his shoulder and he walked with his head down. I told him not to cry, that everything would be all right, that he would surely have better days. I was quite wrong in this prediction, for if anyone was to have better days it was to be Jeff Chandler. My cousin, at the age of sixteen, was to have his head blown off by a sawed-off shotgun fired at close range by a sniper during a street-gang war. Jeff Chandler is now the World Boxing Association bantam-weight champion. The fates of these boys, poor black boys of the streets, far from being unique, take on a sort of dreary, deadening, clichéd familiarity. Both fought for street gangs as adolescents and either could have drawn the other's fortune or misfortune. Chandler could very easily have ended up on a slab in the morgue, and my cousin might well have become a professional fighter. This is perhaps not only how the Bigger Thomases of black America are born but also how they are made.

Although my cousin lived and died in West Philadelphia, his funeral took place in a South Philadelphia funeral home. The deep oddity of that fact is that the funeral came very close to not taking place at all in that location. The South Philadelphia street gang nearest to the funeral home was the Fifth and South Streets gang, the very gang that Jeff Chandler was then fighting for. And these boys were not going to have their turf invaded by the comrades-in-arms of a fallen West Philadelphia gang member. I remember that at the funeral there were nearly as many cops as bereaved relatives and friends, and such a guarded atmosphere that one might have thought some cruel political dictator was being buried. If there had not been so many police officers present, my cousin's funeral might very well have sparked more bloodshed.

I do not think any group of people could have felt more diminished and deranged by all this than my family did. Here, after all, was a young, wayward Jehovah's Witness boy who was murdered according to the arcane but deadly rules of the ghetto rites of passage. My family, both its South Philadelphia and its West Philadelphia branches, had never thought it even lived in a ghetto, much less that it would be brutalized by its hard reality. My mother was stunned to learn that Gino was a member of a street gang. I was an undergraduate at the University of Pennsylvania at the time, and this whole horrible incident made me feel degraded.

Jeff Chandler is a very good professional fighter, amazingly good when one considers that he has had no amateur career to speak of. He had a few amateur fights, then decided that it would be better to fight for money and glory than for trophies and glory, especially since the amount of effort would be about the same. He has beaten everyone in his weight division worth beating, and would love to fight his Latin counterpart—Lupe Pintor, the World Boxing Council bantamweight champion—in a title unification bout. But the young Mexican wants nothing to do with Chandler, so the hard Philadelphian will probably move on to the featherweight division and hope that he can make more money fighting bigger fellows. Because of the death of Tyrone Everett, the retirement of Joe Frazier, the deterioration of Matthew Saad Muhammad and Jimmy Young, and the unfulfillment of Curtis Parker and Frank Fletcher, Chandler has become the top Philadelphia fighter. That is quite an accomplishment because that town produces many good fighters, and the training sessions, both in the gym and on the streets, are wars of the bloodiest and most demanding kind. Chandler, to put it simply, is a survivor in a place and an occupation where most are swallowed whole in mid-career.

II. THE KINGS IN THE TOWER

1

Alexis Arguello, great champion of the featherweight, junior lightweight, and lightweight divisions, is known to be a friendly, easygoing fellow outside the ring. He numbers among his friends many fighters who are potential rivals. He seems particularly proud of his friendship with Sugar Ray Leonard, who despite his retirement is still a potential rival because everyone knows that retirement announcements in boxing do not mean much. The story goes that once in a social context Arguello met Roberto Duran, great champion of the lightweight and welterweight divisions, and came up to shake hands and chat with him. At this time Duran was still considered, by those who are supposed to know, pound for pound the best fighter in all of boxing, and there was more than a little talk of a possible big-money bout between him and Arguello. Duran, known for his haughty disdain for and intense dislike of opponents, looked aghast at the approaching Arguello and, while backing away from him, screamed, "Get away from me! I'm not your friend! Get away from me!"

As crazy as it seems, Duran merely took one of boxing's learned inclinations to both its neurotic and its rational limits. It would seem only to complicate matters a great deal to be friendly with the men one is required to fight. A boxer must inflict a lot of punishment in the normal course of a fight in order to expect to win, and it would seem that he might feel less compromised or uneasy in his actions if the opponent was not a friend. On the other hand, it is quite natural for people who share a particular profession also to share friendships; who can know better than a prizefighter the rewards of achievement or the frustrations of defeat in the prizefighting profession?

Duran does not wish to be friendly with boxers who may be potential opponents because it makes the psychological part of training that much harder. This is often referred to as "psyching yourself up," which means creating an artificial hatred for your opponent, so that you may more efficiently and brutally beat him up. There is more at work here than the incredibly fierce sense of Darwinian competition that characterizes the spirit of play in other professional sports. Boxing, after all, is the only sport whose object is to hurt your opponent—to place him in such pain, to inflict such severe injury upon him, that he cannot or will not continue to fight. The emotional incentive for this must be deeper than the mere quest for championship belts and big money, although, to be sure, those latter items do spur fighters on. Boxers must be driven by other needs as well when they enter the ring: they must have "something to prove," or they must "hold a grudge" against their opponent for some imaginary or petty slight, or they must feel like particularly evil bastards who can, to use John L. Sullivan's phrase, "lick any son of a bitch in the house." In short, the bouts become quests for manhood. *Rubbish — it's all about money I can't dignify this brutal sport w/ manhood*

Former boxer Leonard Gardner's fine novel about second-rate boxers in California, *Fat City,* contains a scene in which the reader sees the pathetic desperation of this psyching up of the boxer, this dredging up of courage from the spirit to stem the tide of the deep fear of it all:

> "Hoping never done nothing," [said Buford Wills.] "It *wanting* that do it. You got to want to win so bad you can taste it. If you want to win bad enough you win. They no way in hell this dude going to beat me. He too old. I going to be all over him. I going kick him so bad, everytime he take a bite of food tomorrow he going think of me. He be one sore son-of-a-bitch. He going *know* he been in a fight. I get him before he get me. I going hit him with everything. I won't just *beat* that motherfucker, I going *kill* him." Buford was small and thin. His hair, divided at one side with a razor-blade part, was cropped close. His nose turned up, his nostrils flared, his lips were soft and full and his hooded eyes were narrowed in a constant frown. The year before, only fourteen, he had lied about his age and won the Golden Gloves novice flyweight title in San Francisco. Tonight he was

fighting the champion of Fort Ord. "You want to know what make a good fighter?"

"What's that?" [asked Ernie Munger.]

"It believing in yourself. That the will to win. The rest condition. You want to kick ass, you kick ass."

"I hope you're right."

"You don't want to kick ass, you get your own ass whipped."

"I want to kick ass. Don't worry about that."

"You just shit out of luck."

"I said I wanted to kick ass."

"You got to want to kick ass *bad*. They no manager or trainer or pill can do it for you."

"I want to kick ass as bad as you do."

"Then you go out and kick ass."

I have spoken in an earlier essay* about the general cultural significance of prizefighting, but I would like to be a bit more specific here. One of the two interrelated cultural needs that boxing serves suggests that the antagonism of the opponents is very much like that of a morality play, a morality play about the very nature of capitalistic society. Despite the fact that boxing is an international sport, practiced everywhere on the globe, America has become and has been for some time the center of professional fighting. Most of the best fighters are Americans; most of the big money originates here, and most of the publicity as well. In short, boxing is an American pastime. Moreover, one must not lose sight of the fact that modern professional boxing in its traceable history was a product of Britain; boxing in its course to its present identity is not just Western, not simply American, but particularly Anglo-Saxon. It should come as a surprise to no one, knowing modern prizefighting's national and racial origins, that the sport extols most simply and directly the values that the Anglo-Saxon male has historically cherished most: the indomitable will of the individual, aggressive conquest, and contempt for humiliation and submission. It is, perhaps, intended to be the height of irony that Wills, the black boy, the historical victim of the Anglo-Saxon's will to power, should teach Ernie Munger, the white boy, the Western values of male conquest. Wills's little speech sounds as much like the street-corner version of the philosophy of Robinson Crusoe as it does like the advice of a senior boardroom executive to a junior upstart. It is one of the striking ironies of the novel that boxing, a sport that so ruthlessly symbolizes the success ethic of American society, produces men who are so ill equipped to be anything but failures. Thus, one of the true oddities of the symbolism of boxing is that the minority male, in becoming like the paradigmatic, mythological Anglo-Saxon male, wears a kind of white face.

Duran's little episode with Alexis Arguello might remind one of the

---

*"Hot Spicks Versus Cool Spades: Three Notes Toward a Cultural Definition of Prizefighting."

incredible invisible burden of the champion boxer, the great "asskicker." Gardner's novel is exclusively concerned with pugs, or as Camus called them, "low-brow gods." But the intensity of emotional commitment is greater when the fights mean more; more money, more prestige for the winner, more humiliation for the loser. Duran's insecurity has its source in the very deep doubt he must have about his self-image in his chosen profession. Duran is afraid, not so much of being beaten, but of being reduced, lessened, by showing any signs that would make him less committed to his line of work. One must remember that it was Duran who once said after beating an opponent that if he had been in shape he would have sent him to the morgue, not the hospital; it was Duran who once saluted Sugar Ray Leonard's wife by pointing his middle finger and calling her *puta* ("whore"); and it was Duran who spat in Leonard's face at the end of their first bout. This need for the commitment, the overwhelming identification not with boxing but with what it means to be an asskicker, is probably the main reason that Duran is still fighting even though he should have retired a few years ago. Duran is more the mythical Anglo-Saxon male than the Anglo-Saxon himself, and if that identification proves meaningless, then Duran is forced to ask himself what his blustering quest for manhood means. This is why he is still fighting and embarrassing himself. He does not want to think about what it would mean to stop: then he would be like a soldier without a war.

2

A film that clearly presents, in a huge metaphorical gesture, the secret fear of the male is the 1950s science fiction classic *The Incredible Shrinking Man*. Slowly, as the hero's body becomes smaller and smaller, the audience finds him overwhelmed not by life generally, not by his job, his government, his culture, or by his general intercourse with other people—but by his home and his wife. The woman becomes an overprotective giant and the home a wild hive of booby traps that threaten him at every turn. One is, of course, reminded of Leslie Fiedler and his talk about those many nineteenth-century American Adams who were trying to escape the very things that Herman Melville's Tommo was returning to at the end of *Typee*: home and mother. In *The Incredible Shrinking Man* there is a parodic inversion by which the man finds himself being swallowed by his home and his wife (whose relative largeness and maternal concern make her a mother figure); he must do battle against objects of his own home: a cat and a spider. The hero thus discovers that living in his home has become the ultimate pioneering adventure as he hunts for food and water and, in the final symbol of pathetic power, uses a straight pin for a sword. Grant Williams, who portrays the hero, ultimately loses his battle and his body simply vanishes by the end of the film.

   This neurotic vision, or rather this dream or parable of the neurotic trapped male, poses an essential question about the sport of boxing: What is its secret, primeval appeal to its viewers? Part of the answer, no doubt, lies in the boxer's puritanical regimen: the hard training, the abstinence from sex before a fight, the Spartan diet. The boxer's leanness and physical conditioning become a sign of his virtue, a virtue worth a great deal in a land where the fatness of sin is the sin of fatness. But more deeply, the answer rests somewhere in the fact that the male is not needed as a cultural image for his courage, stamina, and heart, all of those manly virtues about which he has woven myths; he is needed as a psychological emblem to illustrate the capacity of dumb suffering. It is the torment and disfigurement of the male body that help the male to achieve the godhead. Norman Mailer would find in a film like *The Incredible Shrinking Man* the most endearing symbolism.

The first section of Mailer's *The Fight* opens and closes with images of the male body; the opening chapter describes "the Prince of Heaven," Muhammad Ali, in a training session, the beautiful body hiding both power and grace within its limbs:

> To the degree that boxing is carnality, meat against meat, Ali was master when it was time to receive, he got the juice out of it, the aesthetic juice of the punches he blocked or clipped, plus all the libidinal juice of Bossman Jones banging away on his gut....
>
> Now it was as if Ali carried the idea to some advanced place where he could assimilate punches faster than other fighters, could literally transmit the shock through more parts of his body, or direct it to the best path, as if ideally he was working toward the ability to receive that five-punch combination (or six or seven!) yet be so ready to ship the impact out to each arm, each organ and each leg, that the punishment might be digested, and the mind remain clear. It was a study to watch Ali take punches.

The descriptions seem complementary. In the first, the body as mythic image lies between art and sex; and in the second, the body is the mechanism that must be controlled and manipulated by the mind. Both denote so precisely the precarious precision of the boxer's psychological tightrope-walk between seizing and creating the moment, and squandering it. Mailer is indeed concerned with the wider symbol of the black male's tightrope-walking. But Mailer's representation is not so much a psychology of the male body as it is an anthropology of the male body. Somehow, through the imagery at the beginning, of Ali's body as self-fulfilling sex, as art, and as machine, and the imagery at the end of the first section, of the spindly, ugly body of Ali's talkative trainer, Drew Brown, the reader is presented with the history of male culture, from prince to clown, from the improvisations of the body to the improvisations of language (when the body, as in the case of Brown, fails as adequate symbolism). The polar realities of Brown and Ali as male figures symbolize the morality of masculinity: Ali puts his body on the line and is thus a hero-warrior. Drew Brown weaves with his mouth and is like a jester, a gnome, or as Mailer calls him, the King of the Flunkies. It is

Brown who creates Ali's chants and poetry and it is with Brown that Mailer "plays the dozens." So although Ali was known as "the Mouth," Mailer's fascination and that of the entire Western culture with Ali have, in truth, always been with his heroic body. Boxing becomes, for Mailer, the most primitive yet the highest moment for the male psyche. The one-on-one encounter, the rewards of its brinksmanship, the egotistic excesses of its one-upmanship are what boxing and the male body mean.

The major problem with Mailer's fight book is that he spends a good number of his pages, far too many really, writing about race. This comes about because this book, like most of Mailer's fight pieces, is about Muhammad Ali, and with Ali as a subject I suppose one is, perforce, confronted with the issue of race. Yet I think white writers like Mailer use Ali as an excuse to write about race, or more precisely, about blacks: what a wonderful opportunity to clear the chest and spleen of numerous phobias and neuroses! When Mailer writes about race or about blacks he invariably is going to sound like the writer who penned that inglorious essay "The White Negro"—which means that he is liable to sound foolish. He will not sound utterly foolish, just foolish enough to make any knowing reader accept his good portions with a great deal of suspicion. Consider these passages:

> But [Norman Mailer's] love affair with the Black soul, a sentimental orgy at its worst, had been given a drubbing through the seasons of Black Power. He no longer knew whether he loved Blacks or secretly disliked them, which had to be the dirtiest secret in his American life. Part of the woe of the first trip to Africa, part of that irrationally intense detestation of Mobutu...must be a cover for the rage he was feeling toward Blacks, any Blacks....
>
> His animosity switched a continent over to Black Americans with their arrogance, jive, ethnic put-down costumes, caterwauling soul, their thump-your-testicle organ sound and black new vomitous egos like the slag of all of alienated sewage-compacted heap U.S.A.; then he knew that he had not only come to report on a fight but to look a little more into his own outsized feelings of love and— could it be?—sheer hate for the existence of Blacks on earth.

Mailer was in Zaire to report on the heavyweight championship fight between Ali and George Foreman that took place in a hastily constructed stadium in the fall of 1974. Thus, the reader is confronted with Mailer's image of the land of bogeys and boots, the land without rational order; and the image becomes a quest on Mailer's part for the legitimation of his own rational white mind and his confessed inability to understand that mind which symbolizes for him the nonwhite other. It is Mailer's being in Africa and covering a fight between two black fighters that ultimately leads to the sort of psychic flatulence that the two quotations reveal. For Mailer, the black is always the id-dominated beast, the heart of the white man's darkness; and always, in Mailer's tone, there is that juvenile penis envy that might as well be hate because it amounts to such an insulting kind of love. He writes elsewhere in the book:

So much resentment had developed for black style, black snobbery, black rhetoric, black pimps, superfly, and all the virtuoso handling of the ho. The pride Blacks took in their skill as pimps!

It is no wonder that Mailer loves boxing, or rather loves the symbolism of boxing. His engagement with the black experience has always been limited to the male side of all matters—when Mailer says "Blacks" he means male (an observation also made by Michelle Wallace in her book *Black Macho and the Myth of the Superwoman*). And his engagement with boxing has come about largely because its symbolism can be worked out in such an exclusively male arena and in exclusively male terms. What is amazing, in this regard, is Mailer's lack of growth in the years between the publication of "The White Negro" (1957) and *The Fight* (1975). Jazz and the black subterranean urban life served the same purpose in the pages of the essay as boxing and traveling in Africa do in the book. Consider the similarity to the book in tone and content of these quotations from the essay:

Turgid Crap.

> Knowing in the cells of his existence that life was war, nothing but war, the Negro (all exceptions admitted) could rarely afford the sophisticated inhibitions of civilization, and so he kept for his survival the art of the primitive, he lived in the enormous present, he subsisted for his Saturday night kicks, relinquishing the pleasures of the mind for the more obligatory pleasures of the body....
>
> It is therefore no accident that psychopathy is most prevalent with the Negro. Hated from outside and therefore hating himself, the Negro was forced into the position of exploring all those moral wildernesses of civilized life which the Square automatically condemns as delinquent or evil or immature or morbid or self-destructive or corrupt....But the Negro, not being privileged to gratify his self-esteem with the heady satisfactions of categorical condemnation, chose to move instead in that other direction where all situations are equally valid, and in the worst of perversion, promiscuity, pimpery, drug addiction, rape, razor-slash, bottle-break, what-have-you, the Negro discovered and elaborated a morality of the bottom.

Mailer expresses a very simple and very old idea here, namely, that the black male is metaphorically the white male's unconsciousness personified. What is of deeper interest in that formulation is Mailer's homogenization of the black male personality; in effect any black male, from jazz musician to boxer to pimp to bank robber, any black male who is estranged from bourgeois culture for whatever reason (and the reasons and the choices are far from being the same) is, for Mailer, the same outcast, the same uninhibited, uncivilized self, the same untraumatized noble savage. Ironically, if the black or Latin prizefighter within the code of his own world has absorbed the masculine rites and morality of the Anglo-Saxon West, then as symbol in the larger world he is simply a new type of minstrel, a black face hidden behind an even deeper blackface: the secret shadow-self of the white man's mind. In Mailer's vision, the boxers become clockwork psychopaths; each round in a fight is nothing more than a three-minute drill in regulated aggression, orchestrated and articulated by the writers outside the ring who have come to see boxing not as a sport but as imagistic psychotherapeutic ethics. For Mailer, the good id (Ali) whips the bad id (Foreman). One wishes that Mailer had taken to heart D. H. Lawrence's warning about "cherishing illusions about the race soul, the eternal Negroid soul...."

There is nothing easier than to rake Mailer over the coals for his sexism. I do not intend to do that—first of all because he has been a frequent and quite easy target for feminists in recent years. Secondly, any male who really enjoys boxing is drawn to it at least partly because it is an all-male province, no matter how silly its bravado or how pointlessly dangerous its risks.

The reason why Mailer's book would be open to attack by feminists is related to his conjuring up of Ernest Hemingway whenever he gets the opportunity. Hemingway haunts Mailer and, in this particular instance, one is apt to think that *Death in the Afternoon* looms like a large shadow over Mailer's text. And it is the image of Hemingway that makes one think that Mailer's love of the all-male world of boxing is not the simple recitation of a particular preference but an actual statement of repudiation of any sexually mixed world. To chant the name of Hemingway is merely to give the imprint of genius to any meditation on a world without women.

But in the end, Mailer did not take Hemingway's advice. He tried to write an epic about boxing. The actual fight between Muhammad Ali and George Foreman had to be one of the most boring on record. The only reason it was of any interest is that everyone in the world was convinced that Ali would lose badly. After all, Foreman had bounced Joe Frazier and Ken Norton around like rubber balls, and those two last fighters gave Ali fits in the ring. But as Angelo Dundee has said, "Styles make a fight," and for this fight with Foreman, Ali had the right style. It was exciting *that* he won, but not *how* he won. The fight took on the same pattern round after round: Ali leaning against the ropes covering up while Foreman flailed away like a windmill. Finally, Foreman was too tired to hold his arms up anymore and Ali knocked him out in the eighth round; a flyweight could have knocked Foreman out by then. Ali's strategy worked only because Foreman was such an abysmally stupid fighter. And the long-term bodily effects of the rope-a-dope strategy, which a very lazy Ali adopted as a main feature in his subsequent fights, have yet to be fully realized. Suffice it to say that in the long run Ali may be the big loser. Mailer devotes nearly forty pages in his book to describing the actual combat, a rather dangerous thing to do. A third-rate writer for *The Ring* could have described it in a thousand-word column. Mailer wants to write an epic; he wants to invest his writing with the images of larger-than-life heroes and villains and larger-than-life tragedy and drama. But as Hemingway wrote, "Nor is overwritten journalism made literature by the injection of a false epic quality. Remember this too: all bad writers are in love with the epic."

3

"I am a sports romanticist," wrote the late Nat Fleischer, great boxing historian and biographer, founder and publisher of *The Ring* magazine, "the Bible of Boxing." This statement opens what Fleischer considered to be or at least what was publicly announced as his autobiography, *50 Years at Ringside*. One supposes that Fleischer, certainly not the best of writers even by a fairly liberal standard, though a solid journalist, was indulging in a bit of grandiloquence: he might just as easily have said that he was a sports fan (or more particularly a boxing fan since Fleischer made his reputation as a writer on that single sport and nothing else) and left it at that. But "romanticist" might, after all, be the right world to capture Fleischer's obsession. For Fleischer, boxing had long ceased to be an escape from reality, an adjunct of reality, or a component of reality; the prizefight had become reality itself. Is it not one of the major characteristics of the romanticist to flood and enrich an emblem incessantly until not only does that emblem explain the world but all actions in the world, however distant, are seen as simply replicating the emblem? And is not that act seen as applying, to use Jacques Barzun's phrase, "energy, morality, and genius" to "the problem of reconstruction"? The romanticist, finally, is a reconstructionist. And surely Fleischer was quite dedicated to the task of reconstructing prizefighting.

Having described in the most minute detail in his dozens of books and in his columns and editorials in *The Ring* and other publications the thousands of fights that he witnessed or read about from the golden age of bareknuckle fighting to the era of Muhammad Ali, Fleischer seemed fairly certain that what happened in the prize ring and why it happened were the only experiences worth knowing. This devotion far exceeds that of even the most rabid fan who is usually satisfied by merely collecting and hoarding certain objects, a devotion that not only is parasitic and simply a sign of neurotic consumption but also abhors producing anything. Fleischer's obsession, not unlike that of black scholar Carter G. Woodson, was indeed most closely akin to that astringent devotion of the scholar; for what he really wanted to know was the unknowable: the essence of his love, the essence of boxing, the thing that made it what it was. And he searched for that essence as diligently as, perhaps even more so than, say, a nineteenth-century specialist would seek the essence of Victorianism or the essence of Marx or the essence of Matthew Arnold. Consequently, his production as a writer was prodigious: a five-volume set on the history of blacks in pugilism from its beginnings in England to the era of Joe Louis (which would not have been possible without the existence of Pierce Egan's *Boxiana* and other histories of British Regency boxing and the *National Police Gazette,* the best historical source of American boxing in the late nineteenth and early twentieth centuries); full-length and short biographies of Stanley Ketchel, Jack Dempsey, John L. Sullivan, James Corbett, Gene Tunney, Benny Leonard, Ben Hogan, and others; several general histories of prizefighting and the heavyweight championship; books and pamphlets on such matters as how to train a fighter, how to be a second, how to be a manager, and how to referee a fight; in addition to articles and editorials in *The Ring* for over fifty years. According to *Newsweek,* Fleischer wrote about 40 million words on boxing during his lifetime.

Of all his books, Fleischer was most proud of his multivolume set on black fighters. In the introduction to the first volume he writes:

> Now that the task has been completed, the writer believes that he has done a job for colored fighters which parallels that done by Pierce Egan for fisticuffs in general. But for Egan's splendid *Boxiana* which appeared in parts from 1812 to 1828, the story of the beginnings of the sport would have been lost.

He goes on in this vein:

> In writing the story of the negro [*sic*], the author went far beyond the method used by Egan. Pierce found his story in newspaper files. The writer had to delve through ancient pamphlets, forgotten magazines, copies of newspapers which flourished long before the United States became a nation.

And at last we arrive at the heart of the matter:

> In developing the story of the Negro [*sic*], the writer discovered that a new treatment of the subject was necessary. The model laid down by Egan could not be followed. Even more arduous research than had been gone through by Egan was necessary, because never before had anyone attempted the story of the colored fighter without prejudice to that fighter.

Within the space of a few short paragraphs, Egan is transformed from the hero historian who must be emulated to the rival historian who must be overcome or overthrown: a bold exposition of Fleischer's anxiety of influence and his vision as a reconstructionist. If Egan, now known to historians not as a historian himself but as the frivolous author of the rather minor Tom and Jerry adventures, a text Thackeray branded as not one-half so good as Cruikshank's accompanying pictures, could write the equivalent of a five-volume set on the most socially outcast men of his day, with a few exceptions (prizefighting was, indeed, a criminal offense in Regency England), then Fleischer, of course, could write a five-volume set on the most despised of the socially outcast: the black prizefighter. If Egan could describe the fights of Jack Broughton, which he never saw, then Fleischer could describe the fights of Richmond and Molineaux, the great black fighters he never saw of the late eighteenth and early nineteenth centuries. But what separates Fleischer from Egan and their monumental achievements in the fields of sportswriting and cultural history is that Egan as romantic historian was not a Puritan and Fleischer was. Egan gave the world such fanciful words as *bruiser* (boxer), *bunch of fives* (fist), *chopper* and *chops* (mouth), *clout* (blow), *conk* (head), *game* (brave), *ivories* (teeth), *up to scratch* (ready to fight), *mug* (face), *peeper* (eye), *sneezer* (nose), *upper story* (head), *lark* (adventure), *bottom* (courage), *the fancy* (followers of boxing), and a score of others. Egan loved slang, puns, and the ambience of the life of the prizefighter. Egan was a hedonist. Fleischer was an ascetic: The life of a fighter is simply the fights he has fought, a truth so fundamental that it is nearly as profound as it is simple-minded. First, for Fleischer, a fighter is good, then, at his prime, then, slowly coming apart, and finally, completely finished. The inevitable warp and woof of what to Fleischer is a commonplace tragedy is his only concern and his only pattern. Fleischer dedicated his energy and moral vision to the ultimate failed energy and partial moral vision of the prizefighter. For Fleischer, in every instance, the fighter eventually breaks the covenant with his own body, with his own athletic purity, with the sacred mission of the sport. Fleischer's writing contains no puns, no thick and hectic descriptions of the world of prizefighting, and only the most standard slang: "mitt" for glove, "claret" for blood, "orb" for eye, and so forth. In short, Egan was wildly inventive, reimagining and re-creating the fights and the fighter's world he wrote about so vividly, whereas Fleischer was ponderously consistent and prosaic; not interested in *conceiving* fights, he simply *reported* them with elephantine tenacity. During Fleischer's—and for that matter twentieth-century sportwriting's—heyday from the 1920s to the 1940s, prizefights were made a good deal more frequently than they are today. A good fighter during the twenties, except Dempsey, might fight as often as once a month; some, especially black fighters who had to overcome the constant difficulty of being demanded to throw fights to white opponents, fought almost weekly, in some cases daily. So Fleischer's mill was always, as it were, grinding, grinding away, and his writing, despite his unending opportunity to practice his craft, always had the texture of pulverized substance or in this case pulverized thought, fights so minutely described that they seemed atomized parodies of journalistic descriptions.

Of course, lost in all of Fleischer's books, in this plethora of words, this sea of comprehensive accounts of prizefighting, were the objects of Fleischer's search. In seeking the essence of prizefighting, he was searching not for more and more words about fights or more and more boring descriptions of fights or even ultimately to slay the father figure of Pierce Egan; he was seeking what every scholar truly wants: the one perfect *redaction,* that very small set of words that would say better everything contained in all of the volumes of the world.

He finally discovered one sort of redaction when he wrote "I'm a sports romanticist" to open his autobiography and then, a few pages later, added, "There is romance in boxing." He found one gesture of temperament that explained and contained all of his other gestures, that essence of eloquence that contained all his grandiloquence, the emblem in the emblem. His tautology is absolutely necessary: If he is a romanticist and he loves prizefighting, then prizefighting must have romance. And if prizefighting has romance, and he loves the sport (love is essentially a romantic pretext), then he must be a romanticist. It is substantially not only a self-justifying discourse but an ontological proposition. It is this redaction of the romantic temperament that Fleischer, a Jew, shared with the other American Jewish writers who have dreamed about and written about prizefighting, who were attracted to prizefighting because it offered a kind of solidarity beyond a Jewish sensibility or marginality, those two writers being A. J. Liebling and Norman Mailer. For these very unathletic Jews, although each of them did on more than one occasion step into the ring and train with professional fighters, to love fighting was an intellectual test of being able to explicate an inexplicable love, to justify loving an object that was surely not worthy of either the love or the justification. In a captivating way, being a Jewish intellectual in love with boxing was equivalent to replicating and mocking the aesthetic and political condition of being a Jew.

But because Fleischer is a romanticist and there is romance in boxing, because the object he loves confirms his existence as much he confirms its reality, all fighters, in the end, become simply two fighters, a winner and a loser, a bloodied specimen of humanity and one less bloody. And every fight becomes the same fight, the same tense drama, or the same relentlessly mundane factuality of socially permitted violence endlessly repeated. Only a romanticist could stand this type of repetition; indeed, only a romanticist would crave for its insistence, for the security of the one gesture being fatuously reenacted. Today we might call Fleischer not a historian or a biographer or a romanticist but rather a mythologist. For is not myth the essence of reality, the redaction, the all-consuming gesture, and is not its first and foremost requirement that it must be endlessly repeated and endlessly endured to be truly what it is? That the mythologist must be as voracious in his need to absorb the same expression as the myth is extravagant in its immutable ability to express sameness? And is not myth ultimately an attack against materialism, an attack against any reality (super, mundane, ultra) external to perception or external to the ability to idealize? And has not materialism always been the object of attack for romanticists? So what is a romanticist but someone who does not want the world or the actions of humanity to be subsumed under some impersonal reality, a materialist universe. And Fleischer's prolific endurance was his act of idealization, not to say something new about the fights he saw but to be moved, inspired that the fights so compellingly called forth the need to be witnessed in the same way. What makes Fleischer, on one level, so much more interesting as a writer than Mailer, Liebling, even Egan, was his refusal to call attention to himself as a writer, to resist utterly the attempt to make it all interesting by flights of rhetorical fancy. But there are occasions when the romanticist creates the very thing he is fighting against. Endless descriptions of fights may produce the very clockwork, depersonalized, *trivialized* reality that the romanticist wants to avoid. Fleischer did not understand this, which is why, unlike Egan, who did, he continued to report about prizefighting until the very hour of his death.

4

If Ernest Hemingway's presence overshadows Norman Mailer's fight pieces, then A. J. Liebling is haunted by the old Victorian fight journalist Pierce Egan. Liebling's book on boxing, *The Sweet Science* (the title is derived from a phrase coined by Egan), is doubtless the best nonfiction book on boxing since Egan penned pieces on the bareknuckle brawlers of England in the publication *Boxiana*. Liebling's essays, which originally appeared in *The New Yorker,* are a purist's journey through the major bouts of the fifties: Sugar Ray Robinson's fights with Joey Maxim and Randy Turpin, Marciano's two bouts with Jersey Joe Walcott, his two bouts with Ezzard Charles, and his fight with Archie Moore. Liebling also covers an early Floyd Patterson fight, Moore's battle with his arch-nemesis Harold Johnson, and a minor Sandy Saddler fight.

Liebling writes as a journalist; he is not obsessed with the epic, so his pieces are not pretentious like Mailer's. At his best, he reminds one of the best of Red Smith. Indeed, Liebling positively revels in the seedy hotel, the wrinkled topcoat, the greasy-collar persona of the boxing writer. And because he writes here in the guise of the boxing writer, he is also a purist who loves to listen to the old boys and keep a sharp eye out for the oddballs. The book is filled with presences like Freddie Brown, old-time, raspy-voiced trainer whose last famous pupil was the foul-tempered but brilliant Roberto Duran; Al Weill, manager of Rocky Marciano and seeker of "young broken fighters"; Charlie Goldman, trainer of Marciano, who says, "One of the troubles with fighters now is they don't start before they're interested in dames"; and Runyonesque characters like Prince Monolulu, an Ethiopian prince who plays the ponies in England, preaches Zionism on Sundays, and has moderate success betting on fights.

Yet in reading this book one gets the impression that Liebling is well aware that he has approached the end of an epoch. The boxers and the bouts, the managers and the trainers, the auditoriums where the fights are held, and the audiences who witness them are all part of the past. Liebling sees televised fights as heralding the downfall of the sport:

The immediate crisis in the United States, forestalling the one high living standards might bring on, has been caused by the popularization of a ridiculous gadget called television. This is utilized in the sale of beer and razor blades. The clients of the television companies, by putting on a free boxing show almost every night of the week, have knocked out of business the hundreds of small-city and neighborhood boxing clubs where youngsters had a chance to learn their trade and journeymen to mature their skills. Consequently the number of good new prospects diminishes with every year, and the peddlers' public is already being asked to believe that a boy with perhaps ten or fifteen fights behind him is a topnotch performer. Neither advertising nor brewers, and least of all the networks, give a hoot if they push the Sweet Science back into a period of genre painting. When it is in a coma they will find some other way to peddle their peanuts.

The purist's obsession with standards is not simply a crotchety moralism but a quest for integrity in a world where such a quality is fast vanishing. As it happened, Liebling was right; television absolutely distorted and detached the viewer's ability to see or understand prizefighting and often interfered with the boxer's ability to perform. The viewer is distanced from the struggle and the pain of the ordeal; the vibrating edge of fear and brutality is blunted, is in fact reduced and packaged. Indeed, far from being able to "experience" a fight on television, one is simply manipulated by the camera angles and the commentators. One reacts to the grossness of the occasion without sensing its subtleties. The fighters, in many cases little more than honorable schoolboys who have been advanced too many grades without benefit of instruction, are often in more danger of being seriously injured than would be the case if they were more seasoned performers. Finally, to have taken from the province of the enthusiast and put up for public sale not only the big-money and big-name fights, but the little ordinary ones as well, is to have reduced the sport to its one most prominent and marketable characteristic — the charismatic flowing of blood. As one of the characters in Budd Schulberg's novel *The Harder They Fall* puts it, boxing is "show business with blood."

In the end, it is Liebling's very self-consciousness about his quest for integrity that makes *The Sweet Science* reek of a high-brow, quaint conservatism. To Liebling, the televised boxing match might have been the beginning of a high-tech, grossly inartistic seizure of the manly art of self-defense. But it must be admitted that before television the world of boxing was one of gangsterism, fixed fights, racial baiting and discrimination, severe punch-drunkenness, down-and-out fighters without two nickels to rub together, petty whores, fleece artists, dishonest officials, and a general miasma of corruption and filth. Television was not ruining an art form; it was buying into a money-making den of iniquity. Nearly any sense of this side of boxing is absent from Liebling's essays. Boxing is not, after all, merely a series of cunningly contrived pieces about its characters written in order to make a low-class endeavor palatable to the high-brow readers of *The New Yorker.* This is where Liebling's purist bent leads him astray: the age of the 1940s and the early 1950s in pre-television boxing was not the golden age of bareknuckle fighters that Pierce Egan described during the Regency and early Victorian era. Perhaps the 1810s and 1820s were as innocently bawdy and brawling as Egan wanted his readers to believe, but the 1940s and 1950s demanded more than the picturesque. Liebling's aim, I think, is clear; *The Sweet Science* was meant to be the romance of modern prizefighting, sportswriting as *belles lettres.* Here is an overweight Jewish intellectual who imagined himself the reincarnation of a cocky, loutish nineteenth-century Irishman, emulating Egan's style of dense slang, obscure allusions, sporting-life ambience, and reemphasizing Egan's values, described by one scholar as being "acceptance of social diversity and of the divisions in society with each class pursuing its own pleasures"; "warning against tricksters, moneylenders, procuresses and con-men"; and "rejoicing in the existence of low life." But ultimately *The Sweet Science,* despite the ghost of Egan, is so much less than Egan. The book was not even meant to be historical romanticism like Egan's pieces but rather sheer requiem for the last artists of integrity. This is why the book is framed with the images of two great black fighters who are in the twilight of their careers: Joe Louis and Archie Moore, two supreme artists making their last stands. When Liebling writes that a "boxer, like a writer, must stand alone," the reader knows that the book is making an early claim to its easy moral victory. *The Sweet Science* is nothing more than an effective, long good-bye.*

III. YOUNG MAN STREETFIGHTER:
AN AMERICAN SKETCH

Let me begin by warning the reader that this will not be an unhappy story.

In the neighborhood where I grew up there was a block called Fairhill Street. Every black American ghetto must have one of these streets, where the houses are so dilapidated, so absolutely ruined that the bricks bulge out in a manner that suggest a kind of sterile pregnancy. Even the inanimate objects seem swollen with grief. Many of the houses, as I remember, were boarded up with wood or sheets of metal, and yellow paper signs would be posted on the front doors which read: THIS PROPERTY IS DECLARED UNFIT FOR HUMAN HABITATION. Of course, people continued to live in these buildings and no one thought anything at all about it. If you were to ask these people why they did not move to more suitable quarters, they would tell you simply that they could afford nothing else; they had no place else to live. They were, I think, wretchedly poor, the poorest black people in the neighborhood. The young children would run around barefoot in the summer, with dirty, cut-up feet, mostly because the parents could not afford the fancy PF Flyers and Converses that I and other children wore. The girls on this block were always pregnant before the age of fifteen and the boys in jail before sixteen. In those days, people on welfare did not receive food stamps; they were given government-issued food popularly referred to as "surplus." At school, it was easy to spot the kids whose families received surplus; they always brought lunches that consisted of the whitest white bread in the world and thick, pink, rubbery pieces of Spam or potted meat. Those of us who thought we were better off than our Fairhill Street friends—if only, as in

---

*It is deeply ironic that the greatest fighter of all time, Muhammad Ali, should be a creature of television. The world's greatest ring artist shamelessly sold himself like any sponsor's product. Liebling died in 1963, before Ali won the heavyweight title for the first time. Wherever he is now, he must be terribly chagrined by it all.

the case of most of us, by the fewest of dollars—would revel in our lunches of greasy steak sandwiches and submarines or glazed doughnuts and soda pop bought from the corner store.

On this street was an empty lot, covered with broken glass, garbage, and the occasional dead body of an animal, where one could usually find members of the Fifth and South Streets gang. And it was on this lot that I saw the greatest fistfight of my life, better than any professional fight I have seen before or since. On a certain day in my youth, Frank White, the warlord of the Seventh Street gang, and Tabu, the warlord of Fifth and South Streets gang, fought in that strange ring for the championship of the streets.

It was an extremely hot August day in my twelfth or thirteenth summer. I was loafing in the playground with the boys of the Fifth and South Streets gang. Some of them were playing basketball; most were simply lounging in the shade, listening to R&B on a transistor radio, drinking wine or soda pop, and trying to beat the heat. Tabu was sitting on a bench playing checkers. He loved playing checkers more than anyone else I knew except the old men who played on the front steps of a house on Fairhill Street. Tabu and his opponents always played by the "touch a man, move a man" rule, just as the old men did, which meant that these games were the fastest ever witnessed on a board. Tabu liked me a great deal and this was certainly a curious thing because I had little merit or influence among the boys; I was simply one of the fellows who hung around the fringes. He had a great deal of respect for my intelligence (even in those days I was known for being a bookish boy), which I thought surprising since virtually no one else did. It was an even exchange since I had a great deal of respect for the way he used his dukes. It was a nice friendship; he always called me Slim because he did not like the name Gerald, and I always called him Tabu because I never knew any other name to call him.

Seeing Tabu in my mind's eye, it is hard to imagine that he was the warlord, the best fighter in the gang. He surely had the physique—he was lean and muscular and as hard as steel. But he did not seem to have the temperament. He loved to play basketball and checkers and talk to girls and laugh. He never seemed angry enough with anyone about anything to want to fight. Yet he did fight quite well and quite often and with a bewildering sense of humor. Whenever he had an opponent—whether in a street fight, basketball game, or checkers match—at an insurmountable disadvantage, he would shout gleefully, "It's game time and your ass is mine!"

On this hot afternoon, word began to spread through the playground that the Seventh Street gang was "coming down strong" looking to kick the asses of the "punk motherfuckers of Fifth and South." The air was suddenly electric with excitement. The boys, once assured that this was no idle rumor, gathered their weapons and massed themselves and began moving out of the playground to meet the enemy. I tagged along mostly to watch. Midway up Fairhill Street we could see the crush of black youthful humanity coming to greet us. We had about fifty members and Seventh Street easily had sixty or seventy. I thought we were outmanned—so much so that, discretion being the better part of valor, it was time to consider beating a hasty retreat. No one else felt that way. When the two gangs did meet face to face, there was no violence. The leaders from both groups began to talk, and it was decided, surprisingly, to declare a truce, so that both gangs could unite against the Thirteenth and Fitzgerald Streets gang, the massively manned nemesis of both the Fifth and South and the Seventh Streets gangs. There was some disagreement as to who was to have leadership over this combination and it was decided to have the warlord from each group fight to settle the matter.

The rules of the fight were simple: no kicking, no head-butting, no hitting below the belt, no wrestling, and no rounds. Both boys were to fight until one of them quit. Whoever quit would be the loser.

I did not know Frank White personally but I knew his reputation. He too was lean and muscular but much taller than Tabu. And he had a face that indicated that behind his fire-red eyes was one of the most evil dispositions in all of South Philadelphia. He had a lemon-yellow complexion with freckles and a thick ring of scar tissue around his neck from a knife wound. It was rumored that he had once broken a grown man's jaw in a fistfight. Another rumor was that he had killed a boy in a knife fight and had beaten the rap in court. He looked grim and merciless.

We all sojourned to the empty lot and the principals removed their shirts and shadow-boxed a bit to warm up. It was such a hot day that both boys were sweating heavily even before they faced each other. White had very quick hands and a fluid motion; he looked very, very good to me—much better than Tabu, whose facial expression did not even seem to absorb the gravity of the situation. He was smiling and jocular about all of this. I was afraid for him.

The fight started with both boys exchanging evenly; but White soon pulled out in front, using the advantage of his height and reach. He threw rapid-fire left jabs, then followed up with straight rights and left hooks. He was like a smooth-running machine and he never varied his pattern. First, Tabu's nose started to bleed, then his mouth, then little welt marks started to form around his eyes. Tabu was scoring with punches, too. But his hands were not as fast so he did not land as often. After twenty minutes, both boys were so drenched in sweat that their trousers were soaked and they were nearly exhausted. It was surely surprising that neither passed out from sunstroke. At this point, Tabu was losing badly. Suddenly, he crouched very low as if he were going to spring or lunge a punch. That seemed a sure sign of utter desperation. He stayed in this position for a minute and allowed White to hit with a jab, then another and another. After throwing the left a half-dozen times without missing, White predictably threw a tremendous straight right; it did not miss, although White afterward probably wished that it had. It was the punch that Tabu was waiting for; he timed it so that as the punch was thrown, he jerked out of his crouch and thrust his head forward like a bull charging. The blow landed on the top of Tabu's skull and White immediately gave a howl of pain. He had either jammed his knuckles on Tabu's hard head or broken his hand. In either case, his right hand was useless. Tabu screamed out, "It's game time and your ass is mine!" Tabu swarmed all over White but the fight went on for another twenty minutes before White, after having been struck so vicious a blow on his chest that a surface blood vessel ruptured, finally sat down on the filthy ground and looked up at Tabu and shook his head. The warlord of Seventh Street had quit. It was Tabu's finest hour; he was the undisputed king of the hill insofar as we poor black boys of South Philadelphia were concerned.

As I grew older and no longer hung around with the neighborhood boys, I wondered what had happened to Tabu. About four years ago, when I visited Philadelphia, I learned the news. I was in a record store called 3rd Street Jazz looking through the stacks when suddenly I heard someone call out, "Hey, Slim. Where you been?" I knew the voice right away. I turned and saw Tabu—but what a change from the street days! He was wearing a three-piece suit, carrying a very expensive-looking attaché case, sporting a neatly trimmed goatee and mustache, and looked for all the world like the landed gentry of black folk. Was this the same person who had once been my hero back on Fairhill Street? He told me what he had been doing: he had a degree from Temple University and worked as an administrator for a municipal agency. He was going to law school at night and contemplated finishing that degree in two more years. He was married, with, as he put it, "four beautiful daughters," all of whom had African names that sounded like pure poetry but which I could not recall the moment after he had spoken them. I was never good at remembering poetry. He still had a good physique but he was beginning to develop a paunchy middle. He told me he played racquetball at a health spa he belonged to. He seemed almost sleek with success.

"I had to quit the gang in order to get serious," he said. "I had to stop fighting. You know, some of those cats are still out there. Into the dope thing. Been to prison. And still into the gang thing. Man, they never grew up. Just want to keep street fighting all their lives. You can't go around fist-fighting forever. You got to become a man and put that stuff behind you. I just decided to grow up."

We talked about jazz quite a bit. He had become a big fan of "the music." We were discussing Miles Davis's *Sketches of Spain.* Tabu shook his head in admiration: "It's the baddest album out there. Man, it's like Miles telling the other trumpet players, 'It's game time and your ass is mine.'" I smiled. Some things never really change.

As I said in the beginning, this was not intended to be an unhappy story about a ghetto boy. It is, in fact, an American success story of the most familiar sort. The lesson of the story is this: Tabu, unlike those sweet Sugar Rays (Robinson, Seales, and Leonard), is the only fighter I have ever heard of who was smart enough to quit before, as Pete Townshend put it, he got old.

Ringworld

I. YESTERDAY

When there is a touch of true symbolism,
it is not of the nature of a ruin or
a remains embedded in the present structure,
it is rather an archaic reminiscence.

—D. H. Lawrence, *Apocalypse*

Jeff Chandler, former World Boxing Association bantamweight champion, received, at the end of 1984, the sort of bad news that men in his profession are apt to expect if not to accept. Nineteen eighty-four had not been a good year for him; indeed, it had true Orwellian overtones or, at least, must have reminded him of those blues lyrics that said, "If it wasn't for bad luck, I wouldn't have no luck at all." He lost his title in the summer by being thoroughly thrashed before a national television audience by Richard Sandoval. The loss was particularly galling for two reasons: first, he was so completely outgunned and overmatched by Sandoval that one would not have expected him to win the title again in a rematch; and, second, he had just been referred to as "possibly one of the greatest bantamweights in history" in a cover story on him that appeared in the July 1983 issue of *The Ring*. But in this case injury was added to insult when he required eye surgery this fall for the removal of a cataract and was told by his doctor that he could promptly forget all ideas about avenging his defeat and regaining his title, because, as a result of the surgery, he could never even wipe his eye very hard again, much less fight in a ring. He joins a growing list of professional boxers who, in recent years, either have had to quit because of eye injuries or were unsuccessful in attempting comebacks after eye surgery: Sugar Ray Seales, Sugar Ray Leonard, Earnie Shavers, Harold Weston, and Hilmer Kenty among others. Stories of fighters being beaten to death in the ring give the general public the impression that brain damage and death are the most common and feared injuries for fighters. Actually, relatively few fighters die in the ring, and few are incapacitated mentally as a result of fighting or, at least, no more mentally incompetent than before they entered the ring. Most *do* suffer some eye damage; there are more than a few ex-pugs running around with poor vision or no vision at all because of fists or wayward thumbs thrown their way during fighting days.

In connection with this business about fighters with poor vision, there is a very interesting story about a half-blind fighter who had a half-decent career, better than half decent, really, since he fought for a title, an opportunity few fighters ever procure. (Of course, stories like this abound in prizefighting, a sport that is extremely self-conscious of its own mythology, nearly as much as baseball.) Gypsy Joe Harris, flamboyant welterweight and middleweight of the sixties, fought for many years although he was entirely blind in one eye. He memorized the eye chart in the doctor's office of the Pennsylvania State Athletic Commission, so, ironically, his blind eye was certified as having perfect vision. Harris was good enough, with his one eye, to become a leading contender and even to make the cover of *Sports Illustrated.* I remember as a boy once watching Harris play pool in a pool hall in North Philadelphia. He was well-known for doing his most strenuous training in the pool halls and taverns and cabarets of North Philadelphia. *That,* more than the blind eye, proved to be his undoing when he fought for the championship. A group of us South Philadelphia boys risked life and limb by leaving our neighborhood to go to a North Philadelphia gym to watch Harris train for a fight. We had all decided on an effective and simple course of action should we run into any of the brutally tough North Philly gangs: "haul ass" like Olympic sprinters and pray that we could dodge bullets faster than the enemy could fire them at us. Gang warfare was no longer an engagement involving chains and rocks; knives, pistols, and rifles were the rule. And every gang in the city wanted to make its reputation by "copping a few homicides." When we arrived at the gym, we were told that Harris was in the pool hall down the street. We were, of course, instantly and indelibly impressed when we met him. Probably the ambience of the pool hall, with the radio blaring and all the old and young black men standing around, made a deeper imprint on us than if we had seen him sweating through a workout in the gym. He was dressed in a fancy-cut suit of sharkskin, I think, which was a popular style in those days, wore several expensive rings, had a grandly expensive car parked in

front of the place, and a very lovely woman sitting behind him as he ran balls
with an amazing proficiency and an affected nonchalance. (This remembrance is admittedly at variance with what I knew of Harris at the time and
what I read about him many years later. He was noted for never being
dressed up, for having a fairly plain girlfriend, for being a man of simple,
working-class taste. Yet this is how I remember seeing him and I cannot help
but wonder if I have collapsed the memory with that of another fighter or
perhaps another famous black entertainer. Harris was a pool fanatic; that
much I recall correctly.) His bald head, which the public found so menacing,
was covered by a slight film of sweat. He did not look like a boxer but rather
like a street-smart hustler. Harris regaled the crowd for a time with a bit of
bombastic rhetoric about what he would do to his opponent, which could be
reductively but safely captured by the words: "I'm gonna kick the motherfucker's ass." I have never heard any good fighter speak about his opponent
in any other way. Shortly after, Harris left with the very beautiful woman
on his arm.

One of the old-timers, cigarette dangling, hard-conked hair, who remained
in the hall after many others had cleared out following Harris's departure
began to shoot some pool using Harris's cuestick. He started muttering to
himself about how he knew Ezzard Charles in Chicago back during the days
when "that boy was a good fighter. Yeah, that boy got himself all messed
with the leeches and the bitches. Gypsy Joe's shit is gettin' ragged just like
Charles's. If he don't watch out, he might wind up like Charles, needin' to
pass water and without a pot to piss in." None of us boys knew how Ezzard
Charles, great heavyweight contender of the fifties who had glorious encounters with Joe Louis, Jersey Joe Walcott, and Rocky Marciano, wound up, and
we surely did not care. We knew only that, whatever Charles's past, we
certainly liked Harris's present immensely. Among the boys who were there
was a very, very young Jeff Chandler. Perhaps he was more impressed than
any of us.

I do not know what happened to Gypsy Joe Harris, but I do remember that
a year or two after his retirement a Philadelphia sports columnist wrote a
story telling how Harris needed a job. A few years after that I heard that he
had been working in a meat-packing place for a time but had been laid off.
He was, I was told, less than slick.

There was a black street gang in South Philadelphia known as the Fifth
and South Streets gang, which could never be found on the intersection of
Fifth Street and South Street. In fact, while growing up, I do not recall
anything being on the corner of Fifth and South Streets; even the Jewish
merchants who operated cheap clothing stores in that area for years had
boarded up their shops and escaped to the middle-class nirvana of Mount
Airy. That corner seemed to be not only lonely and blighted, not simply
sucked and drained, but fully charged with a profound cosmic desertion.
Perhaps this was exacerbated by the fact that a mere two blocks away at

Sixth and Lombard stood the oldest black church in America—the grand Mother Bethel A.M.E. Church founded by Richard Allen in 1794. There seemed to be a haunting, almost Manichaeistic contrast between the two locations: the mighty monument of the black urban past and the ghostly emptiness of the black urban present in strange and uneasy proximity.

The boys of the Fifth and South Streets gang could be found some six blocks away on the corner of Fifth and Carpenter, in the glass-strewn main parking lot of the Southwark Plaza projects. I can remember when those projects were built and opened and when the use of the word "plaza" did not sound quite like a shabby stab at something parodically grandiose. The buildings, when they were new, were nice, livable quarters, better than what most of the people in the neighborhood had been accustomed to living in. Times change, as Bob Dylan once noted, and buildings of this sort deteriorate rapidly when occupied by people of this sort. Nowadays, I suppose the animals in the Philadelphia Zoo live in more comfort and less fear than the folk in these highrise projects.

The Fifth and South Streets gang was a very inept outfit, spending most of its time running away from the bigger and stronger gangs in the area: the Thirteenth and Fitzwater Streets gang, Seventh Street gang, and Twenty-third and Tasker Streets gang. Part of the source of the ineptitude was the very small size of the gang; also, internal dissension splintered the gang into at least three separate entities. Third, and most important, was the gang's sheer inability to do what a street gang is organized to do: terrorize those who are outside the fold. I think that during all the years that street gangs were a potent crime force in Philadelphia, the Fifth and South Streets gang may have killed one or two boys, a horrible and horrifying achievement, yet quite insignificant compared to what many other gangs were able to do in this regard. But these boys were no different from the boys in the other gangs. In this ragtag outfit, the boys drank cheap red wine, sniffed glue in brown paper bags, blowing them in and out like a bellows, played basketball endlessly, read comic books, played pinball, and spent the time when they were absolutely bored fighting each other. It struck me even as a child, watching the corner boys from the position of outsider, that they seemed both utterly bored and inexcusably lazy, a most volatile combination.

Two boys whom I remember very well from this gang are TM and LS, partly because I had the dubious distinction of having fistfights with both of them while in elementary school and losing to both of them rather badly, and partly because as young adults they made the front page of every newspaper in the city. LS and another man, both junkies, murdered and robbed two elderly Jews one morning as they were walking down the steps of their synagogue. The booty amounted to ten dollars, which I think came to a ratio of about ten cents for every year of their sentences. TM was a fugitive on a bench warrant; in other words, he failed to appear in court for an outstanding charge while out on bail. The police trapped him in his girlfriend's apartment in the Southwark Plaza projects. In the shootout that ensued, TM killed one policeman but was, quite miraculously, taken alive. He was given a life sentence plus fifty years. In the fourth grade, these two boys were among my best friends; by the seventh grade, they were two of the most vicious boys in the neighborhood; by the eighth grade, they were no longer going to school and were sniffing several bags of glue a day; by the ninth grade, they were heroin addicts and were robbing passersby at knife point. Despite these other activities, they continued to fight with their gang on all occasions upon which they were called. This is an old story that everyone knows; that is, everyone knows the tiresome plot without really comprehending the symbolism. The tale of the city's poor boys is a tough, hermeneutically inscrutable text, after all.

It is out of this cauldron of violence and inertia, depravity and bravado, distorted masculinity and strange fellowship that emerged Jeff Chandler and, indeed, nearly every other good fighter from South Philadelphia currently working his trade. Chandler fought for the Fifth and South Streets gang; Frank (the Animal) Fletcher, a fading middleweight contender, fought with the Seventh Street gang; Matthew Saad Muhammad, known in his youth as Matthew Franklin, and light-heavyweight champion of the world in the late seventies and early eighties, fought for the Thirteenth and Fitzwater Streets gang; and Tyrone Everett, the amazingly talented light-weight who was killed by his girlfriend several years ago, fought for the Twenty-third and Tasker Streets gang.

It is the easiest thing in the world to say that professional boxing ought to be banned because it is savage, corrupt, and a dangerous health threat to the men who participate in it. Yet this moralistic rage of the righteous misses a few major points: First, to ban boxing would not prevent the creation of boxers since *that* process, *that* world would remain intact. And what are we to do with these men who know how to do nothing but fight? I suppose we can continue to lock them in our jails and in our ghettos, out of our sight and untouched by our regard. That, in the end, is precisely what those who wish to ban boxing really want to do: not to safeguard the lives of the men who must do this work but simply to sweep one excessively distasteful and inexplicable sin of bourgeois culture under the rug. Second, those who wish to ban boxing know that they will simply condemn those men to surer deaths by not legally recognizing the sport. Boxing banned will simply become what it was in eighteenth- and nineteenth-century England, a very popular underground, *totally* unregulated sport. Finally, I think it is fitting to have professional boxing in America as a moral eyesore: the sport and symbol of human waste in a culture that worships its ability to squander. And, after all, these men are selling their ability to the highest bidder, getting whatever the market will bear. Professional boxing is capitalism's psychotic vision. Or, as Jeff Chandler said when he quit being an amateur, after his third fight, "If I have to do this for a living, I'd rather get paid, any day."

II. TODAY

Strength and violence are lonely gods. . . .
—Albert Camus, "The Minotaur, or Stopping in Oran"

Can you do the jerk?
Then watch me work.
Can you do the fly?
Then watch me try.
Bring it up. . . .
—James Brown, "Bring it Up"

[handwritten marginalia: What nonsense. Seems to enjoy throwing out meaningless statements to be controversial. People are always good at what they enjoy doing. ? ! ?]

One of the ultimate observations of the ultimate absurdity of the way of things in this world is not that most people are not very good at what they do. In this case we might all imagine doing something, *anything* well enough to achieve a reassuring uncritical and uncriticizable anonymity, the counterpane of slouching invisibility. Rather it is that most people not only are not very good at what they do but are not very interesting or interested in the doing. It is bad enough when our courage and imagination fail in the moment of truth; then we become nothing more than limping lumps of mediocrity. We experience far worse when our standards and ideals and expectations rise up to meet us more than halfway in our slide.

At any local boxing show, such as the one I attended during Christmas while I was in Dallas, rather fancifully entitled "Boxarama"—which, of course, brings to mind some fanciful device of Hollywood during the early 1960s called Cinerama—one expects to see more than a few fighters who would bring no disgrace upon themselves if they quietly retired from the ring and sought another line of work. The true boxing fan shows up at such cards as this in hopes that the wizardry of a Muhammad Ali or a Ray Leonard, the intensity of a Roberto Duran, or the technical skill of a Marvelous Marvin Hagler might be seen in some inchoate form in a young man at an early stage in his career. There is a sheer delightful excitement that is matched by few experiences in this life when one sees potential greatness in a performer. Inevitably, at most local boxing matches, these hopes are dashed rather rudely and the true boxing fan settles back in his chair in a state of relaxed, even cozy boredom, enjoying with a certain relishing and cultivated indifference the sublime differential between what is not there and what is.

A few years ago one would not have expected to find much local boxing in Dallas or in the state of Texas for that matter, except possibly in the areas where Mexicans are dominant, they being traditional lovers and practitioners of the sport. There was not much support for boxing in this state, where football was and still is the provincial obsession. Boxing, just as recently as the middle seventies, was seen by Texans as a sport of the East Coast or West Coast, where thugs and immigrants grew in bunches. One had to go to a city like, say, Philadelphia to see local prizefights, a city where, as heavyweight Randall Cobb once described it, "even the winos know how to jab." Some changes have occurred in Texas in the last six to eight years: First, several boxers from the Lone Star State have achieved national reputations. There are the Curry brothers from Houston; Donald is the current World Boxing Association welterweight champ and Bruce is the former world junior welterweight champ. There is "Rockin'" Robin Blake, current lightweight contender from Levelland; former lightweight champion Ruben Munoz from Dallas; the brilliant, strong, but dangerously psychotic Tony Ayala, middleweight from San Antonio, now in jail serving time for robbing and raping a schoolteacher; and former bantamweight champ Gaby Canizales from Laredo. Texas has produced more than a few good fighters in recent days to live up its past reputation as the state that produced the Galveston Giant, Jack Johnson, the first black heavyweight champ. Also, with the huge influx of northerners and easterners and Mexicans into Texas in the last ten years, an audience has been created for the sport. A sizable swath of the population in the state no longer makes the "hook 'em, Horns" sign as a form of greeting.

The fights took place on a very warm and very rainy evening at a place called the Conquistador Ballroom in the Marriott Market Center, a location better suited for a political fund-raising dinner than an evening of boxing. A fair-sized crowd of 300 or so patrons appeared, including a fair number of women. These women were not simply those who were accompanying boyfriends or husbands, or women who seemed to be groupies, although they were well represented, but rather a good many women who were fight fans—who came out to cheer their favorites as lustily as did the men. Often, women are not taken seriously as true lovers of the sport: they are seen as the adornment on the arm of some man (e.g., the gangster's moll, the politician's mistress), usually wearing a mink coat and fancy jewelry. Or they are symbolically cast as the round girl—the obligatory buxom, scantily clad young woman who walks across the ring after each round during each fight with a card announcing the number of the upcoming round—who becomes the prize in the game itself. In the world of boxing, because fighters are not permitted to have sex during their six weeks of training—"Fucking makes a fighter weak," one trainer once told me—women become, ironically, both the totem and the taboo. Is boxing the psychological quest for the primeval male and his primeval past when the relationship between men and women was imagined to be so much simpler because it was so much clearer? Is boxing the last sport where a man can be an unambiguous hero because the virtues needed for success in this endeavor—the daring, endurance, and heart of the adventurer—are so traditionally and exclusively perceived as male?

Being an outsider and completely unfamiliar with the hometown favorites, I watched the fights with more disinterested curiosity than ardent passion. It is an odd sense of displacement that one has when one cannot root for the local heroes, an essential act of participation for the fan at fights such as these. The crowd, of course, always informed me when the fighters were announced just who the prince of the moment was. I was never in the dark for very long about that. Many of the fighters apparently were from Houston and Tyler but were well received in Dallas nonetheless. The Houston fighters also brought along a sizable contingent of supporters who sat across from me and shouted advice and encouragement to their "homeboys" with an almost evangelical fervor:

"Work the left, Reggie; work the left. Everything off the jab."

"OK, man, beautiful. All night long. Just work the jab all night long."

"Throw that right over the top, Ford. Throw the wild right."

"You's hurting the boy. Go on in. He ain't got nothing."

"Hey, come on, Ray. It ain't nothing but something to do. It ain't nothing but a little work."

"Hurt 'im in the body, man. The boy ain't got no body. Just bust that sucker's ribs."

There were eight fights on the card—originally, it was a ten-fight card, but two were canceled because the fighters did not show up—including two ten-round main events. Of the sixteen fighters only two—Kenneth and Anthony Releford, brothers and both welterweights—displayed enough talent to have any real hope of ever entertaining the possibility of fighting for a title. They each fought a particularly peace-loving, dreadful Mexican fighter who, like a worker with his eyes constantly on the time clock, seemed more interested in collecting a check than in winning the fight. Kenneth stopped his opponent with a powerful right cross in the third round; Anthony stopped his with a barrage of blows in the second. For the amount of resistance that they put up, the Mexican fighters might have done the crowd a favor and called it a day in the first round. They did provide the one service of sticking around long enough so that the Releford brothers could show the crowd a small sampling of their wares. I hope those men will get a chance to fight boxers in the top ten of their division before the end of the year; they are nearly ready for that.

The last fight of the evening was the most interesting because it struck me as the most dismal and distressing. It was a contest between two heavyweights—the big boys are always saved as the highlight of any boxing card—a bald-headed, heavy-muscled Trinidadian named John "Young Duran" Williams and a white fighter from Tyler named Mickey "Rapid Fire" Prior. Williams, whose nickname of "Young Duran" was the mystery of the evening since he did not resemble the renowned champion from Panama in physical appearance or in fighting style, nearly dwarfed Prior in both height and weight. Indeed, despite the fact that both men were heavyweights and weighed over 200 pounds, the fight resembled more an encounter between a heavyweight and a middleweight.

Prior lived up to his nickname and started out very fast, landing a barrage of punches to the head and body of Williams, who simply stood in the corner and absorbed a fearful beating. It would have been a favor to the humanity of the fans, even if they were not aware of it, for the fight to have ended in the first round. Unfortunately, Williams survived the round despite nearly buckling to the canvas twice. From the second round through the tenth and final round, the fight became a very perverse joke. Williams began to land very ponderous rights to the head of Prior, who continued his relentless attack, constantly pinning Williams in the corner and pummeling him furiously. But it became very apparent to me, despite the crowd's vociferous cries of approval for all the "heavy action," that neither of these men knew the first thing about boxing. Round after round, as the crowd screamed with delight, these two men simply bashed each other. In one round it would appear that Williams was finished, but in the next Prior would seem out on his feet. By the sixth round, the drubbing that each man had so primitively absorbed became apparent to the eye of the observer. Prior's mouth was pouring blood like a faucet, so much blood that Williams's white trunks were now a solid pink. Williams, on the other hand, had thick swellings all over his face. I sat in agitated boredom. It was a terrible, terrible fight. There was nothing to cheer in this blood-letting, and ironically, despite all the punches that were being thrown, this fight, because both men were so incompetent, was the most tedious event of the evening. I thought it would never end. The Mexicans earlier on the card had the right idea: it was better to go through the motions of the work and get the check than to get beat up for the benefit and entertainment of, well, of us, the audience. We did not merit witnessing two human beings putting out so much in such an undignified yet strangely poignant way in return for so little. When the fight ended, the audience was on its feet cheering these two hapless, thoroughly whipped, completely fatigued young men. When the fight was declared a draw, usually an unpopular decision with most fight crowds, the patrons cheered again. I suppose the crowd did not see the decision in the same way I did: a draw, it seemed, simply announced that instead of having one winner, which the fighters and the fans always demand, there were two losers. The decision seemed an elaborate con; both men were severely beaten and both now had nothing to show for it. Alas, it never fails to happen to me these days that I am always discomforted by watching some prizefight, that before it is all over I am asking myself why these men are doing this and why I am here. And I must face the ugly fact about myself that I am here because I like boxing more than I dislike it, and I suppose those men are in the ring because they like it, too, and, more important, like me, need to like it. Boxing seems to teach the same lesson to me in recent years, the same very unkind lesson to which I have not hardened myself: The world is either denigrating self-surrender and denial (the used-up Mexican fighters) or it is stupid, pointless affirmation (Williams versus Prior). And why not deny and surrender when the terms of affirmation offer nothing very much better? If the world has taken the best, why not let it take the rest, as Billie Holiday used to sing. And what are those like the

Releford brothers but the illusions that allow us, as Samuel Beckett writes, to go on. Or as I heard an old black preacher once shout to his congregation: "When God's on fire, you can't stand the light; but when the devil's on fire, you love the warmth."

As I was leaving the ballroom I thought about the days when I was a boy and would go to the Uptown Theatre and see all the black R&B stars. My favorite was James Brown. And I used to love it when the M.C. would announce Brown's appearance by saying in a stuttering way: "Can your...I mean, can your...I wanna know, can your heart stand it?" I remembered the days of the corner boys fighting in vacant lots and playgrounds, saying to one another to bolster each other's courage on days of heavy weather: "Your heart gotta stand it. You gotta stand up to the shit and take it like a man."

I had forgotten my umbrella. I realized when I reached the exit door that it was still under my seat. I walked back for it in a hurry; my wife was waiting for me outside. Standing beside the ring, pouring sweat in tiny rivulets was John Williams, the Trinidadian, talking to a small collection of the faithful. He looked disgusted and in a very heavy accent he was telling those who would listen that he thought he had won the fight. He had some sympathetic ones heeding his words. "I had more heart," he said quietly. "I proved I got more heart than the other guy. I had more left at the end." I picked up my umbrella and stopped beside the fighter for about twenty seconds, then turned and departed abruptly. I did not want to hear it. I had heard it all before, long ago. I knew he had more left at the end. I knew *his* heart could stand it. But after all these years of watching fights, I was beginning to wonder how much *I* had left, how much *my* heart could stand it.

The Grace of Slaughter:
Joyce Carol Oates's
On Boxing

Boxing ain't the noblest of the arts.

—Middleweight champion Harry Greb, whose loss to Tiger Flowers in 1926 permitted the first black ever to hold the middleweight title

God didn't make the chin to be punched.

—Ray Arcel, boxing trainer who numbered among his students the legendary Roberto Duran

I. "THE PANTING PURSUIT OF DANGER..."

At that time [Georges] Carpentier was only fourteen and a half years old and I, twenty-one years old. So his first fight was with Georges Salmon at the Café de Paris, Maison Laffitte, and he was making good until the eleventh round; then he blew up. That was really because he was inexperienced on the square circle...but again he was knocked down several times after the tenth round, so I said to Deschamps [Carpentier's manager] to stop it. He said no. So I jumped into the ring and stopped it, picking little Georges up in my arms, and took him to his corner amidst the cheers of the crowd. He was always game to the toes.

—Black American fighter Bob Scanlon recounting the beginning of his friendship with French champion Georges Carpentier

1

Joyce Carol Oates's *On Boxing* seems a sort of culmination or at least a reexamination of several ideas she expressed in her early novel *With Shuddering Fall* (1964). That book, exemplifying so well both the vices and virtues of a first novel by a talented writer, dealt with a character named Shar Rule (the name itself speaks volumes), who is a professional racing-car driver. The similarity among a jockey, a boxer, a racing-car driver, and a bullfighter as far as the nature of their individuality, the brinkmanship of their sadistic/masochistic occupations, the charged, exaggerated mythic version of their masculinity, and the troubling and troubled voyeurism they incite is surely clear enough and is precisely what attracts Oates to athletics: wrath, the ambivalent, oxymoronic iconography of masculine toughness as male suffering, and the pure anxiety inherent in the ritual of male slaughter. She wrote passages like these:

> Max could feel the beauty of Shar's experience in his imagination, while Shar felt it in his very body. At a certain point the speed became his body: he was one with it....
>
> From time to time, he had toyed with the idea that spectators did not really come to see drivers be killed, as most people thought, nor did they come—as Max told him—because they wanted to share in the skill and triumph; they came to share the speed, the danger, the occasional deaths—with exultation, maybe, but with something more than that to force themselves into the men who represented them down on the track. . . . They gave up their identities to risk violence, but they were always cheated because the violence, when it came, could not touch them.

One can see it is not a very far distance for her to travel to this closure:

> One of the paradoxes of boxing is that the viewer inhabits a consciousness so very different from that of the boxer as to suggest a counter-world. "Free" will, "sanity," "rationality," our characteristic modes of consciousness, are irrelevant, if not detrimental, to boxing in its most extraordinary moments. Even as he disrobes himself ceremonially in the ring, the great boxer must disrobe himself of both reason and instinct's caution as he prepares to fight.

Boxing and auto racing are not simply unintelligible; they are anti-intelligible, activities akin to vision quests on the part of the men who participate in them. (Boxing is "obliquely akin to those severe religions in which the individual is both 'free' and determined," Oates writes.) They wish to find their spiritual selves by being in an activity that is relentlessly, ruthlessly physical, but they wish to prove their goodness (i.e., their worth) in an activity that is so self-centered yet so self-annihilating that it can be considered only evil. George S. Bernard, a Catholic priest, argued that very point—the iniquity of being a boxer—in his *The Morality of Boxing,* and it seems a reasonable assertion because boxing poses, on a metaphysical level, such an uncomplex ethical proposition: Beat your opponent until you have weakened him and then, when he is weak and helpless, beat him all the more fiercely in a contrived contest of fictive grievances that prides itself on being without mercy. The spectators are not simply a world apart, they are a morality apart; for the sports of boxing and auto racing turn morality on its head by permitting acts to take place that are so dangerous (high-speed racing and hitting another without malice and not in self-defense) that they are banned outside of certain sacred spaces. It is not simply the thrill of "taboo breaking," as Oates states in *On Boxing,* that makes boxing attractive; it is the fact that the audience recognizes boxing as an attack, a frontal assault upon the very nature of taboo. The death of one of the participants is often wished so that the harsh justice of the taboo itself is made not intelligible but less a cause of distress, more rich as a result of having been empowered by human sacrifice. So death hovers near a certain masculine drama that for the audience may make death frightening but will also make it alluring, electric because it hovers so close to a pointless, intelligible, nearly existential, and very simple, even vulgar excellence. As another character in Oates's novel expresses himself:

> Why should anything be safe?...
>   Look at them all, Shar and the other drivers—their hands all blisters and eyes burnt, cars about ready to explode or fall apart—wheels, axles, anything, but they love it all the way! A man puts in years out on the track—in ten minutes he gets that much living out of it.

And in the later book:

> If boxing is a sport it is the most tragic of all sports because more than any other human activity it consumes the very excellence it displays—its drama is this very consumption...The punishment—to the body, the brain, the spirit—a man must endure to become even a moderately good boxer is inconceivable to most of us whose idea of personal risk is largely ego-related or emotional.

Shar, like a tragic young boxer, dies young, in a literal flame of glory (his car crashes in his attempt to go too fast), consumed by the very instrument that made him great. What is it in sport generally that appeals but that universal morbidity of the instant tragedy of youth used up? (Even in less dangerous sports such as baseball, one feels a great loss when a pitcher like Tom Seaver retires; the golden arm that once brought him fame now all used up by the very act, the very motion that the arm used to achieve its fame in the first place, the "unnatural act," as former Oakland A's pitcher Mike Norris called pitching. One wonders if it is only in sex and athletics that we demand the "unnatural act" as a display of skill and a presentation of excitation.) "All athletes age rapidly but none so rapidly and so visibly as the boxer," writes Oates. Yet their rapid aging is very much akin to that of those illicit and disreputable members of society to whom they are constantly compared: prostitutes. And while all athletes are viewed with a certain distinct distrust and disdain that, I think, arises from the immense and intense adulation they generate, no athlete is held quite as lowly as the boxer. British novelist and former fighter Johnny Morgan, in *The Square Jungle,* constantly makes the analogy between boxers and whores. And in Roman times, as historian Michael Grant points out, gladiators were placed in the same class as women for hire. To sell one's body in performance in order to give pleasure to others ultimately saps the body, perhaps because the body's integrity has been denied, perhaps because the body is simply stupefied by its inability to be thrilled by the thrilling anymore.

At one point in *With Shuddering Fall,* after a race Shar wins by performing a maneuver that kills another driver, two characters shout at each other: "Shar is filled with life!" "Shar is filled with death!" and perhaps it is this essential ambiguity that surrounds the prizefighter as much as it does the racing-car driver that Oates finds so absorbing: Is he filled with life? Or is he an angel of death, he who by his life says that life is impossible, that only the pursuit of death is real?

2

There is no sport that, like [boxing], promotes the spirit of aggression in the same measure, demands determination quick as lightning, educates the body for steel-like versatility. If two young people fight out a difference of opinion with their fists, it is no more brutal than if they do so with a piece of ground iron....But above all, the young and healthy boy has to learn to be beaten. This, of course, may appear wild in the eyes of our present spiritual fighters. But the Folkish State has not the task of breeding a colony of peaceful aesthetes and physical degenerates.

—Adolf Hitler

Hitler liked boxing because it resisted rationality, because its participants were forced to resist rationality. Perhaps that is why many writers have been attracted to it as well (although this difference must be understood: that Hitler worshipped boxing for its psychotic potential in much the same way a murderer worships the purity of his mayhem; Hitler's love of boxing was simply the display of a very depraved infantile taste, but it should serve as a sufficient warning to all who find boxing a seduction). Unlike football, basketball, and especially baseball, boxing cannot be understood through numbers. Its statistics mean nothing; a boxer's record tells no story of the achievements of a career. As Robert Coover showed in his brilliant baseball novel, *The Universal Baseball Association, Inc., J. Henry Waugh, Prop.,* baseball's story can be unfolded through the maze of the purity of its mathematics. Boxing's change of rules in the late nineteenth century, which transformed it from a bareknuckle sport of indeterminate length to a gloved sport of timed rounds and rest periods and eventually bouts of a finite length, was the only concession that boxing made to rationality, to the science and technology of the day. Those changes made boxing more palatable to modern audiences by rendering it more systematic and schematic but only better to exemplify and symbolize the irrationality of the Spenserian struggle of existence. Boxing can be understood only through story: the oral tradition of eyewitnesses or the journalistic narratives of reporters. It is a misnomer to call boxing a science. Boxing does not seek knowing, a truth in its action. It does not seek to explain nature in the way baseball and football can and do. It is, in fact, an action that is meant to be nature itself. Boxing is always seeking its text (like Ishmael Reed's "jes grew") and the ambiguity of the magnitude of its tales. Boxing is anti-science. It is our ancient epic sung to honor a misty past of slaves and warrior-kings and the personification of brute force.

There is an obvious similarity between Oates's *On Boxing* and Roland Barthes's famous essay "The World of Wrestling," indeed, a series of similarities of such a strong nature that one might say that Barthes's essay begat Oates's book, not simply inspired it, but actually provided the method and language to make it possible. To say this is to pay tribute to Oates's work, to its savvy and cunning, by acknowledging that it can be placed side by side with Barthes's paradigmatic essay. Oates's book is the first on the sport of boxing (and there have been many written, of various quality) that has, consciously I believe, emulated Barthes or a Barthes-like approach. The photos, which comment on and supplement the text without pulling the reader into the worlds of biography or history, into individual personalities or social movements, are certainly something that Barthes would have done had he written a book on boxing. The photos suggest a pure world of boxing inhabited only by boxers. "Boxing is not a metaphor for life but a unique, closed, self-referential world," writes Oates. Naturally, in one sense, this is a fiction: for the boxer's world is something quite other than a world of himself and others like him or simply the world of his exploits. (And to talk of a boxer occupying a "world" brings to mind the question Amiri Baraka asked many years ago about the title of a jazz musician's album: Does the boxer really have a world or does he simply occupy a very traditional and related room in a masculine complex? Is he next door to the gloried discipline of the Marine or perhaps the psychosis of the street-corner gang leader?) Oates so powerfully evokes this world, this fiction that the work does not explicate or justify boxing in the end but actually *summons* it forth. Oates wishes to do for boxing and the boxer what Barthes says the wrestler himself does for wrestling and for himself (which may explain why there have been fewer books written on professional wrestling than on professional boxing): make boxing an intelligible spectacle. In this regard, Oates is the true deconstructionist; Barthes is simply a reporter describing a sport that deconstructs itself, whose meaning is self-evident. Of course, boxing can be deconstructed like wrestling, like any combat sport (when will someone tackle Bruce Lee and Mas Oyama's *This Is Karate*?); indeed, boxing is a sport that makes its need and its enticement to be deconstructed, to be decoded in some wizardly fashion, so obvious as to be nearly one of its conceits. ("That no other sport can elicit such *theoretical* anxiety," writes Oates, "lies at the heart of boxing's fascination for the writer."

Claptrap

Barthes writes (in one of the few instances in his essay that he mentions boxing) that "a boxing match is a story which is constructed before the eyes of the spectator." Oates writes: "Each boxing match is a story — a unique and highly condensed drama without words." Barthes argues that "wrestling is the spectacle of excess," that that is, in fact, its virtue; Oates says that boxing is excess because it violates the taboo against violence, that as a public spectacle "it is akin to pornography" (pornographic films and stage acts, I assume she means), which, I might add, means that it is, for Oates, one of the theaters in a complex of entertainments of excess. But it is the naturalism of pornography and boxing that in some sense makes them inferior to professional wrestling as excess. As Barthes writes: "[In wrestling] it no longer matters whether the passion is genuine or not. What the public wants is the image of passion, not passion itself." It is the literalness of boxing and pornography that makes them imperfect because it is that literalness, which is so much, in one sense, the expression of the innocence of the child's literalness turned to the willful immorality of the adult's reductionism, that ultimately deadens the senses. Real blood generously displayed reduces the ability to be awed by the sight of blood, just as real sex copiously produced reduces the ability to appreciate the act of sex. It is this naturalism that tends to reduce every fight to being exactly every other fight that boxing as a social phenomenon tries to overcome by insisting that the fighter become a personality. (Naturalism is the horror of anonymity in modern society.) Boxing is, like wrestling, about showmanship. And the greatest showman and boxer in the history of the sport was Muhammad Ali, who made fights something other than what they were; he made them, for both the blacks and the whites who watched them, the metaphors they wished them to be but principally the battle of good against evil, and it is not an accident that boxing's greatest showman was heavily influenced by a professional wrestler, Gorgeous George. Ali made boxing deal with the one moral issue that fascinates Americans: Is a black man good or evil? Which is the same as asking if he is real or not. Oates's and Barthes's discussions reach a certain critical juncture when they discuss almost in complimentary fashion the very essence of sport and naturalistic expression. First, Barthes:

> Wrestling is the only sport which gives such an externalized image of torture. But here again, only the image is involved in the game, and the spectator does not wish for the actual suffering of the contestant; he enjoys only the perfection of the iconography.

And Oates responds:

> Unlike pornography (and professional wrestling) boxing is altogether real: the blood shed, the damage suffered, the pain (usually suppressed or subliminated) are unfeigned. Not for hemophobics, boxing is a sport in which blood becomes quickly irrelevant. The experienced viewer understands that a boxer's bleeding face is probably the least of his worries.

Ali, like the good wrestler, made the audience care about his injuries: first, the issue of whether he could stand pain when he was unpopular and then, later, the issue of whether he was absorbing too much pain when he was popular. Ali made the moral relevance of injuries an issue, perhaps the only fighter to do so in the history of the sport without having to die in the ring. One remembers his fight with Bob Foster because it was the first time he was ever cut across the brow in the ring. The first Norton bout stands out because he suffered a broken jaw, the first Frazier fight because he was knocked down. It is the very fact that professional wrestling does not demand the realism of boxing that makes it a protest against violence. By showing violence as fakery, as parody, as comedy, wrestling reveals an inner wish to say that violence is utterly impossible as a real act, utterly unbearable. Of course, wrestling is only this protest *theoretically,* and in actual fact a good many wrestlers are injured every year. Even faked violence can be dangerous, which makes the contemplation of real violence all the more frightening. Finally, Barthes argues that "in wrestling . . . defeat is not a conventional sign, abandoned as soon as it is understood; it is not an outcome, but quite the contrary, it is a duration, a display, it takes up the ancient myths of public Suffering and Humiliation." And Oates makes nearly an identical observation about boxing: "Boxing is about being hit rather than it is about hitting, just as it is about feeling pain, if not devastating psychological paralysis, more than it is about winning." What is interesting here is that both assert that boxing and wrestling, symbolic violence and naturalistic violence, are not really competitive ventures in the sense that we normally think professional sport is. They are both elaborate statements about withstanding not necessarily to overcome but simply for the reality of enduring. Boxing and wrestling, we learn from Oates and Barthes, are the only activities in modern American and European societies that give us the enactment, the drama of shame without guilt.

Despite its being a text that I think in many challenging ways carries on a dialogue with Barthes's essay, *On Boxing* occupies its own space. It is, to be sure, not the first nonfiction book on the sport to be written by a prominent literary person (although it is the first, to my knowledge, to have been written by a woman). But it is clearly not intended to present the author as George Plimpton (*Shadow-Box*): the bumbling, well-meaning journalist who cannot get out of the way of the stage; nor is it in the guise of Norman Mailer (*The Fight* and other works), the hot male predator, haunted by Hemingway, trying desperately to make the act of writing a book a blood sport. The book is neither bumbling innocence, sham egoism, nor hot competitive drive. The book is, at last, not A. J. Liebling (*The Sweet Science*), the worldly wise intellectual in the low-life jungle. It does not slum or try to show boxing as being picturesque. It celebrates neither inadvertence nor its own prowess. *On Boxing* is a cool book. It is a book about the audience, about the voyeur and what he or she sees at a boxing match and how he or she is, in effect, what he or she sees.

During the past two or three years, quite a few books on boxing have been published, including the autobiographies of trainer Angelo Dundee (his first) and Jake LaMotta (his second), biographies of Joe Louis, Jack Johnson, and Sugar Ray Leonard, a history of bareknuckle prizefighting in America, and an inside look at boxing as a business. It is not my contention that Oates's book is the best of the lot. Which book is the best has a great deal to do with what the reader wishes to know about boxing and the format he or she finds most stimulating. I do believe that *On Boxing* is a quite sophisticated book, possibly one of the most sophisticated books to have been published on the sport. It is the most critically alert.

II. ". . . IS THE PURSUIT OF LIFE ITSELF"

To be a man, the male must be able to face the threat of masculinity within himself by facing it in others like himself.
—Walter Ong

You no longer have to come from the ghetto to know how to fight. People with a good upbringing are now learning to box. They're looking at it as an art, rather than as a kill-or-be-killed type of thing.
—Michael Olajide, middleweight contender

Any man with a good trade isn't about to get knocked on his butt to make a dollar.
—Chris Dundee, boxing promoter

"The referee makes boxing possible." This statement alone may be worth the price of admission, the price of the book. There are, in essence, two types of statements in *On Boxing:* those like the above, which are brilliant and unquestionable, and those like the following: "[Boxing] is the only human activity in which rage can be transposed without equivocation into art," which are brilliant but debatable. Oates's accomplished analysis of the role of the referee explains not only why a fight is bearable but why a fight is actually taking place. The fight is an act of hope, a plea that warring sides, through the active presence of a disinterested but compassionate noncombatant, can be reconciled not only to each other but to the restless, self-destructive nature within ourselves. Prizefighting is about man's preoccupation with trying to live in an adversative Eden, a world that loves and hates him, made by a God who both comforts and ignores. As Oates writes: "Love commingled with hate is more powerful than love. Or hate." With the presence of the referee, modern prizefighting is the irrationality of pure force confronting the humane conscience of the modern world.

The second quotation is a bit problematic; the rage in boxing, after all, is not genuine but rather fictive, and the viewer hardly knows its source or its objective. The boxer himself may not know either. It is the fact that rage in boxing is completely fake in the enactment of the contest itself that makes this statement troublesome. Boxing seems to say that the articulation of real rage in our society is utterly impossible unless, of course, it is utterly pointless, which is what the contrivance of the boxing match means. The true art form of rage is the duel, of which boxing is the modern rationalization: Why fight to the death for honor when one can fight to the maiming for money? And suddenly the burden of masculine expendability as sport and performance fell upon the lower classes. The possible art form of rage (with equivocation) is revolution or rebellion, about the only worthwhile vessels for the obsessions of the poor. Of course, boxing has always been popular — television ratings tell us that — but cover articles such as the one in the British fashion magazine *The Face* and Oates's own piece on Bellows's boxing pictures in *Art and Antiques* lead us to believe that it is fashionable (in other words, hip) in the way that Michael Olajide says it is, although few middle-class persons in their right minds are going to perform such a sport for a living. And if it is fashionable, can the rage (pun intended) possibly be real? On the whole, *On Boxing* is a series of tableaus that offers perhaps some of the most stunning surfaces imaginable about boxing. There are penetrating discussions on machismo, on boxing as the sport that is not a sport, on time and the prize ring.

But while I find Oates's book impressive, it does have its weaknesses. The section on writers and prizefighting, for instance, does not mention one black writer. And it must be remembered that blacks have had an enormous influence on American popular culture through the sport of prizefighting. To be sure, no major black writer has written a full-length treatise, fiction or nonfiction, on boxing, but there have been several important essays produced by the likes of Amiri Baraka, Eldridge Cleaver, Richard Wright, Jervis Anderson, Larry Neal, and others. Also, two of the most important scenes in all of American literature that involve fights were written by blacks: Frederick Douglass's fight with Covey, the slavebreaker, in the 1845 edition of Douglass's *Narrative,* and the Battle Royal scene in Ralph Ellison's *Invisible Man.* It would have been of some interest to hear what Oates had to say about them. Such a discussion would have given statements like "The history of boxing — of fighting — in America is very much one with the history of the black man in America" a bit more validity.

Generally, the writing about race is the least persuasive in the book and might have been jettisoned without hurting the work as a whole. Ethnicity and boxing, ethnicity and American sports are simply too complex to be handled well in the short space that Oates gives herself. I think her refusal to see boxing as a metaphor hurt her discussion here as well. At some point in American social and political history Jack Johnson, Joe Louis, and Muhammad Ali (the three most important blacks of the twentieth century) ceased to be men in the American mind (both black and white); they even ceased to be fighters in the ordinary sense and became something quite legendary but also something specifically inhuman. Once blacks became a force in boxing, the sport automatically became a metaphor. Indeed, what is race in America but the Melvillian doubloon hammered in our consciousness that bedevils us endlessly and turns anything it shines upon into a metaphor as well.

Some minor quarrels: (1) Her statement that "the bare-knuckle era...
was far less dangerous for fighters" is simply not true. Fewer punches were
thrown under London Prize Ring Rules, but the wrestling, cross buttocks,
gouging, spiking, scratching, biting, pulling, and poking left the old bruisers
more disfigured than modern fighters generally are. Besides, it must be
remembered that audiences in the eighteenth and nineteenth centuries
were a good deal more bloodthirsty than audiences today (after all, for a
good part of their history, bareknucklers had to compete against public
executions as a form of popular entertainment), the fights were a great deal
longer, and medical care for injured fighters was quite primitive, to say the
least. (2) Her assertion that "boxing is contrary to nature" does not take
into account the fact that virtually *all* sports are contrary to nature. Boxing
is not special in this regard: running a marathon, balancing oneself on an
elevated balance beam, or not flinching while trying to hit a 95-mph fastball
are all acts that are contrary to nature. (3) "Baseball, football, basketball—
these quintessentially American pastimes are recognizably sports because
they involve play; they are games. One *plays* football, one doesn't *play*
boxing," writes Oates. There are two responses to this: On the one hand,
certain sports, like football, have a certain limited *playing* sphere. Professional football player Curtis Greer put it this way in explaining why he
chooses to continue to play despite a bad knee: "It's not like baseball,
basketball, golf, or tennis, a sport that you can continue as a recreation once
you retire. When you leave football, you just can't go up to the rec center and
get into a game." So the play element in all sports cannot be characterized in
the same way. Moreover, there are several different types of boxing: sparring, exhibition matches, as well as competitive fighting for titles and the
like. Some nonserious boxing does involve an element of play. Sometimes
sparring is serious and sometimes there are other things going on. Exhibition matches are almost never serious. So to say that one cannot play boxing
is not quite true; it depends on how competitive the participants wish the
bout to be and precisely what is at stake. I remember as a child a game
played among black boys called "slap-to-the-head," in which both participants,
laughing most of the time, would, with open hands, cuff each other lightly on
the head to see who had the fastest hands. It seemed a more physical
demonstration of the dozens, for it was considered in quite bad form ("You're
nothing but a chump!") if one got angry at being shown up at this. Yet it was
a purposeful display of one's boxing abilities.

Her criticism of the arguments for the abolition of boxing are sometimes
telling but ultimately not as compelling as other parts of the book. Doubtless,
no sport compromises the humanity of its participants as much as boxing,
and it is hard, in the end, to overcome the frightening and bitter impact
of that truth. Oates's position, if I might be so bold as to attempt a summary,
is that of distressed ambivalence about boxing as a sort of tragic romantic
rite of male expendability, a position that I have a great deal of sympathy
for, as I once occupied it myself. But finally, I believe it a bit too disingenuous,

too self-consciously self-defensive. It seems merely a strategically convenient stalking ground. There is a tendency, when one occupies this position,
for the whole business of boxing, to borrow Richard D. Altick's words, to
cause "a delicious *frisson* rather than a shudder." Oates likens the arguments
concerning the existence of boxing with those over the morality of abortion,
an apt analogy but an incomplete one, for the arguments about boxing can,
with profit, be likened to past historical debates of great importance: over
slavery before the Civil War, over prostitution during the white slavery/
reformist era of the late nineteenth and early twentieth centuries, over
Prohibition during both the nineteenth and the twentieth centuries, debates
which greatly shaped our national character.

On Boxing is a book with an incredible amount of intense energy, compassionate yet relentlessly scrutinizing. One is often moved by passages
because the author herself is moved. Boxing is, at last, not only our national
sport of utter heartbreak but of how *sometimes* heartbreak is heroically
endured by the boxer and even by the audience. Oates tells her part of the
story of grace through slaughter (is boxing Puritan, as she suggests?) with
astonishing compulsion and an extraordinary sense of humane concern. To
be sure, her book does not have the investigative detail and narrative
exactitude of Barney Nagler's *James Norris and the Decline of Boxing* or
Thomas Hauser's *The Black Lights,* the chatty coziness and insider's view
of A. J. Liebling's *The Sweet Science,* Trevor Wignall's *The Sweet Science,* or
Fred Dartnell's *Seconds Outs,* and it lacks the historical guile and wit of the
volumes by Pierce Egan on eighteenth- and nineteenth-century boxing and
the books by Nat Fleischer on the history of black boxing. Nevertheless, it
possesses a certain critical audacity that none of these other books comes
close to having. It makes up in critical height what it lacks in the kind of
width we have become accustomed to boxing books having. José Torres's
biography of Muhammad Ali and Floyd Patterson's pieces in *Sports
Illustrated* and *Esquire* are still necessary reading for anyone who wants to
understand this sport, but so is Oates. She has established the possibility
and the necessity of our best writers' writing about sport in a way that is
finally free of sentiment, romance, and a deadening and juvenile yearning
for the purer (whiter?) past. She has freed us from reading the intellectual's
entrapment of writing about boxing as if it were the fulfillment of a masculine
golden dream of wonder or as if it could produce only a text that is nothing
more than a *j'accuse* writ with orgiastic eloquence. Along with Hauser's *The
Black Lights,* Oates's work is one of the more absorbing texts that I have
come across on this topic in quite some time.

American Prizefighter:
Chris Mead's Champion:
Joe Louis, Black Hero
in White America

The realization of fantasy is one of our dominant cultural traits—from Disney-land to Sacramento.

—William Irwin Thompson, *At the Edge of History*

Joe Louis missed the father who did not miss him.

—Margary Miller, *Joe Louis: American*

I. WE THREE KINGS

In June of 1946, Joe Louis was trying to get his career as heavyweight boxing champion back in order. Fresh from four years in the army and a tour of duty both at home and overseas that matured him as a man but left him in deep debt to his promoter, Mike Jacobs, his manager, John Roxborough, and the United States Internal Revenue Service, Louis desperately needed a big money-making fight. On the nineteenth of the month, he was to fight Billy Conn again in what he hoped would be a bout the world had been waiting for. When the two men fought five years earlier, in June of 1941, Conn, little better than a light-heavyweight, came within two rounds of winning the title. He was knocked out in the thirteenth round of a fight he had in the bag. It was one of the most exciting fights of Louis's career and one of the most financially successful. As Louis trained at Pompton Lakes for his first *paying* title defense since the outbreak of the war, he learned on June 11 that Jack Johnson, the first black ever to become heavyweight champion, holding the title from 1908 to 1915, had died in an automobile accident at the age of sixty-eight. Johnson had always liked fast women, fast cars, and fast horses, and one of these was bound, one supposes, to be the death of him. Louis's reaction on hearing about the death of the only black to have preceded him as champion was characteristically restrained, the only sort of seemingly laconic response one could expect from a man who had it drilled into his head from the time he started his climb toward the champion-ship in the early 1930s not to say much and not to smile much and absolutely not to emulate in any way the life-style of the only black man ever to have held prominence equal to his own in the sporting world and in American popular culture. Louis was quoted in *The New York Times* as saying, "Johnson must have been a great fighter, as my trainer, Jack Blackburn, knew him well and said he was great." That statement must have struck all the knowing coves as a bit of strange news. Blackburn, who had died while Louis was in the service, hated Johnson and, in fact, taught his star pupil, Louis, to hate him as well. Blackburn had good reasons: he was fired as Johnson's sparring mate back in 1906 or so for not allowing Johnson to look good in the ring. Blackburn also knew that Johnson had tried to take his job as Louis's trainer back in the mid-1930s before Louis became champion but when Louis looked like a sure meal ticket before his devastating loss to Max Schmeling in their first fight. Johnson, frankly a hustler of quite vulgar proportions, wanted a piece of a good thing, but John Roxborough would have no part of it, and when the two men met and Johnson proposed the idea, Roxborough, also black, spat out a string of vituperation of such an ardent nature that Johnson likely thought he was reliving his days as a fighter when white ringside customers insulted him freely. When Johnson failed to acquire the job, he badmouthed Louis whenever he had the opportunity, and, seem-ingly, the opportunities for this stylish and sly raconteur were endless. When Louis prepared to fight Jack Sharkey in August 1936, Johnson gave his assessment of the fight this way to *The New York Times:* "Sharkey looks very good and should beat Louis. Sharkey is faster and knows how to use his hands. Louis is a sucker for a right, and, after they are through teaching him how to avoid a right, he will be a sucker for something else." Louis went on to win the fight quite easily, and, as Roi Ottley reported for the New York *Amsterdam News,* Johnson had to run for his life from a group of very angry Harlem citizens who did not appreciate his criticism of their hero.

Even after Louis's greatest victory, his one-round knockout of Max Schmeling in their return match in June 1938, Johnson was only making a snide gesture toward conciliation when he wrote the following for the *Pittsburgh Courier:* "On the basis of what I saw tonight, I am forced to reverse my opinion about Joe Louis. Tonight I witnessed a great fight by a great champion, a man who had vastly improved his style of attack and his defense since he met Max Schmeling in their first engagement two years ago." But Johnson, great egotist and grand *auteur* of the platforms from which he displayed his enormous neurotic concern about being upstaged by any Negro alive, finally brought the matter at hand around to himself:

White people were inclined to think that the victory of a black man over a white man was indicative of the racial superiority of the Negro race, but today they think differently and more sanely. We might call this a development of mental processes. But I think the sociologists of the future will be able to trace this change to my fight with [Jim] Jeffries [in Reno, Nevada, in July 1910]. They finally decided that my fight with Jeffries was merely a fight between two men and had nothing to do with racial superiority. As soon as this point was driven home, the road was paved for Joe Louis to come along and fight for the heavyweight championship....

If you want to know the truth, these thoughts were on my mind when I met Jess Willard in Havana [in 1915, when Johnson lost the title]. I was thinking of the Joe Louises who were to come along in my wake. I didn't want to make the road harder for them.

Johnson was the only black person in America in 1935 to believe that particular revisionist version of the history of American blacks in twentieth-century prizefighting. As far as most black people, from important leaders to the ordinary multitudes, were concerned, Jack Johnson and his unruly behavior and penchant for white women had prevented a black athlete from competing for the heavyweight title in boxing for more than a generation. During the twenties, both Jack Dempsey and Gene Tunney ducked and dodged Harry Wills, a top-ranked black heavyweight. If their autobiographies are to be believed, it was not Wills's race that was the problem; they refused to fight him because they did not like him or his manager, as if prizefights were arranged because of the brotherly affections shared among the parties involved. But Johnson was right in one fundamental way: when he lost the title in 1915 to Jess Willard in Cuba—a fight Johnson always claimed that he threw—he became America's greatest ironic hero by virtue of his having been its powerful villain. After all, to lose the fight, whether legitimately or not, was a kind of excessively extravagant gesture of generous disdain from a man who had become, in effect, the prince of gestures. For Johnson, marrying white women had to amount to the same kind of effect, a theatricality that seemed as pathetically wrought as it was furiously responded to. So the drama was all about sex and violence, which made the psychological stakes that much higher. Who did D. W. Griffith have in mind when his 1915 epic, *The Birth of a Nation*—based on two southern romances by Thomas Dixon—depicted scenes of black men asking white women to marry them, a stark contrast to Dixon's novels, where rape is the thing that pricks the conscience of the white man? Johnson's mad gestures cried out for equally mad responses.

Louis had to be very happy in the depths of his soul that Johnson was dead. One king was dead; now Louis was the only king in the realm. Besides, Johnson, who had been a troublemaker, a disturber of the public peace, a violator of the Mann Act, and a fugitive from justice while he was champion, had never really been much of a king anyway. As Louis said in his last autobiography, *My Life,* about Johnson in retirement: "He was working as a strong man in Robert Ripley's flea circus, and by my standards that ain't shit." One wonders, though, if Johnson's retirement work differed that much from being a greeter for a Las Vegas casino, which is what Louis did in his years after fighting. Telling tales and doing stunts in a dime museum does not seem terribly different from being paid to be photographed with a middle-aged, middle-class couple from Iowa vacationing on a second honeymoon and under the impression that casinos are really exciting places to be. "They're all crooked," as Johnson once cryptically said. In some realms, kings, in their abdications, become their own jesters.

In the February 1967 issue of *The Ring*, a ghostwritten article appeared entitled "How I Would Have Clobbered Clay." One is not absolutely sure that Louis himself is convinced he could have beaten the young heavyweight champion Cassius Clay, although, of course, he rehearses a fight scenario between the two of them, and Louis, predictably enough, is the winner. But he concedes a great deal to Clay's skills and readily admits that he never could have beaten Clay by fighting him in the center of the ring. "The kid has speed and can surely box when he has to. There's nobody around to outbox him, and the opponent who tries is in his grave. Especially in the middle of the ring. With room to move, Clay's a champion, real dangerous. But he doesn't know a thing about fighting on the ropes, which is where he would be if he were in there with me." But the piece seems more an analysis of Clay's character ("He's a guy with a million dollars' worth of confidence and a dime's worth of courage"); as such, it gives the impression of being a jeremiad, the older generation warning about the declension of the younger generation of athletes:

> Trouble with Clay, he thinks he knows it all. Fights with his mouth. He won't listen. Me, first thing I learned in the fight game was to keep my trap shut and my ears wide open, especially when my wise old trainer, [Jack] Chappie Blackburn, was telling me things for my own good.

Clay responded to Louis's assertions in a May 1967 article in *The Ring*, written by the magazine's editor, Nat Fleischer: "Louis clobber me? Joe must be joking. He was a great fighter, but no fighter who shuffles in to meet his opponent, as Louis did, could tag me. I beat such fighters to the punch." Clay was a braggart and talkative where young man Louis was quiet and to all appearances humble; Clay was a draft evader where young man Louis was a loyal and honored recruit; Clay was the black militant and eastern romantic where young man Louis was simply an American and unchurched; Clay was the fast, clever boxer where young man Louis was a plodding, quick-fisted puncher; it was time, in the 1960s, for a generation of young blacks to disavow the generation of their fathers. Clay had to slay the father figure of Louis; Louis had to condemn Clay for betraying the tradition. It is the old story of how styles change and how names are made.

Red Smith's column in *The New York Times* on April 13, 1981, two days after Joe Louis died, contained the following anecdote:

> Early in Muhammad Ali's splendacious reign as heavyweight champion, he hired Joe Louis as an "adviser" and they appeared on television together.
> "Joe, you really think you coulda whupped me?" Ali said.

"When I had the title," Joe said, "I went on what they called a bum-of-the-month tour."

Ali's voice rose three octaves, "You mean I'm a bum?"

"You woulda been on the tour," Joe told his new employer.

On October 2, 1980, Muhammad Ali, thirty-eight, and no longer capable of fighting competitively, was savagely beaten by Larry Holmes in Las Vegas in what was billed as a heavyweight champion fight. One is grateful that Ali did not come out for more punishment in the eleventh round. He thus became only the fourth heavyweight champion or ex-champion to lose a title match by sitting on his stool. Jess Willard was the first, when he quit after three rounds in his second and last title defense against one Jack Dempsey in Toledo, Ohio. Dempsey had knocked Willard down seven times in the first round and fractured his jaw in several places. The other fights in which a champ or ex-champ sat down in a title match both involve Ali: Sonny Liston bowed out after six rounds with the Louisville Lip in Miami in 1964, claiming a shoulder injury; and Joe Frazier gave up after thirteen rounds of bruising in the Thrilla in Manila. It is the last and most disconcerting way that a fighter can lose a bout—simply to quit. It goes against a fighter's trained instincts, his sense of courage, to quit. In championship fights, particularly, it is a rare happenstance. Every fighter gives at least cursory affirmation to the declaration of a young Roberto Duran: "I'd rather die than quit." (Duran was, of course, forced to eat his words in the end when he quit in his second fight against Sugar Ray Leonard.) So ended Ali's career (not counting the final coda against Trevor Berbick, which no one remembers) in just the manner in which he swore in his youth it would not end. He ended his career as Joe Louis had ended his: fighting when he was too old to be in the ring, because he needed the money and the roar of the crowd again, because, ironically, he couldn't quit. Like father, like son.

II. THE HERO OF THE BLUES

In art both agony and ecstasy are matters of stylization.

—Albert Murray, *The Hero and the Blues*

To outlive one's greatness is an especial destiny of the champion athlete whose period of greatness is so intense because it is so brief and so contextual, a fling during a godly and incredibly beautiful youth. Joe Louis surely outdistanced his greatness, about as completely as a runner in the middle of a long race has left behind the starting block. When he died in 1981 at the age of sixty-six, he seemed even more used up than his age would have indicated. He seemed the way everyone always imagines great athletes and especially great boxers to be in their dotage. He was particularly to be pitied because he had gone crazy in his last years, an occurrence that most of the public mistakenly thought came about as a result of his time in the ring. It was, as one Louis biographer, Barney Nagler, implied, and as most medical experts believed, a case of heredity. His father had gone mad when Louis was a child and died in a segregated asylum shortly after Louis became a headline fighter.

At the time of his death, of course, Louis had not fought a memorable fight in nearly two generations; the last was at the end of his prime in the late forties; and it was difficult for younger sports fans, especially young black ones who cared nothing for nostalgia and love, instead desiring only the newest currency in the improvisations of style and moves, to picture the old man with the receding hairline and paunchy belly who was predicting George Foreman would destroy Ali in Zaire as anything more than a tired old man. This was a new generation that admired Ali and was not even born when Louis was an active fighter. Every time Louis predicted Ali would lose, which he did fairly often and quite without malice, never wishing for Ali to lose, the men on the stoops would say, "Joe talkin' crazy again. He ain't never called a fight right in his whole motherfarmin' life"; or, "If Joe say the other guy gonna win, then all my money goes on Ali." It was hard for those of us of the generation of civil rights marches, black power, and the Eastern approaches of exotic names and religions to believe our fathers and grandfathers who told us he was not only the greatest fighter in America but the most famous black man in history at that time.

As a pop cultural symbol, he had been thoroughly revised by that great showman, Muhammad Ali. But try as he might, Ali, who was in truth always trying to slay the father figure of Louis, could never quite obscure him. Louis was, as in the Zaire drama, always in the background, and his fame and ability and downfall were the measuring rods for Ali and for Ali's public, both black and white. Could Ali match Louis's thirteen-year reign? Could he match Louis's knockout record? Would he wind up broke like Louis? Louis's long shadow resulted partly because his period of success was unusually long for an athlete, particularly a champion boxer. He was more the king of an era than any fighter before him including Jack Dempsey, Jack Johnson, and John L. Sullivan, who each held the heavyweight title long enough during their respective reigns actually to be considered the maestro of an epoch in American social history. In fact, except for Ali, no fighter after him has been able to match the magnitude of his myth and his longevity. No fighter has ever been able to match his consistency, not even Ali or Larry Holmes. In his prime, Louis had a methodical excellence that bordered on being uncanny, slightly bizarre and eerie in its disciplined power. It is true, doubtless, that most of his opponents were inferior fighters, but then what heavyweight champion has made a career of greatness fighting anyone other than stiffs and bums for the most part? His opponents, on the whole, were better than Dempsey's and Johnson's challengers during their championship periods and were probably the equal of Ali's, whose only prime first-class foes were Joe Frazier (his nemesis and alter ego), George Foreman, and Ken Norton. It is, alas, hard to find big men who fight well. But Louis was and is our most mythical athlete, our most beloved athlete, which means, in the end, he was luckier than most fighters who are usually loved by the public in only a kind of amused or cast-off way. Louis became, as Chris Mead points out in his generally fine biography, "a symbol of national unity," something that no black had ever achieved before or has ever accomplished since. And certainly no prizefighter ever has. Even Jess Willard, the great white hope who defeated Jack Johnson in Havana in 1915 and returned the title to "the white race," was never a symbol of any kind of unity, racial or national. He was simply both an essence and a sign of the white male's pathological preoccupation with white supremacy, nothing more. In fact, Willard was not even liked much by the white public and, within a year of winning the title, was humiliated by Harry Houdini in front of an audience in California and hooted from the theater. It is hard to imagine this ever happening to Louis, for whom Jim Crow customs bowed down and white folk made entranceways. But Louis's heroism has been misunderstood by the public that insisted, in Louis's later years, that he must be a victim, that it must be recognized that he was used, that he was the prototypical pawn in the white man's game. It has become for both blacks and whites necessary to see him in this way largely to assuage their very different but undeniably real senses of guilt about his last years. The whites say we should not have let this happen to an American hero. The blacks say we should not have let this happen to a black hero. It is a horribly misguided reduction of the man and the divinity of his stature. And it reveals more about our collective unease about prizefighting and the meaning of black male heroism in popular culture than it does anything about the concern over Louis's fate, which did not seem to have made him nearly as unhappy as it did a distressed American public. Those vestiges of Victorianism that linger like a remnant in our cultural subconsciousness make it impossible to accept a prizefighter as a bona fide hero unless we can qualify it in some way, such as making him a victim. But we do not wish to make him a victim of America's social or political structures but rather, in a vague sort of social protest, a victim of his origins, of some sort of trap from which the impoverished, no matter how wealthy they become in their endeavors, can never escape. There is the possibility that Louis may have been used by his managers, his promoters, his government, by a white public that represented an alien and sometimes hostile culture. But perhaps in the end Louis was not used more than any hero is used by the society that creates him and needs him. There was always a great sense of both irritating condescension and deep, touching innocence in America's relationship with Joe Louis. One fact is perfectly clear, despite everything else: Louis was the greatest, the most expansive and mythical blues hero in twentieth-century America, nothing less.

One of the great features of Chris Mead's biography of Joe Louis, published in the fall of 1985, is that, unlike the five previous major Louis biographies, Edward Van Every's *Joe Louis, Man and Superfighter* (1936), Margary Miller's *Joe Louis: American* (1945), Barney Nagler's *The Brown Bomber* (1972), A. O. Edmonds's *Joe Louis* (1973), and Gerald Astor's *". . . And a Credit to His Race": The Hard Life and Times of Joseph Louis Barrow* (1974), Mead comes closest to understanding Louis as a blues hero, to understanding his life as if it were the utterance of one simple yet crucial phrase: How I got over. In a very vital sense, no one was more determined not to lose than Joe Louis. Yet his victory was not one of achievement but rather of process: "how I got over," a phrase used by both black preachers and black hustlers, the autobiographical summing up of both the sacred life and the profane life. "How I got over" is the sign of the underground victory, the rebel victory that is not simply enduring one's adversities but outslicking them. Mead's greater understanding in this regard occurs in part because he places Louis within the context of Afro-American culture, shows Louis to be a product of it. No other biographer had ever done what now appears such a natural and necessary thing to do. The result in Mead's work is that the reader sees Louis more as the complex meshing of two distinct cultural attitudes, a meshing that is not always balanced and does not always work well. But one comes to see Louis as more than a kind of stereotypical put-upon and distressed black American male. For instance, as Mead writes about Louis's last years as a greeter for a Las Vegas casino:

> He was happy in Las Vegas and did not think of his circumstances as pathetic. He was not the type of person who worried about justifying his life in terms of achievement, who measured his self-worth in terms of a regular job and money in the bank. Even if he had, his success in boxing would have been more than enough. He had far outstripped the most grandiose dreams of any boy growing up in the Detroit ghetto during the Depression. Nor would Louis have ever thought that there was anything wrong with working for a casino. He accepted the world as he found it.

This explains why Louis was such close friends with Sonny Liston when Liston moved out to Las Vegas in the sixties, despite the difference in their ages. Or perhaps because of it. Louis was the father Liston never had. They were both black male delinquents who now found themselves strolling along the ways of the glittering American wasteland of garish entertainment. They understood each other well because they knew the fates they would have suffered had they not become boxers, the fates of working-class men, black and white, who lived anywhere: a life of crime or a life of ordinary manual labor, the life of the urban serf. They both refused to be condemned to those lives of utter degradation when they discovered that people were willing to pay to see them fight in a prize ring. There they found a degradation that was almost quaint in its hypocrisy, and they themselves became nearly quixotic cynics, the type of people whose favorite word is "bullshit" and who are more inclined to watch the world warily than to comment on anything that happens in it. Of course, the black bourgeoisie rejected Louis at first, rejecting the idea of having the "genius" of the Negro race represented by a mere prizefighter in much the same way that whites rejected him at first as representative of American manhood and masculinity. Whites came around because Louis seemed inoffensive; he even became "the man who named the war" when, during a speech for the Navy Relief Society on March 10, 1942, he said, "We're on God's side." As Mead notes, those words became among "the most famous...to emerge from all the overblown oratory during World War II." The black bourgeoisie came to accept him for the same reason that the black masses did: he was beating up white folk in the ring. (Louis had only one black opponent during his championship reign until he fought Jersey Joe Walcott shortly before his retirement.) And blacks, starved for any kind of heroism, felt their frustrations about their status in American society released every time Louis punched out a white fighter. A generation later, neither blacks nor whites were willing to accept Sonny Liston. "God help us!" blacks said when Liston entered the ring. "He's a jailbird!" said the whites. But Louis and Liston were the same men: poor, big, dumb country boys up North who went into prizefighting because they had nothing to lose. Each could have had the other's fate.

Mead touches upon a very vital point, a point we must understand if we are to appreciate exactly the kind of hero Joe Louis was. For a prizefighter to wind up working in a casino is not an unusual or shameful destiny; anybody who is knowledgeable about the history of boxing is aware that, since the days of the English Regency, it was the standard ambition of every ex-pug to wind up owning a tavern. As Alan Lloyd writes in *The Great Prizefight,* Tom Sayers, the British openweight champion of the 1850s, "dreamed of becoming a prize-fighting publican" because all he could see around him were taverns owned and operated by fighters. If Louis wound up in a den of liquor and gambling, it was after all the money from such dens that supported him during his career. The relationship between the boxer and the underworld or netherworld of respectable society has always been a close one for two reasons. First, since the days of the bareknuckle brawls of Jack Broughton in the eighteenth century, prizefighters have always been the socially outcast men of bourgeois society. Who else but such a man would be willing to take the risks involved in the gouging, spiking, wrestling, and endlessly endured punishment that bareknuckle fighting was? It had to be someone who had nothing to lose and everything to gain by going into the endeavor on a professional level. And always those men with nothing to lose in our society have been the outcast, the criminal. It has always been a sure sign of not belonging to the order of things when one has nothing to lose. As former heavyweight champion Floyd Patterson wrote, "How else can Negroes like [Cassius] Clay and myself, born in the south, poor, and with little education, make so much money?" Or as Sonny Liston observed, "Most colored boys who go into boxing are poor, and boxing offers them a chance to make money, to get somewhere." It was not so unusual that Liston and

Patterson, two very different men, indeed, should agree upon this point. The boxer knows what the game is about. But as much as the poor male may need boxing, the bourgeois society needs the boxer and the entire ritual of degradation in the prize ring, not only to give these potentially dangerous men something "safe" with which to occupy their time, but also to give us a framework in which we can admire them while feeling superior to and removed from them. The miracle that Louis wrought was that he was the only boxer in history who has ever been described as possessing dignity. Without doing anything in particular except beating fighters and enlisting in the armed services during wartime, Louis made the sensibility of the poor boy a respectable ethos in American culture. "He is truly one of us," we said.

The second reason the fighter is attached to the underworld is that fighters have always been poor boys, used to being socially outcast and around the socially outcast: to being disreputable, to fighting in clubs and saloons. Logically, after retirement, despite whatever notice he may have received from the bourgeois world, he would want to return to the world not of his origins, but the world that most appreciated his success and esteemed his talents; for the autobiographical utterance of the old heads on the corner, the prostitute, the confidence man, and the gambler is also "how I got over." As James Brown, former prizefighter and, despite his associations with rock and roll, the greatest bluesman of the last twenty years, is wont to sing, "You got to use what you got to get just what you want." The world that the prizefighter comes from is one that understands the hypocrisy surrounding the commercialization of the body in a bourgeois, Calvinist-tinged culture.

There are other impressive features of Mead's work: how he places the presence of Louis within the scheme of American popular culture.

> Louis was the first black American to achieve lasting fame and popularity in the twentieth century. When he began to box professionally in 1934, there were no blacks who occupied positions of public prominence, no blacks who commanded attention from whites. Historians recognize W. E. B. DuBois and A. Phillip Randolph as the most important black leaders of the 1930s; white Americans of that era would have been hard pressed to recognize their names, still less their faces.

Also, Mead's social and cultural analysis of sports writing is quite fine; this is an area of literary criticism that is long overdue in its emergence. Mead's reading of these pieces provides us with an important interpretation of Louis through the eyes of those scribes of popular taste and makers of popular heroes, and an interesting psychological examination of the men themselves. (The discussions of Grantland Rice and Paul Gallico are especially intriguing.) We can see through the shift in the sports columns on Louis throughout the years of his reign not only how the mythology of his heroism was constructed, but also how deeply complex it was. His account of the second Schmeling-Louis fight, the most symbolic and probably the most important sporting event in American social history, is the best available. (Although I must add here that the blow-by-blow descriptions of this and other important Louis fights are a bit tedious and still fail, despite their detail, to give at least this reader a real sense of the fight. Unlike baseball, a fight cannot meaningfully be described merely by plotting its action.)

But Mead's book is, in the end, puzzling. Despite the grand historical scaffolding and the lush care for certain types of critical detail and interpretation, the work never really becomes a biography. Louis remains uncaptured and, to a certain degree, unknown by book's end. We learn little of Louis's southern origins or the experiences he had as a youth growing up in the ghetto of Detroit during the Depression. Virtually nothing of his personal life is revealed. His marriages are recounted very sketchily and his love affairs with such women as Lena Horne and Sonja Henie are not even mentioned. This sort of stuff is not just gossip (although gossip has its critical uses in biography and psychology) but necessary detail in understanding the man as a psychological and emotional being. Mead also does not provide very much insight about Louis's relationships with other men, particularly other black fighters. He does not mention Louis's friendship with Liston at all, and this seems to me a serious omission, for much about the inner workings of both men could have been revealed by a rigorous examination of their friendship. Louis was a pallbearer at Liston's funeral (Liston died of an apparent drug overdose in 1970), and he seemed to have been deeply shaken by Liston's death and somewhat disoriented at the funeral. Also, much more should have been provided on Louis's own drug addiction and his mental illness. Both problems plagued him from the 1950s on. Mead does a good job discussing Louis's anxiety-of-influence relationship with Jack Johnson, but a much lesser job of considering Louis's example as a psychological barrier or a source of inspiration for the black champs who followed him, particularly Floyd Patterson, Sonny Liston, who openly admitted his undying admiration for Louis, and Muhammad Ali, whose response to Louis as father figure seems in some respects the most bitter and the most touching. Some of these details concerning Louis's southern origins, his marriages, his drug addiction, and his mental illness can be found in fuller and more compelling accounts in the Nagler and Astor biographies. So despite the tremendous amount of information of a historical and cultural kind that Mead's book provides, it will not supersede the existing Louis books. Perhaps in all fairness, Mead did not intend his book to do that. In which case, we still await the necessary psychoanalytic biography of Louis, the equivalent of Erik Erikson's *Young Man Luther* or Dr. Bernard Meyer's *Houdini: A Mind in Chains.* After all, what do we really know about the psychological makeup of any champion boxer? For instance, consider the similarities between Louis and Sonny Liston, both country boys who wound up migrating to big cities, both estranged from their fathers, both nearly illiterate until well into their adulthood, both too big to be in their class at school, and both winding up with ties to organized crime. Perhaps the next Louis biography should start with these details and make something of them.

We still need to try to answer the epistemological questions: What is a prizefighter? How does our culture know him? How does our culture make him? Albert Murray's observations about the matador in his *The Hero and the Blues* are, I think, applicable to our appreciation and definition of the prizefighter:

> Not only is the matador a volunteer who seeks out, confronts, and dispatches that which is deadly; he is also an adventurer who runs risks, takes chances, and exposes himself with such graceful disdain for his own limitations and safety that the tenacity of his courage is indistinguishable from the beauty of his personal style and manner.

The prizefighter, like the matador, provides his culture with a heroic stylization in which personal meaning and the symbolic ritual of triumph and defeat can be played out. He is, more so than any other athlete, the hero and devil of absolute anarchy and of absolute absurdity. And to answer the epistemological questions is of paramount importance for us as Americans when we realize one dimly recognized fact: The three black persons who have exercised the greatest influence upon our social reality and our mythical selves have all been men and have all been prizefighters: Joe Louis, Jack Johnson, and Muhammad Ali. How shocking it is to think that the victims of our order should be the beautiful princes of our disorder.

Finally, I would like to quote once more from Joe Louis's article about Cassius Clay, the same piece I mentioned earlier. Toward the end, Louis tells this little story:

> Once I happened to walk along when Clay was hollering "I am the Greatest!" to some fellows outside the Theresa Hotel in Harlem. When he saw me, Clay came over and shouted to the crowd: "This is Joe Louis. *WE* is the Greatest!"
> That was nice. Cassius Clay is a nice boy and a smart fighter.

Fathers and sons. Sons and fathers. It is a very good story. In fact, it is one of the best short stories in all of American prizefighting. Like Queequeg and Ishmael, the pagan and the reformed Calvinist, the cynic and the mad Muslim go off together arm in arm, at last. The prize ring has always been the most profound of all of America's realized fantasies.

James Baldwin's Neglected Essay: Prizefighting, the White Intellectual, and the Racial Symbols of American Culture

Civilization founders upon its inability to be a civilization for everybody.
—Patrick Brantlinger, *Bread and Circuses*

I. COOL BREAD

It is, perhaps, one of the most stunning omissions in the history of Afro-American intellectual and cultural criticism that so few Afro-American writers have written about sports. One would think sports to be a natural, almost shamelessly obvious place to consider the important collision and collusion between the Afro-American and broad aspects of American popular culture, the most intellectually intriguing cultural convergence in American society. Jeffrey Sammons's recent book, *Beyond the Ring: The Role of Boxing in American Society,* strikes one with a certain power while eliciting a rampant curiosity, both of which are evoked quite independently from one's reaction to and assessment of the quality of the analysis in the work itself, when one realizes that Sammons is among a very small handful of black scholars who have written full-length academic treatises on sport. Al-Tony Gilmore, Harry Edwards, and Ocania Chalk are three other black scholars who come to mind as having mined the ore of this field.

To be sure, Afro-American intellectuals have written about sports. Writers such as James Weldon Johnson, Jervis Anderson, Larry Neal, Eldridge Cleaver, C. L. R. James, J. Saunders Redding, Roi Ottley, A. S. Young, and John A. Williams, among others, have written anything from essays to chapters in books to, in a few instances, books themselves on sports ranging from horse racing to cricket. The sport that has attracted by far the most intellectual commentary among black writers and thinkers has been boxing. There are several reasons for this. First, boxing has a history of black participation that dates back to the Regency days of bareknuckle fighting in England, when two American blacks, Bill Richmond and Tom Molineaux, made names for themselves, if not fortunes, fighting in England, then the boxing center of the world and the cultural source for nearly all of America's professional and amateur sports; in short, boxing has a longer history of black participation than any other sport in the industrialized Western world. Second, boxing has always been a notoriously self-conscious and self-exploitative sport along racial lines; part of the manufactured drama and mythology of boxing is the symbolic clash of different races in the ring. Third, boxing has been the sport that, in the twentieth century, has produced the three most powerful black male presences in the history of American culture, men who have changed the landscape of American society: Jack Johnson, Joe Louis, and Muhammad Ali.

In this regard, it is worthy of note that three of the four major epochal black male writers who came of age as writers during the period between the Depression and 1955 — which means that their childhoods had been affected in some way by the championship era and the rousing mythmaking of either Jack Johnson or Joe Louis — wrote notably on boxing. Richard Wright wrote several essays for *New Masses* and *The Daily Worker* in the 1930s on Joe Louis and made symbolic references and allusions to the sport in both his fiction and his nonfiction. Wright was seven years old in 1915 when Jack Johnson lost the heavyweight title to Jess Willard in Havana. Ralph Ellison, whose 1952 novel, *Invisible Man,* contains the most famous boxing scene in all of American fiction, the Battle Royal, was undoubtedly reared on folktales and stories about Jack Johnson, since he was just one year old when Johnson lost the title. But Johnson's importance as black folk hero, as several scholars have shown, has been enduring, and it must be remembered that no American black was to win another major boxing title until Tiger Flowers beat Harry Greb for the middleweight title in 1926, when Ellison was twelve years old. The eleven-year span between Johnson and Flowers — Battling Siki, a West African, briefly held the light-heavyweight title in 1922 — simply intensified the Johnson myth. Ellison alludes to the mythology of the champion black prizefighter on several occasions throughout the novel. Amiri Baraka (LeRoi Jones), who wrote an essay in the mid-sixties about Sonny Liston, Floyd Patterson, and Muhammad Ali, and makes several allusions to boxing in his fiction, poetry, and plays, was three years old when Joe Louis won the title, and a teenager when he lost it more than ten years later. In effect, Baraka grew up with Louis as champion.

The noted omission here is James Baldwin, who, in none of his published and collected fiction, nor in any of his collections of essays, ever wrote about boxing or any sport at all. But Baldwin did write one essay on boxing, which appeared in *Nugget* in February 1963. The subject of the essay is the first Sonny Liston–Floyd Patterson heavyweight championship bout, which took place in Chicago in September 1962, a fight champion Patterson lost by a knockout in the first round. Not only has the essay never been placed in any Baldwin literary collection, it is not listed in any Baldwin bibliography or mentioned in any Baldwin critical study. Only two books on Baldwin take any notice of the essay at all, both biographical not critical works: Fern Marja Eckman's *The Furious Passage of James Baldwin* and W. J. Weatherby's *Squaring Off—Mailer versus Baldwin*. Neither provides a citation for it. Why has the essay been neglected by Baldwin critics? Did Baldwin distance himself from the essay because he never liked it, as Weatherby suggests? Did his dislike of the essay stem from his awareness that it was one of his weaker efforts or from its appearance in a magazine that was not as highly regarded as some of the others that made his literary reputation, as Eckman suggests? In short, was Baldwin embarrassed by the piece?

To be sure, *Nugget* was not quite the venue that Baldwin really wanted, not after having written for *Harper's, Commentary, Partisan Review,* and *New Leader.* This is not to say that *Nugget* was a bad publication. It simply never got off the ground in the way that the magazines to which it bore the greatest similarity, *Esquire* and *Playboy,* both of which Baldwin wrote for, were able to. It first appeared in 1955, created and founded by Archer St. John and published and edited by Michael St. John. *Nugget* circulated fairly regularly, but apparently it was difficult to sustain either a bimonthly or monthly schedule through the years of its existence. It finally died in 1965. Among the writers who were printed or reprinted in its pages were Ben Hecht, Evan Hunter, Noël Coward, Nelson Algren, Wallace Stegner, William Saroyan, Evelyn Waugh, and James T. Farrell. Indeed, the editorial printed in the same issue as Baldwin's essay states proudly:

> With the debut of James Baldwin in the present issue, *Nugget* can safely say (not half-safely either, like those inferior brands) that it has snagged almost every exciting writer of the literary generation now riding the 30-to-40 creative crest. Think for a moment—as we often do, with a smug expression on our corporate kisser—of the rocketing talent that has struck our pages: James Jones, Mailer, Baldwin, Kerouac, John Clellon Holmes, Corso, Brossard, Colin Wilson, Wolf Mankowitz, Alexander Trocchi, Terry Southern, William Gaddis, Warren Miller...

It is a tribute to Baldwin's own fame and importance that the magazine would wish to write such a glowing and crowing fanfare about having his work in its pages, but it is also an indication that the magazine wanted very much to be on the cutting edge of modern American writing. It wanted a reputation for provocation and for excellence. It also wanted to be known as, for lack of a better word, hip, at least hip as it was understood in such pieces as Norman Mailer's 1957 essay "The White Negro": the quest for the satisfaction of masculine appetites (usually white) in order to ward off mental and physical illness, the release of energy in order to become a better receptacle of energy, the simplistic cosmic and metaphysical ethic of male dominance in the beginning of the age of nuclear weapons and the cold war. The subtitle of *Nugget* was "The Man's World," which, of course, echoed *Playboy*'s "Entertainment for Men" and *Esquire*'s "The Magazine for Men," or "The Quarterly for Men" when it was first launched in 1933. The preoccupation with the hip explains why the magazine wanted an essay from a hot black male writer such as Baldwin on sports; the magazine had, over the years, run essays on pro football, auto racing, and boxing.

After all, what was sports but another expression of male existential quest for the orgasm of the moment. But pursuit of the hip also explains why the magazine was obsessed with jazz, particularly what was called cool jazz, which as an aesthetic expression was fairly equivalent to how the magazine saw sports. (It is interesting to note in this regard that Baldwin, in the tradition of *Nugget,* makes a comparison between trumpeter Miles Davis and Floyd Patterson at one point in his essay.) In 1958 jazz was still considered hip by many people, although knowing ones should have sensed that the days of jazz as cutting-edge music were over, through its co-option by television, Leonard Bernstein, André Previn, and the like, and its association as a kind of establishment music for status quo–loving urban-living adults, its degradation to a mood music for relaxation and seduction. Rock and roll, which *Nugget* never mentioned, was the new hip. When director Richard Brooks used Bill Haley and the Comets' "Rock Around the Clock" to accompany the opening credits of his 1955 film *Blackboard Jungle,* when the kids in that movie destroyed teacher Richard Kiley's beloved Stan Kenton and Bix Beiderbecke records, it was as clear a cultural sign as any that jazz was dead as a hip music. For in the world of hip, youth must be served. *Nugget,* as well as *Esquire* and *Playboy,* which also had their jazz polls and jazz reviews in the fifties and sixties, hadn't heard the news.

In part, Baldwin, like virtually every black male writer, even those who have written about professional boxing, is not nearly as obsessed with the subject as many white male writers have been. No black male writer has written as extensively on boxing as, say, A. J. Liebling, Norman Mailer, Budd Schulberg, Pete Hamill, and others. Joyce Carol Oates, the latest in a line of white writers to charge up the interpretive hill of boxing, provides a section in her *On Boxing* that, although incomplete because it ignores many of the major white nonfiction writers on the sport, gives the reader the general aesthetic shape and historiography of writing about boxing. No blacks are mentioned, which is not a racist oversight as much as it is an honest and accurate recounting of what minds have been, over the years, in a cerebral heat over boxing. Black writers are simply not as charged up about the mythology and theater of boxing as white writers are. (It is interesting to consider that only white writers such as Ernest Hemingway, Paul Gallico, Liebling, Mailer, and George Plimpton have ever found it intriguing actually to get into a ring and box with a professional fighter. Perhaps it was the validation of experience that comes from, as Liebling put it, "a laying-on of hands" that these writers found especially attractive.) And they are surely not as fascinated with boxers as personalities because they do not generally see boxers as psychological counterpoints to themselves. This explains at least incompletely why Baldwin wrote about boxing only once, despite his having come into his manhood at the same time that Joe Louis symbolized a kind of national manhood for blacks—he was thirteen when Louis became champion, and he admits in his essay that Louis "was the last great fighter for me," despite his having lived through the era of Muhammad Ali, the most startling, nay, the most compelling political symbol of blackness or black symbol of political consciousness in the late 1960s. It may be instructive in understanding better the effectiveness and ineffectiveness of Baldwin's essay on the first Patterson-Liston fight if it is compared with essays on the same fight by two white writers — Liebling's for *The New Yorker* and Mailer's for *Esquire*. It might be safely said that what drew Liebling to boxing was the conceit of wit but what drew Mailer was the more popular American obsession: the conceit of sentimentality, which is, finally, the lens that focuses the American's sense of morality. As I have said in another essay, Liebling wanted to write mere charming essays, but Mailer wanted to write epics. One wanted to compose études, the other Wagnerian operas. A more developed discussion of these essays is best left to another venue.

But there is a bit more complexity in all of this, which explains why Baldwin's boxing essay did not turn out well and why he never wrote another. That complexity can be summed up in two statements: First, Baldwin did not like boxing; second, Baldwin did not like the *mythology* of boxing. As Weatherby so tellingly observed: "Baldwin . . . had none of Mailer's devotion to the fight game; he was as uneasy in a gym as he was on a beach; he had no interest in athletics, in sports, in that kind of competition." It is a truism, or at least it ought to be, that one cannot write about sports unless one is absorbed in the mythology of sports, fascinated by the intense symbolic reality that sports evoke, feeling that sports' special pure and fantastic reality transcends the mundane, grubby reality of manipulation, falsely induced interest, and corrupt motivation of greed that supports it, encourages it, makes it possible; the extremely unspiritual, profane impulse of capitalism cynically creating a desire, then maddeningly oversupplying the market until one is sickened by boxing, by all sports, not because of their violence and competition but because of their sheer inexorable abundance and repetition.

Baldwin generally thought in theological terms; certainly he saw the world in a way that approached a black Christian allegory. The mythology of sports, its grid of purities and dangers, if you will, paled beside the mythology of Christianity, the sheer grandeur of the edifice of sin and redemption. That is the major reason why, in the end, the fight Baldwin is sent to cover does not excite his intellectual engagement; in truth, the essay seems to be stumbling around in search of a subject or a word limit, whichever comes first. Indeed, the fight elicits not even his curiosity, only his unease and, finally, his bewilderment and despair. "[The] fight itself," writes Weatherby, "probably appalled [Baldwin] deep down — the prospect of black boys, brothers, knocking the hell out of each other for the amusement and profit of whites." For instance, Baldwin describes going to the fight "full of a weird and violent depression," whereas Mailer, in his essay "Ten Thousand Words a Minute," which appeared in *Esquire* the same month as Baldwin's essay in *Nugget,* wrote that "[as] the fight approached, [Pete] Hamill and I had been growing nervous in a pleasant way, we were feeling that mixture of apprehension and anticipation which is one of the large pleasures of going to a big fight." Elsewhere in the same essay Mailer continues in the same vein, "But then there is nothing else very much like being at a Heavyweight Championship fight. It is to some degree the way a Hollywood premiere once ought to have been." Alas, for Mailer, as for many white male writers, the interpretative pursuit of boxing is the quest of the hot circus. Mailer wrote his essay because of the fee and because he liked the idea of writing about boxing. Baldwin too wrote his essay because of the fee or, to use the argot of the hip, because "the bread was cool, ya dig?" He certainly didn't write it because he despised boxing, but he surely did despise it as strenuously as any black intellectual ever has.

II. HOT CIRCUS

Of course, since Baldwin was undeniably attracted to a form of paganism — namely, male sex, the question arises: Why was he not drawn to the paganism of prizefighting? (After all, it is boxing's paganism, its power not simply as a competitive *sport* but as an atmosphere-invoking *circus,* that has attracted most male intellectuals.) For the more prurient-minded, one would think that Baldwin's homosexuality would have made boxing attractive for him: the whole crude bit of sweating, well-built, mostly nude male bodies often locked in embrace. But it is precisely that crudity that he must have found to be virtually devoid of interest because it was so devoid of humanity and artistry and so filled with self-loathing. If boxing represents a homosexual paganism, it is exactly the sort of homosexuality, exactly the sort of paganism, that appeals to the latent homosexuality of the "normal," heterosexual, virile male: an eroticism that denies that it is erotic, that announces the chastity of its innocence by insisting on the purity and danger of the contest. Boxing, for the heterosexual male, is a sport of renunciation; it is symbolically homosexual in about the only way a heterosexual male can accept homosexuality in his cultural signs or in himself: by denying that it truly is. Why should the homosexual male be interested in such a brutal farce, in such an insult to homosexuality, to human sexuality itself? What is revealing here is what Mailer wrote in his Liston-Patterson essay about the championship fight between welterweights Benny "Kid" Paret and Emile Griffith that took place in New York City on March 24, 1962, a fight that resulted in the death of Paret at the hands of Griffith, supposedly because in prefight publicity and at the weigh-in before the fight, Paret, a macho Cuban, insulted Griffith, who had a very high voice,* by calling him something equivalent to a "faggot." Mailer writes:

> The accusation of homosexuality arouses a major passion in many men; they spend their lives resisting it with a biological force. There is a kind of man who spends every night of his life getting drunk in a bar, he rants, he brawls, he ends in a small rumble on the street; women say, "For God's sakes, he's homosexual. Why doesn't he just turn queer and get his suffering over with." Yet men protect him. It is because he is choosing not to become homosexual. It was put best by Sartre who said that a homosexual is a man who practices homosexuality. A man who does not, is not homosexual—he is entitled to the dignity of his choice. He is entitled to the fact that he chose not to become homosexual, and is paying the price.

If heterosexuality in the male becomes most clearly defined when the resistance to homosexuality is most pronounced, a resistance with the power of "a biological force," then boxing, the symbolic brawl to signify utter rebellion against homosexual impulses, becomes virulently antihomosexual theater. The prizefight becomes nothing more than a *pure* and *apparent,* an intelligible homophobic act. The prizefight says, in effect, it is better to practice this than to practice homosexuality. Baldwin had undoubtedly read about the Paret-Griffith fight, as it was major national news at the time, and while he probably would not agree with Mailer's views about homosexuality, he may have felt the same way about what caused the tragedy and about the underlying significance of boxing and its antihomoerotic impulse.

There are two elements missing from the Baldwin essay. First, there is an absence of any detail about the sport. As Baldwin reminds us on several occasions: "I know nothing whatever about the Sweet Science or the Cruel Profession or the Poor Boy's Game." "I am not an *aficionado* of the ring."

---

*Jack Dempsey was also bothered by a high voice. He mentions this fact in every edition of his autobiography. The whole business of masculinity and boxing is complex. Latin fighters such as Roberto Duran and Tony Ayala have been known, most dramatically, to insult their opponents' manhood or sexual potency. But that is generally a common form of ritual insulting among boxers. Consider such symbolic manhood insults as John L. Sullivan's boast about being able to beat any "son of a bitch in the house" or, at even earlier date, of Daniel Mendoza losing his championship because he was grabbed by his long hair and pummeled.

"I dismissed my dim speculations, that afternoon, as sentimental inaccuracies, rooted in my lack of knowledge of the boxing world." These free confessions of ignorance explain the lack of any detail whatsoever about either Liston or Patterson as athletes: no accounts of their careers, no accounts of previous fights, no descriptions of their athletic skill as fighters. Moreover, there are virtually no sociological or biographical descriptions provided of either fighter, no mention of Patterson's troubled childhood or of his accomplishments in the 1952 Helsinki Olympic Games, only a vague account of Liston's prison term and of his intense unpopularity:

> Patterson was, in effect, the *moral* favorite—people wanted him to win, either because they liked him, though many people didn't, or because they felt that his victory would be salutary for boxing and that Liston's victory would be a disaster. But no one could be said to be enthusiastic about either man's record in the ring.

And that is about all that is said on that score. Nothing is said about *why* the fighters occupy the particular moral and symbolic categories that they find themselves in. This lack of detail, this rampant ignorance virtually denies any possibility of any *analysis* of the fight as a political, cultural, sociological, or even purely athletic event, just the sort of analysis that, for better or worse, is the meat of Liebling and Mailer, largely because Baldwin finds it impossible to *describe* the fight, the fighters, the world of boxing. It is not simply that Baldwin is lost in the world of sports, although he admits his need for others—Gay Talese, for instance—to intercede for him, indeed, to accompany him and to guide him, in his attempt to interview the two fighters, because he is "not a very aggressive journalist"; it is more that Baldwin does not think the event is truly worth *knowing,* that it possesses nothing intrinsically that would reward the effort of aggressive investigation that is, after all, what any journalism worth its salt is. His timidity, of which his ignorance is but a sign, may be the result of being surrounded by so many "aggressive" white journalists and writers. The essay opens with Baldwin talking about the writers who were in Chicago to cover the fight and it ends with Baldwin going off to a bar to have a drink with Liebling. Although Baldwin never makes an issue of the race of the other writers—indeed, tries to create a sense of community among the writers—it seems quite clear that Baldwin sees himself as an outsider who cannot ask the right questions, who does not share the same interests in the proceedings as the other writers have.

At the fight itself, Baldwin describes himself as "sitting between Norman Mailer and Ben Hecht," although he does omit the important detail that Mailer provides in his essay, that there was an empty seat between him and Baldwin that Mailer thought signified the rift that had come between them, which Baldwin alludes to when he writes, "I had had a pretty definitive fight with someone with whom I had hoped to be friends." Nonetheless, what Baldwin describes, the sense of being enclosed by two white male writers who are infinitely more interested in the fight and in prizefighting generally than he is, brings to mind the scene in *Native Son* in which Bigger Thomas sits in the car between Jan and Mary, two friendly whites who are as enchanted by his blackness as he is terrified by their whiteness.

Baldwin speaks earlier, as mentioned above, of the need to have Gay Talese intercede on his behalf to get him an interview with Patterson. He needed the help of another white writer, Sandy Grady, to get an interview with Liston. Indeed, near the beginning of the piece, Baldwin lists the names of some of the writers who are covering the fight: Jimmy Cannon, Red Smith, Milton Gross, Grady, Liebling, Mailer, Gerald Kersh, Budd Schulberg, and Ben Hecht, and it becomes apparent that, with the possible exception of some representatives from the black press, Baldwin is the only black "literary" figure who is there. This may explain as much as anything why Baldwin's coverage was so lacking, so uninspired. In the face of all these white writers who felt themselves so knowledgeable about boxing, Baldwin became a "timid, ignorant" black writer, much as Bigger was timid and ignorant when enclosed by Jan and Mary in the car. It was not that Baldwin was intimidated or merely intimidated covering the fight. But he must have realized that professional boxing is, finally, a white man's interest.

III. PATTERSON AND LISTON

There are two keys to understanding Baldwin's essay: first, his intense identification with Patterson; second, how he saw the personality difference between Liston and Patterson. Baldwin visits both fighters at their training facilities and is even granted a one-on-one interview with Liston, something, according to Mailer, that Liston did not grant to white reporters ("Liston did not talk to white reporters individually"). From that fact alone, Baldwin must have been cognizant of his special status covering this fight, of his difference. But it is in examining the way Baldwin saw Patterson that the essay becomes truly illuminating. He notes, as both Mailer and Liebling do, that Patterson is training at a Catholic workers' farm, a place that resembles a monastery, and that Liston is training at a racetrack. The sacred and the profane nestled side by side, although such observations were obvious and were made before the fight by magazines such as *Newsweek* ("The Fight: A Sinner Winner?"). What Baldwin does with the image of Patterson as saint is unique:

> And we watched [Patterson] jump rope, which he must do according to some music in his head, very beautiful and gleaming and far away, like a boy saint helplessly dancing and seen through the steaming windows of a storefront church.

He describes Liston's rope-jumping, for which he was famous, less poetically:

> I had already seen [Liston] work out, skipping rope to a record of "Night

Train," and, while he wasn't nearly, for me, as moving as Patterson skipping rope in silence, it was still a wonderful sight to see.

No, This is not What his layers — this is his interpretation of Baldwin prose, that he calls the music of the moment.

So Patterson becomes, for Baldwin the boy saint in a sanctified church far removed from the austerity and whiteness of Catholicism and returned to the glory and blackness of some inner-directed ("music in his head") charismatic power. And thus Baldwin hearkens back not exactly to his own boyhood as saint but to his character from his first novel, *Go Tell It on the Mountain,* the lovely boy saint, Elisha, whom Johnny Grimes (Baldwin) worships so deeply. Liston is skillful and admirable in his exercises. Patterson is transported and transporting.

And it is because Patterson can evoke this image of blackness and glory for Baldwin that recognition from Patterson is so important to him:

> But Patterson hadn't heard of me, or read anything of mine. [Gay Talese's] explanation, though, caused him to look directly at me, and he said, "I've seen you someplace before. I don't know where, but I know I've seen you...." Gay suggested that he had seen me on TV. I had hoped that the contact would have turned out to be more personal, like a mutual friend or some activity connected with the Wiltwyck School, but Floyd now remembered the subject of the TV debate he had seen—the race problem, of course—and his face lit up. "I *knew* I'd seen you somewhere!" he said, triumphantly, and looked at me for a moment with the same brotherly pride I felt—and feel—in him.

What does this tell us about the men?

There is no corresponding desire for recognition from Liston. Baldwin puts it simply enough: "It wasn't that I didn't like Liston. I just felt closer to Floyd." The closeness to Patterson can be explained by understanding that Patterson represented two distinct but related personas in Baldwin's mind. First, Patterson is, as mentioned above, the boyhood hero-saint, the intense, handsome boy of his youth, the boy Baldwin could never become because he felt himself ugly and without physical grace and dexterity. Patterson is the character Elisha; he is also the character Richard, Baldwin's imaginary real father in *Go Tell It on the Mountain,* as well as the boy Richard in *Blues for Mister Charlie.* He is, in fact, every handsome black boy Baldwin ever imagined in his literature. But on another level, Patterson is Baldwin himself, alone, isolated, unrecognized, unheralded. (Baldwin once described himself as "a very tight, tense, lean, abnormally ambitious, abnormally intelligent, and hungry black cat." It is a description that echoes Baldwin's account of Patterson.) If Patterson, according to Baldwin, "is quite probably the least likely fighter in the history of the sport," Baldwin is the least likely writer to cover the sport. If Patterson possesses "that most un-American of attributes, privacy, the will to privacy," if he is "still relentlessly, painfully shy" but "lives gallantly with his scars," then he is, in effect, James Baldwin, the timid, tense (Baldwin used this word to describe both himself and Patterson in different parts of the essay) black writer at what is, in effect, a white event despite the irony that the two principal actors in that event happen to be black. For Baldwin's greatest strength is his will to privacy as well, as symbolized by his desire to meet with both fighters away from the daily press conferences, by his desire to shout to Patterson during that disastrous first round when the champion was about to experience his greatest public humiliation, "Keep your head, baby." And Baldwin has learned to live gallantly with his scars, that, after all, are the subject, to a great extent, of all his autobiographical essays. There is much about Patterson that makes him appealing to Baldwin because there is much about Patterson's position and demeanor that makes him seem so much like a black intellectual. Patterson brings to boxing precisely what someone like Baldwin brought to the activity of American letters: "a terrible note of complexity."

This brings me to the distinction that Baldwin makes between Liston and Patterson, not so much as aesthetic and moral symbols, as Mailer does, or as fighters and athletes, as Liebling does, but as black men.

> I felt terribly ambivalent, as many Negroes do these days, since we are all trying to decide, in one way or another, which attitude, in our terrible American dilemma, is the most effective: the disciplined sweetness of Floyd, or the outspoken intransigence of Liston.

Both men become political strategies as well as unique personalities, yet ironic layers and details belie the simplicity of the contrast. Baldwin believes Liston to be outspoken because during his interview with the fighter, Liston said, "I tell you one thing, though. If I was up there, I wouldn't bite my tongue." But it is Liston who is controlled by white men with connections to the Mob, a control he was unable or unwilling to shake for his entire career, indeed, for the rest of his life, when one considers the bizarre and sleazy circumstances of his death, which occurred in Las Vegas in 1970. There were many legendary Listons who appeared at various stages of his life: Liston the large, dumb country black boy; Liston the jailbird; Liston the thumbcrusher for the Mob; Liston the fearful fighter; Liston the sex maniac. But Liston never *uttered* much of any importance in his life. On the other hand, it is quiet, unassuming Floyd who, before his fight with Liston, demoted his white manager, Cus D'Amato, and, in effect, began to speak for himself, a most radical move for a black fighter, or any fighter, at the time. Patterson was to get in quite a bit of trouble with blacks, most notably with black intellectuals, for articles he wrote in various magazines after the ascendancy of Muhammad Ali to the heavyweight throne in 1964. Whether one agreed or disagreed with Patterson's feelings about Ali and the Muslims, no one can deny that Patterson was certainly outspoken. He never bit his tongue, surely. But even in 1962, could anyone really call Patterson sweet? Perhaps *Newsweek*'s description of him as "at times...irritatingly oversensitive," may be more apt. "Neurotically driven" may be even better. And Liston's well-known easy manipulation at the hands of the Mob hardly makes him seem intransigent. It was certainly thought wise by someone in Liston's braintrust, not Liston himself, to cultivate the friendship of two Catholic priests shortly before the fight with Patterson in an effort to soften his image as a black thug.

But this is not to say that Baldwin is wrong in his assessment of the two men, although it is clear that he knew very little about them. After all, image is everything, and the image of Liston as outside the bounds of respectability, as a street-smart outlaw, and the image of Patterson as inside the establishment —as Mailer so compellingly put it, "a liberal's liberal," whose key words from his autobiography, *Victory over Myself,* as Mailer rightly points out, are *introspective, obligation, responsibility, inspiration, commendation, frustrated,* and *seclusion*—these images were of paramount concern to American blacks because in truth any image of any public black in America becomes a political statement and a political strategy. Patterson and Liston posed for American blacks, in their American dilemma, the restatement of the very same alternatives that American blacks always imagined themselves as having: the choice of being inside or outside, within or without, to see blackness as something that can accommodate bourgeois Western values or as something else that can live in a bourgeois Western culture while being alien both to that culture and to anything else that is Western. Patterson, a longtime convert to Catholicism, and Liston, a kind of Catholic fellow traveler during these days, may have been poor black boys, but they did not come to Catholicism with the same needs, nor did they view it in anyway alike. Indeed, one could argue that one of them was no kind of Catholic or Christian at all. Patterson and Liston symbolized for Baldwin and for many other blacks the two classic ways blacks respond to the meaning of being civilized in a civilization that insists alternately that they cannot be or that they ought be terrifically glad that they have been. It is the painful and absurd existence between those two negative poles, so brilliantly interpreted by Baldwin in his most staggering essay, "Stranger in the Village," that have blacks responding to the trappings of what is still in many respects an alien civilization—although it is, of course, dear home and mother for us all—with hostility, despair, and madness. And it is this sense of being dislocated in the only state of things that people in the Western world have come to know as civilization that has made the black hate himself. As Baldwin once said, "I despised [blacks], possibly because they failed to produce Rembrandt." And what is most disturbing about boxing for the black intellectual is that it seems so richly to symbolize that dislocation and that hatred.

Baldwin's boxing essay reveals some significant aspects of his creativity and his thought, of his relationship to white writers and to black athletes, of the surprisingly guileless yet strikingly unerring nature of his politics, enough to warrant its re-publication and its rightful placement among his nonfiction. What is found in the essay will not disguise the fact that it is, in some respects, a lesser piece, but its subject matter is of deep importance to anyone interested in the intricacies of American popular culture and its African-American possibilities or, conversely put, African-American culture and its popular American possibilities. The event that generated the essay (and the actual writing of the essay itself) came at a critical time in Baldwin's career, between the publication of the best-selling, hotly debated novel

Another Country, at the beginning of 1962, and the best-selling essay *The Fire Next Time,* at the beginning of 1963. In reconstructing that seminal year of work for Baldwin, the boxing essay becomes a vital fragment. And Baldwin is now recognized and accepted as an American writer of such brilliance and presence that every piece in the puzzle is necessary to bring forth the complete picture of his towering literary achievement.

IV

The Case of
LeRoi Jones/Amiri Baraka

I'm Everett LeRoi Jones, thirty years old. A black nigger in the universe. A long breath singer, wouldbe dancer, strong from years of fantasy and study....

—LeRoi Jones, "Numbers, Letters"

"Baraka?" Cecil Taylor, the great jazz pianist, rolled the name on his tongue as if he were tasting a strange wine that was both interesting and inadequate. "Oh, he never knew what he was talking about when he discussed my music." It was a late afternoon in the spring of 1973, and we were talking in the backseat of a very crowded car that was touring along the New Jersey Turnpike headed to Philadelphia from Glassboro State College, where Taylor was teaching a master class in jazz improvisation. I didn't know whether it was the sheer discomfort of riding in the packed car, or the bleak Jersey landscape, or the fact that the interview was going very poorly that made me feel unwell. But it seems to me now that I was responding chiefly to the uncharitable nature of Taylor's remark. It struck me even then as I recalled his comments on musicians like Keith Jarrett and Chick Corea and Stevie Wonder that he was an uncharitable man. But of course it had also to be remembered that Taylor was himself an artist whose difficult work was not likely to be widely appreciated. He had reasons for his attitude of cultivated resistance. But Baraka, I knew then, as I know now, has probably done more than any other writer to popularize black avant-garde music. He may not have understood it, as Taylor asserted, but he certainly adored it. And adoration is a very useful kind of currency in a society of cash-and-carry emotions.

But if Taylor was uncharitable, then perhaps it was only a sort of tough justice, since Baraka has a history of being fairly uncharitable himself, his most recent disagreements with Stanley Crouch and Ishmael Reed being cases in point. Baraka has always been enchanted with the idea of being embattled, and this may explain why he has probably participated in more fistfights than any other writer in American literary history.

One day in 1967, I think, Baraka walked into the SNCC office in Philadelphia, which was located on either Fifteenth or Sixteenth Street between Lombard and South. SNCC had become, as it was so quaintly put by the media in those days, "a militant organization" under the leadership of Stokely Carmichael and the rallying cry of "Black Power." The local office was under the fiery direction of James Foreman, whom I met several years later while we were both graduate students at Cornell University. He seemed in the later years only a shell of his former robust self, done in presumably by his many confrontations with Philly's wonderfully psychotic men-in-blue and Mississippi's delightfully deranged men-in-white. I remember lots of others hanging around that office as well, including Harry Foy; Ivanhoe Donaldson, then the brains behind Foreman, now the brains behind Marion Barry, mayor of Washington; Robo, who loved to get high on cough medicine; Walter Delegal, who later went to New York and became a filmmaker; Ronnie, who became a Moorish American (Philly has always had more black religious cults than either Africa or the Caribbean); Playtell Benjamin with his photographic memory; and my sisters who were the editors of the black newsletter called *Maji-Maji* and the founders of the Black Student Union of Temple University.

But Baraka's presence in that setting was the most impressive thing about it. He walked in surrounded by an entourage of dashiki-wearing, tough-looking guys and a few women wearing gelees. (My aunt was operating an African clothing store a few blocks up the street called The Uhuru Hut where one could get the latest in ethnic garments.) I saw him several times after that but I like to remember him as I saw him at that moment, a short bearded man with a very uncompromising look about him; despite mumblings by some in the office about "New York niggers who think their shit don't stink" (Baraka was, incidentally, living in Newark at this time), he was an utterly magnificent presence. He had, at that moment, the fine, tragic air of Turgenev's Barazov. He was, to my immature, fifteen-year-old eyes, the dark, inscrutable prince of the sixties.

But, in truth, Baraka was not a product of the sixties. He was an intellectual child of the fifties, a time that offered the cornball optimism of the Eisenhower years, the millennial fervor of the civil rights movement, and the sly yet vacuous excesses of primitive rock and roll juxtaposed against the political excesses of capitalist-McCarthyite democracy, on the one hand,

and Soviet Communism with its invasion of Hungary, on the other. The fifties was also the season of the Beats and the Black Mountain poets who launched new schools of poetry that challenged the academics and their poets; and if the fifties gave the public Dave Brubeck on the cover of *Time,* soft cool jazz on both coasts, and the strange mixture of jazz and classical that Gunther Schiller dubbed "third stream" music, then it also offered the budding avant-garde jazz of Ornette Coleman, Sun Ra, Cecil Taylor, Steve Lacy, George Russell, and the youthfully enigmatic John Coltrane. It was an age not so much of transition but of divided impulses; implacable conventions confronted the "scorched-earth" pursuits of innovative artists. A creature of his time, Baraka stood on the same edge, between convention and radical reform, sometimes opting for an adventurism that could become merely faddish. ("Why are the beautiful sick and divided like myself?" Baraka wrote in the poem "Cold Term.") The real paradox in Baraka, though, is not that he is attracted in any way to the conventional or respectable. He is not torn in the ways of Richard Wright or James Baldwin or Zora Neale Hurston, the three great black writers who came before him. Oddly enough, Baraka occupies the center rather than the circumference of his own conceptual world. He uses convention—and for Baraka this can mean political conservatism, literary preoccupation with form, or a set of ordinary chord changes in a jazz solo—as a measure of his rebellion, of precisely what he must fight against. Baraka's edge is located, therefore, between two mutually exclusive sets of ideas, and the act of walking this line is designed to heighten the tension between them. Syncretism has no intellectual appeal to Baraka. He wants and knows to court risks. This, in part, explains the incredible—sometimes exciting, sometimes juvenile—imbalance in most of Baraka's writing, an imbalance that is not easy to define.

But convention never exists wholly in the abstract for Baraka, for the fight is also against the conventional, the respectable proclivities within himself which in his recent autobiography he summarizes in the standard way as "bourgeois." Baraka does not seek to make any sort of peace with any part of the world as it is; hence his rebellion is not only against governments, oppressive political ideologies, false prophets, and bad artists, but against the present itself, against the very idea of a present that seems to tie human beings up in the riggings of life without allowing them to live it. Rebellion of this sort seems to me and ought to seem to Baraka philosophically absurd not only because its affirmation is the quest for the fictive purer self—as expressed by Baraka's fervent wish to be "blacker" during his cultural nationalist days and to be more "revolutionary" now during his Marxist present—but because it requires the constant denial of previous selves as impure or incorrect. Only the present avatar calling himself LeRoi Jones or Amiri Baraka can be trusted as true and real; all others are repudiated. But how can the present form of Baraka be trusted, according to his own philosophical coordinates, when the present world is itself a lie where the truth must be reflected in its inversions? For Baraka, iconoclasm begets a further and endless iconoclasm, so that one seems to be responding no longer to the world at all but to one's previous selves. We arrive, in short, at an elaborate sort of solipsism.

> *I am real, and I can't say who*
> *I am. Ask me if I know, I'll say*
> *Yes, I might say no. Still Ask.*
> —"Numbers, Letters"

This view of Baraka, of the tautologies in which he is bound, may explain in part why Baraka is so intensely disliked by many black intellectuals these days. Each change that Baraka experienced took on the weight, the timely significance of a conversion—from middle-class black boy with pretensions to the fast life to bohemian to black nationalist to Muslim to revolutionary activist—and the conversion experience implied both repudiation of a previous self and influence over other people. Baraka is one of the few artists in American history whose every life passage, whose every neurotic tremor, became the downbeat for a movement among the true believers. And many feel that Baraka has been more than a little irresponsible in the exercise of this influence. It is obvious to anyone even slightly familiar with Baraka's writings that he needed and continues to need these sleight-of-hand identity swaps in order to create the psychological tension he must have to write. "I want to be black and clean and free," he writes at the end of his autobiography. But Baraka, whose desires cannot be so simply and virtuously stated in any case, can be that only as long as he can define the world as unblack, unclean, and unfree. There may also be a good deal of jealousy among some black intellectuals and writers concerning Baraka. He was the most influential black person of letters over the last twenty years, particularly influential among young blacks, and he had a striking ability to communicate to people who had never read his books. It is not likely that any black writer or intellectual will generate a similar power anytime in the near or foreseeable future.

The Autobiography of LeRoi Jones/Amiri Baraka, the latest in a series of books which signal a resurgence on Baraka's part, is a very important work even if it is not a very good or insightful book. First, Baraka is an important American writer; he has written one substantial and incisive study of Afro-American music, *Blues People,* an impressive collection of essays, *Home,* at least one superlative volume of poetry, *The Dead Lecturer,* and at least four first-rate plays: *Dutchman, The Toilet, The Slave,* and *The Baptism. Tales, The System of Dante's Hell,* and *Preface to a Twenty Volume Suicide Note* are flawed but compelling works. Baraka has proven that he can be, when he wants, a very fine poet and an impressive playwright. To be sure, Baraka has written his share of junk, and much of the stuff from both his cultural nationalist and Marxist periods would fall into that category with the exception of a few absorbing plays like *The Great Goodness Life* and *Slave Ship.* But Baraka has always been a daring writer, and even his didactic nonsense is head and shoulders above other stuff in a similar vein that was being written by other black authors during the same period. He certainly never wrote a poem as bad as those of Nikki Giovanni or a piece of fiction as labored, dull, and cliché-ridden as *If Beale Street Could Talk,* Baldwin's dismal attempt to write a "relevant" work for the masses. Baraka has displayed both an understanding of and an ability to succeed creatively in a number of literary genres.

Second, the autobiography gives us a remarkably sharp picture of the engaged artist. Baraka, an activist in the truest sense of the word, one who often mistook passion for clarity of thought, was and is a deeply committed man. He even served time in prison as a result of an altercation with the police during the Newark riots of 1968. While a Beat, Baraka not only wrote poetry but started and edited several literary reviews; his home became a salon for many poets of his generation. When he became a nationalist, he went to Harlem and started the Black Arts movement, initiated the whole concept of street theater and community art shows, and led the drive to articulate a politics of Afro-American culture. When Baraka returned to Newark, his place of birth and education, and launched the Spirit House Movers, he not only was one of the prime figures behind numerous black power conferences that took place in the late sixties and early seventies but was one of those instrumental in the election of Kenneth Gibson as the first black mayor of Newark. In short, Baraka had much to do with the acceptance of the idea that blacks ought to have control of local politics in areas where they form the majority of the population. His many activities surely impaired Baraka as an artist to some degree, if only because he was unable to devote as much time to his art as he might have. Surprisingly, Baraka, who was never one to write several drafts when one would do (as he once wrote, "Say only what you know/Clearly & freely & swiftly, as it comes/ Springing from / the heart!"), continued to write substantially despite his distractions or perhaps because of them, since they provided the raw material he would continue to need.

Third, Baraka's autobiography gives detailed accounts of life at a black college (Howard University) and of other locations often ignored in standard treatments of American social and intellectual history. And although many persons Baraka names in his autobiography may have a different tale to tell about the matter of their common involvement (I would particularly like to see alternative accounts of Gibson, black nationalist Ron Karenga, former Black Panther Eldridge Cleaver, and the "fat, little, white wife" Nellie, Baraka's first spouse, all of whom are more or less savaged in the book), this is still the fullest, most coherent account of the reformist, counterculture America of the fifties and sixties that has been written by a participant.

Two major problems prevent the autobiography from being a good book. First, though it competently shuffles along as narrative, the prose of the book is hackneyed and stale. Baraka, who abhors the dictates of form, has always been enamored of style, even when it has cost him clarity and precision. But here the noted Barakian linguistic zooms and flights of fancy are attenuated. Mostly, the book gives us the impression that it was spoken through a microphone and then transferred to paper. And I find irritating the insouciance and offhand manner of this oral style, of an Amiri Baraka speaking a self-conscious patois of street language, quasi-Marxist analysis, occasional Rastafarian rant, occasional, ineffective poetic turns of phrase, and plain journalism.

The book also disappoints in offering scant discussion of Amiri Baraka as writer or of his works. Baraka spends a good deal of time setting the record straight about his first marriage, his sex life, and his various public functions as editor and as guide of Black Arts, Spirit House, the Congress of Afrikan Peoples, Black Community Development, and other groups. He talks most directly about himself as a writer during his account of his early years in the Air Force and in Greenwich Village. We learn that while in the Air Force he began to read voraciously, particularly the leading literary magazines and reviews and books cited in the *New York Times Book Review* best-sellers list. He also read the works of Joyce, Melville, James, and Dylan Thomas. In the autobiography he gives us a striking, rather poignant episode summarizing his estrangement from this world of high-brow and middle-brow literature:

> One afternoon I had gone to San Juan by myself. I had found some places in Old San Juan I could walk around....I'd stopped at a bench and sat down near a square. It was quiet and I could see a long way off toward the newer, more Americanized part of the city, the Condado Beach section, where I could go if in uniform, so they would know I was an Americano and not a native. I had been reading one of the carefully put together exercises *The New Yorker* publishes constantly as high poetic art, and gradually I could feel my eyes fill with tears, and my cheeks were wet and I was crying, quietly, softly but like it was the end of the world. I had been moved by the writer's words, but in another, very personal way. A way that should have taught me even more than it did....But I was crying because I realized that I could never write like that writer. Not that I had any real desire to, but I knew even if I had had the desire I could not do it. I realized that there was something in me so *out,* so unconnected with what this writer was, what that magazine was that what was in me that wanted to come out as poetry would never come out like that and be *my* poetry.

The discovery of Allen Ginsberg was Baraka's sudden realization of the voice within himself:

> I had been moved by *Howl* because it talked about a world I could identify with and relate to. His language and his rhythms were real to me. Unlike the cold edges and exclusiveness of *The New Yorker* poem that had made me cry, Ginsberg talked of a different world, one much closer to my own.
> I thought the book *Howl* was something special. It was a breakthrough for me. I now knew that poetry could be about some things that I was familiar with.

He later admits that he "took with the Beats because that's what [he] saw taking off and flying and somewhat resembling [himself]. The open and implied rebellion—of form and content." And he says that his own poetry "was much influenced by the [Charles] Olson-[Robert] Creeley–Black Mountain hookup." But there is little else, especially after the chapter on the Village and the Beats, about Baraka as writer. We discover that he wrote *Dutchman* in one night and that his first wife disliked *The Slave,* that *Blues People* was his first book to be published by a major press and that he wrote the poem "Preface to a Twenty Volume Suicide Note" for a child who had not even been born. Yet we learn next to nothing about the forces that drove him to produce these works, or what he takes them to say about the man he has become. And there is virtually no discussion of the writing he did as a cultural nationalist or how he came to regard his relations with older, established writers such as Gwendolyn Brooks (who is not mentioned once), James Baldwin, and Ralph Ellison. And though Baraka read considerably in Afro-American and African literature, he makes no mention of any compelling voices who influenced or even touched him.

Ultimately, the autobiography is most revealing in letting us see how little a certain kind of black intellectual can understand himself. The book presents itself, and its title certifies this interpretation, as part of the tradition of black *Bildungsroman* autobiographies, conjuring up images of *The Autobiography of Malcolm X* and *The Narrative of the Life of Frederick Douglass.* Yet the book also takes on the guise of a picaresque narrative, with its various low-life characters, unrelated adventures, a praise song for marriage and family at the end, and an ambiguous hero who may very well be a talented confidence man donning various masks in a most spirited way. In fact, Baraka never entirely dispels the suspicion that he is simply a rogue in search of endless kicks, the latest being the liberation of "the oppressed masses." The issue of his own imposture is something that Baraka approaches with a great deal of naiveté and a surprising lack of grace for someone who loves self-dramatizing and mythmaking as much as he does. The book suggests that Baraka was only seemingly a middle-class boy who wanted ordinary success in life but was really a bohemian searching for spiritual freedom and liberation from the philistines; later he was only seemingly a bohemian but was in truth a black nationalist who wanted spiritual freedom and liberation from whites; finally he was an apparent black nationalist who was in truth a Marxist desiring spiritual freedom and liberation from capitalist oppressors. He was never really what he thought and said himself to be at any given time; his true being was always somewhere else. And so there is no reason to suppose that Baraka is at present anything but a seeming Marxist and that he will wind up, like the transcendentalist Orestes Brownson who shifted ground in similar ways, an orthodox Catholic seeking spiritual discipline and liberation from sin. Baraka never exploits the rich psychological ambiguities inherent in all of this: though he admits his "mistakes," his male chauvinism and his posturing bohemianism and so on, he is principally eager to defend himself by utterly putting down those for whom he no longer has any use. Thus, the white bohemians were, by and large, racist, hedonistic, self-centered, and vampirish, an effete, tedious lot. The black nationalists were a bunch of feudalistic (one of Baraka's favorite words), psychotic, self-aggrandizing, false prophets. They were also—like the Afro-American writers he condemned twenty years ago in *Anger and Beyond*—bad writers and philistines. One can only wonder what the Marxists will seem to Baraka ten years from now.

Another disturbing aspect of Baraka's psychology that he can hardly begin to deal with is revealed in his constant references to popular culture figures, especially movie stars (someone always looks like Paul Newman or Jack Palance), athletes, and comic-book heroes. Baraka admits that radio shows and comic books deeply influenced his imagination when he was a kid:

> I heard heroes and saw them in my mind and imagined what evil was and cheered at its destruction. In the movies too, in film after film, evil could be destroyed. By Errol Flynn—*Robin Hood* will probably be ruled subversive by Strom Thurmond in a minute—and Tyrone Power, and Douglas Fairbanks, Jr., Gregory Peck, Jimmy Stewart, John Garfield, Humphrey Bogart, Gene Kelly, Stewart Granger, John Wayne, Alan Ladd, Gary Cooper, Henry Fonda. They taught us that evil needed to be destroyed....And I believed that—impressionable as I was at those young ages—but the trick is that I still believe it!

The influence is apparent in many of his writings; in *The Dead Lecturer,* for example, he uses the Green Lantern's code as an epigraph, a code that he always misquotes. And when he went to Cuba in 1960, he found the Communist revolution there to resemble moral plays he had grown up with: "I had been raised on Errol Flynn's *Robin Hood* and the endless hero-actors fighting against injustice and leading the people to victory over tyrants. The Cuban thing seemed a case of classic Hollywood proportions." All of this has had a tremendous influence on how Baraka sees life—both his own life and life in general. Always he has tended to believe in a kind of simplistic struggle of good and evil, in categories that are absolute and mutually exclusive. As a result, he has tended to see himself as the embattled self. In the Air Force, he stood against the racist, vulgarian, mad bombing loyalists. As a bohemian, he pitted himself against the academics and the intellectural conformists. As a nationalist, he pitted himself against the whites and all of Western tradition and history. As a Marxist, he pits himself against the middle-class boors and the upper-class manipulators of power, the so-called power elite and their agents. Such a moral grid is not only innocently, hopelessly unable to engage itself truly with the problems of this world; it is, in fact, dangerous because it is indeed so removed from the complexities of human reality or the problems raised by the fact of evil. The lurid qualities of the evil conjured by pop culture presuppose a concomitantly inflated conception of heroism. In searching for a framework in which the writer can see himself as a hero, he has often mistaken his outsized passion and sense of commitment for true courage.

It would be nice to see Baraka as the heroic figure he too often takes himself to be, nice to believe that someone who wants so badly to change the

world has the kind of self-knowledge that would make his judgments relia-
ble. Both as writer and as intellectual he has surely had a powerful effect on
his time, particularly on younger black intellectuals excited by his uncompromising vision. That this has also had a damaging effect on the ability of
some of our people to deal with reality in an effective way ought not to be
denied. It was exhilarating to learn, years ago, that a black writer could use
language to stir terror in the hearts of readers, both black and white, and
that he could refuse the blandishments typically offered to black "talent" by
white administrators, publishers, and academics. But the price to be paid for
sustaining that posture is something that black intellectuals will have to deal
with in a way that may be permanently beyond Amiri Baraka.

Addendum:
Jackie Robinson, Amiri Baraka, Paul Robeson, and a Note on Politics, Sports, and the Black Intellectual

In *The Autobiography of LeRoi Jones/Amiri Baraka,* the famous poet, playwright, and essayist reminisces about seeing Negro League baseball games as a boy growing up in Newark, a major stop on the Negro League circuit. There is nothing particularly surprising or informative in this. Baseball is a sport that tends toward an intense nostalgia among its most rabid male fans; it is, for every white intellectual who has an ounce of poetry in his soul and who followed baseball as a boy, the Wordsworthian Tintern Abbey of remembrance once he is grown. Baraka, for a few pages, gives us the black version of the same impulse but not without his political moral for this lesson/story of corrupt American culture. (After all, remembrance that aspires toward being apolitical is nothing more than bourgeois, reactionary politics at its most destructive because it is at its most sentimental, and heaven forbid that Baraka should be guilty of that venial sin!)

> The destruction of the Eagles, Greys, Black Yankees, Elite Giants, Cuban Stars, Clowns, Monarchs, Black Barons, to what must we attribute that? We're going to the big leagues. Is that what the cry was on those Afric' shores when the European capitalists and African feudal lords got together and palmed our future. "WE'RE GOING TO THE BIG LEAGUES!"

Baraka continues his political interpretation by attacking Jackie Robinson:

> So out of the California laboratories of USC, a synthetic colored guy was imperfected and soon we would be trooping back into the holy see of racist

approbation. So that we could sit next to drunken racists by and by. And watch our heroes put down by slimy cocksuckers who are so stupid they would uphold Henry and his Ford and be put in chains by both while helping to tighten ours....

But the scarecrow J.R. for all his ersatz "blackness" could represent the shadow world of the Negro integrating into America. A farce. But many of us fell for that and felt for him, really. Even though a lot of us knew the wholly artificial disconnected thing that Jackie Robinson was. Still when the backward Crackers would drop black cats on the field...we got uptight, for us, not just for J.R.

I remained a Giant "fan," cause me fadder was, even when J.R. came on the scene. I resisted that First shit (though in secret, you know, I had to uphold my own face, alone among a sea of hostile jerks!).

(So what? So Jackie came on down to DC town and they got his ass to put Paul Robeson down! I remember that, out of the side of my head I checked that. I wondered. What did it mean? What was he saying? And was it supposed to represent me? And who was that other guy—Paul Robeson? I heard that name...somewhere.) (Ellipsis Baraka's)

That Baraka incorrectly identifies Robinson's college as USC (Robinson attended, although he did not graduate from, UCLA) is a fairly typical mistake that results from Baraka's admitted disinclination to revise. In one respect, the mistake is crucial, for no one with any knowledge of Negro League baseball or Jackie Robinson would have made such a blatant error. Robinson's attendance at UCLA was well known and well publicized, as he was a star athlete there, as was Woody Strode, who went on to play professional football for the Los Angeles Rams (signing on May 7, 1946, almost a year after Robinson signed to play with the Brooklyn Dodgers' Montreal farm team) and who, after his football career ended, became an actor, mostly playing noble savage-type roles in movies such as *Spartacus* and *The Ten Commandments* or the victimized black in the socially conscious *Sergeant Rutledge.* I remember vividly seeing Woody Strode in a good many jungle B movies on Saturday afternoons, being flattened by some white Jungle Jim or some Tarzan, much to the embarrassment of all us young black boys; and I mention all of this because it was such common knowledge for any black male who grew up listening to older black men talk in barbershops about the history of blacks in sports from Joe Gans to Big Daddy Lipscomb. It is always with Baraka that his brilliance is touched by some sense of being counterfeit, for he constantly subverts the very credibility of his knowledge.

On one level, Baraka's politics here, such as it is, might be easily dismissed. It is mostly the art of name-calling (white racists are "slimy cocksuckers" and those blacks who supported Robinson were "hostile jerks") and arrogance (Baraka is always more right and more intelligent than anyone who disagrees with him) disguised as self-justification. On another level, the simplicity of his dismissal of such a complicated and admittedly often disturbing and unappealing man like Robinson seems motivated largely by Baraka's own *adult* feelings of mortification about the entire act and meaning of racial integration in America. (Baraka is not moved simply by

Robinson's "sellout" testimony; after all, a radical black leftist writer, Langston Hughes, was to testify rather meekly before HUAC a few years later.) Racial integration has been and continues to be a nearly intolerable burden on blacks who must prove themselves worthy of entry. Baraka's outrage over this is an outrage that many blacks feel but ultimately an insult that those who "want to get ahead" must pocket. For Baraka, Robinson—the Frankenstein's monster of American racial pathology (Robinson's integration of baseball was called "the noble experiment," thus the source for Baraka's image)—sinned thrice against black political interests as Baraka understands them: first, he agreed to integrate baseball as an *individual* (not as part of a group but rather as a symbol of a group); second, his success created the paradigm of black integration into white America—it must always be the black who brings about a change of heart in the white by bearing the burden of his racial stigma instead of the white's bearing the burden of his irrational racial phobias; third, he sealed the acceptance of these terms when he attacked Paul Robeson publicly in 1949, something that Robinson regretted in his 1972 autobiography, *I Never Had It Made:*

> I was not sure about what to do [about the request from the House Un-American Activities Committee to come to Washington to testify against Robeson]. Rachel [his wife] and I had long talks about it. She felt I should follow my instincts. I didn't want to fall prey to the white man's game and allow myself to be pitted against another black man. I knew that Robeson was striking out against racial inequality in the way that seemed best to him. However in those days I had much more faith in the ultimate justice of the American white man than I have today. I would reject such an invitation if offered now.

Apparently, Baraka when a boy knew Robeson only as a name, which is actually mildly surprising since Robeson was from New Jersey (he became a football legend at Rutgers, the State University of New Jersey), as was Baraka, and that Robeson's years of great fame occurred during Baraka's boyhood and early adolescence. Robeson was certainly talked about in black communities nationwide and was written about in the black press with great frequency. His very ignorance about Robeson would tend to undermine the assertion that he thought as a boy that Robinson's testimony was contrary to black interests, unless he was annoyed that one black would publicly voice an opinion that was critical of another black. Of course, Baraka's philippic ultimately becomes a kind of digression about the epistemology of racial unity (he himself is an outsider in his dislike of Robinson just as Robeson was an outsider, that much identification the youthful Baraka had to be aware of in order to have the passage make any sense at all), a unity he imagines would be well served if he is free to criticize but poorly served if others are victimized by unjust criticism, and after all, blacks, like many oppressed people, have had a crab-in-the-basket mentality, cannibalizing each other simply to get notice. Baraka's response to this has always been a kind of intellectual fascism, which is why he has been drawn to absolutist systems (black cultural nationalism, Marxism) that insulate against criticism by propounding doctrines instead of generating propositions.

The whole affair involving Robinson's public criticism of Robeson is worthy of some scrutiny as it is both compelling and complex. First, the very icon of Robinson testifying had become fixed in the public mind by 1950, when the film bio of Robinson's life (with a rather portly Robinson portraying himself), *The Jackie Robinson Story,* was released. The film ends with Robinson, having been told by the actor who played Branch Rickey, the president and general manager of the Dodgers who signed him and became a sort of father figure for him, that he could now "fight back" and express himself after having "endured" for the first two years of his major league career, going to Washington (Robeson is not mentioned in the film) to testify in a scene that is framed by images of the Capitol Building and the Statue of Liberty. In an era when Hollywood glamorized the informer (*On the Waterfront,* 1954, winner of eight Academy Awards), it is intriguing that Robinson's apotheosis as American is completed when he becomes, in a sense, an informer as well. Second, Robeson was a man of some importance, having established a lucrative if not totally satisfactory and satisfying career as a singer, stage, and screen actor, otherwise why have Robinson testify at all, and somehow a clash between the two men as "Representative Negroes" in American popular culture was inevitable.

Robinson was asked to testify in July 1949 by Georgia Congressman John S. Wood of the House Un-American Activities Committee "to give the lie to statements by Paul Robeson," so the telegram read. Although he does not say so in his autobiography, one has to suspect that Robinson had to feel a bit uneasy about being asked to testify by a Southerner. After all, Congressman Wood had called the Ku Klux Klan "an American institution." Oddly, Wood was not present when Robinson and several other prominent blacks testified. Robeson asserted in a press conference at the Hotel Theresa after Robinson's testimony that Wood did not appear because he didn't "want to call Jackie 'Mister Robinson.'"

Robeson, who was, at this time, as Harold Cruse wrote, "the most controversial Negro figure in America and the most widely known in all the world," had said earlier that year in Paris that blacks would not take up arms to fight against the Soviet Union. Actually, at the press conference after Robinson's testimony, Robeson denied saying precisely that. What he did say precisely was this: "It is unthinkable that American Negroes could go to war on behalf of those who have oppressed us for generations against the Soviet Union, which in one generation has raised our people to full human dignity." There is a certain naiveté in Robeson's statement, and a certain truth in that, at that point in American history, if blacks were indifferent to the question of fighting *against* the Soviet Union, some were surely thinking of the possibility of not fighting *for* America. Robeson's attachment to Communism, which started in 1934 when he visited that country for the first time, seemed ultimately both untenable and, for his position as a black intellectual, blatantly unusable. (Certainly Robinson thought this, as it formed the basis of his criticism. However, Robinson's own association with the Republican Party after his retirement from baseball was to be just as untenable and just as unusable.) Robeson maintained his popularity among blacks for some considerable time after he had fallen from grace generally largely in spite of his left-wing politics, not because of them. Indeed, his quasi–Pan-Africanism made many blacks think for a long time that Robeson was actually a nationalist, which his 1956 book, *Here I Stand,* should clearly have dispelled.

In any case, it was at this particular moment in post–World War II history that Robinson made his testimony, which consisted of two key statements: "I've been asked to express my views on Paul Robeson's statement in Paris to the effect that American Negroes would refuse to fight in any war against Russia because we love Russia so much. I haven't any comment to make, except the statement, if Mr. Robeson actually made it, sounds very silly to me. But he has a right to his personal views, and if he wants to sound silly when he expresses them in public, that's his business and not mine. He's still a famous ex-athlete and a great singer and actor." And then this, with a sarcastic reference to Robeson at the end: "I can't speak for 15 million people any more than any other one person can; but I know that I've got too much invested for my wife and child and myself in the future of this country, and I and many other Americans have too much invested in our country's welfare, for any of us to throw it away for a siren song in bass." And so the two mythical black men, one an athlete who had broken the twentieth-century color barrier to America's most venerated sport, and the other a former professional and college athlete who had, in 1946, at the invitation of Judge Landis, pleaded with baseball owners to integrate the game, the two angry black men who were not, in the end, really angry at each other, rhetorically rehearsed the dilemma of blackness in America: that all gestures signify a politic that wishes to free itself of the signification of all gestures (the true meaning of the bourgeois phrase "to be free") but which becomes, at last, a realized politic act of psychological debasement.

The story of the relationship between the two men after Robinson's testimony is unclear. Robeson held a press conference the following day but refused to attack Robinson, saying only that HUAC's calling of Robinson and other blacks to Washington "to testify as to their loyalty is a campaign of terror and an insult to the entire Negro people." On August 28, 1949, one day after the beginning of the horrible Peekskill incident, when Robeson was prevented from singing by mobs of riotous white veterans, Robinson bitterly denounced the violence against Robeson in an interview. In *Freedom* magazine in April 1953, Robeson wrote "An Open Letter to Jackie Robinson," which largely encouraged him to continue to speak out against oppression and racism, although with more than a bit of a world history lesson thrown in. There are two anecdotes related by two Robeson biographers that may be apocryphal but which in essence tell the same tale: In the first, which takes place at the Red Rooster, a Harlem bar, in the 1940s, pitcher Don Newcombe of the Brooklyn Dodgers is sitting at a table of admirers when Robeson comes in and someone gets the idea that it would be a momentous occasion if these two men were to meet. Robeson came over to shake Newcombe's hand but Newcombe refused to acknowledge the gesture; he wanted to have nothing to do with Communists, so he said. The second story takes place in a Harlem bar, Small's Paradise, in the early 1950s. Robeson is there with some friends when he notices Robinson and Newcombe at another table. Robeson sends a message to have the baseball players join him and Robinson supposedly replies, "Fuck Paul Robeson." When Robinson and Newcombe leave, Newcombe stops at Robeson's table and apologizes for Robinson. It is impossible that both of these stories are true, and it is highly possible that neither is (although we now know from Martin Duberman's exhaustive biography of Robeson that at least a version of the first story is true. Newcombe did have a run-in with Robeson at a bar. Apparently, Robinson was not present. Newcombe's slight of Robeson was very unfavorably received in the New York black community). But the breach between Robeson and young black athletes, the breach between Robeson and Robinson particularly, had become the storytelling stuff of gossip, the stuff of legend.

In the realm of his testimony, undoubtedly, Robinson was heavily influenced to behave in the way he did by Joe Louis, the major black athlete who preceded him as a dominant figure in American popular culture. Louis's devotion to American ideals, his patriotism, in short, was never questioned; Robinson may have felt that Louis's example was a proper one. Certainly, prominent blacks at the time were afraid to have their loyalty questioned for good reason: the only result from any criticism of the United States would be the wreckage of their own lives. Should they have been so cooperative is an open question. That the vast majority were is due to a predictable human impulse; men and women do not wish to make their lives any more difficult than they have to. But of course Robinson was not being asked to speak out against the government or against American society; he had to consider the integrity of remaining silent against a black who had spoken out—a different act entirely and a less risky one (although not without its dangers). But Amiri Baraka's insistent condemnation of Robinson, as a rhetorically backward-reaching conceit over decades to bring a flourishingly rich closure of alienation to a mad tale about nothing more than the complete disintegrating anguish of alienation, is finally the fundamentalist's denouncement of sin (political, in this case, instead of theological) without understanding the necessity of it, the sheer power and indeed deep humanity of cowardice in the face of life itself, which is all sin really is: to confess that to be human is just that, after all, and nothing more. Robinson's testimony symbolizes the ambiguity of Robinson's life: Where is the line between debasement and epic? Was his life the epic of debasement or was it the debasement of epic? The problem with Robinson is that he was quite unable to accept this himself, which is why his life, in some sense, so rich with grandeur and a valiant heroism in the face of his compromises, seems so devoid of humanity because he seemed so obsessed with overcoming the degradation of his blackness without understanding and further without being humbled by (not humiliated, which in truth he was) his acceptance of terms that were to be destructive for him. What killed Robinson at the comparatively young age of fifty-three was the acceptance of the athletic code of intense competitive jousting, the morality of acceptance and mobil- ity in the meritocracy in which, because he had been a successful athlete, Robinson so fervently believed. The code he hoped so much would fulfill and prove his life ultimately denied him life. The example of Robinson offers, unfortunately, for Baraka or anyone else, no easy lessons in the end.

What utter crap — Robinson accepted the world of racism to move in it
It didn't kill him

A New Reading
of Herman Melville's
"Benito Cereno"

It goes without saying that writing on Herman Melville is a major industry among scholars who specialize in American literature. I can remember awaking one morning to read an article in *The Journal of Popular Literature* entitled "The Avatars of *Moby-Dick* in Contemporary Popular American Fiction" by a colleague and friend, Elizabeth Schultz, and thinking that the world had come to a pretty pass, not to awaken to Melville himself but to be entangled in the endless web of discourse about him. Dissertations and books on him continue to be ground out with all the prolific zeal of workers making sausage in a sausage factory, and sometimes, one suspects, with as much feeling or understanding; Melville is, after all, a sufficiently "safe" writer to write about, conferring, as he does, eminent respectability, rigorous intellectuality, and a virtual thicket of dense images that one can deconstruct, reconstruct, or psychoanalyze, as is one's wont. Melville studies, with their correct emphasis on hermeneutics as Melville's texts have emerged as the American cabala, have become the equivalent of a kind of Christology, complete with their own version of the blending of history and kerygma: namely that Melville was not only a deep thinker about politics but a radical one as well, and to discover this seems a kind light bestowed not only upon Melville but upon the discoverer as well.

To paraphrase George Orwell in his discussion of Charles Dickens, it seems that Melville has become a writer whom white liberal and leftist scholars are awfully eager to steal, to sweep him away from the clutches of the old-fashioned, conservative (racist, if they were reading "Benito Cereno") positivists who had their sway. It was black Marxist scholar C. L. R. James who brought a decidedly different flavor to Melville criticism with his *Mariners, Renegades, and Castaways: The Story of Herman Melville and the World We Live In* (1953). The books that have come after in James's vein, not necessarily Marxist but seeing Melville clearly as politically radical, are more scholarly rehearsed than James's book was, which some today might call impressionistic, but I think these books were deeply influenced by James's reading of Melville. One of these is Carolyn L. Karcher's *Shadow Over the Promised Land: Slavery, Race, and Violence in Melville's America* (1980), a book that seems very much like something H. Bruce Franklin (one of the mentors for Ms. Karcher's project) would have written had he written his Melville book in the 1970s instead of the early 1960s (*The Wake of the Gods: Melville's Mythology,* 1963); it seems a fair companion piece to his work on black prison literature. Another is Michael Paul Rogin's *Subversive Genealogy: The Politics and Art of Herman Melville* (1983). And a third is Joyce Adler's *War in Melville's Imagination* (1981). But the true political litmus test for Melville is not *Moby-Dick* (1851) or even the entire corpus of his writing. It is, in fact, just one story: the novella "Benito Cereno" (1855), a tale about a slave revolt.

The story, based on a portion of Amasa Delano's 1817 *Narrative of Voyages and Travels in the Northern and Southern Hemispheres,* recounts the encounter between the captain of an American merchant vessel, Delano, and the captain of a Spanish slave ship, Benito Cereno. The tale takes place on board the Spaniard's vessel. Delano, after spying that the *San Dominick,* Cereno's ship, is apparently in distress, becomes immediately suspicious about Cereno and his relationship with his slaves. But he is constantly reassured by the bond shown between Cereno and his ever-faithful servant, Babo. After witnessing several strange incidents on board the *San Dominick,* most of which involve the strange-acting Cereno and his servant, and after having given the slaves and Cereno's small crew food and water, Delano prepares to leave the ship, when Cereno suddenly jumps onto a whale boat with him. It soon becomes apparent to Delano that Babo and the slaves have revolted, seized the ship, and made Cereno their prisoner. It then becomes clear to Delano that Cereno was never the captain of his ship but was only *acting* so under the subversive orders of Babo. Delano's crew pursues the blacks and eventually subdues them. The blacks are tried and punished (here, the story uses nearly word for word the deposition material in Delano's original narrative); their leader, Babo, is executed. Cereno, absolutely debilitated both physically and emotionally by his harrowing experience with the blacks, is taken to a monastery where he dies. The story has been hugely influential on at least two major Afro-American novels. In Richard Wright's *Native Son* (1940), Bigger Thomas's "Sambo" act after he kills Mary Dalton is an exact cognate of Babo's fawning slave routine. (It must be remembered that Bigger's subversive creed was: "Act like other people thought you ought to act, yet do what you wanted.") The image of the bones of Mary Dalton is used in much the same manner (as a fetish) as the bones of Aranda, the slaveholder, murdered by the blacks in Melville's story. In Ralph Ellison's *Invisible Man* (1952), among other literary allusions, a quotation from "Benito Cereno" is used as an epigraph. (Ellison links the thematic threads and philosophical propositions of Ishmael's encounter in the black church where the preacher's text is "the blackness of darkness" with the ambiguity about racial roles in "Benito Cereno" to inform the thematic and philosophical structures of his own novel.) Incidentally, the shaving scene in *The Color Purple* (1982), both book and movie, comes directly from the shaving scene in "Benito Cereno."

In interpreting the story, one can be on the side of either the old folk such as Rosalie Feltenstein, Richard H. Fogle, or Stanley T. Williams, who tended to see the story as a discussion of human depravity and darkness (Babo, the slave leader, symbolizing both); or of the new liberals or the new historicists such as Rogin, Karcher, Adler, Allan Moore Emery, Eric Sundquist, and Glenn Altschuler, who feel that the story is denouncing slavery and racism and is clearly critical of the innocent American captain Delano; they are inspired, in part, by Robert Lowell's dramatization of "Benito Cereno" in *The Old Glory* (1965). When I read the "old school" criticism of "Benito Cereno," I was put off by the smug racism of those critics enough to think that the business of literary criticism was a fairly shoddy exercise in obscurantism indeed. Or, to put it another way, as a black reader I felt that Melville desperately needed to be rescued from that nonsense. However, the "new school" readings did not reassure or comfort me.

I had read a few Melville biographies, Newton Arvin's, Leon Howard's, Edwin H. Miller's, and I did not see anywhere stated that Melville ever knew any black people well or intimately (if his portrayals of blacks in his pre-*Pierre* novels are any indication of his actual acquaintance with them on board ships, I would not say his knowledge was especially deep, although it must be admitted that he wrote about nonwhites with a great deal more sensitivity than nearly all of his contemporaries); that he ever read a book written by a black; that he never read *Uncle Tom's Cabin* or any of the leading antislavery literature of the day; that he was ever remotely involved in the cause of abolition. I have been quite impressed by the impeccable scholarship of the "new school," and their readings of "Benito Cereno" certainly made me feel a great deal less insulted as a black reader, but I was not convinced entirely about the liberal or radical politics of Melville. I remember Houston Baker once saying to me that he simply could not believe that a white man living in America in the 1850s was as radical as younger white scholars wanted to make Melville out to be. I felt rather much the same way. If Melville was so vehemently against slavery, it seemed to have been largely an armchair, meditative defiance.

I am no Melville scholar, which, considering how many there are these days, makes me an interesting exception to a quite blanket rule of conformity.

But I have always been interested in Melville, especially "Benito Cereno." There are two observations I would like to make about the story, neither of which is meant to go against anyone else's reading but which are simply my own responses as a black reader to Melville's very puzzling tale about slavery and a way for me to understand Melville without making him anything more than an exceptionally gifted American white writer of the 1850s.

I. NICHOLAS AND BLACK PETER

*...all thy strange mummeries not
unmeaningly blended with the black tragedy of
the melancholy ship, and mocked it.*
— Melville writing about Pip in *Moby-Dick*

I generally agree with Carolyn Karcher's and Michael Paul Rogin's readings of "Benito Cereno." Karcher analyzes the story by considering the important question: For Melville, what are the moral implications of Delano's racism in Delano's world in the 1850s? She answers it by offering a cogent interpretation of the story as a critique of the racist scientific theories of race of the day. Rogin deals with the question of paternalism—a theme, incidentally, of major importance in both *Native Son* and *Invisible Man*. Rogin argues that "Melville's slave mutiny as masquerade inserted itself between two opposed perspectives on the master-slave relationship in antebellum America, and unsettled both. Abolitionists invoked the Declaration of Independence to justify slave revolt at sea. Southerners and their Northern sympathizers (like Delano) defended slavery as a familially based alternative to the competitive deceptions of Northern free society."

Paternalism seems to have been a crucial concern in the nineteenth century and particularly so among Americans thinking about slavery at mid-century. Southern apologists used paternalism as a defense of slavery as a noble institution benefitting both slave and master. As Eugene Genovese wrote in *Roll, Jordan, Roll: The World the Slaves Made* (1974):

> For the slaveholders paternalism represented an attempt to overcome the fundamental contradiction in slavery: the impossibility of the slaves ever becoming the things they were supposed to be. Paternalism defined the involuntary labor of the slaves as a legitimate return to their masters for protection and direction. But, the masters' need to see their slaves as acquiescent human beings constituted a moral victory for the slaves themselves. Paternalism's insistence upon mutual responsibilities, and ultimately even rights—implicitly recognized the slaves' humanity.

Historian James Oakes adds that a "paternalist assumes an inherent inequality of men: some are born to rule, others to obey." David Roberts indicates further in his study *Paternalism in Early Victorian England* (1979) that the assumptions that most aptly characterized paternalism were that society was authoritarian and that the paternalist's first duty was to rule.

But while southerners used this reactionary social and political idea to defend slavery, others such as Frederick Law Olmsted in his *A Journey to the Back Country in the Winter of 1853-54* (1860) were questioning it:

> It is difficult to handle simply as property, a creature possessing human feelings, however debased and torpid the condition of that creature may be; while, on the other hand, the absolute necessity of dealing with property, as a thing, greatly embarrasses a man in any attempt to treat it as a person. And it is the natural result of this complicated state of things, that the system of slave-management, is irregular, ambiguous, and contradictory—that it is never either consistently humane or consistently economical.

Harriet Beecher Stowe in *Uncle Tom's Cabin* (1852), through her depictions of the benevolent slaveholders Shelby and Augustine St. Clair, openly attacked paternalism as a fraud; for Stowe, contrary to the apologists' arguments, paternalism protected neither the humanity of the slaveholder nor the slave.

The southerner Rogin had most in mind was George Fitzhugh, whose *Sociology for the South* (1854) and *Cannibals All!* (1857) argued brilliantly, as Eugene Genovese in his *The World the Slaveholders Made* (1969) has pointed out, against capitalism, and just as strenuously, if less successfully, for paternalism. (Although it must be stated here that Fitzhugh's views were not representative of the southern master class as a whole, which, as Genovese points out, was uncomfortable with many of Fitzhugh's assertions. Oakes points out further in his study *The Ruling Race: A History of American Slaveholders* [1982] that the South was not really a feudalistic society in many aspects, perhaps most aspects of its economic and social relations. No southerner wanted a feudal aristocracy at the expense of white democracy.) Rogin, who scaffolds his formulations with considerable contemporary political history—including references to Marx and Hegel which, though interesting and suggestive, seem a bit off the track since Melville probably had not read the works of either philosopher—makes a convincing case. I am wiliing to concede that Melville was probably a sensitive, perhaps even unusual, thinker on the subject of racial politics and politics generally during his time. But his art must be interpreted through what he was likely to know and to be interested in and not through a modern formulation of what constitutes significant matter in the intellectual and social history of his times.

I agree that the story is about racism and, more important, paternalism. Both of these thematic preoccupations are collapsed in one icon that Melville undoubtedly knew and thought about. What I am thinking about is the Dutch legend of St. Nicholas, which Melville knew because of his Dutch ancestry, his membership in the Dutch Reformed Church, and his having grown up in an area in New York where a good many Dutch traditions remained alive, including those connected with the celebration of the Feast of St. Nicholas on December 6 and Christmas. (Remember the *Pequod* in *Moby-Dick* sailed on Christmas Day.) Alice Kenney in her *Stubborn for Liberty: The Dutch in New York* (1975) discusses the use of Dutch culture and folklore in several of Melville's works. Melville probably learned even more, if that was necessary, from traveling with Dutch sailors on the ocean voyages he took as a young man. (A Dutch sailor is mentioned in virtually every one of his sea-going novels.) As Adrianus D. De Groot points out in his *Saint Nicholas: A Psychoanalytic Study of His History and Myth* (1965), "The sailors' patronage has been part of the Western Nicholas-cult from the very beginning. In the Greek tradition, it appears in several legends, the oldest—which also was widely known in Western Europe—being the *Praxis de Nautis,* the story of the seafarers." So it can be confidently stated that Melville knew about the Nicholas myth. In learning about it, Melville would have known that St. Nicholas traveled with a black helper named, appropriately enough, Black Peter. De Groot states:

> It is only in the Western—and specifically in the Dutch—tradition, however, that the Saint and the Black One have become such an inseparable pair.... The Dutch traditional "Black Peter," the now harmless companion, was originally a devil, a subdued devil.

De Groot continues:

> Let us...consider "Black Peter." His paraphernalia—the sack filled with spice nuts, and the rod—are quite recognizable images of what he originally represented. As for the rest, he is small, not much to look at (black), still full of mischief, a trifle terrifying especially in the eyes of children, a queer customer and joker—features which are all easy enough to identify. Further, his original task was that of "chimney sneak for St. Nicholas" (which chore could in itself, by the way, account both naturally and morally for his blackness: soot and sin hang on).

Melville would have learned something else as well, something especially intriguing in the story of this Dutch saint:

> Although St. Nicholas lived in Asia Minor and was buried in Italy, the Netherlands' belief is that he comes from Spain. How is this to be accounted for?...It seems reasonable to explain this by reference to Dutch national history. Through many centuries the Netherlands were closely associated with rich, powerful Spain, not only politically—ending up with the Eighty Years' War of independence—but also through various kinds of trade relations. A "ship from Spain" was apt to bring a rich cargo of uncommon goods worthy of St. Nicholas. The final step in connection may have been due to Black Peter, who was sometimes called "the Moor." Of course Moors came from Spain, and *Spanish lords often had black valets; so whoever had a black valet must be a Spanish lord.* (Emphasis mine)

But if the legend tells us that a black valet presupposes a Spanish lord, Melville's story reverses the order so that a Spanish lord presupposes a black valet: "There is something in the negro which, in a peculiar way, fits him for avocations about one's person. Most negroes are natural valets and hairdressers, taking to the comb and brush congenially as to the castanets." In a story that introduces the reader early on to an icon "of a dark satyr in a mask, holding his foot on the prostrate neck of a writhing figure, likewise masked," and that hinges upon the almost Alfred Hitchcock-like voyeurism of its principal character (*Rear Window* comes to mind instantly), Delano, it seems reasonable to think that a larger icon may govern the text externally. The icon on the side of the *San Dominick* is ambiguous, at least when one considers it in the light of the two schools of criticism about the story: Is the dark satyr the bestial black man who has taken over the ship or the bestial white, Delano, whose "right foot...ground the prostrate negro" when the revolt was finally uncovered?

The governing icon of St. Nicholas and Black Peter is meant to be less problematic.* The legend informs us that it is important to see Cereno and Babo as an actual representation of a cultural idea that was common not only in European secular life but in European religious life as well. Delano's assumptions, in whose sources is buried deeply this idea of the partnership between Nicholas and Peter, are, I think, more complicated and dense that the mere label of "racist" or "depraved" can ever hope to describe. Cereno, the Spanish lord, has taken control and tamed Babo/Peter, who is the devil, degraded humanity, and a loyal servant. The fact that St. Nicholas is also the patron of procreation and that, at one point in the development of the legend, Peter, the devil, would have represented evil sexuality creates waves of suggestive inquiry that go beyond the immediate scope of this essay. What I have tried to uncover in connecting the relationship of Cereno and Babo to that of Nicholas and Peter, whom De Groot called "a pair both grand and somewhat ridiculous," is that the paternalist relationship between white lord and black servant has deep psychosexual and psychocultural origins that have become part of the cultural unconsciousness of a person like Delano. It is necessary to add the icon of Nicholas and Peter to the reading of religious symbols that H. Bruce Franklin discovers in the story for two reasons: it locates the mythical source of Delano's paternalistic assumptions, and it emphasizes the idea of mummery.

The Nicholas legend is closely associated with the European pagan tradition of mumming processionals, celebrations performed by masked or disguised persons, because his sainthood, his very symbolic importance, became tied to the winter calendar of festivals.† Charles W. Jones, another

---

*I have isolated only a small part of the Nicholas myth. Books such as those mentioned in the text as well as Charles W. Jones's *The St. Nicholas Liturgy and Its Literary Relationships* (1963) provide the complete story. There are times when Delano appears as a Nicholas type or a parody of Nicholas. He provides food and drink for the stricken and ultimately rescues Cereno and his crew, in feats attributed to Nicholas by the sailors who formed his cult.
†Nicholas's was the only legend treated in Church (miracle) plays that are extant and complete. The history of the Mummers' plays is provided in R. J. E. Tiddy's *The Mummers' Play* (1923). These are separate but related strands of English folk drama.

St. Nicholas scholar, writes in his *Saint Nicholas of Myra, Bari, and Manhattan: Biography of a Legend* (1978) that "the Black Man [Black Peter] had a mummer's part" in his role as servant to Nicholas. But Herbert Halpert in his essay "A Typology of Mumming," in *Christmas Mumming in Newfoundland: Essays in Anthropology, Folklore, and History* (1969), which discusses the mumming tradition in Newfoundland, emphasizes that both Nicholas and Peter were mummers. I think that there are some aspects of the Christmas mumming tradition as practiced in Newfoundland that are especially illuminating when considering "Benito Cereno," a story whose entire plot turns upon mumming or disguise. Melville probably learned about this tradition in any one of several ways: from Newfoundland sailors, from books and sources on fisheries which he used in his research (Newfoundland is one of the world's major fisheries), or from his own Dutch background and his extensive acquaintance with Dutch folklore, whose St. Nicholas tradition also involves some mummery. Also, because the mumming tradition in Newfoundland is similar to that practiced in Britain, he could have learned about this from British sailors or British sources. Finally, the practice of Christmas mumming is quite popular in Latin America, as Halpert points out, especially in Quito, Ecuador, and Melville seemed knowledgeable about certain aspects of Latin American traditions and culture. It is especially intriguing that this mumming practice is quite well known in Quito, because the Doubloon in *Moby-Dick* bears the name of this place in bold letters.

There are several important elements of Newfoundland mumming that Melville borrowed for his story: Halpert describes the house visits of Nicholas and Peter as "visitations by inquisitors": Nicholas and Peter "come in the role of inquisitors or judges of the children's behaviour." Halpert also stresses that mumming involves disguise, "disguise of face and body with varying degrees of elaboration, and with sex-reversal (the man-woman figures) as a frequent pattern." I think it is fairly apparent how Melville used these ideas for his story. The image of Nicholas and Peter as inquisitors ties in with not only the imagery of the Spanish Inquisition that scaffolds the story but also the two internal inquisitions, the accountings of the behavior that takes place within the story. The first is when Babo, after having seized Cereno's ship, tells the captain to "keep faith with the blacks," and the second is when the blacks are tried after their capture by Delano's crew. In both cases, the victims are not allowed to speak in their defense; their behavior, in Cereno's instance as a slaveholder and in Babo's instance as a rebelling slave, must speak for itself. The disguises are used by Melville in a deeply ironical way. Babo and Cereno have changed places, the slave is now the master, the master now the slave. Yet the masks they adopt, instead of being true role reversals, are merely more ingrained intensifications of their original relationship. The mummery here takes on a deep deceptive complexity that reflects endlessly, like mirrors showing an infinite row of the same image. If Delano's role is that of the friend who is traditionally charged in mummery with guessing the true identities of the mummers, then his situation is nearly hopeless to begin with because he has no sure idea that a game is being played, although there are moments when he senses such:

> To Captain Delano's imagination, now again not wholly at rest, there was something so hollow in the Spaniard's manner, with apparently some reciprocal hollowness in the servant's dusky comment of silence, that the idea flashed across him, that possibly master and man, for some unknown purpose, were acting out, both in word and deed, nay, to the very tremor of Don Benito's limbs, some juggling play before him.

And, of course, in order to keep himself and Delano alive, Cereno must make sure that Delano never learns the true nature of the play.

II. THE TWO CAPTAINS, OR, NOTES ON IMPOSTURE

O Brave New World
That has such people in't!
—Shakespeare, *The Tempest*

William Godwin, in his 1794 novel, *Caleb Williams, or Things As They Are,* a book Melville procured in 1849 and undoubtedly read, has the two antagonists, Tyrrel and Falkland, confront one another in a key scene. Tyrrel says:

> "Zounds, sir, do not think to put your conundrums upon me! Is not my estate my own? What signified calling it mine, if I am not to have the direction of it? Sir, I pay for what I have; I owe no man a penney; and I will not put my estate to nurse you, nor the best he that wears a head."

Falkland responds:

> "It makes one's heart ache to think that one is born to the inheritance of every superfluity, while the whole share of another, without any demerit of his, is drudgery and starving; and that all this is indispensable. We that are rich, Mr. Tyrrel, must do everything in our power to lighten the yoke of these unfortunate people."

D. H. Munro has characterized this contrast by calling Falkland "the spirit of Monarchy, and Tyrrel...the spirit of Despotism," a useful parallel that can be applied to Cereno and Delano in "Benito Cereno," which I will consider momentarily. The contrast between the aggressive instinct of conquest, ownership, and authoritarian paternalism of Tyrrel and the benevolent, helping paternalism of Falkland shows the antithetical yet joined sides of the capitalistic coin in bold relief: the imperialistic absorption of property and privilege versus the welfare state. Tyrrel is the primitive adventurer; his is the sort of mentality that set the European voyages to the

New World in motion. Falkland, on the other hand, is the latter-day capitalist, the man who realizes that a social order that will safeguard his position and power can emerge only through a certain set of reciprocating duties between the privileged and the lesser classes. Falkland, who has, as Munro put it in his *Godwin's Moral Philosophy* (1953), "all the charm, the wit, the scholarship, the delicacy of perception that Tyrrel lacks," is indeed Daniel Defoe's ideal gentleman described in *The Compleat English Gentleman* (reprinted 1890). Education is essential for Defoe's gentleman for "*Manners make the Man* and...modesty and virtue and humility are the brightest ornaments of the gentleman." Defoe's ideas about the gentleman were commonplace in the seventeeth and eighteenth centuries in Europe and became one of the sources for the antebellum idea of the southern gentleman.

I do not intend to review or even summarize the entire novel here, since the plot of the story is not germane to this discussion. I do wish to emphasize the use of two key words, one of which appears in Tyrrel's statement and the other in Falkland's. Tyrrel's use of the word "conundrum," which, in a vital sense, describes paternalism, implies that character's understanding of the complexity of a newfangled order, a complexity he finds unnecessary and would much rather do without. Falkland's use of the word "demerit," in keeping with his character, implies something a great deal more sinister. If the lesser classes are poor and downtrodden not because of any particular defect in character or intellect or virtue but because of the operation of some inexorable social laws or because of the inscrutable will of God, then the implication is that it is virtually impossible for either the rich or the poor to change positions or escape their roles. As B. J. Tysdahl writes about *Caleb Williams* in his *William Godwin as Novelist* (1981): "Rich and poor alike are imprisoned—symbolically and sometimes literally—by the social system of which they are a part."

I think it is, to some degree, quite apparent what elements of *Caleb Williams* Melville used, consciously or unconsciously, for "Benito Cereno." Godwin's novel did clearly teach him about several subtle aspects of paternalism. First, the contrast between the republican Delano and the aristocrat Cereno is not unlike that between Falkland and Tyrrel. Both Cereno and Delano are gentlemen and both are paternalists; and it is largely because they are both gentlemen and paternalists and that they believe in a hierarchic, organically bonded, rigidly organized universe that the story gives such an overwhelming impression of the characters being locked into their particular positions. The story's ambience, emanating from the paternalist's idea of social Calvinism, is symbolic and literal entrapment for all three major characters. As Rogin points out, "Benito Cereno" is about "the inability of its characters to break free." Cereno is trapped, "shut up in these walls, chained to one dull round of command," trapped by Babo into acting as the white lord was expected to act. Delano is trapped by his innocent voyeurism: "Trying to break one charm, he was but becharmed anew. Though upon the wide sea, he seemed in some far inland country;

prisoner in some deserted château, left to stare at empty grounds, and peer out at vague rods, where never wagon or wayfarer passed." Babo is trapped by his blackness: "And so still presenting himself as a crutch, and walking between the two captains, [Babo] advanced with them towards the gangway; while still, as if full of kindly contrition, Don Benito would not let go the hand of Captain Delano, but retained it in his, across the black's body." (The image of Babo's entrapment reminds us of how the Invisible Man is enmeshed in a web constructed over his body (and mind) by Norton, Emerson, the doctors at the company hospital, and Brother Jack. Also, it brings to mind Bigger's sense of entrapment when he sat between Jan and Mary in *Native Son.*) The reader feels that all of the characters are trapped within the walls of a monastery—the image that frames the story. But in large measure, this sense of entrapment and hierarchic structure is the result not only of the pretended relationship between Babo and Cereno but also of Delano's perception of it.

Delano is the benevolent paternalist, "a person of singularly undistrustful good nature..." a man whose "conscience is clean," whereas Cereno is forced to act out the role of the authoritarian paternalist. It might seem that Delano's "republican impartiality" would make him unsuited to the paternalist's point of view. But it is during the same scene that Delano's republican nature is mentioned, when he distributes water to all the distressed persons on board the *San Dominick* without regarding social station, that the reader discovers that Delano does indeed recognize the natural hierarchy of racial rank after all. Delano "would have given [to] the whites alone, the soft bread, sugar, and bottled cider." Throughout the entire story, of course, Delano perceives a thoroughly structured racial chain of being, thinking blacks "too stupid" for any white to become so far "a renegade as to apostatize from his very species almost, by leaguing in against it with negroes." Also, Delano is generally concerned about the lack of order on board the ship, something that he feels is largely the result of both "the absence of those subordinate deck officers to whom, along with higher duties, is intrusted what may be styled the police department of a populous ship" and the fact that "had Benito Cereno been a man of greater energy, misrule would hardly have come to pass." The narrator reinforces Delano's view by describing the *San Dominick* as being

> in condition of a transatlantic emigrant ship, among whose multitude of living freight are some individuals, doubtless, as little troublesome as crates and bales; but the friendly remonstrances of such with their ruder companions are of not so much avail as the unfriendly arm of the mate. What the *San Dominick* wanted was, what the emigrant ship has, stern superior officers.

This is just the sort of Melvillian description that resonates in many wickedly ironic ways: The reader knows that the slaves were surely *not* the same sort of emigrants that Europeans were, but to say that in some respects a slave ship resembles an emigrant ship is to imply that masses of blacks or masses of the European underclasses need and are subject to the same type of policing.

Also, the passage echoes with the imagery of 1848 in Europe, when the political situation resulted in harsh policing in France and Prussia, for example.

The fact that both Cereno and Delano are gentlemen is quite crucial. In fact, the first part of the story, before the masquerade is revealed, revolves around Delano's suspicions that Cereno, "a gentlemanly, reserved-looking, and rather young man," is no true gentleman:

> Under the circumstances, would a *gentleman,* nay, any honest boor, act the part now acted by [Cereno]? The man was an imposter. Some *low-born* adventurer, masquerading as an oceanic grandee; yet so ignorant of the first requisites of mere *gentlemanhood* as to be betrayed into the present remarkable indecorum. (Emphasis mine)

Inasmuch as paternalism, to use James Oakes's definition, "was the ideological offspring of a nobility for whom it was less an ideal than a simple description of reality," Delano's fear that Cereno may not be a gentleman, that Cereno may not be a member of "one of the most enterprising and extensive mercantile families in all those provinces...a sort of Castilian Rothschild...a true off-shoot of a true hidalgo Cereno" is quite a serious matter. If Cereno is no gentleman, then Delano would realize that his assumptions about the world are based upon appearances and not a solid reality, that his assumptions about the world have been undermined by a kind of iniquitous mummery. It would imply a fluidity, a more protean order of human affairs than the paternalist would be willing to admit. In short, Cereno as imposter would subvert the very idea of a hierarchical world, the very idea of social Calvinism.

Moreover, Delano fears that Cereno, who appears both too lax and too strict by turn, may be like Defoe's ignorant boorish gentleman, who through sheer ineptitude would undermine the natural order: "[Delano] easily inferred that the young captain has not got into command at the hause-hole, but the cabin window; and if so, why wonder at incompetence, in youth, sickness, and gentility united?" Cereno as a master, to use Defoe's words about the incompetent gentleman which fit perfectly, "is haughty, imperious, and tyrannic or else soft, easy, and capable of being wheedled, imposed upon and drawn in by every sharper and into every bubble, till first he is exposed and then undone." For Delano, incompetence becomes a kind of imposture. The possibility that Cereno may be an imposter by virtue of either a false nobility or a defective one is intensified by Delano's Anglo bias against Spaniards; it is when he notices Cereno's "small, yellow hands" that Delano arrives at his opinion of incompetence quoted above. Defoe's prejudice against the Spaniards, their inability to be true gentlemen, seems fairly typical of the seventeenth-century Englishman, and all indications point to Delano following in that tradition. Defoe writes: "We have one strange example in Europe, and it is national too, where a whole people have cast off all claim of blood from their real ancestors, and reject the very race they are descended from, only because of the infamy of their character, and this is the Spaniards." Defoe continues: "Let any man examine the countenances of the Spaniards, and especially of the Portuguese, and see if there is ordinarily not something of the Moor and the Negro in their very features." Finally, Defoe warns against the profligate and dissipated practices of the British gentleman in failing to keep strict account of his money and tight management of his estate with this woeful denunciation: "What havoc has this absurd *Spanish* temper made among our nobility and gentry!" (emphasis mine). Benito Cereno is described throughout the story as effete: "This distempered spirit lodged, as before hinted, in as distempered a frame. He was rather tall, but seemed never to have been robust, and now with nervous suffering was almost to a skeleton. A tendency to some pulmonary complaint appeared with lungs half gone—hoarsely suppressed, a husky whisper." He also is referred to, as I mentioned earlier, as having "small, yellow hands" similar to the "yellow arms" of "Malay pirates" mentioned later in the story, and is called "the dark Spaniard." Delano himself thinks that "these Spaniards are all an odd set; the very word Spaniard has a curious, conspirator, Guy-Fawkish twang to it." Delano concludes his thought in an oddly condescending way: "And yet, I dare say, Spaniards in the main are as good folks as any in Duxbury, Massachusetts." Delano's own liberal sentiments are undercut in the very next sentence when he expresses relief at spying *Rover,* the whaleboat, coming to fetch him. In short, Cereno's imposture as a gentleman, because of his nationality and because of his seeming temperament and leadership abilities, is just as important in undermining the assumptions of paternalism, at least from Delano's perspective, as the fact that Babo is revealed at last to be the imposter who undermines paternalism from the reader's perspective.

Finally, all of this is in keeping with the view of paternalism taken by Godwin in *Caleb Williams,* part of whose main theme seems to be the gentleman as imposter. The fact that Falkland murders the evil Tyrrel and that he is discovered by the book's hero, Caleb Williams, to be hideously evil himself is equivalent to saying that the choices between authoritarian paternalism and benevolent paternalism amount not to choices between good and evil but to choices between two sorts of evil. Thus, the very system of paternalism is undermined by the psychopathic preoccupations of the men who control it, the primary obsession being the gentleman's code of honor and the obligations of gentlemanly conduct. What is most striking about Falkland is not only that he murders Tyrrel because of a minor insult but that he contrives to place the blame on an innocent man because he is determined to keep his unspotted reputation at all costs. A more insidious danger makes itself apparent in all of this: Falkland is never suspected of killing Tyrrel largely because of the charismatic way he exploits his gentleman's position. His dependents are intensely loyal not only to the man himself but to the larger ideas of both his character and his status. Don Benito, in Melville's story, may be just that sort of charismatic gentleman as symbolized by his beautifully ornamental clothing of "loose Chile jacket of dark velvet; white small-clothes and stockings, with silver buckles at the knee and instep; a high-crowned sombrero, of fine grass; a slender sword, silver mounted, hung from a knot in his sash—the last being an almost invariable adjunct, more for utility than ornament, of a South American gentleman's dress to this hour."

Delano clearly expresses his fear of Cereno's possible charismatic power when he speculates that "if Don Benito's story was, throughout, an invention, then every soul on board, down to the youngest negress, was his carefully drilled recruit in the plot." Readers who are familiar with Melville's novels before "Benito Cereno" (although even some of the latter ones such as *The Confidence Man* [1856] and *Billy Budd* [1924] make use of this theme), particularly the sea stories and most especially the relationship between Ahab and his crew in *Moby-Dick,* are aware that the conjunction of authority and charismatic power was a deep intellectual and philosophical concern with Melville. So I do not think it is unreasonable that Melville may have learned from Godwin's novel the very elements that I have isolated. If so, then we find another aspect in locating the origin of Delano's paternalist views—the concept of the well-bred gentleman—as well as some fertile grounds for exploring the relationship between Cereno and Delano.

III. MYTHOLOGY

Eric Sundquist discusses Melville's incredible abundance of double negatives in "Benito Cereno": "The instances of the double negative are numerous, but in almost all cases they are rhetorical embodiments of information or assessments that are at once asserted and denied—or to put it another way, of a rebellion in consciousness or language that takes place almost but not quite and thus remains in suspense." Melville's use of the double negative seems to endorse the idea that language can produce only propositions and their antitheses but no real rhetorical or philosophical spaces that can contain a statement and its opposite. Melville's double negatives, his "not un-" constructions seem to thwart the very purpose of language since in the end they fail to describe anything at all. Indeed, Melville's double negatives are really a form of linguistic mummery, language used not to highlight and amplify a multiplicity of meanings but to mask and hide utter and complete nonmeaning. Melville's double negatives simply admit the impossibility of language to encompass its own merged contradictions.

The story is a mystery, but it seems to be a displaced one since mystery is never truly engaged in ambiguity in perception but rather in the absence of perception. The mystery is the quest for the assurance, the rational text beneath the possibilities of the text *seeming* to be incoherent. "Benito Cereno" is a mystery that does not hinge on the rational text of depositions that are appended to it because, unlike most mysteries, to know what happened in this case does not explain why it happened. The sources that can unravel the mystery of "Benito Cereno" lie not in one's perceptions of "objective reality" or the ability in one's perceptions to conjure up something that we can all agree is that; it is rather located in one's understanding of certain archetypal myths that inform the white Western mind: the St. Nicholas myth, paternalism, and the concept of the gentleman, for instance. "Every myth," writes Mircea Eliade, "shows how a reality came into existence, whether it be the total reality, the cosmos, or only a fragment—an island, a species of plant, a human institution."

So, while Melville's story takes the form of the conventional mystery, its mythological sources inform it as a sacred text, Melville seems more interested in the unresolved ambivalence of human relationship, in "trailing the genealogies of these high mortal miseries." "Benito Cereno" is a story about race and slavery, and to use a phrase of both Melville and Ralph Ellison, the blackness of blackness, but ultimately it seems to point to the masking of human relationship in such a way that one is never sure whether bonds are symbolic of our power or of our benevolence, and whether our benevolence is a function of our sense of our power. As in the actual mummer's plays of early English folklore, with which I feel Melville must have been familiar, perhaps human relationships can be symbolized by the battle between the two protagonists. In any event, Cereno has located the very nature of the deceptive essence of human relationship when he remarks to Delano at the end, "So far may even the best man err, in judging the conduct of one with the recesses of whose condition he is not acquainted." In any relationship, one never knows what one is really confronting, and perhaps if one is strong enough to conquer or weak enough to submit perhaps one really never need know. Perhaps conquest and submission are ways of saying one really does not want to know.

As I am not a Melville scholar, I do hope that the group that considers itself that is not too upset by this incursion from an amateur. I know how turf-oriented many scholars can be. Obviously, I have supplied my own reading of Godwin's novel, not Melville's. And how or even if Melville used St. Nicholas and mummery in his story is still open to question. I have conclusively proven only that he knew these things. The rest is the sort of speculation that the critical reconstruction of literary texts is really about. I have reconstructed Melville's story to satisfy myself as a black reader of Melville so that I can live with what the story is about while not making special claims for Melville's politics or his concern for black people (if he had any). Of course, the real complaint from scholars will be that this is not really scholarship, which it is not trying to be. It can be dismissed, as scholars are wont to do, as being "merely impressionistic"; but there have been some noble impressionists who really could think, contrary to what Jacques Barzun said about Thoreau. To be in company with Emerson, Louis Armstrong, Count Basie, Sojourner Truth, Jesus Christ—impressionists all—is not such a bad thing at last. There is certainly enough Melville scholarship floating around, good, bad, and indifferent, that those oceans needn't have my small bucket thrown on top. But for me, at least, while this may not be scholarship, I guess it will have to do until the real thing comes along.

The man is arrogant to think that he can pontificate on sthg he knews so v little about + deem it to be, (impressionistic) + use the company of other thkers as the mantle for him to spout such gibberish.

Needed:
Useful Black Literary History

...innocent lunacy or wicked imposture.

—Herman Melville, "Benito Cereno"

It must be remembered that the oppressed and the oppressor are bound together within the same society; they accept the same criteria, they share the same beliefs, they both alike depend on the same reality.

—James Baldwin, "Everybody's Protest Novel"

William L. Andrews, in his review of *The Slave's Narrative,** writes that "the central issue facing students of nineteenth-century Afro-American literature [is] the question of *how* to analyze and evaluate the autobiographical tradition of the ex-slave" (emphasis mine). The statement seems to have dual significance: The core of the nineteenth-century black literary experience is the autobiography of the ex-slave or the slave narrative; and the major concern with this literature is the methodology to be used for its proper study. How does one analyze and evaluate this material? Is it largely historical and sociological in nature? Or is it in the domain of the literary theorist and

---

*Henry Louis Gates and Charles T. Davis, eds. *The Slave's Narrative* (New York: Oxford University Press, 1985). The quotation is from Andrews's review in *Black American Literature Forum,* 20, nos. 1-2 (Spring–Summer, 1986), p. 203.

textual critic? In short, do these books have a literary worth quite apart from their value as documents generated by one of the most important social protest movements in American history? In a sense, this series of decidedly naive and disingenuous questions has been posed about most of the books that make up the Afro-American literary canon. To paraphrase Leslie Fiedler, what is Afro-American literature? Do the works of Willard Motley, Samuel Delany, and Frank Yerby belong in the canon despite the fact they are rarely about black characters? Are *The Greatest: My Own Story* by Muhammad Ali and *Message to the Black Man in America* by Elijah Muhammad worthy of literary analysis in the way that *Invisible Man* is? When Afro-American literature of the late 1960s is finally strenuously evaluated, will it pose the same methodological problems as slave narratives of the antebellum era because both periods were preoccupied with literature being subsumed under the cause of political and social change? It seems to me that a book like Andrews's is helping to change the way we see both the American and Afro-American literary canons, one of several works in recent years to do that.

Andrews has elaborately and extensively tried to answer the question of how to analyze and evaluate slave and other types of black autobiographies in the eighteenth and nineteenth centuries by fusing the crafts of the historian and the literary critic. On the one hand, he has rehearsed and designed a full-scale historical schema in which these various works can be filed and classified and seen as evolutionary phenomena of independent black creativity: from early spiritual and crime autobiographies of the late seventeenth century, largely managed by white ghostwriters and editors and scarcely self-realized as political or artistic works, to the antebellum narratives of William Wells Brown, Frederick Douglass, Harriet Jacobs, and J. W. C. Pennington, composed exclusively or in large measure by the slave writers themselves—fully articulate expressions of political protest and artistic will. Thus, in the beginning of his book Andrews writes: "White acceptance of a slave narrative as truth depended on how judiciously the slave had censored the facts of his life into something other than the whole truth." And by the end, using the narratives of the 1850s as closure, Andrews writes: "Self-realization for the black autobiographers involved the finding of one's voice, the reclaiming of language from the mouth of the white other, and the initiation of the arduous process of fitting language to voice instead of the other way around." In short, the black autobiography started out as the story of a buried life and a buried consciousness and ended its first century of existence with a triumphant showcasing of emerging mind and self: the movement from "how I endured" to "how I got over."

There is nothing new or startling about the historical contexts developed by Andrews for these slave narratives, but his study is surely more richly intellectual and more detailed, almost littered, with scholarship than any previous treatment of these works. Andrews states about as well as anyone who has ever written about slave narratives the importance of their historically realized, humanistic thrust: "They were antagonist works in two senses: (1) they functioned as ripostes against racist charges against black selfhood and (2) they resisted the fragmenting nature of objective autobiography, which demanded that a black narrator achieve credence by objectifying himself and passivizing his voice." The black autobiography, in other words, has always been in a state of becoming; even from its crudest beginnings in such pietistic works as the narratives of Briton Hammon and John Marrant, the work always sought the ownership of its own voice so that it might achieve its state of being, so that it might show the black's consciousness not as an alien or enemy consciousness, but as a socially redeemed one. The major question that always surrounded this early quest for the Afro-American writer was, as Andrews phrased it, "Could black 'tellability' and white propriety coexist in a discursive situation...?"

But if Andrews's book were merely a more scaled and erudite version of what we have already learned from other studies, then it would scarcely have been worth writing and probably not worth reading. After all, we do have such capable works as the Ph.D. dissertations of Margaret Young Jackson and Marion Wilson Starling (the latter recently published as *The Slave Narrative: Its Place in American History*), Charles Nichols's *Many Thousand Gone: The Ex-Slaves' Account of Their Bondage and Freedom*, Stephen Butterfield's *Black Autobiography in America* (informed by something akin to the Black Aesthetic), and Frances Smith Foster's *Witnessing Slavery: The Development of Ante-bellum Slave Narratives*. Therefore, any new probe in this area must offer us something fresh, not simply another round of, to borrow Count Basie's signature, "one more once." In short, we have had enough of the dutiful; it is now time to be daring.

What Andrews has done, on the other hand, is to bring to bear upon the slave narrative the latest literary theories (reader response, deconstruction, speech act theory, limning the autobiography) in an attempt to elevate the entire enterprise of discussing this literature by elevating the language and ideas by and through which we speak about it. This process, of course, has occurred with virtually all Afro-American literature, formalistic, positivistic readings having been thrown out the window. There is nothing wrong with this particular development except that at times I cannot help but suspect that in his eagerness to sound like a philosophical anthropologist, the "postmodern" literary critic comes strangely close to sounding like a mountebank. There have been literary critics who have given more or less literary or more or less "new critical" readings to some slave narratives (Douglass's 1845 *Narrative* has been a particular favorite of the critical fancy): Houston Baker, Jean Fagan Yellin, Henry Louis Gates, Charles T. Davis, H. Bruce Franklin, Eric Sundquist, and Robert B. Stepto have been most conspicuous in this area of analysis. But Andrews is the first to devote an entire book, not simply an essay or a chapter or two, to this approach to pre–twentieth-century black nonfiction narrative. I think that this sort of pursuit of the text is wholesome as scholarship (not to mention politically valuable since it bestows upon Afro-American literature the sort of high-powered attention it deserves). But I sometimes wonder if this is being done simply because the critic has the power to do it, or if analysis is really in service to the text and to the act of reading. Consider this passage from Andrews's book:

> We should recognize, however, that even if directives became the slave narrator's alternative mode to assertives, the slave narrator was still boxed into a "prison-house of language." For whether the slave's words served as assertive representations *of* the world or as directive models *for* the world, they remained bound *to* the world, to an alien ("distanc-iating") locus of reference and signification. This assumed and expected linkage of words to world in either or both directions was, of course, arbitrary and culturally determined. But how was the slave narrator to be liberated from such assumptions and expectations? (*To Tell a Free Story,* p. 83)

Gibberish

After having negotiated the dangerous shoals of the technical terms "directives" and "assertives" (to be joined later by their cousin, "expressives"), one is left wondering whether the above is just a fancy way of reworking the old Black Aesthetic idea that the language of whites effectively foreclosed—politically, linguistically, and artistically—the ability of black mythmaking: a point, incidentally, that was made in 1855 by Herman Melville in "Benito Cereno." The blacks in that story never fully come to human consciousness because they can never fully seize the language of the text. Babo is first trapped in Delano's text and seen as a liar and fawning slave; then he is trapped in the legal language of the depositions at the story's end where he is seen as a liar and a devil. I think that the whole business of directives, assertives, and expressives might be more convincingly applied to the Melville story than to slave narratives. But Andrews's book, on the whole, is accessible and readable; unlike many other current critics, he does not often sacrifice clarity of thought or the simple act of making sense on the altar of sounding profound.

Held your own criticism

I have two complaints, however, about Andrews's book. First, I think he gives a simplistic and unfair reading to Harriet Beecher Stowe's *Uncle Tom's Cabin.* I think there is more in Stowe's novel than a mere rehearsal of the romantic racism of the day (a thesis more elaborately developed by George M. Fredrickson in *The Black Image in the White Mind*). In truth, *Uncle Tom's Cabin* changed the entire nature of the political discourse on slavery: in popular culture, the victims of slavery were now perceived as women and children; slavery was an assault on the domestic values of home and the holistic plenitude of the family not simply because people were bought and sold but because slavery was simply another example of the white male's obsession with pursuit. For the white male mind, according to Stowe, everything was pursuit: wealth, sex, land, even play. This is symbolized most clearly in the twin hunting scenes that open and close the novel: at the beginning, Haley and two slaves, on their horses—animals associated with male sport in the South (one simply has to read *The Spirit of the Times* or *The American Turf Register and Sporting Magazine,* two antebellum sporting publications, to realize that American men thought a great deal about breeding thoroughbreds)—hunt a woman and a child; and, at the end, Legree and his black henchmen, using dogs (the other animal written about in the above-mentioned magazines), hunt down a woman and teenage child. (As white historian Richard Hildreth demonstrated in his 1837 anti- *Never heard* slavery novel, *The Memoirs of Archie Moore,* republished in 1852 as *The* *of this must* *White Slave,* slavery had become nothing more, from a feminist point of *track down* view, than the white planter's crazed hunt to seize and sell his own misbegotten half-cast children.) If anything, by exposing this preoccupation with pursuit, Stowe shows that paternalism, the main argument used by southern intellectuals, was an unreal apology used to justify a pathological social order. Andrews states that the death of Uncle Tom and the exile of George Harris "was the most comforting and popular way for white America to think about black liminality in the crisis years of the mid–nineteenth century." But like most critics who make this point, he overlooks Aunt Chloe, the "perfectioner" (an interesting malapropism) and the other blacks who are set free by George Shelby the younger. I think that the assertion that black "responses to *Uncle Tom's Cabin*...point to a campaign of literary revisionism in black autobiography of the 1850s, an unacknowledged but evident effort to prevent Stowe's novel from becoming a literary plenitude" is clearly wrong. Stowe's novel helped focus the antislavery movement on paternalism. Consider that Frederick Douglass's revised 1855 autobiography and Harriet Jacobs's 1861 feminist narrative are both attacks on paternalism and the patriarchy (which Andrews freely admits); also consider that the major pro- and antislavery works after *Uncle Tom's Cabin,* such as *Aunt Phillis's Cabin,* "Benito Cereno" (I concur wholeheartedly with Michael Rogin's reading of this story in his *Subversive Genealogy*), and George Fitzhugh's *Sociology for the South* and *Cannibals All! or, Slaves Without Masters* all are about the ontology of paternalism.

I will deal briefly with my second complaint: I would have wished for a bit more discussion about the tension that existed between the slave's past and his present status as a freedman. Slavery was both mad imposition and "wicked imposture," and perhaps one is never sure who is playing what role, or if it really matters if one is playing a role or really believes in what he is supposed to be. It is the one insistent strain of the slave narrative that the slave is better than the slave's life, that the black is better than the black's life. This is not simply a false idea; it is a hideous sort of sentimental delusion, that one can oppose the innocent pose of a justified oppressor with the innocent pose of an incorruptible victim. What does it mean for a slave, whether freed or not, to live under a morality that condemns him although he is forced to accept its terms, to live both *under* and *with* his social death, his utter nonbeing? In his discussion of Samuel Ringgold Ward's autobiography, Andrews asserts that this is the only slave narrative that suggests that the slave cannot repudiate his slave past when he escapes bondage, that his escape does not "enable a fugitive to transcend

his dwarfed self in slavery and become someone different—the free man":
in this Andrews touches upon what I am talking about. Also, his chapter on
marginality and his references to Du Bois's famous formulation of the
black's double consciousness explore this question as well. But I suppose I
await the philosophical investigation that starts this way: why did the slave
narrator never say, "I am what slavery made me, so I decided to be what
slavery made me"? *but I'm now free to break the Sovereign bondage*

   To Tell a Free Story is an excellent book, a fine study of a difficult
literature, and a clear indication of where Afro-American literary criticism
is, and where it is tending. *Have v. grave doubts as to whether one can credit his recommendation.*

Langston Hughes
Festival Keynote Lecture

I have always associated Langston Hughes with my childhood. I think this is only partly because he wrote so many children's books, such as *The First Book of Jazz, The First Book of Negroes, The First Book of Africa,* and *Famous Negro Heroes of America,* books whose naive and hilarious titles could be acceptable to and taken seriously by children only. It is also partly because he wrote so many adult books that a child could read: the Simple books, both volumes of the autobiography, most of the poetry and fiction, and the pictorials in partnership with Milton Meltzer. But finally I associate Hughes with my childhood because he was the only black writer anyone ever talked to me about during my youth. My mother liked him. His column appeared in the local black newspaper. So that meant my mother's friends and other black adults I knew heard of him and liked him as well. The fact that my mother liked him is quite significant because I do not recall my mother ever reading more than a dozen books during the first eighteen years of my life. I reasoned as a child that with that kind of selective reading list the fact that she had heard of and liked Hughes meant he was someone worth reading; otherwise she wouldn't be wasting her time on him.

It is the acknowledgment of the fact of his popularity that I think concedes

This lecture was first delivered to the faculty and students of St. Louis Community College at Forest Park on October 21, 1987.

the enduring truth of his genius. Hughes appealed to black folk who normally never read books, never read poetry, who would not consider themselves to be in any way literary.

They liked Hughes because he himself never seemed literary and so he seemed to talk directly to them in a way that few other black writers in American history have done. Ordinary, poorly educated black folk of my mother's generation may have been proud of Frederick Douglass, may have admired the mainstream acclaim given Richard Wright and James Baldwin (seeing *those* writers talked about in the local white papers, in the national mainstream publications, and of course, in *Ebony*), but they *read* Hughes. He didn't seem to be writing for whites, which for most black American writers has never been a common practice, and he never condescended to an audience of plain people. In the late sixties, which I remember quite well as it was the time of my late teenage years and thus the time of my personal rebellion, all the poetry readings and street-theater productions that became so popular with the militant black literati as a way of bringing literature and art to the masses were really nothing more than a tribute to Hughes. He had done all that sort of stuff before, in many cases before some of the members of the militant black literati were even born, let alone before any of them were even remotely thinking about theories of a working class-oriented system of aesthetics. And, of course, Hughes had done it better because he was so much less ostentatious in his desire, so much more sincere in his hope that literature and art were something, human activities that all could share in. I am convinced that the rap records being made today by such stars as L.L. Cool J and Run-DMC, the whole business of hip-hop and urban black youth culture, would have fascinated and delighted Hughes very much if he were still alive; how he would have richly relished it, the idea of ordinary street-wise black folk making a popular rhetorical art form from the patterns of their speech and the everyday interests of their lives, a world of black Robert Burnses. He could remember the days when he pioneered—before Gil-Scott Heron, the Last Poets, Muhammad Ali, the Beats and Amiri Baraka—the marriage of black music and black poetry. If he were here today, he might even have made a few rap records himself.

So I read a good many of Hughes's books as a child, which was good in one sense but very bad in another. For when I reached my young adult years, I refused to take him seriously as a writer for adults for a quite long time. He was for a time not simply a children's writer for me but a childish one, or, more correctly, a childlike one. I suspected a certain gilded artifice in it all. He seemed to lack sophistication, and his poetry was too apparent. Of course, in making that assessment I forgot such poems as "A House in Taos," which is quite as dense as anything:

RAIN:
Thunder of the Rain God:
And we three

Smitten by beauty.
Thunder of the Rain God:
And we three
Weary, weary.
Thunder of the Rain God:
And you, she and I
Waiting for nothingness.
Do you understand the stillness
Of this house in Taos
Under the thunder of the Rain God

SUN:
That there should be a barren garden
About this house in Taos
Is not so strange,
But that there should be three barren hearts
In this one house in Taos—
Who carries ugly things to show the sun?

MOON:
Did you ask for the beaten brass of the moon?
We can buy lovely things with money,
You, she and I,
Yet you seek,
As though you could keep,
This unbought loveliness of moon.

WIND:
Touch our bodies, wind,
Our bodies are separate, individual things.
Touch our bodies, wind,
But blow quickly
Through the red, white, yellow skins
Of our bodies
To the terrible snarl,
Not mine,
Not yours,
Not hers,
But all one snarl of souls.
Blow quickly, wind,
Before we run back into the windlessness—
With our bodies—
Into the windlessness
Of our house in Taos.

To learn, as I did at one point in my life, that the poem is about Mabel
Dodge Luhan's actual house in Taos and her relationship with her Indian
husband, Tony Luhan, and her black—white?—lover, novelist Jean Toomer,
is to become aware instantly that the poem is undeniably funny, poking fun
at a group of pretentious people seeking the world of the spirit when what
they really want is old-fashioned, earth-bound sex, which although it is an

exciting enough engagement is not likely to do anything for the spirit one way or the other. To realize what is behind the poem is to marvel at how well the poem is put together, how well Hughes is able to evoke the sort of New Age mysticism that this group reveled in, in order to satirize it.

But I really did not think of Hughes's more complex poems when I went through my phase of dismissing him as an important writer. It would hardly have mattered if I had remembered them, because I had then entered a phase in which I completely misunderstood Hughes. The fact that Hughes's poetry was readable was sign of my immaturity, not Hughes's inability. For Hughes's apparent simplicity did more than allow generations of blacks to read him; it also inspired many younger blacks, such as myself, to become writers.

Hughes made it seem so easy that we all thought, fatuously, that we could do it too. But it is important that in misunderstanding Hughes's power we were not daunted by the project of creative writing, that is to say, good creative writing. Simply put, Hughes was, for a good many literary-inclined black children, the first black writer they read and almost assuredly the first important poet, black or white, whose poetry was entirely readable. How many of us can I think of — Toni Cade Bambara, David Bradley, James McPherson, Ishmael Reed, Rita Dove, Leon Forrest, Alice Walker, Cecil Brown, and several more — who owe our start in our careers as writers to having read and emulated the writings of Hughes as children? Why, even Ralph Ellison, in his essay "The World and the Jug," admitted to reading Hughes when he was in grade school. Hughes has become, in one sense, the black version of schoolhouse poets such as Whittier and Longfellow. What an incredible role model he has been! And what an incredible burden his reputation has had to bear, the entombment of being in the schoolhouse, of being the black schoolmarm's or black librarian's poet.

But in trying to dismiss Hughes I kept being haunted by him. I kept running into his words all over the place. I looked up to confront the title of the most celebrated play by an Afro-American playwright, Lorraine Hansberry's *A Raisin in the Sun,* which is a line from Hughes's poem "Harlem" (incidentally, I might add that Hughes's own play *Mulatto* was the longest-running black play on Broadway before Hansberry's *Raisin* appeared), and anytime any black woman wanted to declaim theatrically in public, the choice was inevitably Hughes's "Mother to Son," a poem that had to be an ironic comment on his relationship with his own mother, which was not always a happy or inspiring one. Hughes's presence in Afro-American culture seemed pervasive.

Without question, Hughes was the most prolific black writer in the history of American letters (not even excepting Frank Yerby, who has been cranking out romances over the decades much as an auto assembly line spins out cars). And I would liken this productiveness to Hughes's favorite art form, jazz. ("I wouldn't give up jazz for a world revolution," Hughes once said back in the thirties as he returned home from Russia.) Hughes spun out work much as a jazz musician endlessly creates solo improvisation. The fertility of his imagination seemed endless, which does not mean that his work was always good but that he, as an artist, was always engaged in and by the processes of the creative act. I remember doing some research on a project once by reading old copies of the famous black newspaper *The Chicago Defender* and discovering that Hughes had a column in the early 1940s called "Here and Yonder." It was quite a good column, and I found myself fascinated by the range of subjects he explored weekly—the blues of Memphis Minnie one week, the poetry of Walt Whitman the next. I would look in the library and find Hughes's Spanish translations. I would look somewhere else and find him talked about during the McCarthy era. Turn again and his name is prominent in the civil rights movement of the sixties. In graduate school, my best friend, whose family apparently knew Hughes well, could not stop talking about Langston Hughes. There was simply no escaping him.

If he had written nothing but poetry he would have been one of the most renowned writers in twentieth-century America. But Hughes also wrote novels, short stories, travel pieces, translations, plays, scripts, song lyrics, and journalism. And he managed this kind of productivity while still maintaining an extremely energetic social life and conducting extensive lecture tours. Hughes almost never refused to read his poetry at any sort of institution, a college, an elementary school, a retirement home, a cocktail party, on a street corner. And he did not let a little matter like someone's inability to pay his fee stop him from appearing. He was virtually a literary Johnny Appleseed, dropping poems on the public as if, when he awoke every morning, he could comb them out of his hair.

In the end, about eight or nine years ago, I returned to Hughes; in fact I returned to one of the very poems I remember reading when I first encountered him in the Southwark Branch of the Free Library of Philadelphia when I was a child. The poem is one of Hughes's most famous: "The Negro Speaks of Rivers," and I heard jazz alto saxophonist Gary Bartz adapt the words to music in a very moving and powerful rendition on a live album he made back in the early 1970s. The poem made an excellent song. And it was not the first time someone had been moved to put Hughes's poetry to music; in fact, it was not even the first time that "The Negro Speaks of Rivers" was set to music. But hearing Bartz sing the words made the poem resonant for me in new ways that both surprised and pleased me. A certain compelling realization hit me about the nature of Hughes's poetry, how close it was to capturing the essential beauty and design of black music. It was only when I began to understand the meaning of Afro-American music that I finally appreciated what Hughes's poetry was about. This poem itself began to take on the quality of its main image; it seemed as full and life-giving as the rivers of which it spoke.

I've known rivers:
I've known rivers ancient as the world and older
than the flow of human blood in human veins

My soul has grown deep like the rivers.
I bathed in the Euphrates when the dawns were young.
I built my hut near the Congo and it lulled me to sleep.
I looked upon the Nile and raised the pyramids above it.
I heard the singing of the Mississippi when Abe Lincoln went down to
*   New Orleans, and I've seen its muddy bosom turn all golden in the sunset.*

I've known rivers:
Ancient, dusky rivers.

My soul has grown deep like the rivers.

This poem was published in *Crisis,* the journal of the NAACP, in June 1921, when Hughes was just nineteen. Some of you might know that Hughes dedicated the poem to W. E. B. Du Bois, one of the founders of the NAACP and one of the most impressive scholars and intellectuals of his day. There is a certain maturity and ease about the poem that seems almost startling for someone only nineteen years old. And it was such a fitting poem to dedicate to Du Bois, who himself embodied so much black history because he lived and did so much that he seemed like a river with a limitless amount of silver silt on the bottom.

Hughes died in the same year, 1967, as jazz saxophonist John Coltrane. Their deaths were only a few months apart. I think it is safe to say that the jazz world has never recovered from the death of Coltrane; certainly, no one has emerged with the same type of leadership. Perhaps there is no clearer indication of how impoverished the jazz world has become since the death of Coltrane than the saxophone solos by current jazz artists, all of whom seem to be waiting and wishing for Coltrane to put out a new record so that they might get some new ideas. Alas, it was the same dilemma for the jazz world when Charlie Parker died in 1955. Hughes's death is just as big a blow for black letters because his presence was, if anything, even more seminal than Coltrane's was to the jazz world. There is no black writer today who speaks with the authority and grace as the conscience for his or her generation as Hughes did for his, not even Baldwin who came the closest or Baraka who tried most vehemently. Hughes was the very personification of black letters in America, and there is no black writer working today who is not doing something, operating in some field that Hughes did not touch, whether it be lyrical poetry, humorous sketches, folklore, leftist politics, or theater. Hughes's presence is not so much the mountain that must be overcome but rather the complex inspiration that has to be savored and absorbed.

If, as William Dean Howells once said, Mark Twain is the Lincoln of American literature, then Langston Hughes must be something close to its Mozart; he was that versatile and that endlessly inventive, so gifted that he did not ever feel the burden or anguish of his creative ingenuity. In some ways, especially in the nature of his prolific production and his broad concern for humanity, he resembles George Orwell. (His newspaper reports on the Spanish Civil War rank with Orwell's *Homage to Catalonia*.) In other ways, he resembles Twain himself. Indeed, one can scarcely imagine an American writer other than Hughes who has come close to duplicating Twain's literary power as a humorist, satirist, and observer of human nature. To say this is to say a great deal toward understanding the importance of Hughes. As one great writer once said: "Great men are too often unknown, or what is worse, misknown." I offer an example of what I mean: Ralph Ellison, in his review of the first volume of Langston Hughes's autobiography, said the following: "In the style of *The Big Sea* too much attention is apt to be given to the aesthetic aspects of experience at the expense of its deeper meanings." This amounts to saying that Hughes was not a profound or philosophical writer, that he was, in effect, not even a literary writer because, according to Ellison, he did not understand the potential of his own artistic capabilities or how to exploit them (a critical complaint similar to one Baldwin would make several years later). Ellison, an astute critic in many respects, simply does not understand the man who was instrumental in helping him launch his career. I think Ellison felt, in part, that he had to distance himself from Hughes in order to create a space for himself. He did not, after all, as a black writer, wish to be mistaken for Hughes or for someone who wanted to do a version of the Hughes creative project. But Ellison made the common mistake of thinking that simplicity has no virtue other than being self-evident and self-apparent; in short, that simplicity has no virtue other than being simple, being artlessly contrived. In the back of his mind Ellison has always been convinced that a black could not succeed unless he was flat-out virtuosic in such a way that there would be no ambiguity surrounding the question of his skill and thus of his right to be a writer worthy of a certain kind of critical notice and acclaim. In this sense, Hughes resembles the late jazz pianist Thelonious Monk. The debate is the same: Can he really play (write)? Is his art the reification of genius or the artless contrivance of reductionism? Yet it was Thomas Carlyle in his *Sartor Resartus* who said: "The beginning of all Wisdom is to look fixedly on Clothes...till they become *transparent*." In other words, there is much to learn from looking at surfaces. Indeed, surfaces are depths, in the final rendering of things. Neither Monk nor Hughes ever claimed to be doing anything other than looking fixedly at surfaces (clothes) in their art—in fact, they never wished for their art to aspire to be anything more than what it was—but obviously, implicit in their art was the credo: Of course, we look at surfaces. Why bother to look at anything else, anyway?

To begin a discussion of Hughes's life, I think one must start with the opening paragraphs of the first volume of his autobiography entitled *The Big Sea*:

> Melodramatic maybe, it seems to me now. But then it was like throwing a million bricks out of my heart when I threw the books into the water. I leaned over the rail of the S.S. *Malone* and threw the books as far as I could out into the

sea—all the books I had had at Columbia [University], and all the books I had lately bought to read.

The books went down into the moving water in the dark off Sandy Hook. Then I straightened up, turned my face to the wind, and took a deep breath. I was a seaman going to sea for the first time—a seaman on a big merchant ship. And I felt that nothing would ever happen to me again that I didn't want to happen. I felt grown, a man, inside and out. Twenty-one.

I was twenty-one.

This was, of course, the pose that Hughes was to adopt for the rest of his professional life: the writer who disdained the pretensions of the intellectual, the writer who refused to live his life from books or to see the world through books. If writing is indeed the necessary product of experience, the guarantee of experience, Hughes was offering his credo in the opening of this autobiography that his writing would stem from the living of life and not from the reading of books. Hughes did remain a voracious reader all of his life and one might say that he was indeed an intellectual, although not necessarily a man of ideas in the strictest sense that we mean that phrase. Yet this pose was essential, for Hughes never wanted to be estranged from his audience, never wanted to be the alienated artist. And there was something about being too much attracted to living the life of the mind that Hughes wanted to avoid, especially if he were to have a sizable black reading audience of ordinary people. His democratic impulses would not allow him to become a sort of aristocrat of the mind. I think Hughes in the opening of the autobiography felt that a writer's most important function was to write for people and not for other writers or intellectuals. Moreover, Hughes probably felt as a black writer that he could not afford to live in an ivory tower, that he had to be able to voice a plainsong of social protest for the black masses that they could in fact understand as protest. He certainly felt that he could not be engaged in the rather esoteric game of protesting the idea of protest or, put another way, obsessed with the Hamlet-like question: What does it mean to be a black writer? Hughes was, throughout his life, the committed and engaged writer. And this he would have been even if he had not been a Communist sympathizer in the thirties, for he had a very broad sense of justice and a Whitmanesque acceptance of variety in people. But, more important, he was preoccupied with being able to identify with the ordinary, not to elevate it, but to celebrate the power of being common. "Oh," his works collectively seem to say, "You feel that way. Well, what a coincidence, I happen to feel that way myself. I wonder why we do?"

James Mercer Langston Hughes was born in Joplin, Missouri, on February 1, 1902, the second son of James Nathaniel Hughes and Carrie Mercer Langston Hughes. His mother's uncle was John Mercer Langston, lawyer, politician, college administrator, autobiographer, first black congressman. There are several important implications in these facts. First, we know that Hughes was named after his famous great-uncle. In effect, he was burdened with a name in much the same way that Ralph Waldo Ellison was burdened with being named after Emerson. One wonders if Hughes was, in some manner, driven to be a great writer to be able to live up to his name or simply to be able to live it down.

I suspect there was always a kind of anxiety-of-influence that governed Hughes's ambition his entire life. Indeed, part of his downplaying the sense that he felt driven by an ancestral presence was never to appear as if he were ambitious. Second, Hughes was undeniably a midwesterner. That is a fact that most people lose sight of when they associate Hughes with the Harlem Renaissance or with his return to Harlem in the 1950s and 1960s or with the circle of writers he hung out with while in Carmel, California, during the 1930s or with globetrotting when he visited Russia, Spain, Haiti, western Africa, Japan, China, and Cuba. But the fact that Hughes was born in Missouri, spent his formative years with his grandmother in Lawrence, Kansas, and went to high school in Cleveland is as important in under-standing the man as it is to know that Miles Davis is a midwesterner and that Charlie Parker was a midwesterner and that Toni Morrison is a midwesterner. To be from the Midwest is to be from the ambiguous heart and center of the American landscape. New England, the South, and the West are mythical regions of the American geography of the mind: they are *definite* places in America. To be from the Midwest is, in effect, to be from nowhere or perhaps I should say nowhere in particular. In truth, every midwestern artist becomes Dorothy of the famous Oz books who must constantly juxtapose a mythical landscape of some gorgeous proportions to a home which one hopes will induce a kind of self-exile. This is why, I think, in the end, Hughes gave the overwhelming appearance of being rootless, of drifting across the continental divide as if he were in search of something and of nothing in particular. There is in that sort of a quest which is not a quest something peculiarly male and American, the urge to be a hobo of sorts, out at the elbows, looking for a job of work. One can imagine Hughes, like Woody Guthrie, another famous midwesterner, going around the country with his typewriter bearing the same legend as the famed folksinger's guitar: "This machine kills fascists." Midwesterners are the displaced personas of the American imagination, and to suffer from that kind of vast sense of being lost but of not being at all desperate about it can make a particularly spirited and powerful writer as I think the sense of displacement did with Hughes.

If Hughes suffered from the anxiety of influence because of the name he bore, he also suffered from the anxiety of influence because of his parents. He very much did not want to be like his father, who, after separating from Hughes's mother, became a quite successful businessman in Mexico. Hughes went to live with his father after he graduated from high school (which is, incidentally, how he learned Spanish and first became interested in Latin American and Caribbean literature) and he found the experience of being with him very difficult. This is how he described him in his autobiography:

But my father was certainly just like the other German and English and

American businessmen with whom he associated in Mexico. He spoke just as badly about the Mexicans. He said they were ignorant and backward and lazy. He said they were exactly like the Negroes in the United States, perhaps worse. And he said they were very bad at making money.

My father hated Negroes. I think he hated himself, too, for being a Negro. He disliked all of his family because they were Negroes and remained in the United States, where none of them had a chance to be much of anything but servants — like my mother, who started out with a good education at the University of Kansas, he said, but had sunk to working in a restaurant, waiting on niggers, when she wasn't in some white woman's kitchen. My father said he wanted me to leave the United States as soon as I finished high school, and never return — unless I wanted to be a porter or a red cap all my life.

Being with his father so depressed and disturbed Hughes that he thought of committing suicide. Certainly, if Hughes wound up being the black poet who championed blackness it was in part because his father so hated blackness and Hughes wanted so much and consciously to be the antithesis of that.

His father who was so money-grubbing and so business-oriented was to produce a son who could never manage money well, never made any considerable sums of it, and was never aware of himself as a commercial entity during his writing career. Hughes at times surely wrote for money but never saw his career as a money-making venture, only as an enterprise to keep body and soul together. In effect, I think some of Hughes's posturing as an adult, some of his ideas, and certainly the way he decided to live his life were in direct conflict with the values of his father, in part out of hatred for his father and in part out of fear that he might become like his father if he did not radically make himself something else. His father wanted him to go to Columbia University to become an engineer. Hughes tried it for a semester but left, disgusted with the racism of many of his professors and his peers, and completely disillusioned with the regimen of academic life. (Hughes was a graduate of Lincoln University in Pennsylvania, an all-black school, in the mid-1920s.) It is, I think, very meaningful that he should open the first volume of his autobiography with the scene of tossing books into the sea. This happens right after he has left Columbia and is about to become a knock-about on the sea; the books are many he accumulated at Columbia. So the scene really announces his emancipation from his father and his father's particularly rigid set of inhumane values. His father, in short, was a puritan, and Hughes, all of his life, like H. L. Mencken, hated puritanism. The tossing out of the books is the rejection of the practical career, the bourgeois career of male competitive desire. The father wants Hughes to become an engineer, a practical career and one in which he could, as the father envisions it, join the father in commercial enterprises (so the "million bricks" symbolize an edifice that would read "Hughes and Son") in Mexico. Hughes's refusal to stay at Columbia was tantamount to a refusal not only to be an engineer but to engage seriously the father's way of making peace with being a black man in a world of white sensibilities. In short, he is saying to his father, "You have nothing to offer me as a father and nothing to teach as a black man." It is a stunning renunciation. One might normally expect in the autobiography of a writer the scene where he or she describes the dramatic entry into the world of books, how books and the world of the creative imagination saved him or hér. (This is particularly true of the classic black male autobiographies: consider the importance of the discovery of books in the autobiographies of Frederick Douglass, Richard Wright, and Malcolm X.) Hughes turns the expectation on its head as he presents himself as the writer who had to liberate himself from the world of books in order to be sprung into the life, the true subject of his writing.

But Hughes also distanced himself from his mother, and he never adopted her values either. In his autobiography he writes in this way about his mother and his stepfather:

> My mother and step-father were interested in making money, too....But they were interested in making money to *spend*. And for fun. They were always buying Victrolas and radios and watches and rings, and going to shows and drinking beer and playing cards, and trying to have a good time after working hours.

I think the problem that Hughes had with his parents was best summed up by Faith Berry in her biography of Hughes when she wrote:

> Perplexing traits of his mother matched equally perplexing traits of his father. *Her* insensibility against *his* austerity, *his* taciturnity against *her* garrulity, *her* lack of discrimination against *his* snobbism, *his* harsh prudence against *her* indiscretion.

Hughes's parents, in effect, represented a kind of polarity that Hughes had to negotiate all of his life. His father was everything that was wrong with middle-class morality and the cultural mythology of the self-made person. He was a black version of a Matthew Arnold Philistine. She, on the other hand, was everything that was wrong with lower-class life, self-indulgent, inclined to self-pity and complaint, living in a world of fantasy. (Although, of course, it was she who introduced him as a boy to the world of art, taking him to concerts and libraries. For that she endeared herself to him forever, in a way.) It must be remembered that although Hughes wrote very sympathetically about lower-class blacks and knew many intimately, he never *lived* that life himself as an adult despite his bouts with poverty.

He liked blues music but he was never as acquiescent in his view of life as the persona in a blues song. It always is a dangerous endeavor to read too much autobiography in any writer's work, even a book that professes to be an autobiographical novel such as Hughes's first novel, *Not Without Laughter.* Yet one cannot help but think that the fictional relationship between Anjee and her son Sandy was Hughes's attempt to come to grips with his relationship with his mother. The account is far from flattering: Anjee is a weak, whining woman who is constantly running behind her irresponsible husband, JimBoy, constantly abandoning her son, yet, when he finally reaches his maturity, she is ready to make selfish demands upon him. The major one she makes is that he mustn't continue his education anymore but rather must go to work to help her out. This happened to Hughes in his young adult life virtually every time he lived with his mother. The same bitter conflict, the same obsessive demand. Essentially, I think Hughes thought his mother to be without ambitions and, what is more important, without any real understanding of his. It was his mother acting as a drain and a burden upon his finances, especially with her bad health in her later years, that prevented Hughes from saving any money at all. It is difficult to say if Hughes honestly disliked his mother, although he may have "loved her hopelessly," Arnold Rampersad writes. I think it is safe to say that he felt sufficient tension in their relationship actually to feel guilty about it to some degree. It was a topic—the demanding unsympathetic mother and the aspiring son—that he was to return to a few years later after publication of *Not Without Laughter* in his one-act play, *Soul Gone Home.*

But one wonders, despite all the gifts and psychological incentives and drives that Hughes possessed, if he would ever have been a writer if there had been no Harlem Renaissance, no social and political movement of his youth that provided him with a context, a collection of colleagues, a setting, a group of mentors, and the inspiration and encouragement to write. Writers, in the end, despite their autobiographies to the contrary, do not create themselves; their cultures create them and create the moment for the works by defining the necessity of its production. It takes a great deal, both accidental and intentional, for a culture to nurture a writer, and in many instances the nurturing fails; the writer fails to produce at all or his or her works never fulfill their promise. It is somehow getting through that period in his or her life when the writer is burdened with the expectancy of promise that is most perilous. For Hughes and, oddly enough, for modern Afro-American literature, that period of promise was the Harlem Renaissance.

But the Harlem Renaissance did more than provide young black writers like Hughes with a framework and emotional support; it provided publications. And young writers need journals and magazines that will publish their work more than they need bread or meat. Publications, even without pay, are the very stuff that keeps them going. The major publications of the Harlem Renaissance were *Crisis,* the organ of the NAACP, *Opportunity,* the organ of the Urban League, *The Messenger,* the socialist magazine of Chandler Owen and A. Philip Randolph, and *Negro World,* the organ of Marcus Garvey's United Negro Improvement Association. Hughes's work was to appear in virtually every mainstream literary and commercial magazine in America including *The New Yorker* and *The Saturday Evening Post,* but it was publications such as those black magazines and the literary awards that both the NAACP and the Urban League sponsored that gave Hughes his start. As Hughes wrote: "Jessie Fauset at the *Crisis,* Charles Johnson at *Opportunity,* and Alain Locke in Washington were the three people who midwifed the so-called New Negro literature into being." And

Hughes's eyewitness account of the Harlem Renaissance in *The Big Sea* remains the most vivid and the most strikingly shrewd of all that were produced. "I was there," Hughes writes cunningly, "I had a swell time while it lasted. But I thought it wouldn't last long....For how could a large and enthusiastic number of people be crazy about Negroes forever?"

The Harlem Renaissance officially began with the 1923 publication of Jean Toomer's fascinating novel-cum-miscellany, *Cane,* and culminated with the 1925 publication of Alain Locke's anthology, *The New Negro,* and it ended with the Crash of 1929 or, as Hughes and other black folk put it, it ended with the death of Harlem's leading and richest citizen, A'Lelia Walker, in 1931. The Renaissance was made possible by the northern and urban migration of southern, rural blacks before but especially after the First World War. (Incidentally, an excellent novel by an Afro-American writer about the black migration to the North is William Attaway's 1940 work, *Blood on the Forge.*) Not all blacks went to New York, of course. Jazzman King Oliver left New Orleans and came to Chicago to be followed a few years later by his protégé, Louis Armstrong. The family of future heavyweight champion Joe Louis, like many other blacks, went to Detroit to work in the auto plants. Others drifted to Kansas City, Philadelphia, and Boston. The twenties saw the resurrection of black political consciousness with the rise of black trade unionism, socialism, and the Back to Africa movement. This decade saw blacks in shows on Broadway written by blacks, and saw two blacks — Battling Siki and Tiger Flowers — become boxing champions of the light-heavyweight and middleweight divisions, respectively, the first blacks to hold any kind of professional sports title since the reign of heavyweight champion Jack Johnson ended in 1915. Jazz came into its own as an art form with such artists as Oliver, Armstrong, Duke Ellington, Earl Hines, Fletcher Henderson, W. C. Handy, and Sidney Bechet. And blues could be heard in practically every black neighborhood with records by Mamie Smith, Bessie Smith, Ma Rainey, Ida Cox, Sippie Wallace, Bessie Jackson, and others blaring on the Victrola.

And of course it was the era of literature: W. E. B. Du Bois, Eric Walrond, Countee Cullen, Rudolph Fisher, Thurman Wallace, George Schuyler, Nella Larsen, Jessie Fauset, Zora Neale Hurston, and Claude McKay were some of the important writers who produced major works during this period. And Langston Hughes was right in the middle of all this. He encountered the Renaissance largely through Alain Locke, was sustained by the same white patron who supported Zora Neale Hurston, tried his hand at editing a radically different literary magazine, *Fire!!,* along with his friends, and finally, entered the new decade of the thirties as thoroughly disillusioned and enlightened as the new crop of black writers who were to make their way writing uncompromising, naturalistic social protest. Hughes, like many of the younger more rebellious writers of this era, wanted very much to capture the form and flavor of the expressive culture of the ordinary Afro-American; that is to say, he did not aspire toward the creation of bourgeois literature or the literature of bourgeois sensibilities. (Perhaps the influence of H. L. Mencken here, as Charles Scruggs argues in his fine study of the Harlem Renaissance, *The Sage in Harlem*.) As Hughes wrote: "The ordinary Negroes hadn't heard of the Negro Renaissance. And if they had, it hadn't raised their wages any."

Obviously enough, Hughes was certainly not interested in a black novel of manners or a novel of black manners in the sense that he did not find the peculiar position of the middle-class or light-skinned black (for all intents and purposes, being middle-class and being light-skinned were fairly synonymous) worthy of excessive sympathy or intense psychological scrutiny. After all, this class of blacks, from the time of the slave narratives, many of the most famous ones having been written by mulattoes, including Frederick Douglass, had their advocates. Hughes, at times, when he wrote about the black middle class sounded a great deal like E. Franklin Frazier did in his famous treatise *The Black Bourgeoisie*. This is from *The Big Sea*:

> These upper-class colored people consisted largely of government workers, professors and teachers, doctors, lawyers, and resident politicians. They were on the whole as unbearable and snobbish a group of people as I have ever come in contact with anywhere. They lived in comfortable homes, had fine cars, played bridge, drank Scotch, gave exclusive "formal" parties, and dressed well, but seemed to me altogether lacking in real culture, kindness, or good common sense.
>
> Lots of them held degrees from colleges like Harvard and Dartmouth and Columbia and Radcliffe and Smith, but God knows what they learned there. They had all the manners and airs of reactionary, ill-bred *nouveaux riches* — except that they were not really rich. Just middle class. And many of them had less fortunate brothers or cousins working as red-caps and porters — so near was their society standing to that of the poorest Negro. (Their snobbishness was so precarious that I suppose for that very reason it had to be doubly reinforced.)

The subject matter of Hughes's work was a revolt against black middle-class values but it was, more deeply considered, a revolt against not only what his father stood for but what his mother's side of the family — the James Mercer Langston side — stood for as well. He stated his position innocently enough: "Anyway, I didn't know the upper-class Negroes well enough to write much about them. I knew only the people I had grown up with, and they weren't people whose shoes were always shined, who had been to Harvard, or who had heard of Bach. But they seemed to me good people, too." Hughes is not being simplistic here; he is being disingenuous. He is writing about common black folk not because they are the only type of blacks he knows but they are the only blacks he feels who can be portrayed in a way to create a powerful new Negro literature. He does not express his preference as an artistic corollary but it is exactly that in the end. (And he was to express a kind of artistic creed quite formally in his 1926 essay, "The Negro Artist and the Racial Mountain," a piece written in response to George Schuyler's "The Negro Art-Hokum," and which was spiritedly defended by Chicago poet and Hughes disciple Fenton Johnson.) Great literature must be great stories told about common people. Moreover, to be himself, he found that he could not aspire to be part of a tradition that was hardly a tradition at all but a dreadful pathological stance against the ravages of an inferiority complex. Hughes's writing, among other things, sought the avenue of discovering just what it was to be a well-adjusted Negro. For Hughes, that meant the broad acceptance of black culture itself; it was a self-discovery akin to that of the Invisible Man when he eats the yam midway in Ellison's novel.

The fact that Hughes in his early works such as *The Weary Blues, Fine Clothes to the Jew* (which biographer Arnold Rampersad feels is Hughes's finest book), *Not Without Laughter,* and *The Ways of White Folks* was able to establish himself as a "jazz poet," a "blues poet," and a proletarian, social-protest writer is not entirely because he made himself those things. The culture provided avenues for these artistic roles. Indeed, Hughes was, in essence, a writer dealing with aspects of popular culture.

It must be remembered that although jazz and blues in their most authentic forms were still a race or ethnic music in the twenties, the terms themselves, as well as diluted forms of these musics, were so sufficiently diffused throughout the culture that white literary critics could refer to Hughes's allusions to and appropriations of the forms of these musics without mystifying their readers. Diluted forms of jazz and blues in the twenties were, after all, popular music. It was the Jazz Age. The invention of the phonograph and the radio made these musics a mass art experience. Moreover, an interest in socialism and leftist thought, while never truly popular in this country (except possibly during the Depression of the 1930s), was not a totally unacceptable political exploration for a black writer during the twenties, especially among the black masses who were more tolerant of deviant or subversive political expression, though too cynical to be seduced by it. In short, Hughes was seizing upon the new cultural expressions open to a black writer at that time, open not simply because of the Harlem Renaissance but also because of technological innovations and a general shift in mainstream white American culture, in much the way one might expect. Hughes came along at a time when Black American culture, often in a confused and distorted but a real and powerful way, was making an enormous impact on popular American culture itself, and much of his writing reflected the vitality and possibilities of that conjunction. Hughes certainly opened the creative doors for his two good friends Richard Wright and Ralph Ellison to come after and make further artistic investigations along the same lines: the connection between popular culture and the Negro. Isn't *Native Son* in part about a Negro boy who bumps into the monstrous image white popular culture has of him? Does not the black boy in *Invisible Man* keep bumping into various avatars of white popular culture? In the end, Hughes's greatest achievement during the Harlem Renaissance may have been the fact that he survived it and continued to write.

There are few other prominent persons from that era about whom one could make that claim. Such diverse personalities as Florence Mills; Tiger

Flowers; Battling Siki; Rudolph Fisher; A'Lelia Walker, daughter of a businesswoman, hot-comb magnate; and Madame C. J. Walker either did not see the new decade of the thirties at all or saw precious little of it before expiring. Before the thirties were over, Marcus Garvey would be jailed and deported, Bessie Smith would die in an automobile accident, Claude McKay would be ill and no longer writing, James Weldon Johnson would die in an auto accident (during the same week that Joe Louis beat Max Schmeling in a heavyweight title fight in New York that was heard around the world), W. E. B. Du Bois would have departed from the NAACP, Wallace Thurman would die of alcoholism. Only three fiction writers associated with the Renaissance would continue to produce major work after the twenties: Zora Neale Hurston, Arna Bontemps, and Langston Hughes. And of these three, only Hughes and Hurston, who after an early friendship were destined never to get along well, would produce work that would obtain them significant critical stature (although Bontemps's work is worthy of more critical attention). It was after the Harlem Renaissance that Hughes produced such important work as both volumes of his autobiography, the Simple books, most of the short stories and plays, and all of the anthologies including those on African literature and Afro-American folklore.

Hughes continued to write, and he never became dated, never became a parody of himself. His last book, a collection of poems entitled *The Panther and the Lash,* was just as timely and compelling when it came out in the mid-sixties as anything that was being written by the young Turks of that era: Amiri Baraka (LeRoi Jones), James Baldwin, Don L. Lee. Hughes survived in part because he never caused factions, never alienated others; in the twenties he traveled with the known black writers of the day, finding it just as easy to converse with Jessie Fauset as with Eric Walrond. In the thirties, he encouraged and aided Wright and Ellison; in the fifties he could praise Gwendolyn Brooks and Lorraine Hansberry equally. Hughes never seemed jealous about the accomplishments of other black writers or disturbed when their opinions or approaches differed sharply from his own. And Hughes never looked back to the past, never lived in a bygone era. The only black writer we know of with whom Hughes did not get on well, other than Hurston, whose difficulties were not his fault, was James Baldwin, and when one considers how temperamental writers are as a lot, how prickly, surly, egotistical, vain, and shallow many of them can be, it is a remarkable thing that Hughes got along with so many from so many different eras. But Hughes also survived because he possessed the quality of endurance. He seemed capable of growing, expanding, changing, without being disrupted by the force, speed, or extent of his maturity. He never gave the sense that he feared depletion or exhaustion. Thus, he never indulged in the self-destructive behavior so common among writers. It was his demeanor of well-adjustedness that accounts for this and for the fact that his supposed homosexuality never became a public personification of torment and distress but rather a private image of sexual ambiguity.

There is little that remains to be said. Hughes's achievement as a writer was staggering, not simply in its overall quality or in its amount but in its sheer and quiet abidingness; and we are only just now beginning to appreciate it and give it the critical attention it deserves. It is not an accident that Hughes was the first black writer with an academic quarterly devoted to the study of his work: the *Langston Hughes Quarterly*, edited by George Bass of Brown University. Other black writers surely deserve a journal as well: Richard Wright, James Baldwin, Ralph Ellison, W. E. B. Du Bois, Amiri Baraka, the entire Harlem Renaissance—and it is pleasing to know that there is now a *Zora Neale Hurston Forum* which comes out of Morgan State—but it does the heart and soul good to know that Hughes was the first black writer to be so honored. I am sorry that my words are so paltry. They scarcely touch the man, his work, his great endearing soul. So, perhaps, at last, only a kind of awed silence can be the only real tribute. As Miles Davis once told his fellow jazz musicians about Duke Ellington: we need to go down on our knees every night and thank God for giving us Langston Hughes. He made the whole business of modern Afro-American literature possible. It is as simple as that. To borrow from songwriter Paul Simon, Hughes was one of the few American writers who could straddle so humorously and tellingly in his work both the worlds of "bodegas and the light of Upper Broadway." He had diamonds on the soles of his ordinary shoes.

V

Play Without Ceasing:
Thelonious Monk and Earl Hines

I. THE GATHERING OF STONES

I may be crazy but I ain't no fool.
—Black vaudevillian Bert Williams

Every morning during a six-month span in 1977 when I was Communications Supervisor for the Crisis Intervention Network, a gang-control agency (how I loathed that term!), I would arrive at work at 8:15, before anyone else, sign on with the City Hall dispatcher and turn on the shabby, scarred AM-FM radio to the college FM jazz station. Soon, the bluesy strains of Gene Ammons or Yusef Lateef would purr through the room. Invariably, by 9:00 or 9:30 when one of the other dispatchers or a team member would come into the office, someone would switch the radio to the FM soul station. This did not bother me very much since I found it difficult to enjoy any kind of music while I was working. I have always been one of those aesthetic purists who feel it to be the worst sort of sin to relegate any music worth experiencing to the position of background drone. From 8:30 till 9:00, before the day officially began, I enjoyed the music in solitude; once the other workers arrived I promptly forgot it.

After a time, I had come to suspect that the fellows I worked with—all of whom had fought with some of the toughest teenage street gangs in Philadelphia and some of whom had served a stretch in Holmesburg

Prison—thought that my listening to jazz was one of my University of Pennsylvania airs, a college-boy pretension. There were two other University of Pennsylvania black graduates working for the Crisis Intervention Network; and I believe the fact that all of us were office workers, paper pushers, and supervisors, the fact that we had never set foot in the streets to help combat the savage slaughter of the teen wars really, in some minds including my own, amounted to the sort of house nigger/field nigger schism that has always existed among black folk. There existed the classic example of the status-seeking, middle-class "Us" versus the street-corner-hardened, uncouth "Them." Of course middle-class black boys who attended Ivy League colleges listened to jazz because it was so much more intellectual and refined than the jungle bunny's boogie. But many a modern black listener of jazz has forgotten that in music's gutbucket roots, jazz was a nasty music; indeed, "jazz" was a nasty word.

One can only suppose that between lower-class and middle-class blacks there exists a certain "anxiety of influence" insofar as music is concerned. In the end, one seems constantly confronted with the question, "Which class are you in?"

"So you really like jazz, huh?" asked Mike Carpenter, a member of the West Philadelphia team, in an extremely sinister way.

"Yes, I do," I rather hesitantly replied. "It is a music of great dignity and rich in black cultural heritage."

I thought that to be a truly innocuous statement, but it must have offended Mike. He looked at me with the sort of disdain any lower-class black ought rightfully to feel when his middle-class brother pontificates like a condescending ass.

"You ever heard of Hank Mobley?" he asked.

I nodded, recognizing the name of a former Miles Davis sideman and a fine bop and mainstream saxophonist.

"Well," he said as he strolled out of the Communications room with a certain secret relish, "you can see him out on Greys Ferry Avenue anytime, as drunk as a motherfucker. He can't even keep his horn out of hock. That's real dignity and culture for you."

The only person beside myself who worked at the Crisis Intervention Network and liked jazz was Reds, the leader of the South Philadelphia team. At fifty-five or so, he was the oldest worker in the organization. He had a splotchy red complexion, and he always wore a stingy brim to cover a bald pate, which in his younger days was probably covered with red hair. His voice had that whiskey-drenched sound of a man who has consumed lots of strong liquor over the years in the cheapest, darkest dives. He was undoubtedly a zootsuiter in his youth, hanging out, as he told me, getting wise in the streets of Philadelphia and New York, and listening to jazz in places where only musicians, pimps, prostitutes, gangsters, and serious music lovers would dare to tread. Darting in and out of the Communications room, singing snatches of "Lush Life" or "Don't Get Around Much Anymore," or telling stories about some jazzman he knew (and he seemed to have known them all), he struck me as a tough old bird, no one to fool around with. Unlike Muddy Waters, Reds was not "hard again"; I doubt if he were ever anything in life but hard and swift, swift, swift as a lightweight boxer. Most of the guys thought him to be a foolish Uncle Tom, largely because he never had anything good to say about blacks.

One afternoon when a bunch of workers had gathered in the Communications room to luxuriate in the deep leisure of our weekly bull session—Happy, Spaceman, Bird, Bat, Robert Jarrett, Master Spoon, Eric Lark (our equivalent to the March of Dimes poster kid because he had been paralyzed for life by a stray bullet fired during a street-gang rumble), Brown, Tony King, and Rudy Mormon, all partaking of a conversation that hung suspended between political discussion, playing the dozens, and absurdity—Reds, after listening for a bit, broke in:

"I ain't never met a group of people more full of shit than niggers. You talking about Africa? What them niggers in Africa got? You couldn't get me to go to Africa if you offered me a million dollars. Say, I used to know Nkrumah. I used to see that nigger on the corner of Broad and South with a bunch of robes on talking about 'Get rid of the European imperialists.' That's when he was a student at Lincoln. I used to party with the nigger, go to Peps to hear Miles. I done heard all that shit you niggers talking about African liberation. I heard that shit thirty years ago, and it was tired then!"

"Hey, man," Tony King shouted, twisting his toothpick to the side of his mouth, "look, we don't wanna hear all that old Uncle Tom stuff. If you heard it all before, that's fine. We ain't saying that it's new. You old niggers ain't never satisfied unless you dragging down everything."

"You wanna call me a Tom?" Reds bellowed, getting very animated, "Go ahead! I don't care. But you know that a nigger ain't shit. If it wasn't for black women covering your asses there wouldn't be no niggers in America. Niggers hate anything another nigger do."

At this point Reds rushed over to the radio from which was seeping the latest Commodores' hit and switched the dial to the jazz station while turning the volume up to its limit. Lester Young's saxophone came blasting through the tin speakers in an ugly cloud of distorted sound. It was like a rooster squawling over a bullhorn. The Pres, who always wanted to play pretty, sounded hideous.

"You niggers want to talk about black pride. Jazz is a music made by black people, but you won't ever support it or listen to it. That's Lester Young playing there. I used to hang out with Lester in New York—"

"Hey," Happy shouted, jumping up to turn down the radio, "you crazy or something? You snapping out? You trying to make everybody deaf?"

"I wanna tell you about Lester Young," Reds replied.

"Well, I don't wanna know about Lester Young," said Happy with a great deal of finality in his voice. He turned off the radio.

"You all are just ignorant," Reds said more calmly, "and you want everybody else to be ignorant. Let me go around and pick up the stones."

And saying that, Reds went around the room stopping in front of each person, except me, and pretended to pull stones from each one's pockets and dropped them into an imaginary bag.

"What you call yourself doing?" asked Brown.

"I'm getting the stones, brother," said Reds.

"What stones?" asked Tony King, winking.

"The stones you gonna bust my head with and bust the radio with. That's all niggers ever use them stones for, to bust each other with them."

After Reds had gathered the stones, he quietly left the room. Everyone began to laugh.

"That old Tom nigger done snapped, jack," barked Tony King.

"Hey," said Spaceman, "somebody turn the radio back on; I want to hear some music."

The conversation continued for several minutes more, but the spirit of the thing was broken. There was something about what Reds did that was a bit disquieting to us all. As he went from person to person collecting the stones, I felt as if he were making good, on not some make-believe debt, but a divine one. It was a strange ritual and we, though unbelieving, knew it to be some secret powerful theology. I think what may have been extracted from us was the weapons that the living use to ward off the dead. We all felt strangely defenseless. The jazz music was coming through softly on the radio. No one had changed the station; Lester Young was still playing. Reds popped his head into the room.

"The dead is trying to communicate with the dead." He laughed and his head quickly disappeared. His hat blurred in a tweedy streak.

The fellows, laughing a bit more defensively and nervously, filed quietly out of the Communications room, by twos and threes.

"He's just crazy," said Happy, as he turned off the radio. "Don't nobody care about no Lester Young."

II. BIRD SAID, "PLAY!"

Ain't it great to be living?

—Oscar Brown, Jr.

Good music is something you enjoy. It's pleasing to you. It's good to your ear. Anything that sounds good to your ear, a nice type of sound, is music.

—Thelonious Monk

I once knew a poet named Yusef Rahman who hung around with and was, I believe, briefly promoted by Amiri Baraka. This was back during the days of the Spirit House Movers, dashikis, and rap-session poetry readings. These were the days when hip black people looked like dancers for the chorus line of a Sun Ra musical, when Walt Palmer, James Foreman, and Playtell Benjamin were black Philadelphia's heroes. Rahman was what one might call a jazz poet akin to Ted Joans but much better. He wrote one book of poetry that I know about called *Alhomdilillah* and gave something called a "Kosmic Kiddie Koncert," reading poetry and playing bells for children. It was delightfully droll. This was also the time of the rise of Jimi Hendrix, when voodoo met the enlightened of the Kundalini. Rahman's poetry was that strange halfway house between Eastern mysticism and black revolution, between vegetarianism and gun smuggling.

It was certainly one of the more interesting times to be black in this country. Black folk were discovering some colorful ways to deal with adversity. Rahman never made it in the poetry game, a casualty of the serious battles fought in the art world. What I remember most clearly about Rahman was that inadvertently he introduced me to Thelonious Monk. In looking back, I could think of no better historical ambience to have learned about someone like Monk than during those days; finally, a young black could truly appreciate the fact that some of his race's great achievers not only rose from the streets but managed still to be inspired by bad places and foul air in spite of their success. Every place where jazz was played became for me a kind of Funky Butt Hall all over again. This was, at the time, particularly soothing to the neurotic middle-class black. Jazz was and is the great example of that sort of advance against adversity which did not always mean, to use trumpeter Buddy Bolden's phrase, that one had to let the bad air out. Jazz's heroes had become as respectable as Douglass and Booker T. Washington.

I was not unfamiliar with jazz when I finally encountered Thelonious Monk. My sisters had records by Miles Davis, Nina Simone, and Max Roach (the legendary *Freedom Now Suite* album; I was the only kid on my block who not only could hum the latest Motown hit but could recite all the lyrics from "Driva Man," which for me was the most moving music I had ever heard)—no watered-down, commercial jazz either; no greasy soul food by Booby Timmons, no African waltzes by Cannonball Adderley, no flaccid blues by Les McCann. Indeed, when I think of my early teenage years, I can clearly remember each of my sisters poised by the cheap hi-fi, holding records with a sort of careless attention that always characterized the true music lovers from mere record collectors. I will always remember hearing Nina Simone singing "Pirate Jenny" and "Mississippi Goddam" and Hubert Laws's flute and piccolo on "Miedo" flittering down the steps like flower petals on grass.

But I was still at heart an R&B man, sitting all evening in a room listening to the radio blare out Darrell Bank's "Everlasting Love," Aaron Neville's "Tell It Like It Is," Otis Redding's "Mr. Pitiful," Junior Walker's "Cleo's Back," or Dyke and the Blazers' "Funky Broadway." Little Willie John and Sam Cooke gave me chills of delight when I heard them sing. (John's "Talk to Me" is still one of the best soul ballads ever cut.) Most jazz left me unmoved. Largely, this stemmed from the fact that I, like most people, found an intricate instrumental music like jazz very difficult to follow aurally. But more important, I had not learned that jazz was telling the same story as R&B.

I heard my first Thelonious Monk record at the age of seventeen when I was living in San Francisco with my eldest sister. It was, in fact, one of Rahman's records, an old Riverside label issue entitled *Monk's Music,* with such people as Coleman Hawkins, Gigi Gryce, Art Blakey, and the great John Coltrane.

Unlike many first-time listeners to Monk who say that the music went over their heads, I, with an untrained ear, loved what I heard immediately. This record was not really one of Monk's better efforts, but at the time I did not realize that Hawkins was floundering in deep waters (he had come a long way from Fletcher Henderson's 1920s band, or had he?), that Copeland's trumpet solos were bland, and that Coltrane was still finding it difficult to negotiate Monk's harmonies, although I think he had been playing with Monk regularly at the time this record was made. Monk's melodies and solos (which really amount to the same thing since his solos are built around the permutations of his melodic lines; in short, his surfaces and depths are one) were the only aspects of the record to which I really paid any attention. It was more than a year later when I finally began to pay attention to the other musicians. It was Monk who made me aware of the R&B element in jazz. Monk played like an edited gospel pianist who was kicked out of the church because he played too much of the "devil's music" when no one was watching. (Monk had actually spent his teenage years serving as an accompanist for a woman evangelist.) His playing reminded me a good deal of Ray Charles—not Charles's playing but his voice. There was in Monk's method the deepest sort of testifying, the headiest type of bearing witness. He sounded positively possessed of the Holy Spirit, not in a frenzied way of church as theater but in the deliberate calm of religion as wisdom. It was never really the college boy's cool that led to jazz; I have always loathed fey music.

I decided, after listening to that record until my sister was ready to climb a wall, to buy some other Monk albums. The first one I bought was called *Monk's Blues,* on Columbia, a bunch of big-band sessions he did in L.A. in 1968 using Oliver Nelson's arrangements. It is probably one of the worst Monk records ever made; Nelson and those studio musicians succeeded in making Monk's songs sound like TV show tunes. Still, I enjoyed the record thoroughly. Next I bought *Monk's Greatest Hits,* another dismal Columbia collection which, although it contained Monk's best compositions, such as "Straight, No Chaser," "Epistrophy," "Round Midnight," "Ruby, My Dear," and "Bensha Swing," did not offer the listener the best renditions of those tunes. (It was not until I became a much more experienced jazz listener that I learned that Monk did his best work from the late forties through the late fifties on the Blue Note, Prestige, and Riverside labels. Columbia got him when he hit the big time and had gotten a little stale.) Moreover, the packaging of Monk's music as if he were a top-40 pop star, as if his canon can be rightfully and meaningfully understood by designating some tunes "greatest hits" seems to me in retrospect both absurd and insulting. Songs like "Nutty," "Brilliant Corners," "Jackieing," "Humph," "Evidence," and "Four in One," some of Monk's most musically challenging pieces, were not included. Nonetheless, I played the album until it was white.

This was the sort of power that Monk had over me. I could hear his music in the most unsympathetic and uncongenial settings, and the whole world would simply stop for me. That is the power of the great ones, as pianist Cecil Taylor once pointed out, the power to suspend the listener between conscious reality and a state which may possibly resemble death. (Pianist Keith Jarrett once described his improvised solo concerts as being inspired, in part, by the idea of death. I might think that the trancelike state he some-times affects for himself, and, vicariously, for his listener, is an example, of sorts, of what I am talking about.) Perhaps it is simply dreaming. But in this state the mind feels most clear because it is so unaware of itself. The highest tribute to be paid to a musician is to say that his art makes the listener quail and tremble before the great, aching, impersonal glory of this world and this life. Monk's music could do that for me, could do what those great gospel-trained voices of those sweaty, greasy-headed men and women of the R&B world could do: tell me the tale of how black folk soar above adversity. I realized that black music was the most telling criticism of American life.

Monk, more than any other jazz musician, made me realize that R&B and jazz were of a piece, part of a grand continuum in black life. The R&B people I grew up listening to, from Johnny Ace, Joe Loco, and Bobby Day to the Coasters, the Jaynettes, Sonny Til and the Orioles, the Shirelles, James Brown, and Ike and Tina Turner, always sang and performed with dignity and grace. I remember these men and women were always well dressed, even if sometimes gaudily so, for their performances. And often catching these acts at Uptown Theater at Broad and Dauphin Streets in Philadelphia, we little black kids would emerge from the darkened magic talking about buying a pair of shoes at Florsheim's that would match what we saw Smokey Robinson wearing, or the girls would talk about getting their hair done in the style of the lead singer of Brenda and the Tabulations. The performers on that circuit had to be "clean"; they had to wear their clothes with style and execute their dance steps, their routines, with the greatest precision and aplomb. The members of the Modern Jazz Quartet may have thought that their formal attire gave their music the elite status of a classical music concert, but black folk knew that the Temptations, Major Lance, and Jackie Wilson all wore suits too. Monk's funny hats were just as appropriate for his dark suits as the R&B performer's huge, wild process hairdo was appropriate for his own stylish wear. It was a kind of easy meshing of the outlandish and the staid, this ability to embody the incongruous with the depths of character: that is what made the black performer "clean."

But, oddly enough, in addition to being "clean," the black performer had to be "funky." This rather formidable irony, which Albert Murray touches upon in his *Stomping the Blues,* brings in the element of play, because while the artist, either jazz or R & B, is supposed to give everything he has on the stage, he is supposed to be enjoying it and never losing his cool.

The effort has only to look hard. For underneath the mask of funk and sweat is always the cool, clean black, detached and unruffled. It was, in my salad days, a put-on but of a very different kind from the put-on of the darkie entertainer in the early part of the century. What R&B and jazz made clear is that the black entertainer wears no longer the masks that white culture forced upon him but rather the two masks of either side of his own mythic, archetypal self. It is no longer the grinning Sambo encasing the desperate, self-hating black, but the passionate virtuoso encasing the disinterested artist. And in hearing Monk I finally understood the story of the black triumph over white adversity: Blacks had learned to combine the hot and the cool into such a density of expression, into such a special rhythm, that they had learned a kind of special code in life. Monk's playing was, at times, a kind of parodic version of that special awareness. What was in Monk's music was the epistemology of the black artistic enterprise: Was Monk a gospel or a blues pianist? Or was he Tin Pan Alley in the same way as Will Marion Cook and Rosamond Johnson, inventors of the Broadway musical? Could he even play the piano or was he just an unschooled tinkerer? (He did attend Juilliard briefly, but he never formally studied the instrument.) The whole of Monk's art was the playing around with these elements of his own self-created ambiguities without clarifying anything. He played around with a kind of multilayered doubleness.

I saw Monk perform in the early seventies in Philadelphia at a place called the Aqua Lounge. By this time most of the jazz watering holes in town had dried up. I could remember roaming Broad and South as a kid and discovering that Yusef Lateef would be holding court at Peps, Horace Silver would be around the corner at the Postal Card, and Johnny Hartman would be down the block at the Showboat. These were only a few of the major jazz houses, and besides these the locals who liked the Hammond organ sound could always catch Groove Holmes or Jack McDuff or Jimmy Mcgriff at a small bar. But that whole jazz, like the R&B shows at the Uptown Theater, was all part of another time. The Aqua Lounge was making the last stand against indifference, changing neighborhoods, and economic hard times.

Paul Jeffries was on tenor sax and Monk, Jr., was on the drums in this edition of the Monk quartet. It was a good evening filled with solid music. Monk had aged, on the whole, fairly well and on this particular night the quaint vapidness which had crept into his music over the last few years was absent. Monk did not play anything new; he sounded very much like a man who was at peace with himself. He had allowed electronics and the avant-garde to pass him by as if he were standing still. Monk, unlike the old R&B

singers who perform at revival shows, was not living in the past. If anything, he had been grappling with the meaning and the measure of his artistic past, which is why he felt so compelled to repeat it without ceasing. He had paid his dues in the ass-kicking business of music making. He had been an original, so he certainly did not need to be novel.

In the past, many, both laymen and musicians, thought that Monk could not play, that he was a bungler, that his solos were, as guitarist Joe Pass once put it, "dumb and ugly." But Monk was able to hang out with the big boys; Bird and Diz loved him and Charles Christian could hardly wait to get away from Benny Goodman to jam with him at Minton's Playhouse in Harlem, where, we are told, the new music called bebop was born or at least very lovingly nurtured. Miles Davis, John Coltrane, and Sonny Rollins all acknowledged their debts to him, and his compositions have endured longer and aged better than those of any other composer from that era. (Only Gillespie's "A Night in Tunisia," Tadd Dameron's "If You Could See Me Now" and "Good Bait," and Parker's "Donna Lee" and "Confirmation" are played as much by jazzmen as Monk's tunes.) Bud Powell was undoubtedly the greatest piano *player* of this period, but Monk was the greatest thinker on the piano. Powell could play the ivories, wail, cook, and burn, to use the jazzman's argot, but Monk understood the *sound* of the instrument. Monk was one of the first players to realize that virtuosity was not enough and should never be an end in itself. This is not to say that Monk eschewed technical proficiency; he simply became virtuosic in his own personal language. In a sense, Monk was, in Ralph Ellison's phrase, a "tinker-thinker."

If part of the concern on the part of the black musician's constant search for technical advancement was to prevent whites from copying the music and thus stealing or perverting its identity, Monk's playing was so rooted in the atavistic memory of bad, out-of-tune pianos, storefront churches, whorehouse jam sessions, and black funerals that no "white boy" in this world could ever succeed in copying it. In this way, as great as pianist Art Tatum was, he was, at last, not nearly as inventive on the instrument as Monk. If Miles Davis is jazz's brooding, arrogant *artiste,* if Coltrane was its patron saint, if Art Blakey is its raconteur, and if Parker was its existential hero, then Monk was its mysterious shaman, protector of the rites and sacraments.

In the tradition of African-American improvisational music, Monk would rank behind only Duke Ellington as the premier composer in this genre. That is a great compliment, because Ellington was the finest composer America produced in the twentieth century. No, it is not a compliment. It is simply the truth. Ellington, Monk, and Charlie Mingus — good company for anybody to keep. What a rocking corner of heaven theirs must be! What marvelous sounds must be emanating from that nigger paradise or from the deepest pits in hell! Descend those circles with your literary guide, and you will not find Satan in a frozen pool but Mingus writing furiously at the piano while cursing everything in sight, Ellington bathing his hands in lotion and baby powder in preparation for his sleight-of-hand, and Armstrong, wearing an Aunt Jemima kerchief, laughing through his horn as he plays for all the squares and bohemians "I'll Be Glad When You're Dead, You Rascal You."

As I watched Monk perform, as I saw how perfectly at ease he was playing those tunes of his again for the millionth time, the lines of Wordsworth came to mind:

His is by nature led to peace so perfect that the
young behold with envy, what the Old Man hardly feels.

I feel no need to retrace the Monk career from the hard early days of the bebop wars through the neglected years of the fifties to acceptance and a *Time* magazine cover in the sixties. If we consider the type of music he played and the type of man he was, he probably got as much recognition for his genius as any black man can hope for from the *Herrenvolk*. He was, I am told, a very gentle man who believed in song. That sort of magisterial dignity and grace characterized his music.

It is, I think, fitting that Monk died during Black History Month (February 17, 1982). He was, after all, the link in modern jazz that connected the early black piano wizards like James P. Johnson, Fats Waller, Eubie Blake, and Jelly Roll Morton to the young lions of the post-bebop era. If Monk continued the African-American art of playing the piano by performing such tunes as "Memories of You" and "Honeysuckle Rose," then his own compositions have become, at various times, standard fare in the repertoires of Cecil Taylor, McCoy Tyner, and Anthony Davis.

Some jazz artists are totally worn out at the time of their deaths. Names like Charlie Parker, Ben Webster, Lester Young, Bud Powell, Louis Armstrong, and Billie Holliday come to mind. Others die prematurely and, thus, have given the music its sense of deep tragedy: Rashaan Roland Kirk, Herbie Nichols, Hampton Hawes, Booker Little, Lee Morgan, John Coltrane, Albert Alyer, Booby Timmons, Cannonball Adderley, Eric Dolphy, and Jimmy Garrison. These people still had a lot of new music left in them. But in the case of both groups, they were, in large measure, killed by the constant adversity that the jazz life forced them to confront. I am not sure if Monk was artistically or emotionally worn out at the time of his death. It is pretty to think that somehow he could have played his music forever, but I tend to doubt if he could have. He did succeed against the greatest odds imaginable in getting all of the music in him out into the world. His death was, ironically enough, the closing of the story of how one life won out over adversity at last.

III. FLOWERS FOR FATHA

Before our heads go under we take a last look
At the killing noise

Of the out of style, of the out of style,
The out of style.
—Jimi Hendrix

My mother never liked Earl Hines's toupee, a bit of affectation he adopted in the sixties when the thinning of his hair must have reached the plateau of baldness. It was, I suppose, a homely thing; it looked so obviously like a toupee that I wondered why he wore it. I have thought that if a man were vain enough to wear one, he ought to have the decency to buy something that would not call attention to itself, that would not announce to the world its own falseness. Toupees in particular and wigs in general must be subtle; but Hines wore something as shameless and brazen as those leaning towers of horsehair that Diana Ross and her Supremes used to sport.

What made Hines's hairpiece so gauche was that it would have looked more suitable perched atop the head of a white man. "He doesn't have straight hair," said my mother, "so why is he wearing a toupee like that?" What my mother meant was that, in the parlance of black folk, Hines did not have "good" hair, that is, hair like a white person. Although the hair may never have been good, it had been straight, chemically straightened in the old conk style which begat the process which begat the curly perm and the era of wearing a plastic bag to keep the grease in place and the straightening capacity in effect. In short, despite the differences in style, Hines wore his hair in the same "do" and with the same grease as disco singer Michael Jackson. And the substance that has straightened the hair of black men for generations is lye, the stuff some people use to make soap and others use to open clogged sinks. I remember as a boy seeing young men walking around the street with purple medicine stains on their scalps; they had ruined both their hair and their skin by overapplying the burning, acidlike "conkolene."

I suppose that after all those years of wearing straightened hair, Hines decided that the best way to cover his balding pate was with straight hair, a white man's hairpiece. Of course, Hines's wig revealed the tremendous difference between a black person with straightened hair and the hair of a white person. I think Hines's toupee, much more so than his conked hair, embarrassed a good many black people; to many it symbolized the sort of Sambo inferiority complex that Louis Armstrong's big grin and white handkerchief did. The hairpiece seemingly made apparent what many black people thought Earl Hines always was: a black entertainer from the old school, the school as old as minstrelsy; and the wig may have made him seem like nothing more than a clown. In an odd, paradoxical way, the man known as "Fatha," who, in many ways, was the progenitor of modern jazz, symbolized, in the sixties and seventies, the very sort of jazz musician blacks wanted not only to avoid but actively to demythify. Jazz had come full circle, and in the person of Hines the black musician confronted the very essence and origin of his modern self; and, in keeping with the inability of the average American to understand anything about his past, most of the modern cats were distinctly ambivalent about Hines.

I suppose "serious" is the key word here, for Hines always seemed like someone who was never serious about playing, who never quite understood the pose of the *artiste* or even the necessity of that pose. He was, in attitude, an artistic primitive. This is why most people, even musicians, have not really comprehended, would find it almost impossible to appreciate that Hines was one of the greatest piano players in the history of American improvised music. Many of the young jazz musicians are making tribute albums to Thelonious Monk, not only because his music sounds more modern, but because his image seems more modern as well. (After all, bebop was an inchoate form of social protest; is it really an accident that Richard Wright's *Native Son,* the greatest social-protest novel in the history of American literature, and the stardom of Charlie Parker, the greatest iconoclast figure in American art, should have occurred in the same decade?) Hines is the forgotten great man of jazz, and his being forgotten is symbolic of the haphazard way that cultural tradition, black or white, gets passed along to another generation. Tradition in America is characterized by the most intense sort of alienation and by the most intense sense of longing; in the end, we are either hopelessly sentimental or crudely cynical.

Without Hines, Monk would not have been able to evolve as he did; indeed, without Hines, there would have been no Monk, for it is clear to anyone with at least a passing familiarity with the musics of the two men that Hines is the key, the root in Monk's playing. If one listens to Hines playing a piano solo such as "Blues in Thirds" and then listens to Monk's blues originals such as "Functional" or "Blue Monk," the similarity is startling. Anyone who even casually listened to jazz knew that there was plenty of slow blues in Monk's bebop, but it is surprising to realize how much bebop there was in Hines's playing, how much of his best playing anticipated bebop. Perhaps one should have expected this since Hines's famed Grand Terrace band of the thirties had such players as Dizzy Gillespie, Charlie Parker, and Mister B—Billy Eckstine—holding down chairs. And these wound up being associated with the "New Jazz," the modern stuff, in a big way. Yet despite all of this, one still feels that exhilarating sense of new discovery, that special vertigo of aesthetic displacement when one learns that Earl Hines on the piano does not sound like an old fogey.

There was in Hines's playing not only the natural modernity of true genius but the conscious keeping abreast of new things, new happenings, and this is not an easy thing to do in jazz where so much of the newness is simply not worth much; in most cases, it is the novelty of the player coming upon, usually with more luck than daring and always with more daring than logic, a new style. And jazz musicians are obsessed with seeking new styles—which is why that music has evolved more rapidly and often more superficially in sixty years than classical music did in three hundred. For Hines, there were only two requirements for the music: it must swing and it must give pleasure to its listeners.

And Hines, as is indicated by the autobiographical section in Stanley Dance's book *The World of Earl Hines,* was a great raconteur. He loved to talk and loved to tell stories about the old days. The inarticulation of many modern jazz players who were to follow Hines, such as Miles Davis, Thelonious Monk, and John Coltrane, may have resulted more than merely from being hip or from the uncompromising stance of the politically aware black artist; it may indicate the frightening instance of a lost tradition, the tradition of oral history so vital in jazz life and black life in America. Perhaps it means that jazz is no longer, in any sense of the word, a folk music or that black people, in any sense of the word, are any longer a folk. And all that "rappin' and stylin' out" business is nothing more than the quaint mannerism of a group of highly self-conscious people who, in the end, maybe would really rather own BMWs and Mercedeses and wind up as pedestrian and philistine as any middle-class person anywhere in the world.

Hines's autobiography is filled with lovely stories such as this one:

My father had about fourteen men in his band, and we would go out to the picnics in Kennywood Park in four or five streetcars. They'd have them all lined up, and my dad and his band would sit in the first car, with as many children as could possibly get around them, and they would play music all the way out to the park with the other streetcars following. They were summer cars, with the running board along the side, but no windows. All they had in case it rained was something similar to the Venetian blinds we have today. You could still get a bit wet through them if it rained hard.

Or consider this picture of Chicago in the 1930s:

Along with so many of the bad traits people said Al Capone had, he had some good traits, too. He used to run a restaurant twenty-four hours a day where poor people could get free meals, and he took over real estate where these same poor people could move in and live. He used to come by the club at night, and if I met him by the door he might put his hand up to straighten my handkerchief, and there would be a hundred-dollar bill. Or he might give me a handshake and put a twenty-dollar bill in my hand. Some nights the heads of the organization used to come in and tell Ed Fox [the owner] to close up. "This is our night," they'd say, and give him a thousand dollars. They would always pick a slow night, too, so Fox loved that. We'd play one show, and after that everybody used to come off the stand, and then you didn't know what you were, a musician, a show person, or a gangster. Everybody was mixing, having a great time. So there was fun along with the headaches during the reign of the racketeers.

Guns were often drawn at the Grand Terrace—even the waiters had guns—but no shots were fired because of the risk of hitting innocent customers. Rival parties from different parts of Chicago would fight sometimes, and throw ice and bottles at each other. I remembered getting under the piano one time, and by then we had a Bechstein grand. I found a lady already there.

"What are you doing here?" I asked.

"I'm a guest. What are you doing here?"

"This is my place. I work here."

These passages were not chosen at random, nor were they chosen simply because they are well-told episodes of a kind of Americana. They are endlessly rich in their complexity and what they reveal of the author. I think that Hines always associated music with the fast life, the sporting life, which was, indeed, a common association made by most respectable people in those days, and these too, for that matter. From the time he was quite young, Hines was obviously drawn to music partly for this reason. Undoubtedly, the sight of his father riding down the street with the members of his band was a very impressive one; after all, most black people probably did not own streetcars in the early part of the twentieth century. To be a musician was to have a certain amount of infamous status. And I believe it is the dubious status of the gangster that impresses Hines as much as the dubious status of the jazz musician at the turn of the century in a tiny black community. There was certainly a great amount of flash in all of this. So we learn that Hines was attracted to men who possessed a certain dubious status because, in effect, these men possessed a kind of magical power. In the case of his father, "surrounded by little children," it was the magic of the Pied Piper. And with Al Capone, it was the daring of Robin Hood. To be a musician was to be privy to certain interesting fantasies. Hines never takes the fantasies too seriously; the episodes end with a sort of off-beat, humorous note: his father getting rained on; a brawl at the club. He manages to make his heroes look slightly ridiculous.

Hines suffered the misfortune of always being overshadowed by jazz's mythic figures: he could have claimed being the most important instrumentalist in the formative years if he hadn't had the ill luck of arriving on the scene at the same time as Louis Armstrong. The waxing of the great *Weatherbird* is symbolic of his relationship with Armstrong. Hines's playing on that record is stunningly alive, rich in easy splendor, yet it will always remain Armstrong's record, Armstrong's great moment of staggering artistic triumph. He might have become known as jazz's greatest bandleader if Duke Ellington and Count Basie had not come along. His reputation as a pianist was overshadowed first by Art Tatum, then by Bud Powell, then by Oscar Peterson. When the young moderns such as Bill Evans, Herbie Hancock, and Chick Corea arrived on the scene during the late fifties and early sixties, Hines was a respected figure but hardly revered. He was also no longer recording music and seemed to have been forgotten by the public at large. He was rediscovered in the late sixties and the dozen or so years before his death in 1983 were quite productive. He probably recorded more than fifteen albums during this period. Hines, in this way, did prove one point before his death: He put out more consistently good music than Armstrong and remained active for more years than either Armstrong or Ellington.

When Hines says in his autobiography, "I've never been what is commonly termed an Uncle Tom," it seems a strangely distressing plea. Anyone with feeling for his music is made more than a little uncomfortable that a man of his stature should be forced to make it. It is the keen and bitter demand—keen because it is so deeply wrought and bitter because it is so undeniably petty—that black people make of their artists—that they must be great in their art and somehow always "current" in their politics—that engenders such a plea. One would find this sort of demand more bearable if blacks were not so quick to condemn their artists for being out of style, so easily able to disengage themselves from engagements of awesome worth. In the end, black people relate to their artists in a way that is both ardently romantic and profoundly nihilistic. And perhaps what we have always thought of as penetrating engagement is, in truth, a most complex alienation. It may very well be the process of manipulating their collective alienation that has enabled black artists to overcome and survive their adversity. Many people did not know this fact: Earl Hines, like most great black artists, outran and outrode the out-of-style all of his life.

IV. THE SULTANS OF SWING

It was a saxophone solo by Lester Young. He didn't recognize the tune, but it had the "Pres" treatment. His stomach tightened. It was listening to someone laughing their way toward death. It was laughter dripping wet with tears. Colored people's laughter.

His thoughts took him back to the late 1930s—the "depression" years. When he and Digger had attended a P.S. on 112th Street. They'd hear Lester Young playing at the Apollo, swapping fours and eights with Herschel Evans on their tenor horns.

Pres! He was the greatest, he thought.

—Chester Himes, *The Heat's On*

I had never thought myself liable to be stricken by that peculiar variety of disease known as homesickness. But in the fall of 1983 it occurred to me with a decided suddenness that I had not been to Philadelphia since I had resigned my position with the Crisis Intervention Network and started graduate studies at Cornell University in 1977. It had been what I now think a somewhat immature resolution on my part, my intention, once I left Philadelphia, never to return. I did not like the place; and this dislike was not the result of any personal injuries, either psychic or physical, that I had sustained but rather stemmed from the massive carnage I had witnessed that has erased nearly half the black boys of my generation. Philadelphia had been more cruel to these fellows than any center of "urban reality" had a right to be. I attribute my survival to the fact that I was a good deal nastier in the clinches than most people ever suspected. Moreover, not even the idea of visiting family could sway me in my determination. My folk are not the sentimental type and their close-knittedness seems to breed that special sort of subtle contempt that arises from unrelieved familiarity. I must add, though, that this enforced absence, to some extent, was made easier by the fact that my family always came to see me. I must confess that I did not reward them by seeking out truly interesting places in which to live: first, Ithaca, New York, and now, St. Louis. I suppose that learning over the summer about my grandfather's severe illness sparked the flames or shall I say sparked a banked fire of homesickness. I was never very close to my grandfather—he took me to see the Phillies when I was a kid; his rabid support of them struck me as being quixotic—but I knew I would be crippled with guilt if I did not make an effort to see him before he died, if dying he was. (It turned out that he was not, in fact, dying, and the old fellow may outlive us all. Long may the Phillies be cheered!)

When the fall began, Philadelphia was no longer, in my mind's eye, dirty, cramped, ugly, and murderous. It had suddenly become profoundly lyrical, rich with vibrant beauty, very good bookstores, and much live jazz music. I could hear more good jazz music in Philadelphia in one day than one could rightly expect to hear in St. Louis in a year. And I very much wanted to hear *those* boys (and girls) at play. My childhood memories were no longer bitter; indeed, at worst, I thought my childhood benign and at best, it was positively privileged. Half the fellows I grew up with may have lost their lives or have been incarcerated, but the other half was still alive and kicking. By the beginning of October, I was overwhelmed by a desire to return to my hometown. Alas, I had no money. But my prayers, like everyone else's sooner or later, were answered in this regard in the most unexpected way.

St. Louis had the dubious distinction of being invaded by a television filming crew during the months of September and October. The show being filmed was entitled *The Mississippi* and starred Ralph Waite (formerly of *The Waltons*) as a lawyer who rode up and down the Mississippi on his boat helping the victimized or something like that. He had two assistants who traveled with him whose names I cannot remember and whose careers would be best served should they continue to live in anonymity. A television show such as this seems an awful thing to have to acknowledge on one's résumé. I certainly would never have crossed paths with some of the persons involved in the making of this show if Waite had not had the temerity to want to do an episode that featured black characters. How Warner Brothers' studios got hold of my name is a mystery to me and why they wanted it is an even deeper enigma. One afternoon a woman by the name of Laura Hoffman called me and asked if I would be willing to read a script that was to be filmed featuring black characters. I said I would, and she came to take me to Ralph Waite. Miss Hoffman turned out to be a production assistant, whatever that is, and it seemed to me to be nothing more than a glorified go-for; she was a trim, blond woman with very tired eyes who propelled me to Waite's trailer. (They were doing some exterior shots.) I use the word "propel" because she drove her car as if she were flying a jet aircraft. Waite, it turned out, was a white liberal who knew James Baldwin (he said this after I told him I taught black literature) and who knew nothing about black people and who wanted to do a script about an orphan black boy. The script as written was abysmal. He wanted me to authenticate the language used by the blacks in the script. It is never enough, of course, for someone to watch a program and see that a character is black; the viewer must always be reminded by every sign imaginable that this is indeed a black character. My first inclination when I read the script—incidentally, entitled "Joey"—was simply to tell Waite to cast white actors in the roles instead of blacks. I saw no reason why a race that was already psychologically overburdened should be further traumatized by garbage that it could neither digest nor regurgitate. But I was afraid that if I told him that, I would not be paid. So I tried to improve the script although I wondered why I, a literature professor with absolutely no experience in scriptwriting, should be doing something that several blacks in Hollywood would be infinitely more qualified to do. I do think that I improved the script immeasurably, although I doubt if any of my changes was used. I did not try to make the characters more *black;* I tried to make them more *human* and in this way their blackness became that much deeper. In the main, I decided to take the money and run—always the sanest thing when dealing with people who do not know what they are doing or who have no business doing what they are doing. I certainly did not care whether my changes were used or not, although I am sure that my suggestion to make the orphan boy a lover of poetry was thrown out of the window with a particularly derisive grunt of disapproval. I wanted to go to Philadelphia, not to Hollywood. I wanted more than anything else to hear that good live jazz. I very much appreciated the fact that the television people pay very promptly.

What stopped me in my tracks was that it was an old song by the Savoy Sultans being played on a downtown street in the middle of the afternoon. It was strange enough to hear that but even stranger to hear this jumping tune being played by a flute and a tenor saxophone. There was an emptiness in hearing these wind instruments sing a cappella—without a rhythm section of piano, bass, and drums—that made me think about a Japanese instrument, the shakuhachi, playing traditional Japanese music. For a moment, I thought the setting and the instrumentation to be terribly inappropriate, but then I realized that jazz was just as fitting on a street corner as anywhere else. "Music," as Sonny Rollins once said, "is an open sky." And good jazz could be played on anything from an accordion to a kazoo.

A small knot of people, perhaps a dozen, stood before the two men on the pavement of Chestnut Street. The flutist was an older man, probably in his fifties, very dark-skinned and quite overweight, with a black beret tilted jauntily on his head. The saxophonist looked like a mere boy, no more than twenty at the most, with thin, sensitive hands and fingers and an expression of the utmost seriousness on his dark face. He may have been the older man's son or nephew. He certainly looked the type who would talk about "the music" as if it were "the godhead." Their music cases were on the ground behind them, and a small iron pot, resembling the type that old black grandmothers cooked turnip greens or chitlings or string beans and fatback in, stood between the two men for contributions. They had no sheet music.

They played the melody together, very rapidly yet very patiently. Then the flutist played a very competent solo, surprisingly heavy, drenched in a kind of blues syrup of thickness and density. He made the flute sound almost like a blues harmonica in the hands of a Delta sharecropper. The saxophonist quietly but rhythmically riffed in the background as if he were in Basie's reed section. It was the saxophone, ironically, that sounded light and airy, almost chirpy. The young boy had his eyes closed, and the veins in his neck were pronounced as he blew. He gave the impression of being an altar boy praying fervently to a very impersonal god. But the sound of the instrument was so unlike the grave boy; it was humorous, sparkling, refulgent, soaring. Some of the lines sounded like laughing paradiddles one would drum on a tabletop with one's fingertips. In a word, it was triumphant. One became totally unaware of the fact that the saxophone was being played with absolutely no accompaniment except the riffing flute. Most the time, when one hears the saxophone played alone it sounds like someone practicing. A saxophone does not have the same solo capacities as a piano, a guitar, a violin, or even a flute. Yet the boy did not sound as if he were practicing. There was such a depth of lyricism in his playing that one almost wanted to dance before the beauty of the sound. Indeed, when the old head and the young boy started exchanging riff patterns in a call-and-response way, many in the crowd began to tap their toes and nod their heads. I thought I had heard that sound before; it was so old-fashioned. No one played like that anymore; it was out of style. But it surely felt good; these two men were outswinging that legendary Harlem dance band whose song they were playing. It all sounded as familiar as home.

The small audience applauded when the men finished, and a few dropped coins or dollars into the iron pot. As I walked forward to make a contribution, I heard one of the auditors say to the flutist: "Your young saxophonist sounds like Lester Young." And when I heard that, I was able to place my finger on the source of the familiarity in the saxophonist's sound. He *did* sound *exactly* like Lester Young. I found it hard to imagine that a boy so young would copy such an antiquated style of playing. Most of the young players want to sound very modern and hip, so the fact that this boy not only had heard of Lester Young but had so completely absorbed his style was somewhat disconcerting. I was thrown for a loss about the whole. The fact that a young boy played like an old swing saxophonist struck me as either an absurd paradox or as a continual sealing and healing of the unbroken circle. I suppose the old flutist settled the issue when he responded: "Oh yes, we always play in the tradition."

On Good Morning Blues: The Autobiography of Count Basie

I. THIS NIGHT, THESE EYES

I was around thirteen years old when I went through a momentary fascination with Count Basie or with the Count Basie Orchestra. I am never quite sure, when I have looked back on this, whether I was attracted to the man himself or to his orchestra. I can safely say that at that age I was not particularly attracted to his music. I had heard my uncles play Basie's records on the phonograph and was quite fond of the Neal Hefti tune "Lil Darling" and the original version of "One O'Clock Jump" but the rest of Basie's repertoire did not interest me overly much. Even then I had a great deal of respect for Basie's music in part, I suppose, because I knew of no black people who did not revere Basie in a way. And so I did too. Men in the barbershops used to argue over who was the best bandleader: Ellington, Basie, Gerald Wilson, Lionel Hampton, Cab Calloway, or some others. And always we young boys had to bow to the superior knowledge of the old heads: we frequently had no idea about whom they were talking. "You young boys don't know shit about no music except that rock and roll you hear on the radio. Rock and roll ain't new. Cats was playing that shit thirty years ago," and with such statements as that we were effectively put in our place. But somehow by the age of thirteen I had a tremendous desire to see the Basie orchestra live and to hear that band play a number entitled "The Night Has a Thousand Eyes." For some reason I had fallen madly in love with that tune after hearing John Coltrane's quartet play it on an album that my sister owned. Coltrane himself did not do much for me then, but I thought the song was extraordinary, even the title seemed marvelous. And I had gotten it into my head, in some totally inexplicable, weird way, that I wanted to hear the Basie band do the song on the stage.

At that time, Philadelphia, the city where I was raised, had a theater that was a considerably lesser version of New York's Apollo. It was called the Uptown and it was a major stopping place for a good many R&B artists on what was called the chitling circuit. Marvin Gaye, the Supremes, the Temptations, James Brown, the Shirelles, the Drifters, Ben E. King, Solomon Burke, Otis Redding, Carla and Rufus Thomas, Aretha Franklin, Sam and Dave, James and Bobby Purify, the Jive Five, Dee Clark, Little Willie John, Art and Aaron Neville, Shep and the Limelights and a score of other famous and minor soul acts graced the Uptown's stage "for ten, big exciting days," as the d.j.s would say, during the fifties and sixties. I had learned about the Apollo Theatre in Harlem around the time I developed my obsession with Count Basie and "The Night Has a Thousand Eyes" and I learned that Basie made an annual pilgrimage to that "sepia Mecca," as it was called in *Jet* magazine. But Basie had never appeared at the Uptown. I remember asking my mother about this, about why Basie never appeared at the Uptown, and she looked at me as if I had gone slightly mad: "Boy, are you crazy?" she said. "The Uptown can't hold no Count Basie band."

This remark, I discovered, had nothing to do with the size of the place, which was cavernous. It was a big, run-down showplace in the middle of a huge, sprawling slum that went on for blocks and blocks as if one were walking the streets of the wild side of eternity. My mother meant that the Uptown, no more shabby in truth than the Apollo, could not contain the myth of Basie, the power of Basie. And when I went, on occasion, to the Uptown during my thirteenth year to see shows and I would sometimes look at the walls, the ceiling, the floor, the cracked leatherette seats, the place would seem so much like some Xanadu, some glitterdome gone in the teeth, I figured that my mother was right after all. Harlem and the Apollo had history and the magic of New York even if the Apollo was simply another "raggedy-ass joint," even if Harlem was simply row upon row of cut-up tenements and teeming projects. It was a place, a series of places—the Apollo, Harlem, New York—where black people wanted to be. The Uptown and Philadelphia were simply ugly places—a nigger theater in a ghetto where no one, except the people who lived there, would ever be caught. And even they could find no reason to want to be there.

When I finally saw the Basie band in person a few years ago in St. Louis at the Fox theater, a grandly refurbished glitterdome of epic proportions, it was as though I had waited too long, as if I were actually too late really to see anything. Basie was not even physically capable of leading the band. He came out on a little motor scooter, was helped to the piano bench, played with the band for a few tunes, never soloed, then got back on the scooter and rode offstage while the band played without him. Basie was no longer the rotund man who wore the yachtsman's cap, the man whose picture I saw on the albums that I used to finger in record stores when I was thirteen, absolutely bewildered by the stars he played with: Sammy Davis, Sarah Vaughan, Frank Sinatra, and Tony Bennett. He was, at the Fox on that night, from my vantage point, just a little old man who seemed very sick and weak. And the band itself did not sound legendary. It sounded like Woody Herman's band or the K. U. concert band or any good, competent college band filled with good, competent college-educated players performing good, sprightly arrangements. It seemed the ultimate sin had been committed: the Basie band was simply an imitation of itself, a kind of clockwork banality as it rattled off tune after tune in an effortless faceless pastiche. It sounded exactly like the *Tonight Show* band, a band that could have been a Las Vegas lounge act. And of course, the band did not play "The Night Has a Thousand Eyes," which relieved me a great deal. As someone told me later, that song was never in Basie's book.

God, how I wish that Basie, when he was great, had played the Uptown. How I wish he had played the Uptown when I was thirteen. Its blasted, dilapidated room, like those which were the true home for Bill Basie and his music, was just such a room that a weak, sick Bill Basie should have played at the end.

II. THE MIGHTY BURNER
AND THE GIANTS OF JAZZ

The death of Count Basie was announced by the media and received by the public unlike the death of virtually any other American jazzman with the possible exceptions of Duke Ellington, Louis Armstrong, and most recently, Benny Goodman. (Some argue that the great "symphonic jazz" band leader and popularizer of Gershwin's "Rhapsody in Blue" Paul Whiteman might be a possible exception as well. He was certainly the best-known and the highest paid band leader in the history of American popular music till 1960. However, Whiteman himself has been largely forgotten as an important figure in jazz.) And even with these latter three, who had, of course, achieved a status of respectability as artists and marketability as name commodities that matched Basie's (otherwise their deaths would not have been noticed at all or would have been discussed only because of the tainted scent of some scandal), even here, there is a difference.

With Duke Ellington, for instance, there is always this unease in American critical and academic circles (largely resulting from the Pulitzer Prize Committee's refusal to grant him that award in music back in the early seventies) about his importance as a composer in a musical form that many feel to be so dubious. It is true that Ellington gave a concert at the Nixon White House on the occasion of his seventieth birthday and that Yale University established a fellowship in his honor in 1972. Yet for many, he remained always and only a jazz musician who, in the end, to some ears, such as those of Soviet poet Yevgeny Yevtushenko, sounded "a bit old-fashioned." Perhaps this critical anxiety about Ellington occurred because, for some, jazz and the art of composition seem almost to be contradictions in terms.

Basie does not present that problem since he never took himself seriously as a composer and, although he arranged many things in his head, probably never wrote a single composition down on staff paper in his entire life. It is Basie's unschooledness—his lack of interest in creating concertos, masses, musicals, and ballets—the high-brow musical enterprises of Ellington—that I think makes him so much easier to embrace for the musical establishment. Basie wound up being considered a musical genius of sorts, ironically, not despite the modesty of his talents but rather because of it. He was not a brilliant composer; he was not a brilliant arranger; he was not a brilliant pianist (although he was, stylistically, a very important and intriguing one). Ellington, at various points in his career, could lay claim to being all three. And it is perhaps the very grandeur of Ellington's jazz genius, the sweep that may at times border on the mannered and the pretentious, that finally makes Ellington such a difficult artist for the American mind to grasp. Ellington's genius has gotten in the way of the recognition of his genius, or I might say, the assumptions of his genius have gotten in the way of an understanding of what his genius assumed. Even the tunes from Ellington's early years, works such as "East St. Louis Toodle-oo," "Creole Love Call," "The Jeep Is Jumpin,'" and "Ko-Ko" (Charlie Parker's "Ko-Ko" was a bit of related-unrelated musical revisionism), are all dense pieces that Ellington tended to make parodic or arcane during the course of his career, although they never ceased to be listenable. Basie, on the other hand, was so much like the music he played, or at least so much like people thought his music was: the mighty burning of the unassuming.

Jazz historian Stanley Dance was probably right when he wrote that in effect Basie was a source of influence while Ellington was a source of inspiration. Ellington was even an inspiration for Basie himself. In *The World of Count Basie,* the great bandleader says the following about Ellington:

> My biggest thrill as a listener came one night back in, I think, it was, 1951.
> The so-called progressive jazz was going big then, and here comes Duke Ellington on opening night at Birdland. He had just revamped his band, and no one knew just what he'd have. We all dropped in to catch him—and what we heard! What a thrill that was!
> The Duke was swinging. All this "progressive" talk, and the Duke played the old swing. He scared a lot of people that night. It was just wonderful. Of course, the Duke has always had the greatest band at all times. There's never been another band for me, year in and year out.

In his autobiography, Basie devises the rhetorical strategy of comparing Ellington to Joe Louis, not only the highest compliment that a person of Basie's generation could pay to another black person, but also an indication that Basie felt that Ellington's achievement as an artist was comparable to Louis's as an athlete. They both met and defeated white supremacy on its own turf:

> He was just glorious. I loved him so much. I used to get a kick out of being near him. Just like I also used to get so much of a kick every time I'd get a chance to be next to and talk to another champion, one by the name of Joe Louis. Standing next to him, you felt so big. Just to sit down by Duke did me a world of good.

Louis Armstrong was surely the most beloved of any American musician, black or white, in the history of white popular taste in America. Yet in recent years, even before his death in 1971, the Armstrong image of mugging, grinning, and singing pop songs and coon tunes like "Snowball" and "Sleepy Time down South" had become increasingly distasteful to blacks and a source of concern to many thoughtful whites. Did the whites love Armstrong for his undeniably powerful musicality or because he was a one-man revival of minstrelsy without blackface? What did they think they were watching when they saw the old black man in his final years singing "Hello, Dolly" and "C'est Si Bon" on television talk shows? Could his genius be contained only by having it entrapped in a halo of intolerable nostalgia, of degrading sentiment about darkies on the southern campground? The cool imperturbable Basie is not and does not present an image problem, although Basie possessed no more political consciousness than Armstrong, and some might say after reading the autobiography that he, in fact, possessed less political awareness than Armstrong. No one can recall Basie making statements against Governor Faubus of Arkansas during the school integration days at Little Rock's Central High in the 1950s. Armstrong did. Here are a few examples, culled from the autobiography, of what I mean about Basie and politics:

> Truthfully, I really didn't know anything about all those things Marcus Garvey was into. But of course everybody in Harlem knew about him because his people used to be in those parades. But my main thing in those days was show business and stumbling in and out of these joints, digging music, and trying to cop another gig.
>
> As for going down into the Deep South for the first time, I've been asked about that many times, and some reporters have written up what *they* thought it *must* have been like, but truthfully, I didn't actually think about Jim Crow and things like that much.

I do not mean to imply here that either Basie or Armstrong was an Uncle Tom, although Armstrong was perceived by the black public to be pretty much just that. The case about politics and the black artist cannot be so easily stated and so easily dismissed. Basie never aspired to live in an integrated world. Many blacks of the 1920s and the 1930s did not, especially blacks who were not middle class. Therefore, they were not bothered by segregation very much at all. Basie says, for instance, in the autobiography, that he rarely ventured beyond a ten-block area while in Kansas City, those ten blocks being the black ghetto of the city where the music was happening. He said that he never once set foot in downtown Kansas City and, in fact, had no idea how the rest of the city looked. He did not venture into downtown Kansas City not because he *could* not go there; he simply did not *want* to go there. Also, I don't think Basie ever wanted his blackness to be used by liberal whites for a cause. I think this is certainly suggested in the second quotation above when Basie speaks about Jim Crow. He never wanted to be presented as a down-and-out, victimized black man.

But more important in explaining the fact that Basie got away with being nonpolitical while Armstrong did not, is that neither Basie's presence nor his music conjured up images of the American past that seemed to present blackness as a dangerously ambiguous condition or state of mind—which, in effect, is what Armstrong did. In part, this is because Basie was never self-conscious about himself or the implications of his self-mythology as Armstrong was. Also, one supposes that somehow Kansas City, where Basie cut his musical teeth as a young man, is a good deal less ambiguous, less foreign, less self-conscious in providing people with a sense of place (and a sense of unthreatening modernity) than New Orleans, the place where Armstrong developed his talent. The one city in the entire American landscape that remains irresistibly and frighteningly alien to the dominant Protestant American sense of self is New Orleans. Basie made matters less complicated by being a transplanted midwesterner and so the mighty burning of the unassuming was freed from bad politics and suspect myth.

Benny Goodman's presence in the history of jazz as a major innovator has always been viewed with suspicion, contempt, anger, dismay, or some combination of the four by most blacks. As LeRoi Jones (Amiri Baraka) wrote in *Blues People,* his famous study of Afro-American music:

> By the thirties quite a few white bands had mastered the swing idiom of big-band jazz with varying degrees of authenticity. One of the most successful of these bands, the Benny Goodman orchestra, even began to buy arrangements from Negro arrangers so that it would have more of an authentic tone. The arranger became one of the most important men in big-band jazz, demonstrating how far jazz had gotten from earlier Afro-American musical tradition. (Fletcher Henderson, however, was paid only $37.50 per arrangement by Goodman before Goodman actually hired him as the band's chief arranger.)

Goodman's presence is to jazz what Elvis Presley's is to 1950s rock and roll, a sign of oppression and cultural theft, at least to some; or a sign that the art of black folk can be legitimized only by whites who copy it. This distorted view has power inasmuch as, like any distortion, it reveals a very important truth. But the relationship between black American artists and white audiences and white patrons is surely more complex than most people think. Consider the quotation from Jones above. First of all, black big-band jazz of the 1920s and 1930s had become an arranger's music. Henderson had been arranging pieces for his own band for years; so had Ellington, Cab Calloway, Bennie Moten, Andy Kirk, Louis Armstrong, and nearly every other black performer working with a big band used written arrangements, so this was not a new feature introduced into Afro-American music by "trained" whites. True, blacks did use a lot of head arrangements as well (musicians just making up riffs on the spot and tossing together an arrangement from memory), but it is a mistake to think that a large number of professional black musicians of this era could not read or write music or that black jazz is more authentic or less inhibited by white cultural standards, as it were, because head arrangements were sometimes used. Second, Jones implies that Henderson was down and out and was being used by Goodman. Henderson was still running his own band when Goodman first asked him to write arrangements. And Henderson's band, over the years, was a respected and commercially successful one. Moreover, Jones fails to note the significance of the Goodman band's hiring a black, at *standard wages,* to be an arranger. (It might be added that Paul Whiteman hired black classical composer William Grant Still and saxophonist/arranger Don Redman to do arrangements for his band *before* Goodman hired Henderson. Whiteman also paid well over $50 per score.)

It is a strange fact of American culture that while it is true that whites made Benny Goodman an artistic and commercial success, they also made Count Basie a success in the same way. Basie's band could have wound up like Erskine Hawkins's or the Savoy Sultans or Alphonso Trent's or the other good black bands who played for black audiences almost exclusively. Long before Michael Jackson and Prince, black artists had crossover audiences: Fats Waller, Art Tatum, Billie Holiday, Duke Ellington, Count Basie, and Bessie Smith, just to name a few. As jazz historian James Lincoln Collier has pointed out ("The Faking of Jazz," *The New Republic,* November 18, 1985), jazz has always had a strong and sympathetic white audience willing to support black artists. In fact, if it had not been for the support of this white audience and several white patrons, black jazz would never have been recorded or have developed as rapidly as it did. Besides, it is always difficult to tell who is copying whom: Glenn Miller's hit recording of Erskine Hawkins's "Tuxedo Junction" is an obvious case of a white artist "covering" a black tune for a white audience in order to make it more acceptable and to make money. But Goodman's band was in full flower before Basie left the Reno Club in Kansas City to become a big name. In fact, Basie was first introduced in the East as the band discovered by Benny Goodman (a point that Basie mildly resents in his autobiography). And it was Basie who borrowed Goodman's arrangements for one of his performances when he was in need of music, and not the other way around. But the feeling of unease is there.

The presence of whites such as Goodman in jazz and his enormous success and fame, achieved by playing what was in essence a black music, have become a discomfort for some whites and a point of outrage for most blacks. Was Goodman's success purely on the basis of his artistry or did the existence of American apartheid in the 1930s and 1940s necessitate that black swing music, growing ever more popular with whites, be coopted by a white male presence? Does the presence of whites deny the authenticity of Afro-American music? Can whites even play it? Basie does not present dilemmas of this sort for the American public. His blackness, for better or worse, makes him the real thing, the uncrowned king of swing, for both whites and blacks. In short, Basie's death could be greeted in the manner that it was largely because Basie's life and music were so unproblematical. "Mighty burning" is authentic nonambiguity.

Basie's death was seen as the loss of a cherished institution or a cherished tradition. It is always a bit disconcerting and dislocating for any artist who has reached that status to die because it almost always means that he has lived too long and has virtually been embalmed for a number of years before his death. This was not particularly true with Basie, or at least not true before his major heart attack in 1976 and the other health problems that began to plague him in the late 1970s. In the seventies until that point, Basie was recording very fine music on Pablo, jazz impresario Norman Granz's latest label; these recordings featured small groups with Zoot Sims and Sweets Harry Edison, the big band, jam sessions with an assortment of past and present Basie men, duets with Oscar Peterson, and accompaniment for Ella Fitzgerald. But certainly from the late seventies until his death in 1984, Basie's life as any kind of artist was over. He was simply physically unable to lead the band anymore. And even the extraordinary stream of albums in the seventies did little more than consolidate his gains, rearticulate his artistic creed. Basie as a true force in contemporary jazz saw his end when Joe Williams left his 1950s band. But the rearticulation of the seventies was quite necessary to assure his position as a cherished tradition, as a cherished institution.

I am forced to wonder if Basie would ever have written an autobiography, ever have bothered to try to collect the scattered materials of his memory and life to finish one if his capabilities as a musician had not been diminished to the point where reflection became not only the greater part of valor but the greater part of being alive, so that the band itself had begun to recede in importance. Basie was always an extremely reticent man and so the publication of his book, to me and many other jazz fans, came as something of a shock. Bill Basie talked for 400 pages? Incredible! I don't think he would ever have felt the need to do the autobiographical project if the band had still been able to speak for him. He simply would have continued talking about doing an autobiography, would have continued talking about doing a project that required talking about himself as if this talking about the act of talking about were a sort of game.

"You were always moving on to the next gig," Basie writes near the end of his book, and one cannot help but think that Basie realized a sort of existential absurdity in this. Perhaps he was tired of moving on to the next gig. Perhaps the next place was just like the last one. Maybe the book was a way, at last, of keeping still for a moment. Maybe Basie wrote his autobiography because he was weary of the Basie who was simply moving on to gig after gig. Finally, after Basie became ill, what else was there to think about but other things, not one's work or one's sex life, but one's self in relation to some meaning beyond work and sex, straddling the difficulties of testimony and confession? The passages of one's life are truly the stages of one's faith.

Or maybe Basie really wanted to write an autobiography because he wanted to free himself from his band; for his greatness, the very fixture and diction of his stature as an artist, was tied to a corporate entity: Count Basie's Orchestra, the Basie band, Sixteen Men Swinging. There was a d.j. in Philadelphia back in the 1960s named Sonny Hopson who called himself the Mighty Burner. After having heard the original version of "One O'Clock Jump" when I was a boy, when I went through my period of fascination with the Basie band when I was thirteen, I concluded there was really only one mighty burner and it was not that d.j. In fact, it was not even the Basie band but little old Bill Basie himself. I remember standing around in the barbershop one afternoon listening to the old heads talking about jazz while some others were getting their heads cut. (One never gets a haircut in a black barbershop. One is always getting one's head cut. In the black beauty parlor the women are getting their heads done, not their hair.) And I, quite timidly, interjected a little note about Basie:

"He's a mighty burner," I said.

And one of the older men laughed loud and raucous, saying:

"Why, lookahere, the young boy tryin' to snap out. The young boy tryin' to know something. Why, one day, he might even know who Bill Basie is. But he learning."

It was Bill Basie and no one else who made the Basie band possible and it was time for him to step forward and tell the tale. And time for all of us to learn it.

III. FIRST MOTEN, THEN RENO,
THEN BIRDLAND

I was with that band. I was with the Blue Devils. I was a Blue Devil, and that meant everything to me. Those guys were so wonderful.

Few know that Count Basie was born and raised in Red Bank, New Jersey, and few need to know it. The only important fact that one needs to know about Basie's childhood — other than the fact that he took piano lessons — was that, like most great black men, he did not want to grow up and be like his father:

My father had been trying to talk me into going into work with him cleaning up those houses and cutting lawns on those big estates. I really couldn't see myself getting into that line of work.

Later, Basie describes the breakup of his parents' marriage and what amounted to the final estrangement from his father. Basie remained close to his mother for the rest of her life but his father became a remote figure.

Perhaps he could not forgive his father for not going back to his mother, although the breakup occurred after Basie had left home and was out struggling as a jazz pianist:

> Meanwhile, every time I was back in Red Bank from then on, I would try to talk my father into patching things up. I remember one time in particular.
>
> "Let's just straighten this thing out," I said, and he just looked at me like I was still a little boy in knee pants. "If you all don't straighten this thing out, I just feel like I don't ever want to come back down here no more."
>
> "Well," he said, "if that's the way you're going about it, that's the way it'll have to be. Because, after all, she's your mother, and I know you love her, but she was my sweetheart and my wife."

The conflict with his father that culminated not over the issue of Basie's role as son and heir who had just flown the coop but over the father's role as husband and lover was probably responsible for generating Basie's own peripatetic personality and his own failure in some respects as a husband, lover, and father, a failure that was inevitable since he was never home. Basie's rootlessness was a response, a defensive response, to the precarious nature of his father's own *rooted* experience of menial labor and a busted marriage. In other words, Basie's fascination with show business as a child and an adolescent had to be partly a result of his own awareness that such a life offered him a built-in excuse should he fail in the way his father did in a domestic life. In fact, show business nearly gave him the right and opportunity to fail. He could, after all, claim that being in show business meant succeeding at one kind of life at the expense of another. This is why I believe he is right when he asserts that joining the Blue Devils was such a momentous episode in his life. Basie had finally found a group of young black men exactly like himself: rootless, consumed with a sort of ambition for artistic and commercial success, in desperate need of an identity. It was precisely men of this sort whom Basie was to be around for the rest of his life, the nomadic tribe of lonely men who make up the road show of American jazz. It was always to be for Louis Armstrong, Duke Ellington, Coleman Hawkins, Lester Young, Jo Jones, Ben Webster, and Basie himself the dogged quest of assurance and employment, even when assurance was not necessary, even when jobs could be had for the asking. The life was always, in Basie's own words quoted above, "stumbling in and out of these joints, digging music, and trying to cop another gig."

So the first important fact in Basie's musical life is his meeting with the great Harlem stride pianist Fats Waller, and then his membership in the great Oklahoma territorial band the Blue Devils. Meeting Waller in New York was important for several reasons. First, Basie learned how to play the organ from Waller and vastly increased his fund of musical knowledge. Second, he learned how to play along with silent movies (Waller taught him to play the organ at a movie theater), and this enabled him to get a job at the Eblon Theater in Kansas City and keep himself going when things were rough in the early days. Third, Waller gave him the confidence he needed to continue in his attempt to become a professional musician. The scene where Basie describes in detail the lessons Waller gave him is a very good one and a rare moment of cooperation between an older established musician and an unknown novice. (It should be compared to the scene where Basie as a young cat on the make is "cut" on the piano by the legendary Art Tatum, whose reputation, along with those of Willie "The Lion" Smith and James P. Johnson, frightened the average pianist out of his skull.) Jazz, the reader discovers in this book, is a tough fraternity to join; initiation is painful and aggressive in a particularly masculine and peculiarly Afro-American way. Jazz is highly competitive, and one always lived in fear that when one showed up for the gig that night that there could be a new person blowing or strumming or beating your instrument on the bandstand. It was one of the hazards of a fiercely predatory existence. Someone "cuts" you out of a job and so you must "cut" someone else. But it was just this kind of pressure exerted doubly by the forces of economics and shame that honed the skill of the jazz musician as sharply as if he had attended a conservatory.

The Basie career really begins when he joins the Blue Devils in 1927 after having heard the band while in Tulsa, Oklahoma, on tour with another group. The other stuff of Basie's early career, playing black vaudeville shows and going on the TOBA (Theater Owners' Booking Agency, which marketed black acts, better known as Tough as Black Asses) circuit with various bands, was simply juvenilia; he learned some important aspects of the black musician's life (and so does the reader) but he was simply getting his feet wet. Going to Kansas City was Basie's real entry to a university, for it was there that he played with the Blue Devils and met the nucleus of musicians (Jimmy Rushing, Walter Page, Hot Lips Page, Eddie Durham, Ben Webster, and others) who were to form the core of the Bennie Moten band in the early 1930s, and it was the Bennie Moten band that became to a man the famous Count Basie orchestra that John Hammond, jazz writer and record company executive, was to hear at the Reno Club and to bring back to New York by way of Chicago.

But what kind of place was Kansas City during the 1920s and the 1930s? Why did it become a mecca for black jazz music? Ross Russell, whose *Jazz Style in Kansas City and the Southwest* is the only major study to have been done on the history of black music in that region,* writes the following series of explanations:

Kansas City was just another one of those large, unremarkable, untidy, and undistinguished cities located somewhere on the American plain. Yet it was here in Kansas City, Missouri, that the same kind of musical renaissance that had occurred in New Orleans was about to take place, though with somewhat altered material, a different cast of players, and a different set of backdrops: for the honky-tonk we substitute the cabaret; for the street parade, the jam session.

*Nathan W. Pearson's *Goin' to Kansas City* was published after this essay was written.

Kansas City jazz started from scratch. From the beginning it was a grass-roots movement, and so it was to remain for the greater part of its life....

Another remarkable feature of Kansas City in those years was "Pendergast prosperity." Free spending and easy money were common enough all over America until the stock market crash of 1929. In Kansas City, night life carried on at the same old pace, and employment for musicians reached its best levels. As a result, Kansas City bands managed to stay together through the panicky years from 1930 to 1934 when theaters, nightclubs, and dance halls were folding all over the country, when many of the name orchestras were obliged to disband, and when practically all recording activity ceased. Those were just the years needed to bring Kansas City style to its full flower....

A jam session is a foregathering of jazz men to engage in a musical free-for-all. Its locale is most frequently a nightclub, but musicians will jam in public halls, ballrooms, backstage at a theater, or even a hotel room. Their purpose is to play for the sheer fun of playing, without any commercial restrictions on what they are doing, to extend their ideas as far as they will reach by means of free improvisation, and to test their ability under competitive conditions. The jam session was a Kansas City specialty.

Albert Murray, coauthor of the Basie autobiography and a fine jazz writer himself, describes the scene in Kansas City in this way in *Stomping the Blues:*

It was a good-time town where a lot of people went out to eat and drink and socialize every night. So there were big bands as well as combos, quartets, trios, and accompanied soloists working somewhere all during the week as well as Fridays and Saturdays and holidays; and when on special occasions the big ballrooms and outdoor pavilions used to sponsor a battle of the bands as an added feature, the excitement, anticipation, and the partisanship would be all but indistinguishable from that generated by a championship boxing match or baseball game.

Murray goes on to describe the jam session:

The Kansas City jam sessions, whose influence on most contemporary blues musicianship has been far more direct than, say, the old New Orleans street parades, were already a matter of legend and myth even then. Most often mentioned are the ones at the Sunset, the Subway, the Reno, and the Cherry Blossom. But as almost everybody who was there remembers it now, since there was a piano (and as often as not, a set of drums also) in almost every joint, there was no telling when or where the next one would get going. Nor was there ever any telling when one would break up. It was quite common for musicians to improvise on one number for more than an hour at such times, and sometimes the session would run well into the next day.

Kansas City, strangely enough, became the focal point of a geographical area that was bounded on the east by Chicago and St. Louis, on the south by Oklahoma City and Dallas, and on the west by Denver and Albuquerque. And it was in this area, as culturally barren, one might suppose, as any stretch of territory in the United States, that the major contra-Dixieland jazz style developed. Scott Joplin and James Scott created ragtime in Missouri; Basie, Bennie Moten, Lester Young, Ben Webster, Mary Lou Williams,

Charlie Christian and a score of others came from the Oklahoma–Texas–
Kansas City axis and created swing; Miles Davis, Clark Terry (both from
Illinois by way of St. Louis), Charlie Parker (Kansas City), and John Lewis
(New Mexico) became leaders in bebop and cool jazz. Music departments
of such black high schools as Lincoln High in Kansas City and Douglass
High in Oklahoma City produced many musicians of note, including pianist
Pete Johnson, Parker, Christian, Harlan Leonard, Walter Page, and Jasper
Jap Allen. In the Denver public schools, for instance, Paul Whiteman's
father provided musical instruction for future black swing band leaders
Jimmy Lunceford and Andy Kirk. This all became possible, in part, because
blacks had been migrating steadily from the Deep South since the end of
World War I and they were not always settling in Chicago or New York; they
went where they had family members or relatives or where jobs were available. The pressures of southern racism and, later, the Depression combined
not only to make migration a sensible solution to a host of problems but to
make being a musician more attractive than ever for a black male who even
with a college education could find nothing better for life's work than being
a Pullman car porter or working in the post office.

It is in this environment of transition and transiency, corrupt machine
politics and gangsters, a major world crisis in capitalism, and a major
change in black American social history as black people went from being a
rural folk to an urban proletariat that Basie came into his own as a musician.
To be sure, the autobiography is at its strongest describing life in Kansas
City and traveling in the Southwest with the Blue Devils and Benny Moten.
The incidents Basie describes are marvelous reading: playing swing music
while accompanying the silent movies at the Eblon Theater; the jam session
with Lester Young, Herschel Evans, and a freshly repatriated Coleman
Hawkins calling out "for those badass keys" that only pianist Mary Lou
Williams could accommodate; copping free meals from Jimmy Rushing's
father's restaurant; the battles of music with other black bands of the area,
"head-chopping time"; the story of how he joined Moten's band as an
arranger who could not write down arrangements and who needed quite a
bit of alcoholic refreshment to fuel the energies of his muse; the story about
the formulation of the phrase "Every Tub," which became the title of a
famous Basie tune; or what the lingo "throwing your head back" means. All
of this offers a view of black jazz and black life in artistic circles (which is
very different from white life in artistic circles) that is rarely encountered.

I think that after the shocking recounting of the death of Benny Moten and
Basie's heroic determination to put Moten's band back together again the
book falls down. But not before Basie's own understated musical vision is
articulated (a thematic climax), not before we are made privy to the drive
that made the band possible:

By the time we first started getting that band together at the Reno, I already had
some pretty clear ideas about how I wanted a band to sound. I knew how I

wanted each section to sound. So I also knew what each of the guys should sound like. I knew what I wanted them there for....

I have my own little ideas about how to get certain guys into certain numbers and how to get them out. I had my own way of opening the door for them to let them come in and sit around awhile. Then I would exit them.

Once Basie's own artistic method is finally realized with the Reno band, once the reader comes to know clearly and powerfully that that band and all Basie bands are merely extensions of the Basie will, the book is not nearly so interesting. Success seems to bring a life, not of creativity, but of one-nighters, as if the dreary, wearying journey has begun simply in the art and craft of making a living, which is quite different from making music. Nothing can be so defeating for any hero as the discovery that life is not the meaning of life or the poetry of the meaning of life but simply gathering the means in order to stay alive. But Basie never found this life disheartening; he thought it was glorious. Musicians come and go in waves and the reader is constantly given updated rosters. And all the personalities we have come to know and love from the early days such as Rushing, Lester Young, Jo Jones, Herschel Evans, and others begin to disappear. Some of the new people such as Buck Clayton, Buddy Tate, Eddie "Lockjaw" Davis, Joe Williams, Marshall Royal, and Frank Foster are interesting. But the reader learns less and less about the new musicians because Basie himself seems more removed from them.

I think the book picks up with the resurrection of the band from its own ashes at Birdland in New York in the early fifties. At a time when no major big band of the thirties can really make it anymore, Basie, at the urging of singer Billy Eckstine, put together a big unit almost in defiance of the times. It is particularly important that Basie triumphed in the club named for Kansas City's last great black jazz musician, Charlie Parker, great alto saxophonist, hipster extraordinaire, who lived the fastest life of any jazzman born. It was Parker, a progeny of K.C. swing and the Basie riff, who turned jazz on its head by revolting against the simplicity of the Basie edict of mighty burning and launched bebop, another kind of mighty burning, fraught with intimidation for the squares and black political awareness for the outsider. If, as Albert Murray has stated in *Stomping the Blues,* black American music is "a matter of elegance," "a matter of style," then Parker took style and elegance to the very limits of the human imagination. And he pronounced them the last mad bulwarks against and beyond a culture of fear and loathing. It was for Basie and Bird a simple matter of seeing the blues in two related but different ways. It was fitting, therefore, that Basie, the rootless father of the old-fashioned style and elegance, should bring all the children back home for a moment while playing in the temple built in honor of the rootless son, Parker, and his charismatic perversions and revisions.

There are two final observations to make about the Basie autobiography. One is that we learn at last the real story about the origin of the nickname "Count," which means we learn no story at all, because while Basie denies the famous and standard account (which he started) of getting the name from a radio announcer (in much the same way bandleader and pianist Earl Hines got the name "Fatha"), the story that he tells about giving himself the name "Count" while he was still unknown in Kansas City is denied by other witnesses in his own text, most of whom tell the story that Benny Moten used to refer to his unreliable and sometimes tipsy arranger-pianist as "that no 'count Basie" and the name simply stuck as names like that often will. And there is a certain ironic pleasure (both for the reader and for Basie) in knowing that "Count" really doesn't refer to royalty or grandeur but to laziness and irresponsibility, stereotypical black traits turned on their head. The other observation is that Albert Murray, the book's cowriter, as he is called in the text, is probably the best qualified person in America to have written or to have helped write this book. Besides his *Stomping the Blues,* he has written a novel (*Guitar Train Whistle*), and several books of non-fiction (*The Omni-Americans, South to a Very Old Place, The Hero and the Blues*). Basie, like Hemingway, is one of Murray's heroes, and perhaps nothing reveals that more than this comment in *Stomping the Blues:*

> It was as if Count Basie edited the orchestrations for his repertoire of the 1930s to the late 40s on the principles of composition that Ernest Hemingway learned from the style sheet for prose writers at the *Kansas City Star* back in 1917: "Use short sentences. Use short first paragraphs. Use vigorous English. Be positive, not negative. Never use old slang...slang to be enjoyable must be fresh. Avoid the use of adjectives, especially such extravagant ones as splendid, gorgeous, grand, magnificent, etc." Basie stripped his own Harlem Stride-derived piano style down to the point that he could make *one note* swing.

I suspect that the only other writer capable of having coauthored this work is Ralph Ellison (incidentally, an ardent admirer of Murray) who worshipped the ground Basie walked on. Being an Oklahoma boy, Ellison, I am sure, was a Blue Devil at heart himself. But now that the book is here Ellison needn't worry about ever publishing his second novel; for the Ellisonian blues hero who does not gossip, signify, or sell wolf tickets has composed his own. (It could not even be wildly imagined that Basie would have written a sexually frank, put-on, or despairing autobiography such as those by other jazzmen like Charles Mingus, Art Pepper, and Hampton Hawes. In the old school, elegance and style mean of course discretion and grace.) As Ellison wrote about the blues:

> The blues is an art of ambiguity, an assertion of the irrepressibly human over all circumstance whether created by others or by one's own human failings. They are the only consistent art in the United States which constantly remind us of our limitations while encouraging us to see how far we can actually go.

It's all here in Basie's autobiography, the whole story of the blues as the life of one man, as the life of a band, as the life of a section of the United States and the creative instinct of an artistic elite emerged from a group of oppressed people. Basie knows that once you leave the woodshed or the basement, as it were, you just quietly take your ax and take care of the business of chopping heads. So, the Ellisonian blues hero has already told the story of what the Invisible Man does when he leaves his hole. As Basie himself said:

> It's the way you play it that makes it. What I say is, for Christ's sake, you don't have to *kill* yourself to swing. Play like you play. Play like you *think,* and then you got it, if you're going to get it. And whatever you get, that's you, so that's your story.

ESSENTIAL COUNT BASIE DISCOGRAPHY

1. *Kansas City Style: Young Bill Basie and the Bennie Moten Orchestra* (RCA)
2. *The Best of Count Basie* (Decca)
3. *Good Morning Blues* (MCA)
4. *Super Chief* (Columbia)
5. *Sixteen Men Swinging* (Verve)
6. *Count Basie Swings, Joe Williams Sings* (Clef)
7. *Basie Plays Hefti* (Roulette)
8. *Count Basie and His Kansas City Seven* (Impulse)
9. *Satch and Josh: Count Basie Encounters Oscar Peterson* (Pablo)
10. *Basie and Zoot: Count Basie and Zoot Sims* (Pablo)

"And I Will Sing
of Joy and Pain for You":
Louis Armstrong
and the Great Jazz Traditions

I. BIG BUTTER AND EGG MAN

My God, I've got roots!

—Charles Mingus

Then Louis Armstrong hit town! I went mad with the rest of the town. I tried to walk like him, talk like him, eat like him, sleep like him. I even bought a pair of big policeman shoes like he used to wear and stood outside his apartment waiting for him to come out so I could look at him. Finally, I got to shake hands and talk with him!

—Jazz trumpeter Rex Stewart on the arrival of Louis Armstrong in Harlem

Louis Armstrong, like a good many other exceptional African-American musicians, had the terrible misfortune of living well beyond the age of his genius. Many other black artists have had less than gracious "aging processes": Muddy Waters, Dizzy Gillespie, Count Basie, Lester Young, Billie Holiday, Thelonious Monk, Miles Davis, and even Charlie Parker. But what makes this especially tragic in the case of Armstrong is that not only he ceased to be a genius, but after the 1950s he ceased to be musically inventive or interesting. The pain that one feels when Armstrong's television performances of the middle and late sixties are recalled is so overwhelming as to constitute an enormously bitter grief, a grief made all the keener because it balances so perfectly one's sense of shame, rage, and despair. The little, gnomish, balding, grinning black man who looked so touchingly like everyone's black grandfather who had put in thirty years as the janitor of the local schoolhouse or like the old black poolshark who sits in the barbershop talking about how those old boys like Bill Robinson and Jelly Roll Morton could really play the game; this old man whose trumpet playing was just, no, not even a shadowy, ghostly remnant of his days of glory and whose singing had become just a kind of raspy-throated guile, gave the appearance, at last, of being nothing more than terribly old and terribly sick. One shudders to think that perhaps two generations of black Americans remember Louis Armstrong, perhaps one of the most remarkable musical geniuses America ever produced, not only as a silly Uncle Tom but as a pathetically vulnerable, *weak* old man. During the sixties, a time when black people most vehemently did not wish to appear weak, Armstrong seemed positively dwarfed by the patronizing white talk-show hosts on whose programs he performed, and he seemed to revel in that chilling, embarrassing spotlight. To this current generation of young black adults, Armstrong's greatness, if he ever had any, occurred in such a remote, antediluvian time as to bear almost no relation to modern American music or modern American culture. Alas, one does not wish that Armstrong had died young, say, in 1930 after waxing the wondrous Hot Five and Hot Seven recordings; one wishes simply that he had made the demands of American society and of his culture that his genius entitled him to make. It is the tragedy of Armstrong, as it is with most African-American musicians who lived before 1940, that he could not perceive, was absolutely unaware of, how staggering his genius truly was, how great his demands might be.

James Collier's *Louis Armstrong: An American Genius,* surprisingly, the first work of a truly scholarly magnitude to have been done on Armstrong—the first (unlike Albert McCarthy's *Louis Armstrong,* 1961, Hugues Panassié's *Louis Armstrong,* 1971, or John Chilton and Max Jones's *Louis: The Louis Armstrong Story,* 1971) to have been written by someone who was not a starstruck worshipper is, one hopes, the opening literary salvo of a period of several such books to reclaim and reassess Armstrong's greatness. Collier's book, certainly one of the most important jazz studies in recent years, rating in importance alongside Stanley Dance's *The World of Count Basie,* Dizzy Gillespie's *To Be or Not to Bop,* and the newly reissued volumes of Hampton Hawes's *Raise Up off Me,* Albert Murray's *Stomping the Blues,* Charles Mingus's *Beneath the Underdog,* and Dance's *The World of Earl Hines,* reminds us that much necessary scholarly work needs to be done to clarify and order the early years of jazz history, particularly the years of the New Orleans and the Chicago eras. Major studies need to be done on such early black jazz musicians as Jelly Roll Morton (Alan Lomax's book is not definitive), King Oliver, Sidney Bechet, Earl Hines, Kid Ory, and blues singers Chippie Hill, Memphis Minnie, and Mamie Smith. The full-length biographies of Bessie Smith and Ma Rainey that have appeared in recent years have filled in some gaps.

It is, to be sure, not my contention, nor is it Collier's, fortunately, that Armstrong was a "neglected artist." Quite the contrary, Armstrong, at the time of his death in July 1971 was not only quite wealthy but was probably the most famous American entertainer in the history of the American performing arts. But it is not Armstrong the entertainer, Armstrong the performer, Armstrong the darkie minstrel, who needs to be remembered. The great burden most black Americans must bear is that Armstrong will never be forgotten, least of all by whites when they wish to wax sentimental about the good old days of American jazz. It is Armstrong the deeply moving trumpeter and not the showy blower of high Cs and high Fs; Armstrong the master blues musician and not the performer of such execrable tripe as "Zip-a-De-Do-Da" and "Carry Me Back to Ole Virginny"; and Armstrong the "jokifying" singer and pardonist, not the man who, at times, nearly groveled for applause, who needs to be brought to light. Collier's book succeeds in doing just that.

For the first time in any Armstrong biography, the reader is given a clear and well-researched picture of black life in New Orleans at the turn of the century and the sort of intensely musical atmosphere Armstrong grew up in as a child:

> New Orleans was without question the most musical city in the United States, and perhaps the whole western hemisphere. The city was simply drenched in music. There were symphony orchestras, marching bands, and dance groups by the scores. At times there were three opera companies playing at once, and as early as the 1830s there was a Negro Philharmonic Society, which gave regular concerts....
>
> [Music] was customary accompaniment for almost any event. There was music at weddings and funerals—not just organ music, but frequently a full band which played in the church, at the graveside, and again at the wake. Bands played for picnics, parties, store openings, even athletic events, and, of course, just for the pleasure of it.

And of the neighborhood where Armstrong was raised, Collier writes the following:

> Black Storyville was a tough, hard neighborhood of cribs, honky-tonks, and rough dance halls, like the famous Funky Butt Hall, where the legendary Buddy Bolden played. Fighting was routine, gun and knife play was frequent, and murder was not unusual. There was enough drunkenness, drug addiction, disease, and lunacy to do for several ghettos. This area was probably the single most important cradle of jazz—the place where Bolden and the others played the blues for the slow drag dancing that whores and hustlers demanded.

Collier does try to straighten out the early biographical data, so shrouded in the myth-lore that Armstrong himself helped to create. He was certainly not born on July 4, 1910; probably his actual birth was anywhere from 18 months to two years earlier. He was not born Daniel Louis Armstrong and he was surely placed in the Colored Waifs' Home, where he learned to play the cornet, for something more serious than shooting a pistol in the air. He was probably firing at someone. Collier reminds those of us who think that jazz started with Count Basie in Kansas City or with bebop at Minton's Playhouse in Harlem that jazz is a southern music played both by blacks (Buddy Bolden, Joe Oliver) and by black Creoles (Sidney Bechet, Kid Ory) who had to teach northern blacks such as Fletcher Henderson and Duke Ellington what swinging was all about. Jazz was born and nurtured in a place of corrupt carnality, genteel historicity, and sheer filth of a uniquely unrepressed, non-American sort. This is why I think the music's polar matrices run from the gross sensuality of masculine poverty to the indulgent sentimentality of the whore and to a philistine middle class.

Collier, a brass player himself, offers a coherent explanation for Armstrong's lifelong lip problems which often incapacitated him for months and which finally resulted, in his later years, in diminished technical abilities. Armstrong was never properly instructed about his embouchure and, for his entire life, held first the cornet then the trumpet incorrectly on his lips.

What is most striking about the youthful Armstrong is how much a self-taught and original musician he was. Not even "Papa" Joe Oliver, who was to bring Armstrong to Chicago in 1922, exercised much stylistic influence. Armstrong was so sure of his own method of playing, so completely insulated by his own aesthetic vision that he was given to extraordinary dexterity and horrible excesses. On the one hand, Armstrong had a better intuitive sense of playing the blues than any player in the history of jazz music; on the other hand, he had very poor taste in music and was quite taken with ineptly written sentimental coon songs and pop songs and Guy Lombardo's band. This latter is especially odd as Armstrong was not a particularly sentimental person.

Leaving aside for the moment certain aspects of Collier's analysis of Armstrong psychology and of black culture (I shall return to these shortly), the portion of the book that covers Armstrong from his stay in the Colored Waifs' Home to his joining Oliver in Chicago through his Hot Five and Hot Seven recordings to his first appearances in full-length commercial motion pictures in the mid-1930s is the most readable and complete, and altogether finest account of Armstrong's youth and his days as a young artist that exists in print. It is a period that I call "Big Butter and Egg Man," after a late 1920s Armstrong hit. The title seems to capture so accurately and tellingly the man's exuberance and wit, his enormous artistic imagination and his physical zest for living. "West End Blues," "Hotter Than That," "Strutting with Some Barbecue," "Weatherbird," "SOL Blues," and all the rest of the Hot Fives and Hot Sevens, all of which were recorded between 1925 and 1927, are without a doubt the most momentous recordings in jazz. Collier, in describing in detail the musical features of each piece, seems hardly capable of finding superlatives that match the artistic wonders of the music. His enthusiasm almost leaps from the page and his prose seems almost breathless by chapter's end. (Incidentally, Collier must be commended for his clear and concise explanations of various musical terms. Any layman can understand the technical explications of Armstrong's work in this book.)

Armstrong is positively uncanny between the years of 1925 and 1940 because he will let nothing, not a bad lip, terrible arrangements, awful songs, bad management, or personal problems interfere with the beautiful obstinacy of his artistic vision. No other jazz musician, not even Charlie Parker, was so able to transcend for so long and so completely the circumstances that governed the conditions under which he played. Armstrong singlehandedly was able to transform garbage into astonishingly profound art. What is truly remarkable about Armstrong is not that, as Collier wrote, his talent should wind up being wasted over the last two-thirds of his career, but that he should have flowered so gloriously for as long as he did in a culture that both psychologically and physically abused him as a person, misunderstood his art, and depreciated his real worth.

It was during this period, the era of the Big Butter and Egg Man, that Armstrong was a cultural hero among black folk. It was not until World War II and beyond that Armstrong steadily lost his black audience and became, in effect, a "white" entertainer. During the bountiful days of the twenties and thirties, Armstrong was constantly featured in news stories and the gossip columns of the leading black American newspapers. He was unable to walk in a black neighborhood without being mobbed by ardent fans and, like most black entertainers of any age, he was quite a fashion plate; in fact, as Miles Davis was to do twenty years later, Armstrong, as Albert Murray has pointed out, set the trend for black male clothing styles: "a crisply ironed shirt with low-riding widespread collar worn with a smartly tailored three-piece suit and a tie with a large Windsor-type knot." Armstrong was, in the parlance of the street-corner hustler, "sharp as a tack."

But it was not any change in Armstrong's artistic direction that caused his black audience to abandon him after World War II. Indeed, it was because of his adamant refusal to change, his strenuous insistence that he should continue to perform as if social and cultural history in America had stopped in 1930 that he went from being praised as a black cultural hero to being denounced as an Uncle Tom. He had not changed, but the world and especially black America clearly had. That obstinacy, that pierced, oblivious yet narrow vision which had so informed and inspired his genius in his young adulthood had, by the end of the forties, become a kind of mule-headed innocence, maintained at the expense of a total grasp of reality. In a way, his black audience was right for throwing him over because he was an Uncle Tom. He did say, after all, that he needed to be "some white man's nigger," that is, taken under the protective, paternalistic wing of a white man who would "look out for him." He also continued to sing coon songs such as "When It's Sleepy Time Down South," "I'm a Son of the South," and "Snowball" long after such tunes were in vogue and when they could have been excised from his repertoire in homage to his black audience's dislike of them without in any way alienating his sizable white public. Yet if Armstrong ever felt outrage or despair over this abandonment because he thought that black folk had misunderstood him and judged him unfairly, he would have been right, too.

II. KING OF THE ZULUS

I suggested, helpfully: "You mean—like Louis Armstrong?" His face closed as though I'd struck him. "No. I'm not talking about none of that old-time, down home crap."
—James Baldwin, "Sonny's Blues"

Bop is no lovechild of jazz. Bop is something entirely separate and apart.
—Charlie Parker

In 1949 (the same year he made the cover of *Time* magazine) Armstrong was named King of the Zulus for Mardi Gras, which was to signal his complete rupture with his black audience. No matter that, as Collier explains, the Zulus were a black social club who had a long tradition of electing kings and queens. No matter that "among New Orleans blacks, it was a great honor to be chosen King of the Zulus." No matter that all of this was meant to be a parody of the white floats and the white kings and queens of Mardi Gras; indeed, the Zulus' float, with all its heathenish implications, was meant to serve as a counterstatement to the high seriousness of the white Christian Lenten season. What most blacks saw in newspapers all over the country were photographs of Armstrong in blackface (although it was clearly a different type of blacking up than that of the old minstrels), wearing, in Collier's words, "a long black wig, a crown, a red velvet gown trimmed with sequins, black tights, and a grass skirt." To most blacks, especially the "dicty" middle-class ones, there was nothing funny in all of this. Armstrong simply looked ridiculous and he seemed to be holding the entire race up to scorn. If blacks of the sixties were obsessed about not projecting a public image of weakness, then blacks of the forties were surely concerned about their public cultural roles as jesters, clowns, and fools. They wanted to be respected. They wanted no part of being the collective unconscious garbage heap of neuroses for whites. But of course there was no escaping *that:* vanguard whites adjusted by being outlaws, moving from hep to hip, from hot to cool. The white spokesman for America's cultural underbelly was no longer "Mezz" Mezzrow but Norman Mailer.

The creation of bebop, that great artistic movement in which black male jazzmen experienced the collective hysteria of the anxiety of influence, was the beginning of the end for Armstrong. But Powell, Thelonious Monk, Dexter Gordon, Fats Navarro, and most especially Charlie Parker were to redefine the role and the demeanor of the black jazz musician. Bebop, if anything, was the romantic period of black American music. Bebop musicians, despite their stance as militant, socially aware, artistically uncompromising professionals, were no more in tune with the black masses than the older Armstrong and, in some sense, were probably less so. The beboppers' insistence on seeing themselves as artists and not entertainers pushed them much closer to viewing their cultural function in more European terms. To Armstrong and to the black masses, the concept of the artist and of art as it is generally fixed by Euro-American standards is, quite frankly, incomprehensible. Armstrong saw himself as an entertainer who must, by any means, please his audience. And to the black masses generally there would scarcely be a reason for the public performer to exist if he did not feel that pleasing his audience was the prime directive. If jazz musicians wanted to play for themselves, then, according to Armstrong's way of thinking, they might as well blow in their living rooms. The cultivated alienation of the beboppers must have struck Armstrong as bizarre. Moreover, he probably thought that heroin addiction, the sine qua non of bebop life-style, to be further evidence that these younger musicians were simply "crazy niggers." Armstrong enjoyed his marijuana and apparently smoked it throughout his life but he would have found the self-destructive addiction to heroin to be, well, a very "white" thing more fitting for his buddy, Mezzrow, than for a hip black musician like Bird.

Bebop, inasmuch as it was, in part, a counterstatement to the jazz that preceded it (which means it was a counterstatement to Louis Armstrong because he symbolized pre-bebop jazz) succeeded not in capturing Armstrong's black audience but in alienating young and intellectual blacks from him. This, coupled with the rise of R&B and little Harlem dance bands of Louis Jordan, Erskine Hawkins, and Buddy Johnson, which effectively seized the older, finger-popping, good-timing blacks, left Armstrong with no black audience except old-timers who remembered his glory days in Chicago and New York. The boppers, led by Parker, decided, in essence, that jazz music would no longer be governed by the Armstrong concept (although it was still acceptable to plagiarize his solos and breaks; Miles Davis was still getting plenty of mileage from Armstrong's "West End Blues" solo when he recorded his *Sketches of Spain* album), and the growing R&B sector decided that black dance music would no longer be in a vaudeville (i.e., Armstrong) vein. To be sure, Armstrong was not about to play bop and, while it is pleasant to fantasize about the possibility of Armstrong having fronted a band like the Savoy Sultans, he really was not inclined to go the R&B route either. So during the fifties he either reprised the music he made in the twenties or sang insipid easy-listening pop tunes.

The shortcomings of Collier's book are, in part, related to his inadequate understanding of Armstrong's loss of a black audience and how it contributed to Armstrong's artistic failure in latter years. But more important, the shortcomings are tied to Collier's inability to grasp fully the complexities of black culture and his insistence on psychoanalyzing Armstrong using a method akin to Erik Erikson's in his books *Young Man Luther* and *Gandhi's Truth*. The other major problem with the book is that the portion on Armstrong's post–World War II career is much too sketchy.

To begin with the issue that can be most easily dispatched: Much more needs to be added about the second half (or final third, to use Collier's divisions) of the career. The State Department tours, particularly the one to Ghana, need to be thoroughly retold. The significance of that tour cannot be overemphasized; it had a profound effect on Armstrong to go "home," as he put it, and to place himself before black audiences. The television performances should also be examined: What sort of impact did they have on Armstrong's career? Also, Collier totally dismissed Armstrong's second autobiography, *Satchmo: My Life in New Orleans,* published in 1954, which is much superior to the first one published in the mid-1930s, called *Swing That Music.* The second is much truer to Armstrong's own style of writing (he did, in fact, write it) and it poses some very teasing questions about Armstrong's self-conscious myth-making. Indeed, Armstrong's writing as a whole deserves critical scrutiny, and this realization reveals still another problem with Collier's biography. He has no texts from any of the lengthy letters Armstrong wrote to friends and fans over the years. Armstrong not only loved to write letters but wrote extraordinary ones. His language, his syntax, his powers of description, his mastery of the art of storytelling are simply stunning. There are texts from several letters in the biography by Jones and Chilton as well as in Leonard Feather's *From Satchmo to Miles.* It would be a great service to scholars, jazz fans, and students of black culture if these letters were collected in a separate volume. Any biography that does not contain any of the letters and that does not even mention Armstrong's love of letter-writing is, I think, a deeply flawed effort. Moreover, Armstrong wrote many magazine articles, including a piece for *Ebony* and a *New York Times* review of Alan Lomax's *Mr. Jelly Roll.* Collier mentions none of this.

Now, to engage in more substantive matters: Collier overemphasized the barrenness of poor black culture and, as a result, he diminishes or ignores the complexities and extensions of African-American life-style. For instance, in discussing black life in Storyville, Collier writes the following:

> [The blacks] had no novels or poetry because many of them could not read or could read only on a low level. They had no painting, no opera, no theater, no ballet because they were barred from museums and performance halls. They had no radio, no television, no movies, no magazines, few records, and the roughest sort of newspapers....All they had was the music they made and, to a lesser extent, the dances they danced.

First, Collier is describing New Orleans during the early years of the twentieth century, when it would have been highly unlikely that whites had any access to radio, television, or movies, because these devices had not yet become the toys of mass culture. Once television, radio, and movies were available in a mass way, black people, no matter how poor, seem to have been able to enjoy these amenities. Indeed, if sociologist Herbert Gans is to be believed, these contraptions have become the unholy provinces of make-believe for the poor. The black masses made Armstrong, Bessie Smith, Fletcher Henderson, and others big stars during the 1920s by buying their records and they certainly could not have done that unless they owned phonographs. In the 1930s they listened to their favorite musicians on the radio like everyone else. There is no reason to suspect that blacks in New Orleans differed in this respect from blacks in New York.

Second, Collier is simply measuring black culture against a white cultural norm and, inasmuch as black culture resembles any poverty culture, it would appear that middle-class Euro-American culture is superior, at least materially. But poor black folk counterstated the deprivation they suffered by emphasizing in their rituals a refulgence of style. Although the poor black could not read, he did possess speech, so that through a complex manipulation of this medium, blacks created their theater in their barbershops and churches and their history and traditions in their folktales, folk beliefs, jiving, and signifying. Armstrong was not the product of an inadequate culture; if he had been, there would have been no emotional or psychological resources to support his becoming an artist.

This leads me to my final point of contention with Collier, namely, his obsession with wanting to examine Armstrong's adult life in the light of his having been a fatherless boy. Collier's analysis is predictable: Armstrong was insecure about his talent as an adult, felt an extraordinary need to be loved by his audience, and was unable to exert control over his affairs and his career, which at various times were managed by his second wife, Lil, a remarkable woman and the most interesting of Armstrong's wives, and three tough, gangster-connected white men, Tommy Rockwell, Johnny Collins, and Joe Glaser. Collier may be correct in his speculations, but without rigorous sociological study of the cultural rituals that existed in New Orleans black life for a boy coming of age or of the cultural rituals that characterized the relationship between young and older males in black New Orleans they are simply unconvincing. Collier cites Armstrong's jealousy about being upstaged by fellow musicians and his competitive urges to defeat his rivals as an example of his insecurity about his talent. But that can be explained just as easily and perhaps more plausibly by considering the values that were instilled in Armstrong as a child. He may have been told by older black males that once you become the best at something, you must deal immediately and ruthlessly with any pretenders to your throne if you wish not only to save but to enhance your reputation. Since Armstrong, as Collier admits, grew up around black men who were largely musicians and pimps, such advice would have been out of context. In another instance, Collier cites Armstrong's showboating displays of high Cs in his in-person performances as an example of his need to be loved by his audience, a need that arose because he grew up without a father. Once again, another explanation may account for Armstrong's need to please his audience by, in effect, resorting to stunts. As a boy growing up among a good many public performers, he must have discovered that "stunting" was an essential part of any performance; it was the performer's signature as sure as his theme song since a stunt had to be a very individual expression of parodic virtuosity. Besides, Armstrong was aware, even if he could not articulate the concept, that stunting was necessary not only to please the crowd who expected artists to show off in this larger-than-life way but also to serve as a counterstatement to the "deep song" or the true improvisational substance of a performance. After all, a certain amount of pure showmanship exists in even the most exalted art. It was just these sorts of psychological conjectures or psychoanalytic theorizing that marred Collier's earlier book *The Making of Jazz*.

On the whole, this new Armstrong biography is a serviceable study. Yet there is a need for a book that will examine Armstrong's relationship to both American and African-American comic tradition. It is my belief that although Armstrong did some silly and embarrassing make-believe on stage, he bothered black people as much for his personification of the ambiguities of blackness as for his Uncle Tomming. It is time to tease apart in an Armstrong performance the elements that make the average black person quail in fear from the elements that make him cringe in mortification. We do know definitely that Armstrong, unlike many other black performers of his day and of the present, was never ashamed or ill at ease about his blackness. He never harbored secret neurotic yearnings to be white. We also know that Armstrong set the standard for creating not musical comedy but comic music: personalities as diverse as Dizzy Gillespie and Peter Schickele have been, directly or indirectly, inspired by Armstrong's stage art.

It is altogether wonderful, marvelous even, to have the life of this incredible genius of a man before the public eye again, a man with strange, compelling gifts, who used to laugh his rich black laugh as deep as the deepest well, who used to call his trumpet "Satchelmouth" and who used to prance around on stage drenching two dozen handkerchiefs with his sweat, and who, even with a bloody lip that looked, to borrow "Mezz" Mezzrow's description, like a "bursted strawberry," loved "to make pretty for the peoples."

On Marion Brown's Recollections: Essays, Drawings, Miscellanea *and Al Young's* Kinds of Blue

To borrow a phrase from Victorian specialist Jerome Buckley, for some time we have been living in an age of the "subjective impulse." This intellectual tendency toward "inward dwelling" has had a curious effect upon jazz writing. In a field that was once and, though not nearly to the same extent, still is dominated by history and biography, students of jazz find themselves afloat in a mass of memoirs, autobiographies, reminiscences, stylish belles-lettres essays, and what has become the sine qua non of the exploration of the jazz musician's soul, the interview. Now, much of this is good and welcomed with heartfelt appreciation by those of us fascinated by this profound art form. But too much of *this* particular good thing can be confounding, distorting, and ultimately a distressing indication that in this willfully subjective consciousness we have so lovingly constructed, we fail, in a way that almost amounts to decadence, to realize anything beyond ourselves.

Both Marion Brown's *Recollections* and Al Young's *Kinds of Blue* are recent and intriguing examples of this trend in jazz writing that grows out of Amiri Baraka's seminal work, *Black Music* (New York: William Morrow, 1970). I think Baraka's book has had more influence upon jazz writing, particularly among blacks writing about jazz, than any other work produced in Afro-American history. This is surprising in one sense because *Black Music* is not really, at first glance, a good book. That is, with few exceptions, its parts are not impressive. The essays in the volume seem to be exactly what they are: occasional pieces, fillers, and album liner notes, mere intellectual bric-a-brac, more stylish sloganizing and posturing than statement and analysis. Yet it has a power and a presence that adamantly deny its shortcomings, that make it much more than a sum of its parts. For Baraka, *Black Music* was truly a sophisticated kind of autobiography: the listener's guide both to the music and to Baraka's own moods of self-discovery. The book succeeds marvelously in entrancing the reader and in making the reader interested in listening to what many thought to be essentially unlistenable avant-garde music because of Baraka's naive and naked exuberance and his unbridled hope for the mystical virtues of this music. Finally, like any avid listener who is not a musician, Baraka believes in the music more than the music could believe in itself, expecting more of it than it is capable of delivering. Avant-garde jazz holds the greatest of all gifts for a man of Baraka's philosophical inclinations: It holds and offers the gift of promise of even more possibilities lying in wait in its expression of possibility. Not really understanding how music is made, Baraka can think of it as a sort of encoded magic. Lost in the labyrinths of his own poetic sensibilities, he can, like a child or a dreamer, wonder at his own ability to supply a verbal voice, a text, for a virtually mute art, as Jacques Barzun has written, an art of sensation. It is, of course, the fiery optimism of his own well-loved powers of expression that suffuses every page of *Black Music.* There one finds the boyish belief that art must be and can be freed from the taint of the money motive or sexual jockeying, that it must be our purest selves, which means for Baraka the erstwhile nationalist that the black male jazz artist must remain, uncorrupted by "commercialism" and white women. It is this philosophic obsession with refinement and aesthetic revisionism that makes Baraka's portraits of various young jazz artists really variations of poses of himself as the embattled artist against the establishment. In this genre of writing, this book is perhaps the subjective impulse's finest or at least most compelling moment.

If Baraka's book gave us the self as anthology, a form of autobiography popularized among black folk by Du Bois and Baldwin, then Marion Brown's *Recollections* might be called the self as miscellany, for this book possesses a quaint disjointedness. It is divided into several parts containing interviews with Brown (an alto saxophonist of some note who made his debut on the avant-garde jazz scene in New York during the sixties and has recorded and appeared in America intermittently ever since), several stiffly formal essays by Brown, some poems and drawings, and, finally, the scores of five Brown musical compositions. The book is certainly interesting and important but, ultimately, someone not familiar with Brown's music would be better off listening to such albums as *Three for Shepp, Why Not?, Afternoon of a Georgia Faun,* and *November Cotton Flower,* this last consisting of Brown's compositions inspired by Jean Toomer's *Cane* as performed by pianist Amina Claudine Myers. The German editors of this volume would have provided an invaluable feature by supplying a complete Brown discography.

The interviews, conducted by the German editors, are easily the most impressive parts of the book. Brown relates his boyhood days in Atlanta:

> My family, my mother and aunts didn't have many children. Some of the women didn't have any children. Most of the others only had one. I had a lot of uncles and aunts. And so I got a lot of love and attention. Everybody wanted me to be something different. Some of my relatives wanted me to preach. Some wanted me to teach. But none wanted me to play music. Because...I come up in the South, in a very Christian family; and people didn't understand why music could be for any other reason than dancin' and worship.

His early musical influences:

> Charlie Parker and Johnny Hodges were two very essential players. They were princely men. Parker was very princely. And very aloof; and so was Johnny Hodges. Earl Bostic was a very well-hewn man. He looked like the owner of an insurance company, an undertaker, or real-estate man.

His self-definition:

> I only play saxophone. I am a western man. A western Black man. And I live in America. The saxophone for me is the main instrument to express myself on. You can play many things on the saxophone. It's endless.

His church background:

> I went to church every Sunday until I was eighteen....For Black music there are no conservatories. The church is our conservatory.

And his assessment of some contemporary saxophonists:

> So, this idea, this phrase "In the Tradition" is related to two people basically: Anthony Braxton and Arthur Blythe. They use it as a way of saying "Look, folks, don't put me in this particular hole because I'm in the tradition!" But I didn't use the word "In the Tradition." They know that I am in the tradition. Maybe, I'm so far in the tradition that it is too much for people. But I don't know what Anthony means by "In the Tradition." I don't know what Arthur meant by "In the Tradition"—I don't know what they mean.

Brown's essays are unfortunately not very successful either as deft prose or as trenchant discussion. It is momentarily engaging to have a professional musician play the role of amateur critic, but in the end, no more so than having the professional critic play the role of amateur musician. "Notes to the Afternoon of a Georgia Faun" is the most striking and substantial of the essays because Brown is discussing his own music and he seems quite comfortable doing that. In the other essays, one would learn more from reading Brown's sources—André Hodeir and Martin Williams, for instance, in the Duke Ellington piece—than from reading Brown.

The Coltrane essay is particularly disappointing because Brown himself played with Trane on the *Ascension* albums—two of the most difficult recordings to listen to in all of jazz—and one would have thought he had more insight into Coltrane's music. The biggest mistake in this essay is that

Brown tends to characterize all of Coltrane's music from the time of his spiritual awakening in 1957 as being like that of his very final albums. This is not true. In fact, over the ten-year period between his spiritual awakening and his death, Coltrane made albums almost exclusively for Prestige, Atlantic, and Impulse that were "in the tradition" of conventional post-Charlie Parker jazz. Coltrane, it must be remembered, not only recorded with such avant-garde musicians as Eric Dolphy and Pharoah Sanders, but with such traditionalists as Duke Ellington and Red Garland; and his signature tune was not "A Love Supreme" or "Meditations" but a pop tune: "My Favorite Things." The albums, which actually form the bulk of Coltrane's recorded music, must be taken into account before any telling analysis of his music and his spiritual beliefs can be detailed. Moreover, in considering Coltrane's "ultra" music, Brown totally neglects one of Trane's most beautifully realized pieces from this period, "Kulu Se Mama." It is the only record, aside from the ballads he recorded with Johnny Hartman, on which he uses a vocalist and where the spiritualism takes on a decidedly African and political flavor.

Brown's drawings, none of which is earlier than May 16, 1981, the day he started his career as a visual artist, are better than his essays but are not compelling works. Perhaps one can say this about every aspect of the book: Brown as essayist, Brown as poet, Brown as visual artist, all of these psychotherapeutic avatars exhibit a certain dexterous homeliness but not the profundity of true gifts. One senses that this miscellany as the morphology of the self is a misreading and a misrendering of autobiography; somehow Brown's hobbies, the things he plays at, take up nearly as much space as that which he *honestly does,* the real playing as opposed to some fictive playing. He does not talk about the very thing and the only thing that makes him worth knowing. He mistakes his leisure for his work. Brown the autobiographer and the Brown the musician—the most important roles that Brown can occupy for any reader—do not emerge as pointedly or as dramatically as they should. In the end, Brown never seems fully in control of his book and thus it becomes unbounded and digressive. Unlike Baraka, who, incidentally, greatly impressed and influenced Brown with his works, particularly *Blues People* and *Black Music,* Brown is unable, through any sense of vision, to make the whole greater than the sum of its parts.

Kinds of Blue is Al Young's second book of what he calls "musical memoirs." The first, *Bodies and Soul* (San Francisco: Creative Arts Book Company, 1981), was a charming book but as good a writer as Al Young ought to know that while it is not too formidable a task to write *one* charming book, it is almost impossible to write a charming *series* of books on this subject, although *New Yorker* jazz critic Whitney Balliett has tried very hard to convince us that it is conceivable if not truly to be realized. "Simultaneity," writes Young, "has always enthralled me: the ways in which human suffering and joy are endlessly connected. Time and timelessness, soul and spirituality, the physical universe crammed with celestial bodies as the natural extension, in both space and mind, of our own fragile, terrestrial organisms—that is what continues to warm, nurture, and strengthen me in my eternal flight into light." The very grandiose nature of this thematic concern makes it impossible for Young to stretch successfully the format of *evocation* over the space of two books. Simply to see music as the ability to evoke endlessly a reality in the mind (memory and longing), a reality beyond the music itself, is finally to reduce music to a kind of solipsistic romance for the mere nostalgia of music. So, by the time one has reached the end of the second volume, these episodic essays—written in the Whitmanesque spirit of liberal humanism and free association—begin to become the same essay endlessly repeated. One finds oneself faced with a series of prefaces which all seem madly in love with their cunning conceit to talk about the ineffable.

The essays in *Kinds of Blue* are not as uniformly good as those of *Bodies and Soul.* One discovers that when Young is good he is very very good but when he is bad he is simply a passable journalist. "Cast Your Fate to the Wind," about Fantasy Records in Berkeley, California, and "When I Lay My Burden Down," about a husband-and-wife singing duo, are very flat puff pieces. The piece on Mingus contains the best line in the whole book: "Tuned to its grandest level, music, like light, reminds us that everything that matters, even in this world, is reducible to spirit." But it contains very little else in large part because the author cannot convince the reader of any possible significance in his very slight, very passing acquaintance with Mingus. Young was not privy to much when Mingus discussed his auto-biography with him. The sly bassist talked about it with anyone who would listen but shared the actual prose with very few. There is also one minor but irritating mistake in the book: Young mistakenly credits the Shangri-Las with the hit "My Boyfriend's Back." The song was recorded by four nasal-sounding white girls from New Jersey who were called the Angels. The Shangri-Las made two cultish hits: "Remember (Walking in the Sand)" and "The Leader of the Pack."

Despite the brilliant essays that occasionally appear in *Kinds of Blue,* such as "Maiden Voyage," about a cruise to Lisbon; "Green Onions," about working in a research lab, which reminds one of Richard Wright's adventures in such an institution; and the hilarious "Mercedes-Benz"—when one puts both of Young's books together, the absences are dismaying. Other than the essay on Mingus and the reprinted album liner notes from a John Coltrane Prestige recording, no avant-garde jazz figures are discussed. The essay on Miles Davis does not consider any of his music recorded after 1960 and with the exception of James Brown, Stevie Wonder, and Ray Charles, no figures from R&B are discussed. It is hard to believe that no songs by Aretha Franklin, Otis Redding, or Jimi Hendrix evoke memories for Young. I suppose that is the real problem with these books: everyone who has listened to American music over the last few decades has some memories to tell, and Al Young's in the end do not seem as enthralling as, say, my own. This is rather like the trick Nathaniel Hawthorne pulled in one of his short stories when he listed several strange books that he had read. He showed that we all possess some obscure knowledge that will make us seem like geniuses to others. But I am not sure if Young ever shows us anything hidden or tucked away in the attic. One simply hopes that this sort of diarylike autobiography will not go on tediously into an ever-receding horizon.

I think, ultimately, what I do not like about Young's books is that they fail to go after the music. There is no hunt here like Ishmael's intellectual pursuit to describe the whale, to pursue the whale around the globe in order to *know what it is* and not simply to *acknowledge his reactions to the chase.* Ishmael's search is always outward, whereas it is Ahab who is subjective and inner-dwelling. Young's subjectivity is not precisely that of Ahab's but in the end, the music becomes secondary for Young, almost irrelevant, simply signifying that which can evoke another reality. Indeed, both books could have been written without the rather tenuous connection to music and may have been better for it. The problem with subjectivity is that it is likely to take you on a journey to nowhere. This is what separates Baraka's *Black Music* from Young's books and what makes Baraka's work the more profound and the more moving. Baraka is always pursuing the music; Young is only pursuing himself. Baraka truly loves the music more than his ability to describe it. Young does not so much love the music as he does his ability to subordinate it to what he feels is the greater poetry of his own feelings about self-creation. We must see, as Ishmael does, that we must find ways of talking about the qualities that adhere to the objects of this world without getting enmeshed in thinking that the name of the object is what the object is, or without thinking about ourselves thinking about the object.

I suppose that Marion Brown's *Recollections* and Al Young's *Kinds of Blue* are, in some ways, disappointing books. But each contains its own multitude and so there is much here that would be of interest to any student of American music or American autobiography. In this regard, Brown's book is undoubtedly the more important. Young's book would appeal to his fans but to those unfamiliar with his works *Snakes* or *Sitting Pretty* or *Who Is Angelina?*, all good novels, would be better places to get acquainted. Do not mistake this as some sort of reviewer's standard coda. Any book is much more than what one can say about it. To paraphrase William James, the reason we call a certain music jazz is the reason it is jazz. And for those few of us who like to think about those reasons, these books and any scribbling on fugitive scraps of paper are actually indispensable.

The Passing
of Jazz's Old Guard:
Remembering Charles Mingus,
Thelonious Monk, and
Sonny Stitt

Music is your experience, your thoughts, your wisdom. If you don't live it, it won't come out of your horn.

—Charlie Parker, in *Hear Me Talkin' to Ya*

For, while the tale of how we suffer, and how we are delighted, and how we may triumph is never new, it always must be heard. There isn't any other tale to tell, it's the only light we've got in all this darkness.

—James Baldwin, "Sonny's Blues"

I suppose that jazz listening and prizefight watching are my two most passionate avocations, and this is largely so because the origins of my aesthetic urges are in the black working class. At times these avocations are a bit difficult to reconcile: boxers like to train in the early afternoon and jazz musicians like to jam late at night. But I think they are, on the whole, more deeply related than one might suspect. They are such direct expressions, not of emotion, but rather of *emotive power,* and they are such risk-taking endeavors. The most vibrant memories I bear from my childhood are of my uncles crowded around a very small black-and-white television, drinking beer and watching the Gillette Friday-night fights; my aunts would be in another room listening to old jazz records such as Lionel Hampton's "Flying Home" and Billie Holiday's "Don't Explain." The men would join them later to play Charlie Parker records and lots of rhythm-and-blues stuff. I liked those Friday nights as much as I have ever liked anything.

The person I associate most with these remembrances of Fridays past is my Uncle G., who has, for most of his life, struck me as a wonderfully wayward, perennially playful man. I learned a few years ago that he has cancer of the prostate gland. This struck me as the rather absurd sort of insult that fate is very likely to add to a life that has seen its fair share of injury. He lost his eldest son in a street-gang fight that took place nearly in front of his home. One of his daughters became pregnant while still in high school, and he has fought a very unsuccessful battle to keep himself and his ten children off the welfare roll, a pitched struggle where his embattled efforts have been to keep his dignity and eat at the same time, a trick as demanding for the working class as the childish game of patting your head and rubbing your stomach simultaneously.

I remember my Uncle G. on those Friday nights, fresh from being kicked out of the U.S. Army and the war effort in Korea—a slim, muscular man who loved to dance and laughed as raucously as any human being I have ever heard. And he loved to tell stories about his heroes, the jazzmen and the rhythm-and-blues cats of the underworld. It was he who told me about Count Basie's drummer Jo Jones throwing a cymbal at the feet of a fumbling Charlie Parker and shouting, "Get off the stand, motherfucker, you can't play." "Of course, after that, Bird went to the shed," Uncle G. continued, "and he learned how to blow that horn. He did what a man gotta do." I often wonder what it is that men must do and what happens to them when, as in the case of my uncle, the dilemmas of fatherhood and the social demands of manhood seem impossible not only to accommodate but even to bear painfully. When I learned that my uncle, who had been (and, I think, always wanted to be) a gloriously vigorous man with a cocky radiance of power, had cancer, I realized, with a certain formidable, bristling force, how precarious manhood of any sort is in this world: what a strangely perishing thing it is.

I. "I'M ALWAYS MAKING A COMEBACK..."

Now they are nearly all gone—the old guard, the great black male presence that coalesced around bebop and post-bop: Booker Ervin, Lee Morgan, the latter-day Coleman Hawkins, Charlie Parker, Tadd Dameron, Clifford Brown, Bud Powell, Paul Chambers, the early John Coltrane, Charlie Christian, Wilbur Ware, and—most recently—Charles Mingus, Thelonious Monk, and Sonny Stitt. What a sense of loss to be a witness to the tail end, the burning out forever of that magnificent light of great music with its tough carnality and its depth of telling resonance that made not only storytellers but also heroes of its practitioners. They were the last heroes of jazz; never again will there be the likes of Dexter Gordon and Wardell Gray—hair slicked hard, big pants blowing in the wind, hats cocked to the side, pointed-toe shoes walking in rhyme and rhythm with the corner boys—battling on their tenor saxes in an endless version of "The Steeple-chase." Never again will there be a watering hole like Minton's Playhouse, where the experimentation in sound led to bebop and modern jazz. Although Monk once said that he "had no particular feeling that anything new was being built here," the stories are legion about how Monk, Parker, Dizzy Gillespie, Kenny Clarke, and others played weird to scare away the unhip. As Gillespie himself put it: "Thelonious Monk and I began to work out some complex variations on chords and the like, and we used them at night at Minton's to scare away the no-talent guys."

Oh, those young black cats—all in their twenties, full of new ideas, and filled to the point of disgust with the virulent practice of racism as the social norm in World War II America—were more than a little aware of what they were doing. As Amiri Baraka (LeRoi Jones) wrote:

> Bop also carried with it a distinct element of social protest, not only in the sense that it was music that seemed antagonistically nonconformist, but also that the musicians who played it were loudly outspoken about who they thought they were. "If you don't like it, don't listen," was the attitude....These musicians seemed no longer to want to be thought of merely as "performers" in the Old Cotton Club–yellow hiney sense, but as musicians.*

Nowadays, young black musicians are as thoroughly trained as a formal education can make one, and they pontificate, as Yale-educated pianist Anthony Davis does, upon the death of traditional improvisation. As Mercer Ellington put it: "Things ain't what they used to be." But I do not wish to imply that the golden era of jazz occurred before I was born, that now we are experiencing merely the measured, misdirected march of a period of decline and decadence in a once noble art form. I firmly believe that extensive formal education has created a core of musicians who are generally better players than the old guys. Younger musicians such as Wynton Marsalis, Arthur Blythe, and Jay Hoggard are playing music which is as fine as any that preceded it, and many of the younger men pay more than casual homage to their elders. Yet it must not be forgotten that what makes the old bebop cats so vital in understanding post–World War II Afro-American and American culture is not only that they made wonderful music under less than ideal conditions but also that they bore witness to the terrors and anxieties of the young black male coming of psychological age in America. Bebop was a mass performance of a male identity crisis.

But let us start here: To paraphrase James Baldwin, unless a black artist lives as long as Eubie Blake, in which instance he becomes a "cherished institution," then his death is bound to be untimely and tragic. We have no trouble understanding this when an artist dies quite young and accidentally as did Jimi Hendrix or old-time rhythm-and-blues star Johnny Ace, whose

*Amiri Baraka, *Black Music* (New York: William Morrow & Co., 1970), p. 23.

death in the early fifties caused many young black women, my mother included, to weep in the streets. We will even accept this when an artist dies quite unexpectedly in early middle age as did Rahsaan Roland Kirk. It is possibly a bit more difficult to see this point when an artist dies sick, broken, and at an advanced age, as did Coleman Hawkins and Ben Webster. But it must be understood that the latter is, in truth, the most untimely and rudely tragic of all. The black public performer never retires from the scene; his deterioration becomes the spectacle of a bitter public witness. The images of alcohol-ravaged Ben Webster unable to negotiate the steps to the bandstand and of a painfully ill Kenny Dorham being slowly poisoned by failing kidneys and unable to make even an easy run on his horn make me think that jazz musicians—particularly black jazz musicians because they, more than any other artists in our culture, symbolize the psychotic martyr and his attendant dubious honor in the backwater of the American imagination—that these men are destined or were destined to enact their fall as well as their rise. The tragedy of this role entails personifying that "sickness unto death" that has generally become a wretched but ineluctable cultural ritual for many black artists as they writhe in front of their audience. Much of jazz music till the seventies was performed by sick men.

Thelonious Monk, Charles Mingus, and Sonny Stitt were not particularly old at the time of their deaths. Indeed, both Mingus and Stitt were under sixty, and Monk was just a few years over that mark. Two of them were too sick to be able to perform publicly anymore and had, truly, spent their last few public years playing while quite ill. Stitt was still performing until his death but, although he was still able to play well, he had, in recent years, lost his stamina, a trademark of his greatness. I do not wish to imply that this sort of ghastly edge to the jazzer's public life is unique to blacks; the very different, strangely illuminating, slightly repulsive deaths of white alto saxophonists Paul Desmond and Art Pepper would deny such an implication. But I do think that the deaths of black jazz artists in general and of these three men of genius in particular are especially poignant and deeply meaningful. By this, I mean that the deaths of Monk, Mingus, and Stitt are in some spiritual and culturally relevant way tied to our complex fate, the magnificent curse of being black Americans.

Each of these men lived well beyond the period of his greatest work. Each represented a different but major aspect of the jazz music that grew out of the forties: Mingus as the composer who learned from the best in jazz and classical music without resorting to "third stream" fusion; Monk as the composer who knew nothing but black music; and Stitt as the popular disseminator of the virtuosic technique of the language of bop.

It was nearly unbearable to hear about the decline of Mingus and Monk and the faltering of Stitt in their later years. And their deaths were untimely and tragic not only because they meant the closing of the book on a period of great music and the passing from earth of a type of masculine vitality not bound to resurge anytime soon, but also, and most important, because these men died without having the luxury of ceasing to work. They saw their genius stretched out to the point of softness and serene decay; they were not able to die secure in what they had accomplished or in the recognition of that accomplishment. They will always be the old men who lost it. The black male performer is he who in youth conquered adverse circumstances, and he who in old age succumbed to them. There is a tacit admission, a downright undermining and unnerving confession of failure in the careers of most black jazz artists if they live long enough.

It occurs to me that with the deaths of Mingus, Monk, and Stitt in the last few years, I have an opportunity to talk about the passing of great black artists who had lived beyond the term of their greatness, a rare occasion for any writer.

I will talk about Mingus's autobiography, Thelonious Monk's innocence, and the color of Sonny Stitt's horn.

II. "BUT NOBODY EVER TELLS ME WHERE I'VE BEEN"

1. CHARLES MINGUS:
A CALIFORNIA YANKEE STROLLING ON THE GANGES

"He went around with a lot of cheap white women. It was a disgusting book." So said Mari Evans, noted poet, literary critic, and musician, referring to Charles Mingus's autobiography, *Beneath the Underdog*. It was said quite calmly, so calmly that one would hardly have suspected the depth of bitterness that threatened the chitchatty blandness of this dinner conversation like an undertow. The opinion was not taken lightly then, nor is it now. Evans is a sensible enough person not to be squeamish over the details in Mingus's book simply because they are graphically rehearsed. At the core of this complaint is the pathetic outrage that many black women feel when they discover that some black men prefer blondes. I call this sort of emotion pathetic not to denigrate the scope and intensity of the anguish but to say clearly that the men who generate this feeling simply are not worth such painfully wrought attention. In the end, all of us, black and white, are fairly shoddy or positively uninteresting as sexual beings.

The swirling dispute about Mingus and his relationship with white women did not end with his death. Shortly before his death he arranged to have Joni Mitchell do an album of his songs to which she would supply the lyrics. The album was released under the title *Mingus,* and while it was his most successful commercial venture, it was not, in the end, even his album. It was released under Joni Mitchell's name. Not everyone was pleased with the accolades the album received on the review pages of *Downbeat* magazine.

Vi Redd, a black singer and saxophonist, wrote a letter to the editor which read in part:

> What is all this madness about nonsinger Joni Mitchell? Who needs her wailing (which sounds like it's emanating from a maternity ward) to validate the artistry of the giant that Charles Mingus was?

In Ms. Redd's letter, the bitterness reaches an almost hysterical pitch, and it is a bitterness which is unconsciously directed at Mingus and not at Joni Mitchell at all. Like an injured adolescent, she angrily, outrageously asks how he dare allow a white woman to be the instrument through which he should attempt to reach a wider audience. But what black woman pop singer would have been interested in recording an album of Mingus's songs? Diana Ross? Dionne Warwick? Aretha Franklin? It is quite likely that they would not have touched Mingus's material. When I read Ms. Redd's letter in *Downbeat* a few years ago, I recalled something my mother told me when I was a child. She had seen blues singer Joe Williams perform at a cabaret the night before and she was infuriated. She said she hated him and would not see or listen to him again.

"He sang a song called 'I Don't Want No Monkey-Faced Woman,'" she said disdainfully. "And what women do you think he was talking about? Colored women, that's who."

But Mari Evans's comment is, finally, not misplaced. It is Mingus himself who makes his sex life the dominant feature of his autobiography, and it is he who gives the impression that he has slept with every white woman from Maine to Texas.

"I think the book is meant to be a put-on," I replied to Ms. Evans, leaning back in my chair and thinking to myself what a great musician Mingus was. He had achieved something that few other jazz musicians were capable of: he absorbed the lessons of Duke Ellington, America's supreme composer. Mingus was a peerless bassist and he, in that regard, would rank alongside Jimmy Blanton, Slam Stewart, Scott Le Faro, Paul Chambers, Wilbur Ware, and Al Stinson. But Mingus's real importance as a jazz musician is in the realm of composition. He was second only to Ellington as a composer. His great songs, "Goodbye Old Pork Pie Hat," "Song with Orange," "Fables of Faubus," "Mingus Fingers," "Better Get It in Your Soul," and "Pithecanthropus Erectus," were all suffused with Ellington without being derivative of the master. He was able to use avant-garde elements in his works without sounding like someone making random noise with kitchen utensils as so many of the young black musicians of the late sixties did. John Coltrane, Ornette Coleman, and Albert Ayler would have profited much from recording some of Mingus's tunes. And of course, some of the best musicians in jazz played in various Mingus bands: Eric Dolphy, Ted Curson, Jimmy Knepper, Jaki Byard, John Handy, Jackie McLean, Max Roach, and Rahsaan Roland Kirk, whose stunt of playing three reed instruments at one time brings to mind such turn-of-the-century black musicians as Wilbur C. Sweatman and

Horace George. Ah, Mingus, I thought, your music makes up for whatever shortcomings you possessed. Indeed, your music is so glorious that I can be generous and excuse the sins of a thousand other men as well. Mingus, if I were God, your music would have made it possible for a thousand sinners to enjoy the celestial palace when they deserved to burn in hell.

Admittedly, *Beneath the Underdog* is a strange book, not the usual jazz musical memoir about travels on the road and the struggle for recognition. One is struck by the similarity between Mingus's book and Chester Himes's autobiography: neither talks very directly or extensively about the life of a practicing artist.

The one immediate distinction about Mingus in comparison to other jazz musicians of his era that the reader is made aware of is that he was not a dope addict. This is quite a noteworthy fact when one considers that so many musicians around him were. Mingus was as self-absorbed as any other autobiographer but, since he was not addicted to drugs, one learns that he was largely obsessed with the nature of his sanity. He was more afraid of going crazy than of nearly anything else, which probably explains why he wrote such a self-consciously psychoanalytic book.

The book opens with Mingus talking about his three selves, a tongue-in-cheek way of saying that if he is a divided, irrational self, so is the concept of the Christian God. The true nature of his irrationality emerges when he shouts to his psychologist: "I am more of a man than any dirty white cocksucker! I *did* fuck twenty-three girls in one night, including the boss's wife!" For Mingus, sanity is tied to his idea of manhood, and manhood is tied to sex. The only way that Mingus can prove that he is better than a white man is through sex: one of two avenues of expression left open to him as a black man. Far from being unique, Mingus opens his book by making himself a psychological paradigm for every black man. The irrational nature of the black man is largely the result of possessing too many dimensions, too many selves to fit into the roles white America has proscribed for him. His energy is, therefore, dammed up into very confining modes of expression. Mingus has three selves, yet there are only two possible roles for him: a pimp or a jazz musician. The artistic outlaw and the sexual outlaw become, for Mingus, equivalent roles: each provides entertainment for clients who can pay. What Mingus is really railing against in his book is the fact that the black male's heart, mind, and gonads are commodities of exchange in an immoral marketplace. In a sense, sex has become art for the black male in both his emotional needs and his expressive capacity for it. It is through sex that the black male can have moments of being human. And art has become sex not only in the very origin of the word *jazz* (to copulate) but also because it is through this music that Mingus is able to attract women. Jazz becomes the call of the sexual wilds; the nightclub becomes the place where one can act out one's sexual fantasies.

At this point, Mingus's autobiography may sound a bit too consciously clinical. Recalling Erik Erikson's definition for patienthood as "a sense of imposed suffering, of an intense need for cure," the reader realizes that Mingus's book is the descriptive journey of his own patienthood, from the book's opening with a dialogue between Mingus and his psychologist to its culmination when Mingus succeeds in checking himself into the psychiatric ward of Bellevue. That scene, as Mingus retells it, of his attempt to be placed in Bellevue is hilarious in a dark and horrible way, and it puts one in mind of other jazz musicians who have been "treated" as criminals or diseased persons in institutions: Charlie Parker, Billie Holiday, Tadd Dameron, Bud Powell, Thelonious Monk, and Lester Young.

The four major black male characters in the book—Mingus's father, Buddy Colette's father, Billy Bones the pimp, and Fats Navarro, the tragic trumpeter known as "Fat Girl" because he was overweight and had a high-pitched voice—all seem a bit contrived as the father and older-brother figures whom Mingus seeks. The conflation of his white lover, Donna, and his black wife, Lee-Marie, into the composite character he calls Donnalee (after a Charlie Parker composition) seems a bit too much like the fulfillment of a black male's sexual fantasy. All of this business with both the men and the women seems too symbolic of Mingus's state of patienthood to be very useful as literary autobiography or as trenchant psychoanalysis. And Mingus is striving mightily for both. This little volume is fraught, burdened really, with the self-conscious weight of its own significance.

But Mingus makes clear that his concern is not only with patienthood but also with sainthood. Or perhaps, for Mingus, patienthood and sainthood amount to the same thing. Freud was always "struck by the resemblance between what are called obsessive acts in neurotics and those religious observances by means of which the faithful give expression to their piety." Mingus is something of a mystic, and the movement of the book from the West (Mingus was raised in the Watts section of Los Angeles) to the East (the book reaches another culmination with Mingus's arrival in New York) is emblematic of his spiritual concerns. Mingus says in various parts of the book:

> He was busy reading everything he could find in the library that went beyond his Christian Sunday School training—karma yoga, theosophy, reincarnation, Vedanta—and sitting on park benches he often became so engrossed in finding God that he forgot about shining shoes. [Mingus often refers to himself in the third person throughout the book.]*
>
> I hope to God I can really love before it's too late.†
>
> Yes, and we got no directions or visions from the modern holy men who are growing in doubt of themselves.‡

---

*Charles Mingus, *Beneath the Underdog: His World as Composed by Mingus,* ed. Nel King (New York: Knopf, 1971), p. 51.
†Ibid., p. 215.
‡Ibid., p. 257.

> Someday one of us put-down, outcast makers of jazz music should show those church-going clock punchers that people like Monk and Bird are dying for what they believe.*

Mingus's infantile search for religion and the core of spiritual matters was not unusual for a black jazz musician, particularly a jazz musician who was a young adult during the forties and fifties. Most looked toward the East for inspiration and many, as a result, became Muslim. Others, such as Mingus, free-lanced superficially with the terms of Hinduism and Buddhism. It is quite apparent why young black men of this era would be attracted to these religions: they were rebelling against their Western (white) background; these religions gave a sense of history and ethnicity to a group of terribly deracinated men; finally, these young jazzers were able to achieve a sense of recognition—they suffered from a kind of double anonymity of being neglected by the white Western world because they were black and being ignored by an essentially grasping, wealth-obsessed society because they were artists. This last became something like the burden of invisibility compounded by the ache of alienation. It is no wonder that these men were deeply neurotic. One wonders why many of them did not go stark raving mad.

Mingus died on January 5, 1979, in Mexico, where he was being treated for amyotrophic lateral sclerosis (Lou Gehrig's disease). He was cremated and his ashes were scattered along the Ganges River in a Hindu ceremony. Presumably all of this was done on instructions Mingus left behind. So all the spiritual seeking in the book is undoubtedly meant to be a sincere representation of the anxieties of the inner man. I suppose that it was fitting that in death he finally arrived at wholeness and holy annihilation in the East. But Mingus was no true believer in Freud's or Eric Hoffer's sense of the term. If anything, Mingus as holy man was simply another role he, as a black man, was expected to fill, just as he was expected to be a stud for white women. Uncle Tom, the dying, selfless, black male of Harriet Beecher Stowe, is the prototype for the religious black man in the West, no matter what religion he is attracted to. Mingus symbolizes this role through the relation of a conversation between Charlie Parker, the great alto saxophonist, and blind white pianist Lennie Tristano. The contrast could not be more startling, or more obvious: Tristano is an atheist, a composer and player of a very intricate, rather cold, technical sort of cool jazz; Bird, on the other hand, is a believer in God and mysticism, a composer and player of a very intricate but very warm, effusive music. Tristano is revealed to be, as most black people believe white people are, blind in more ways than one, overly civilized and overly cynical. Parker wins the debate by finally saying that God is "a bird without wings." In other words, God is a suffering, effusive, intelligent yet primitive black male. God is Charlie Parker, a Bird without

---

*Ibid., p. 252.

wings. It is very consistent with Mingus's highly wrought sense of patient-hood that he should believe in God and in the special holiness of the black male. After all, the suffering, both Mingus's and that of black men generally, must mean something in the end.

The perfect complementary text to Mingus's autobiography is his finest album, *The Black Saint and the Sinner Lady,* recorded on the Impulse label in January 1963. Mingus made many exceptional records, but on this one his compositional skills reach a culmination never really to be matched again. Everything in Mingus's book is here in miniature. In the title, we have the major religious, sexual, and racial imagery of the book. We discover that the music is meant to accompany dancers, so we are not listening to jazz as virtuosic music but as programmatic music; its identity depends on the strength of the overall texture of composition and not on the strength of the solos by various players. It was as close as Mingus ever got to achieving the artistic, organizational anonymity of, say, the Juilliard String Quartet. And if the following passage from the autobiography is close enough to truth, then Mingus may have always been haunted by the platonic ideality of *players* simply and always in the act of *playing:*

> I've just been listening to Bartók quartets and wow! It's not the composer so much that prompted this writing as the musicians—the players, as Rheinschagen used to say. Their names were not announced, just "The Juilliard Quartet." That's the way it should be. They're good, good players and their names are unimportant.*

Mingus the composer, the arranger, and the orchestrator reigns supreme here. Finally, there are the liner notes. In them, Mingus writes an extensive essay in which he talks about the music; indeed, there is a more concentrated and sustained discussion of jazz here than in the entire autobiography. Mingus's essay is followed by a much shorter one by his psychologist, Edmund Pollock, who discusses the music in a psychoanalytic way. So, as in the book, Mingus insists that his white psychologist act as an alter ego. Mingus gives in miniature in this album the aesthetic mythology of his own patienthood. It is quite a terrifying record to experience. It is full of the fury and "put-on" that was the life of Mingus. No one believed more than Mingus in the psychoanalytic therapy of music, which for him, of course, was equivalent to the psychoanalytic therapy of living. In one brilliant moment, finally and forever, Mingus enacted not simply the *dramatic* but the absolute *drama* of his psychological roles within a completely, almost immaculately, impersonal artistic realization. He did what all great artists must do: use his excesses instead of merely lumbering about with them with the self-conscious sanctity of someone dragging a cross.

---

*Ibid., p. 244.

2. THELONIOUS MONK: GOTHIC PROVINCIAL

When I heard on February 17, 1982, that Thelonious Monk, the great bebop pianist, had died of a stroke, I felt not only saddened but, oddly enough, relieved. It had seemed, for such a long time before his death (excluding the few years of artistic silence that preceded it), that Monk had become tiresome. How many times could one stand to hear him play "Straight, No Chaser," "Ruby, My Dear," or "Round Midnight"? For so many years, actually since the late forties, when Monk recorded his first two albums for Blue Note, nothing really new emerged from the Monkian imagination. The fifties saw Monk refine and distill his art, perfecting his expression in an extraordinary canon of albums for Prestige and Riverside ranging from solo piano versions of Tin Pan Alley stuff to big-band arrangements of his own compositions. The arrival of the sixties was the arrival of Monk: a cover story in the February 28, 1964, issue of *Time* magazine and a lucrative contract with Columbia Records. Then Monk proceeded to commit the terrifying mistake that has beset so many great artists, from Hemingway to George Cukor: he repeated himself; he tried to recapture the moment of his greatest triumphs and he failed. Some of the Columbia records were quite good; most were merely competent; and many were, finally, boring, heartbreakingly so. The slow decline, the quaint staleness began to pervade his music, and his most aware fans realized that the "put-on" had finally and most devastatingly fooled the confidence man himself. Monk's music had been reduced from the controversy of uncompromised artistic engagement to the slouch of bedeviled laziness.

I suspect that Amiri Baraka (LeRoi Jones) knew that Monk would cease to be vital once he gained wide acceptance, and so Baraka wrote the essay "Recent Monk" which appeared in *Downbeat* in 1963, saying in one breath that success wouldn't spoil T. S. Monk, and in another breath, "Say that it ain't so, Thelonious, that you sold out to the moguls on the hill."

But success did spoil Monk in a way that it spoils, destroys really, a fair number of black men in this country. The very persona that Monk encased himself in as the opaque, weird, high priest of the zombies in the forties, a persona so unacceptable to mainstream America then, became quite acceptable in the sixties. What initially made Monk just another outcast black jazzman eventually rendered him attractive and interesting, cute even, to, as Baraka put it, "a pretty good swath of that part of the American population called 'knowledgeable.'" Once Monk was accepted, he was trapped in the image of what made him an "interesting" black man to the white majority. This sort of thing happens very often to many performing black men: Richard Pryor and Muhammad Ali are two recent examples. When Monk was trapped in the image, he was no longer able to grow as an artist. Indeed, Monk, to the popular, simplifying mind, had even ceased to be a man; he had become an innocent primitive. Nat Hentoff, a usually very perceptive jazz critic, in an essay in his book *The Jazz Life,* referred to

Monk as a "child," and the *Time* article made it clear that Monk, after the death of his doting and overprotective mother, had simply transferred his allegiance and his need to be mothered to his doting and overprotective wife. Underneath all of this was the fairly hoary thesis that Monk was the product of black matriarchs and maybe even a white one, if one is to consider Monk's friendship with the Baroness Nica de Koenigswarter (for whom Monk wrote a lovely tune called "Pannonica").

If Monk had become, by the sixties, the noble innocent, then he was simply reenacting a sort of Nigger Jim–Queequeg role for the larger white public. It is quite in keeping that this black man-child, neurotic and mother-dominated, should have an exterior that white people found frightening. Perhaps it is because the appearance is so frightening that the figure has to be reduced: the southern racist calls him a "boy," the northern liberal, a "child." Nat Hentoff describes the incident that led to Monk's temporary stay in an insane asylum:

> In spring of 1959, he was booked for a week at Boston's Storyville. He had been up for some three days and nights without sleep. When he arrived, he came to the desk of the Copley Square Hotel, where Storyville was then located, with a glass of liquor in his hand after having flitted around the lobby rather disconcertedly, examining the walls. He was refused a room, and at first also declined to accompany his sidemen to the Hotel Bostonian where they were staying. At about ten o'clock, he finally went on stand. The room was nearly full of expectant but patient admirers. He played two numbers...and then sat motionless at the piano for what seemed like half an hour. His bewildered sidemen had left the stand after about eight minutes.
>
> Monk began wandering around the club, obviously disturbed at not having a hotel room. He finally registered at the Bostonian, didn't like the room, and left. He tried the Statler, was refused there, and took a cab to the airport with the idea of going home, collecting his wife, Nellie, and taking a room with her for the rest of the week. By that time of night planes were no longer running, and he was picked up by a state trooper to whom he would not or could not communicate. Monk later did reveal who he was, but it was too late, and he was transported to Grafton State Hospital near Worcester for observation.*

The passage seems to abstract the entire Monkian personality: the brooding, sullen demeanor, the dependency on his mothering wife, the inability to communicate through language. I feel deeply ambivalent about the entire episode. There is little reason to doubt the accuracy of Hentoff's account; he was a very close friend of Monk and probably got this account from both Monk and his wife. To be sure, there is no denying the fact that Monk *was* emotionally disturbed, at least temporarily so.

I do not wish to sound like the overly sensitive minority person, but I believe that one cannot overemphasize the fact that Monk was committed to

---

*Nat Hentoff, *The Jazz Life* (New York: Dial Press, 1961), pp. 190–191.

a mental institution mostly because he was a black man who refused to cooperate with authorities. Monk was surely not arrested because he acted like a child. To speak of the black male personality as being childlike — any black male's personality — is merely to describe euphemistically what white society perceives as the black male's psychopathology. Hentoff quotes jazz critic Paul Bacon as saying in reference to Monk that "to become an adult it's necessary to make a lot of concessions." There is a certain amount of truth in this assertion, but it fails to examine the complex depth of cultural resonance in precisely what it means to call a black man a child or the meaning of any black male's refusal to make "concessions." Surely, any half-thinking black male realizes it is only as an adult that the act of refusing to make concessions has any meaning beyond merely asserting the ego, in that such an act acquires a political aspect. Anyone who knows the history of the black male in America — the constant attempt by white society to reduce and restrict his impulses and personality, to make him submissive and tractable — anyone who knows how much black males hated this insultingly familiar diminution would realize that Monk, whatever his emotional disorders, was no child.

I would not even try to explain the whole of Monk's personality in racial terms, for he is much too complex a human being for that. But part of the manifestation of his psyche was largely an attempt to personify and symbolize, albeit subconsciously, the very *unknowableness* of the black male personality. Monk's actions as a public performer were a precise equivalent, a precise cognate for the function of slang or of the X in a Black Muslim's name. For so long had the black male been unrecognized — and I believe bebop symbolized this — that he chose, in response to years of invisibility, to be unrecognizable. In short, Monk is locked up not because he is a child but because he is a threatening, inscrutable black adult. The real ambiguity in role-playing here is the inability of many observers to understand that Monk's *willful* and somewhat deranged dependency is not synonymous with childishness. It is more closely akin to a distraughtly played game of deception.

It is in the great racial overtones of this story that one finds the true source, the touchstone, of Monk's personality: his gothic provincialism. One is reminded, when thinking of Monk, of those Poe heroes, so tortured yet so frightfully self-absorbed. That gothic provincialism had allowed Monk to survive and operate in a white-dominated society.

Monk was born in the South but was raised in New York City and, indeed, lived there all his life. He spent his entire life in practically the same neighborhood, almost on the same block. (That sort of insulation is common with poor urban blacks. I remember working with some tough black kids for a social service agency and discovering that few of them knew how to get downtown. They had never been there!) He seemed to have little inclination to do anything but play the piano and compose, and he wrote many of his best pieces while he was still a very young man. His style of playing may have developed as an act of self-defense as much as for any other reason. He was very familiar with Art Tatum, whom he called "the greatest piano player I ever heard," and the recently deceased Earl Hines, and once hearing these men he realized that there was no need or even possibility of going the virtuoso route. One jazz critic called Monk's playing "fey" but, at times, it almost seems (to me) cowering in its effort to avoid being in any way "artistic."

When his music went unheard and unaccepted, Monk simply clammed up and waited. This was, in a sense, a very brave thing to do. It was, moreover, not only a sign of the depth of his determination but also of the intensity of his provincialism. While waiting, he showed little interest in doing anything else or in approaching anything differently. The cloistered environment of the black in the inner city made that kind of attitude possible. It is difficult to know whether this is lassitude or inner strength. The bourgeoisie have decided that if a poor boy succeeds, then it is inner strength; if he does not, then it is lassitude.

In Monk's case, we have a combination of both. Monk was surely a very great piano player in his way and a profoundly brilliant composer, but the music which was lauded by musicians and fans as being so rife with possibilities finally became quite narrow and restricting, just as Monk's gothic provincialism proved to be a source of tenacious inspiration and, eventually, the pathway to a kind of amazingly busy sloth. The problem lies in the fact that Monk never found a proper avenue for his musical expression. Many thought that Monk was a bluesman, pure and simple, and, to be sure, he was. Yet the essence of his music, where it was really tending, was toward the show tunes and songs of a W. C. Handy, a Will Marion Cook, and a Fats Waller. Most of Monk's music cries out for lyrics, and in another age his music would have been songs with lyrics sung from a stage. By the midsixties, Monk's days as a composer of new material and as a stylistic innovator on the piano were over. At this point, Cecil Taylor of the new school and Duke Ellington of the old school were much more bracing to listen to, as both pianists and composers. But the body of material that Monk wrote could have been mined in other ways. What if Monk had hired a lyricist to pen words to his songs? What if someone had constructed a book around Monk's tunes and created a musical? It is an idea that might yet be realized, but without Monk guiding and supervising such a project, it will be fairly much an empty exercise in commercializing the art of a heavyweight. But when I speak of making real songs from Monk's material, I do not mean to commercialize it but rather to extend further the aesthetic content, to *lyricize* formally a music already rich in lyricism.

It is often said that Monk was ahead of his time, but he really was not. His music was a distillation and recapitulation of all the Afro-American *songwriters* before him. Only a man of considerable genius could have realized how much his cultural past was filled with the sounds of singing and could have exploited this realization with such unassuming deftness and quiet profundity.

3. SONNY STITT:
THE BLUES HERO AS LONG-DISTANCE RUNNER

When Charlie "Yardbird" Parker singled out Edward "Sonny" Stitt as his saxophone successor, he did not present a compliment so much as chant a curse, an extremely successful curse. One wonders if Stitt spent his life trying to live up to Parker's pronouncement or trying to live it down. No matter: Stitt was, all his life, haunted by the ghost of Bird. Even Fate played the most horrible trick by seeing to it that Stitt's most memorable and artistically acclaimed album should be filled with Parker's compositions. *Stitt Plays Bird* was the best album Stitt ever made and all it did, at best, was make people think it was redundant or, at worst, make people put on their Bird sides to listen to the real thing.

Stitt was an incredibly gifted saxophonist who really did have a sound that was distinct from Parker's. Unfortunately, he sounded enough like an imitator of Parker to be forced to go through his career tagged as just that: one of Bird's better imitators. Stitt switched from being exclusively an alto saxophonist to being both a tenor and an alto man, but nothing helped. When he played alto, he seemed to be playing Bird verbatim; and when he played tenor, he was merely doing Bird in a different voice.

Stitt, though, was able to do a few things that Bird was unable to achieve. First, Stitt was a survivor in an area of music that was notorious for its bloodthirsty propensity. Second, Stitt reached an entirely different audience from Bird's. Parker appealed to the white and black hipsters and intellectuals; Stitt, on the other hand, was a great draw for the ordinary, working-class folk whose favorite jazzmen did not have to be cultural rebels or the subject of articles in *Esquire*. The first fact is significant because it shows that Stitt never allowed his excesses or his frustrations to destroy him as a young man. The second fact reveals why Stitt was so important to jazz as Parker's alter ego: he demystified Bird's music; he made it accessible and freed it from the charismatic burden of its creator's shadow; he virtually made it over into rhythm and blues.

I remember Sonny Stitt as the skinny, nervous cat who was billed with Gene Ammons in "the battle of the tenor saxes." He and Ammons would always front an organ combo in a little dingy nightclub filled to the rafters with slick papas with processed hair and finger-poppin' mamas in tight dresses. You rarely, if ever, saw any white people wander into these clubs; they were always in the heart of some black community, sometimes in the same block as some notorious bucket of blood such as the Clam Bar in South Philadelphia, where my uncle once was cut to pieces simply because he was a stranger. These were not neighborhoods that took kindly to strangers.

The patrons of the club would thoroughly enjoy the tenor sax battles, almost to the point of acting as if they were at some sort of holy-roller church service or a revival meeting. During Ammons's solos, people would yell, "Blow it, Mr. Man," or "Preach it, Brother man," or "Brother Gene is saying a taste tonight." During Stitt's solos, the chorus would be: "Make it talk, Sonny, make it talk," or "Blow that shit, my man, and work it on out." The music was extraordinarily loud; on a summer evening you could stand outside the nightclub, as I did when I was a youngster, and hear everything quite clearly.

It was always difficult to tell who won the saxophone battles. Stitt played more notes to a bar, but Ammons had a bigger, bluesier tone. By playing with Ammons, Stitt had forsaken any possibility of taking on Parker's highbrow audience. After all, no one was going to mistake Ammons for anything but a gutsy rhythm-and-blues man who played jazz in order to keep alive a family tradition. But Stitt, I always thought, was a bit more than this. It is a curious thing in jazz that a solo that goes beyond ninety seconds tends to become uninteresting and repetitive. Here were two men, Stitt and Ammons, who played solos that seemed to go on forever, solos that were so long that they seemed to be parodies of jazz, reducing the music to simple rhythmic blocks of cacophony. Yet in all this din, Stitt would sometimes play ninety seconds of extraordinarily well-conceived music. As I grew older, I became convinced that Stitt was the better saxophonist.

I saw Stitt perform about ten years ago in the basement of a church on the campus of the University of Pennsylvania. The audience was small, made up mostly of young white college students; the only drink to be had was organic apple juice. I figured that in this kind of atmosphere Stitt was definitely out of his element. I remember three things most clearly about the performance.

First, Stitt was drunk or at least fairly loaded. He was not very steady on his feet, his eyes were terribly bloodshot, and his speech was thick and slurred. There were stories traveling like bad news through the audience about poor Hank Mobley, once a first-rate tenor man, and his drinking problem. Seeing Stitt stumbling around looking very old, very tired, and very much like a man who had been slowly and viciously used up made everyone feel uneasy. He stood on the bandstand for two minutes with his head down and a cigarette dangling from his lips. I thought for a moment that I was about to witness not merely a tragedy but a very messy affair of bad taste. Stitt finally put the horn in his mouth and began to play; he sounded better than anyone had a right to expect.

Second, Stitt held in his hand the most gleaming, golden Selmer saxophone I had ever seen. It was such an amazing counterpoint to the slightly shabby man—this cold, hard but brilliant piece of metal that scarcely seemed an instrument at all. It more deeply resembled a thing that could take flight, not an animated thing or a living thing, just the impersonal touched with a soaring grandeur.

Third, I remember one moment in the set as Stitt's triumph. He had played in a rather perfunctory manner, not bad but not outstanding. It was simply not his audience nor his element. He would never have that old-time audience again nor that old-time element. Clifford Jordan, a solid tenor sax man with Texas roots, sat in on a few numbers and seemed to lift Stitt out of his lethargy. Echoes of those old tenor battles with Ammons must have reverberated in Stitt's mind for a moment. They honked their way through Bird's "Constellation" like uncontrolled roller coasters careening toward a wall. Stitt then played a slow-tempo version of "Skylark" while Jordan laid out. He returned to his lackadaisical self, giving a rather pedestrian reading of the song; then suddenly, during a two-minute cadenza, he played a solo which was simply the best played by a jazz saxophonist. It not only had the fireworks of technique but was faultlessly constructed. It not only was as good as Bird, but was actually better. For a brief moment, Stitt outdid the teacher; he was the king of the hill. After the cadenza, there was a brief silence before Stitt and his group launched back into the theme. In those few seconds, someone in the audience yelled, "Bird lives." Stitt started to play the theme but he abruptly stopped, peered at the audience a minute as if searching for someone, then said clearly into the microphone, "I don't play Bird." I suppose he meant to say that he didn't play *like* Bird. But that is really open. Perhaps he meant exactly what he said, just as when old black folk say, "The sun do move," they do not mean, "The sun does move." He never finished the theme of "Skylark." He simply walked off the stand. The unfinished set did not matter; he had played for a long time. Perhaps he found out that night he had played too long. As he walked off the stand, he looked quite sad, sadder than any man ought to look. I suppose Hemingway was right: "It is awfully easy to be hardboiled about everything in the daytime, but at night it is another thing."

Appendix

The Fight:
Patterson vs. Liston

by James Baldwin

We, the writers—a word I am using in its most primitive sense—arrived in Chicago about ten days before the baffling, bruising, an unbelievable two minutes and six seconds at Comiskey Park. We will get to all that later. I know nothing whatever about the Sweet Science or the Cruel Profession or the Poor Boy's Game. But I know a lot about pride, the poor boy's pride, since that's my story and will, in some way, probably, be my end.

There was something vastly unreal about the entire bit, as though we had all come to Chicago to make various movies and then spent all our time visiting the other fellow's set—on which no cameras were rolling. Dispatches went out every day, typewriters clattered, phones rang; each day, carloads of journalists invaded the Patterson or Liston camps, hung around until Patterson or Liston appeared; asked lame, inane questions, always the same questions, went away again, back to those telephones and typewriters; and informed a waiting, anxious world, or at least a waiting, anxious editor, what Patterson and Liston had said or done that day. It was insane and desperate, since neither of them ever really *did* anything. There wasn't anything for them *to* do, except train for the fight. But there aren't many ways to describe a fighter in training—it's muscle and sweat and grace, it's the same thing over and over—and since neither Patterson nor Liston were doing much boxing, there couldn't be any interesting thumbnail sketches of their sparring partners. The "feud" between Patterson and Liston was as limp and tasteless as British roast lamb. Patterson is really far too much of a gentleman to descend to feuding with anyone, and I simply never believed, especially after talking with Liston, that he had the remotest grudge against Patterson. So there we were, hanging around, twiddling our thumbs, drinking Scotch, and telling stories, and trying to make copy out of nothing. And waiting, of course, for the Big Event, which would justify the monumental amounts of time, money, and energy which were being expended in Chicago.

Neither Patterson nor Liston have the *color,* or the instinct for drama which is possessed to such a superlative degree by the marvelous Archie Moore, and the perhaps less marvelous, but certainly vocal, and rather charming Cassius Clay. In the matter of color, a word which I am not now using in its racial sense, the Press Room far outdid the training camps. There were not only the sports writers, who had come, as I say, from all over the world: there were also the boxing greats, scrubbed and sharp and easygoing, Rocky Marciano, Barney Ross, Ezzard Charles, and the King, Joe Louis, and Ingemar Johansson, who arrived just a little before the fight and did not impress me as being easygoing at all. Archie Moore's word for him is "desperate," and he did not say this with any affection. There were the ruined boxers, stopped by an unlucky glove too early in their careers, who seemed to be treated with the tense and embarrassed affection reserved for faintly unsavory relatives, who were being used, some of them, as sparring partners. There were the managers and trainers, who, in public anyway, and with the exception of Cus D'Amato, seemed to have taken, many years ago, the vow of silence. There were people whose functions were mysterious indeed, certainly unnamed, possibly unnameable, and, one felt, probably, if undefinably, criminal. There were hangers-on and protégés, a singer somewhere around, whom I didn't meet, owned by Patterson, and another singer owned by someone else—who couldn't sing, everyone agreed, but who didn't have to, being so loaded with personality—and there were some improbable-looking women, turned out, it would seem, by a machine shop, who didn't seem, really, to walk or talk, but rather to gleam, click, and glide, with an almost soundless meshing of gears. There were some pretty incredible girls, too, at the parties, impeccably blank and beautiful and rather incredibly vulnerable. There were the parties and the post mortems and the gossip and speculations and recollections and the liquor and the anecdotes, and dawn coming up to find you leaving somebody else's house or somebody else's room or the Playboy Club; and Jimmy Cannon, Red Smith, Milton Gross, Sandy Grady, and A. J. Liebling; and Norman Mailer, Gerald Kersh, Budd Schulberg, and Ben Hecht—who arrived, however, only for the fight and must have been left with a great deal of time on his hands—and Gay Talese (of the *Times*), and myself. Hanging around in Chicago, hanging on the lightest word, or action, of Floyd Patterson and Sonny Liston.

I am not an *aficionado* of the ring, and haven't been since Joe Louis lost his crown—*he* was the last great fighter for me—and so I can't really make comparisons with previous events of this kind. But neither, it soon struck me, could anybody else. Patterson was, in effect, the *moral* favorite—people *wanted* him to win, either because they liked him, though many people didn't, or because they felt that his victory would be salutary for boxing and that Liston's victory would be a disaster. But no one could be said to be enthusiastic about either man's record in the ring. The general feeling seemed to be that Patterson had never been tested, that he was the champion, in effect, by default; though, on the other hand, everyone attempted to avoid the conclusion that boxing had fallen on evil days and that Patterson had fought no worthy fighters because there were none. The desire to avoid speculating too deeply on the present state and the probable future of boxing was responsible, I think, for some very odd and stammering talk about Patterson's personality. (This led Red Smith to declare that he didn't feel that sports writers had any business trying to be psychiatrists, and that he was just going to write down who hit whom, how hard, and where, and the hell with why.) And there was very sharp disapproval of the way he has handled his career, since he has taken over most of D'Amato's functions as a manager, and is clearly under no one's orders but his own. "In the old days," someone complained, "the manager told the fighter what to do, and he did it. You didn't have to futz around with the guy's *temperament,* for Christ's sake." Never before had any of the sports writers been compelled to deal directly with the fighter instead of with his manager, and all of them seemed baffled by this necessity and many were resentful. I don't know how they got along with D'Amato when he was running the entire show—D'Amato can certainly not be described as either simple or direct—but at least the figure of D'Amato was familiar and operated to protect them from the oddly compelling and touching figure of Floyd Patterson, who is quite probably the least likely fighter in the history of the sport. And I think that part of the resentment he arouses is due to the fact that he brings to what is thought of—quite erroneously—as a simple activity a terrible note of complexity. This is his personal style, a style which strongly suggests that most un-American of attributes, privacy, the will to privacy; and my own guess is that he is still relentlessly, painfully shy—he lives gallantly with his scars, but not all of them have healed—and while he has found a way to master this, he has found no way to hide it; as, for example, another miraculously tough and tender man, Miles Davis, has managed to do. Miles's disguise would certainly never fool anybody with sense, but it keeps a lot of people away, and that's the point. But Patterson, tough and proud and beautiful, is also terribly vulnerable, and looks it.

I met him, luckily for me, with Gay Talese, whom he admires and trusts, I say luckily because I'm not a very aggressive journalist, don't know enough about boxing to know which questions to ask, and am simply not able to ask a man questions about his private life. If Gay had not been there, I am not certain how I would ever have worked up my courage to say anything to Floyd Patterson—especially after having sat through, or suffered, the first, for me, of many press conferences. I only sat through two with Patterson, silently, and in the back—he, poor man, had to go through it every day, sometimes twice a day. And if I don't know enough about boxing to know which questions to ask, I must say that the boxing experts are not one whit more imaginative, though they were, I thought, sometimes rather more insolent. It was a curious insolence, though, veiled, tentative, uncertain—they couldn't be sure that Floyd wouldn't give them as good as he got. And this led, again, to that curious resentment I mentioned earlier, for they were forced, perpetually, to speculate about the man instead of the boxer. It doesn't appear to have occurred yet to many members of the press that one of the reasons their relations with Floyd are so frequently strained is that he has no reason, on any level, to trust them, and no reason to believe that they would be capable of hearing what he had to say, even if he could say it. Life's far from being as simple as most sports writers would like to have it. The world of sports, in fact, is far from being as simple as the sports pages often make it sound.

Gay and I drove out, ahead of all the other journalists, in a Hertz car, and got to the camp at Elgin while Floyd was still lying down. The camp was very quiet, bucolic, really, when we arrived; set in the middle of small, rolling hills; four or five buildings, a tethered goat—the camp mascot; a small green tent containing a Spartan cot; lots of cars. "They're very car-conscious here," someone said of Floyd's small staff of trainers and helpers. "Most of them have two cars." We ran into some of them standing around and talking on the grounds, and Buster Watson, a close friend of Floyd's, stocky, dark, and able, led us into the Press Room. Floyd's camp was actually Marycrest Farm, the twin of a Chicago settlement house, which works, on a smaller scale but in somewhat the same way, with disturbed and deprived children, as does Floyd's New York alma mater, the Wiltwyck School for Boys. It is a Catholic institution—Patterson is a converted Catholic—and the interior walls of the building in which the press conference took place were decorated with vivid mosaics, executed by the children in colored beans, of various biblical events. There was an extraordinarily effective crooked cross, executed in charred wood, hanging high on one of the walls. There were two doors to the building in which the two press agents worked, one saying *Caritas,* the other saying *Veritas.* It seemed an incongruous setting for the life being lived there, and the event being prepared, but Ted Carroll, the Negro press agent, a tall man with white hair and a knowledgeable, weary, gentle face, told me that the camp was like the man. "The man lives a secluded life. He's like this place—peaceful and far away." It was not all that peaceful, of course, except naturally; it was otherwise menaced and inundated by hordes of human beings, from small boys, who wanted to be boxers, to old men who remembered Jack Dempsey as a kid. The signs on the road, pointing the way to Floyd Patterson's training camp, were perpetually carried away by souvenir hunters. ("At first," Ted Carroll said, "we were worried that maybe they were carrying them away for another reason—you know, the usual hassle—but no, they just want to put them in the rumpus room.") We walked about with Ted

Carroll for a while and he pointed out to us the house, white, with green shutters, somewhat removed from the camp and on a hill, in which Floyd Patterson lived. He was resting now, and the press conference had been called for three o'clock, which was nearly three hours away. But he would be working out before the conference. Gay and I left Ted and wandered close to the house. I looked at the ring, which had been set up on another hill near the house, and examined the tent. Gay knocked lightly on Floyd's door. There was no answer, but Gay said that the radio was on. We sat down in the sun, near the ring, and speculated on Floyd's training habits, which kept him away from his family for such long periods of time.

Presently, here he came across the grass, loping, rather, head down, with a small, tight smile on his lips. This smile seems always to be there when he is facing people and disappears only when he begins to be comfortable. Then he can laugh, as I never heard him laugh at a press conference, and the face which he watches so carefully in public is then, as it were, permitted to be its boyish and rather surprisingly zestful self. He greeted Gay, and took sharp, covert notice of me, seeming to decide that if I were with Gay, I was probably all right. We followed him into the gym, in which a large sign faced us, saying *So we being many are one body in Christ.* He went through his workout, methodically, rigorously, pausing every now and again to disagree with his trainer, Dan Florio, about the time—he insisted that Dan's stopwatch was unreliable—or to tell Buster that there weren't enough towels, to ask that the windows be closed. "You threw a good right hand that time," Dan Florio said; and, later, "Keep the right hand *up. Up!*" "We got a floor scale that's no good," Floyd said, cheerfully. "Sometimes I weigh two hundred, sometimes I weigh 'eighty-eight." And we watched him jump rope, which he must do according to some music in his head, very beautiful and gleaming and far away, like a boy saint helplessly dancing and seen through the steaming windows of a storefront church.

We followed him into the house when the workout was over, and sat in the kitchen and drank tea; he drank chocolate. Gay knew that I was somewhat tense as to how to make contact with Patterson—my own feeling was that he had a tough enough row to hoe, and that everybody should just leave him alone; how would *I* like it if I were forced to answer inane questions every day concerning the progress of my work?—and told Patterson about some of the things I'd written. But Patterson hadn't heard of me, or read anything of mine. Gay's explanation, though, caused him to look directly at me, and he said, "I've seen you someplace before. I don't know where, but I know I've seen you." I hadn't seen him before, except once, with Liston, in the Commissioner's office, when there had been a spirited fight concerning the construction of Liston's boxing gloves, which were "just about as flat as the back of my hand," according to a sports writer, "just like wearing no gloves at all." I felt certain, considering the number of people and the tension in that room, that he could not have seen me *then*—but we do know some of the same people, and have walked very often on the same streets. Gay suggested that he had seen me on TV. I had hoped that the contact would have turned out to be more personal, like a mutual friend or some activity connected with the Wiltwyck School, but Floyd now remembered the subject of the TV debate he had seen—the race problem, of course—and his face lit up. "I *knew* I'd seen you somewhere!" he said, triumphantly, and looked at me for a moment with the same brotherly pride I felt—and feel—in him.

By now he was, with good grace but a certain tense resignation, preparing himself for the press conference. I gather that there are many people who enjoy meeting the press—and most of them, in fact, were presently in Chicago—but Floyd Patterson is not one of them. I think he hates being put on exhibition, he doesn't believe it is real; while he is terribly conscious of the responsibility imposed on him by the title which he held, he is also afflicted with enough imagination to be baffled by his position. And he is far from having acquired the stony and ruthless perception which will allow him to stand at once within and without his fearful notoriety. Anyway, we trailed over to the building in which the press waited, and Floyd's small, tight, shy smile was back.

But he has learned, though it must have cost him a great deal, how to handle himself. He was asked about his weight, his food, his measurements, his morale. He had been in training for nearly six months ("Is that necessary?" "I just like to do it that way"), had boxed, at this point, about 162 rounds. This was compared to his condition at the time of the first fight with Ingemar Johansson. "Do you believe that you were overtrained for that fight?" "Anything I say now would sound like an excuse." But, later, "I was careless—not overconfident, but careless." He had allowed himself to be surprised by Ingemar's aggressiveness. "Did you and D'Amato fight over your decision to fight Liston?" The weary smile played at the corner of Floyd's mouth, and though he was looking directly at his interlocutors, his eyes were veiled. "No." Long pause. "Cus knows that I do what I want to do—ultimately, he accepted it." Was he surprised by Liston's hostility? No. Perhaps it had made him a bit more determined. Had he anything against Liston personally? "No. I'm the champion and I want to remain the champion." Had he and D'Amato ever disagreed before? "Not in relation to my opponents." Had he heard it said that, as a fighter, he lacked viciousness? "Whoever said that should see the fights I've won without being vicious." And why was he fighting Liston? "Well," said Patterson, "it was my decision to take the fight. You gentlemen disagreed, but you were the ones who placed him in the Number One position, so I felt that it was only right. Liston's criminal record is behind him, not before him." "Do you feel that you've been accepted as a champion?" Floyd smiled more tightly than ever and turned toward the questioner. "No," he said. Then, "Well, I have to be accepted as the champion—but maybe not a good one." "Why do you say," someone else asked, "that the opportunity to become a great champion will never arise?" "Because," said Floyd, patiently, "you gentlemen will never let it arise." Someone asked him about his experiences when boxing in

Europe—what kind of reception had he enjoyed? Much greater and much warmer than here, he finally admitted, but added, with a weary and humorous caution, "I don't want to say anything derogatory about the United States. I am satisfied." The press seemed rather to flinch from the purport of this grim and vivid little joke, and switched to the subject of Liston again. Who was most in awe of whom? Floyd had no idea, he said, but, "Liston's confidence is on the surface. Mine is within."

And so it seemed to be indeed, as, later, Gay and I walked with him through the flat, midwestern landscape. It was not exactly that he was less tense—I think that he is probably always tense, and it is that, and not his glass chin, or a lack of stamina, which is his real liability as a fighter—but he was tense in a more private, more bearable way. The fight was very much on his mind, of course, and we talked of the strange battle about the boxing gloves, and the Commissioner's impenetrable and apparent bias toward Liston, though the difference in the construction of the gloves, and the possible meaning of this difference, was clear to everyone. The gloves had been made by two different firms, which was not the usual procedure, and, though they were the same standard eight-ounce weight, Floyd's gloves were the familiar, puffy shape, with most of the weight of the padding over the fist, and Liston's were extraordinarily slender, with most of the weight of the padding over the wrist. But we didn't talk only of the fight, and I can't now remember all the things we *did* talk about. I mainly remember Floyd's voice, going cheerfully on and on, and the way his face kept changing, and the way he laughed; I remember the glimpse I got of him then, a man more complex than he was yet equipped to know, a hero for many children who were still trapped where he had been, who might not have survived without the ring, and who yet, oddly, did not really seem to belong there. I dismissed my dim speculations, that afternoon, as sentimental inaccuracies rooted in my lack of knowledge of the boxing world, and corrupted with a guilty chauvinism. But now I wonder. He told us that his wife was coming in for the fight, against his will "in order," he said, indescribably, "to *console* me if—" and he made, at last, a gesture with his hand, downward.

Liston's camp was very different, an abandoned racetrack in, or called, Aurora Downs, with wire gates and a uniformed cop, who lets you in, or doesn't. I had simply given up the press conference bit, since they didn't teach me much, and I couldn't ask those questions. Gay Talese couldn't help me with Liston, and this left me floundering on my own until Sandy Grady called up Liston's manager, Jack Nilon, and arranged for me to see Liston for a few minutes alone the next day. Liston's camp was far more outspoken concerning Liston's attitude toward the press than Patterson's. Liston didn't like most of the press and most of them didn't like him. But I didn't, myself, see any reason why he *should* like them, or pretend to—they had certainly never been very nice to him, and I was sure that he saw in them merely some more ignorant, uncaring white people, who, no matter how fine we cut it, had helped to cause him so much grief. And this impression was confirmed by reports from people who *did* get along with him—Wendell Phillips and Bob Teague, who are both Negroes, but rather rare and salty types, and Sandy Grady, who is not a Negro, but is certainly rare, and very probably salty. I got the impression from them that Liston was perfectly willing to take people as they were, if they would do the same for him. Again, I was not particularly appalled by his criminal background, believing, rightly or wrongly, that I probably knew more about the motives and even the necessity of this career than most of the white press could. The only relevance Liston's—presumably previous—associations should have been allowed to have, it seemed to me, concerned the possible effect of these on the future of boxing. Well, while the air was thick with rumor and gospel on this subject, I really cannot go into it without risking, at the very least, being sued for libel; and so, one of the most fascinating aspects of the Chicago story will have to be left in the dark. But the Sweet Science is not, in any case, really so low on shady types as to be forced to depend on Liston. The question is to what extent Liston is prepared to cooperate with whatever powers of darkness there are in boxing; and the extent of his cooperation, we must suppose, must depend, at least partly, on the extent of his awareness. So that there is nothing unique about the position in which he now finds himself and nothing unique about the speculation which now surrounds him.

I got to his camp at about two o'clock one afternoon. Time was running out, the fight was not more than three days away, and the atmosphere in the camp was, at once, listless and electric. Nilon looked as though he had not slept and would not sleep for days, and everyone else rather gave the impression that they wished they could—except for three handsome Negro ladies, related, I supposed, to Mrs. Liston, who sat, rather self-consciously, on the porch of the largest building on the grounds. They may have felt as I did, that training camps are like a theater before the curtain goes up, and if you don't have any function in it, you're probably in the way.

Liston, as we all know, is an enormous man, but surprisingly trim. I had already seen him work out, skipping rope to a record of "Night Train," and, while he wasn't nearly, for me, as moving as Patterson skipping rope in silence, it was still a wonderful sight to see. The press has really maligned Liston very cruelly, I think. He is far from stupid; is not, in fact, stupid at all. And, while there is a great deal of violence in him, I sensed no cruelty at all. On the contrary, he reminded me of big, black men I have known who acquired the reputation of being tough in order to conceal the fact that they weren't hard. Anyone who cared to could turn them into taffy.

Anyway, I liked him, liked him very much. He sat opposite me at the table, sideways, head down, waiting for the blow: for Liston knows, as only the inarticulately suffering can, just how inarticulate he is. But let me clarify that: I say suffering because it seems to me that he has suffered a great deal. It is in his face, in the silence of that face, and in the curiously distant light in the eyes—a light which rarely signals because there have been so few answering signals. And when I say inarticulate, I really do not mean to suggest that he does not know how to talk. He is inarticulate in the way we all are when more has happened to us than we know how to express; and inarticulate in a particularly Negro way—he has a long tale to tell which no one wants to hear. I said, "I can't ask you any questions because everything's been asked. Perhaps I'm only here, really, to say that I wish you well." And this was true, even though I wanted Patterson to win. Anyway, I'm glad I said it because he looked at me then, really for the first time, and he talked to me for a little while.

And what had hurt him most, somewhat to my surprise, was not the general press reaction to him, but the Negro reaction. "Colored people," he said, with great sorrow, "say they don't want their children to look up to me. Well, they ain't teaching their children to look up to Martin Luther King, either." There was a pause. "I wouldn't be no bad example if I was up there. I could tell a lot of those children what they need to know—because—I passed that way. I could make them *listen*." And he spoke a little of what he would like to do for young Negro boys and girls, trapped in those circumstances which so nearly defeated himself and Floyd, and from which neither can yet be said to have recovered. "I tell you one thing, though," he said, "if I was up there, I wouldn't bite my tongue." I could certainly believe that. And we discussed the segregation issue, and the role, in it, of those prominent Negroes who find him so distasteful. "I would never," he said, "go against my brother—we got to learn to stop fighting among our own." He lapsed into silence again. "They said they didn't want me to have the title. They didn't say that about Johansson." "They" were the Negroes. "*They* ought to know why I got some of the bum raps I got." But he was not suggesting that they were *all* bum raps. His wife came over, a very pretty woman, seemed to gather in a glance how things were going, and sat down. We talked for a little while of matters entirely unrelated to the fight, and then it was time for his workout, and I left. I felt terribly ambivalent, as many Negroes do these days, since we are all trying to decide, in one way or another, which attitude, in our terrible American dilemma, is the most effective: the disciplined sweetness of Floyd, or the outspoken intransigence of Liston. *If I was up there, I wouldn't bite my tongue.* And Liston is a man aching for respect and responsibility. Sometimes we grow into our responsibilities and sometimes, of course, we fail them.

I left for the fight full of a weird and violent depression, which I traced partly to fatigue—it had been a pretty grueling time—partly to the fact that I had bet more money than I should have—on Patterson—and partly to the fact that *I* had had a pretty definitive fight with someone with whom I had hoped to be friends. And I was depressed about Liston's bulk and force and his twenty-five-pound weight advantage. I was afraid that Patterson might lose, and I really didn't want to see that. And it wasn't that I didn't like Liston. I just felt closer to Floyd.

I was sitting between Norman Mailer and Ben Hecht. Hecht felt about the same way that I did, and we agreed that if Patterson didn't get "stopped," as Hecht put it, "by a baseball bat," in the very beginning—if he could carry Liston for five or six rounds—he might very well hold the title. We didn't pay an awful lot of attention to the preliminaries—or I didn't; Hecht did; I watched the ball park fill with people and listened to the vendors and the jokes and the speculations: and watched the clock.

From my notes: Liston entered the ring to an almost complete silence. Someone called his name, he looked over, smiled, and winked. Floyd entered, and got a hand. But he looked terribly small next to Liston, and my depression deepened.

My notes again: Archie Moore entered the ring, wearing an opera cape. Cassius Clay, in black tie, and as insolent as ever. Mickey Allen sang "The Star-Spangled Banner." When Liston was introduced, some people boo'd— they cheered for Floyd, and I think I know how this made Liston feel. It promised, really, to be one of the worst fights in history.

Well, I was wrong, it was scarcely a fight at all, and I can't but wonder who on earth will come to see the rematch, if there is one. Floyd seemed all right to me at first. He had planned for a long fight, and seemed to be feeling out his man. But Liston got him with a few bad body blows, and a few bad blows to the head. And no one agrees with me on this, but, at one moment, when Floyd lunged for Liston's belly—looking, it must be said, like an amateur, wildly flailing—it seemed to me that some unbearable tension in him broke, that he lost his head. And, in fact, I nearly screamed, "Keep your head, baby!" but it was really too late. Liston got him with a left, and Floyd went down. I could not believe it. I couldn't hear the count and though Hecht said, "It's over," and picked up his coat, and left, I remained standing, staring at the ring, and only conceded that the fight was really over when two other boxers entered the ring. Then I wandered out of the ball park, almost in tears. I met an old colored man at one of the exits, who said to me, cheerfully, "I've been robbed," and we talked about it for a while. We started walking through the crowds and A. J. Liebling, behind us, tapped me on the shoulder and we went off to a bar, to mourn the very possible death of boxing, and to have a drink, with love, for Floyd.